3000

RELIGION AND CIVIL SOCIETY

This book presents the first full-length study of the relationship between religion and the controversial concept of civil society. Across the world in the last two decades of the twentieth century religions re-entered public space as influential discursive and symbolic systems, apparently beyond the control of either traditional religious authorising institutions or states. This differentiation of religion from traditional institutions and entry into secular public spheres carries both dangers and possible benefits for democracy, and prompts a rethink of ideas of secularization.

Offering a fresh interdisciplinary approach to understanding religion in contemporary societies, this book provides an invaluable resource for students and researchers in religious studies, sociology, politics and political philosophy, theology, international relations and legal studies. Part one presents a critical introduction to the interaction between religion, modernization and postmodernization in Western and non-Western settings (America, Europe, the Middle East and India), focusing on discourses of human rights, civil society and the public sphere, and the controversial question of their cross-cultural application. Part two examines religion and civil society through case studies of Egypt, Bosnia and Muslim minorities in Britain, and compares Poland as an example of a Christian majority society that has experienced the public reassertion of religion.

Ashgate Religion, Culture & Society Series

Series Editors:

Dr Graham Harvey, *Religious Studies, King Alfred's College, Winchester, UK*
Dr Peter Edge, *Reader in Law and Religion, Oxford Brookes University, UK*
Lois Ann Lorentzen, *Professor of Social Ethics, University of San Francisco, USA*

The Ashgate Religion, Culture & Society Series presents a focused cluster of high profile titles exploring the critical issues of contemporary society and culture, and relationships to and within living religions. Each book offers an accessible, stimulating new contribution to key topics. The series explores constructions of religion and religious issues from a range of perspectives, offering accessible texts by scholars based within and outside traditional religious studies who are able to bring immersion in their own disciplines to the study of contemporary religion, culture and society, enriching understanding across all three elements. The series will prove of particular value to higher level undergraduate students for their course studies in the areas of contemporary culture, society, media, law, and religious studies, as well as to academics, graduates and postgraduate readers worldwide.

Religion and Civil Society

Rethinking Public Religion in the Contemporary World

DAVID HERBERT
The Open University

ASHGATE

Published by
Ashgate Publishing Limited
Gower House
Croft Road
Aldershot
Hampshire GU11 3HR
England

Ashgate Publishing Company
Suite 420
101 Cherry Street
Burlington, VT 05401-4405
USA

Ashgate website: http://www.ashgate.com

British Library Cataloguing in Publication Data
Herbert, David
    Religion and civil society : rethinking public religion in
    The contemporary world. – (Religion, culture and society)
    1. Religion and sociology 2. Civil society 3. Religion and culture
    I. Title
    291.1'71

Library of Congress Control Number: 2002100870

ISBN 0 7546 1332 1 (Hbk)
ISBN 0 7546 1339 9 (Pbk)

Typeset by Martingraphix
Printed and bound by MPG Books Ltd, Bodmin, Cornwall

Contents

Acknowledgements

This book has been forming over a long period, and my debts to those who have helped me are many. In roughly chronological order I would like to thank: Mike Fox and Richard Coupe for early encouragement to take the study of religion seriously; Dermot Killingley, Gerard Loughlin, Isobel Wollaston and John Sawyer for intellectual stimulation at Newcastle; Kim Knott, Al McFadyen, Phillip Mellor, Hugh Pyper, Phil Goodchild, Helen Reid and Phil Lewis for guidance and discussion during my time in Leeds. Thanks to staff at Jagiellonian University in Kraków for their help in Poland; to Elissa Helms, Emina Hadzihalilovic, Rusmir Mahmutahajic and Jo for their help in Bosnia; to Romany Helmy for his help in setting up interviews in Egypt. Thanks to the British Sociological Association Religion Study Group for their support and stimulation, and to José Casanova and Steve Bruce for conversations and e-mail exchanges. Thanks to the Open University for funding trips to Poland and Egypt, for giving me the opportunity to interview many leading thinkers on secularization and Islam and human rights for educational audios, and for giving me time to pursue my research and complete this book. Thanks to the British Academy for funding my PhD and for Small Grant No. 30,339 which funded my trip to Bosnia. Thanks to Sarah Lloyd of Ashgate for her support and to Tracey Black for her patience.
This book is dedicated to my parents, and to the memory of Brian Pearson.

Introduction

The primary question for any cultural institution anywhere, now that nobody is leaving anyone else alone and isn't ever again going to, is not whether everything is going to come seamlessly together, or whether, contrariwise, we are all going to persist in our separate prejudices. It is whether human beings are going to be able, in Java or Connecticut, through law, anthropology, or anything else, to imagine principled lives they can practically lead [together]. (Geertz 1983 p. 234)

The events of 11 September 2001 make the issues addressed in this book more controversial, yet more important to address impartially, open-mindedly and in depth than perhaps ever before. Completing the book during the weeks and months following the destruction of the twin towers of the World Trade Center, a few simple observations can be made. First, it seems that for reasons that were at least partly related to religious (and specifically Islamic) conviction, in the attack terrorists claimed the lives of more than fifteen hundred people, including themselves. Second, it seems clear that while the majority of governments in predominantly Muslim countries have in some sense backed America in its 'war against terrorism', the mood on the 'Muslim street' in those societies is more ambivalent.

Third, it seems clear that American and other Western governments are keen to distance their Muslim populations and Islam from terrorism. Yet the increase in attacks on Muslim citizens, properties and places of worship indicates that the 'Western street' can be less discerning, while many Muslim citizens appear less than convinced of their governments' arguments. A string of successes by the Far Right in French and Dutch national elections, and in English local elections in 2002, underlines the strength of anti-Muslim feeling. Fourth, neither official nor popular discourses in Muslim majority societies nor the West show a clear understanding of the complex way that religions interact with contemporary societies. They tend instead to oversimplify into polar opposites: Islam is either 'peace' or 'fanaticism', the West is the 'defender of world liberty' or an 'evil capitalist oppressor'. This book seeks to deconstruct such dangerous forms of polarization, calling for a reassessment of the relationship between religion and civil society, and hence for a rethinking of public religion in the contemporary world.

Rapid success in the military campaign in support of the Northern Alliance largely relegated debate on the rights and wrongs of military intervention in Afghanistan to history (though the mop-up operations continue at the time of writing, May 2002). But the task of reconstruction in Afghanistan and of the relationship between political and economic development, religious identity and transnational intervention remains. In this context, the first part of the book examines the relationship between religion, modernization, civil society and the public sphere in general. In doing so it uses a range of evidence and case studies from around the world and compares competing theories, with the final chapter of

Part I examining related philosophical and ethical issues. Part II then considers four case studies from Britain, Poland, Bosnia and Egypt in further depth.

Chapter 1 asks why, at a time when globalizing forces are apparently drawing the world closer together, the role of religions in societies seems to be diverging so sharply. How is it that one author can write confidently of the 'death of Christian Britain' (Brown 2001), at a time when a major social–political parallel society can emerge in Egypt around the slogan 'Islam is the solution' (Starrett 1998)? To build a global picture of religious vitality, quantitative evidence from Europe, America and the Muslim world is considered. But such conventional indicators tell only part of the story. Therefore qualitative evidence of the role of religion as discourse, in the way people talk about issues and make senses of their lives, is drawn from three cases studies: on Egypt, Britain and America.

Chapter 2 reflects on the evidence presented in Chapter 1 in the light of the theory of secularizaton, which seeks to explain the relationship between religion and modernization. Can theories such as secularization, based on a common process of modernization, account for such divergence? Is it possible to see revival and decline as part of a common set of global processes? This chapter develops a critical account of secularization theory, and considers alternative views.

Chapter 3 asks what is the relationship of religion to those social practices, networks and institutions that promote trust, and nurture the development of participatory citizenship, all functions ascribed to civil society. Civil society is generally understood as a sphere of associational activity between the state and the private citizen, within which opinion is formulated and feeds into the public sphere. Clearly, such a concept presupposes particular modern institutions and maybe certain cultural conditions, and the extent to which the latter is the case forms part of a discussion that focuses on the compatibility of Islam and civil society. The chapter locates civil society in the context of theories of democratization, and also considers the influence of national cultures on civil society formation.

Chapter 4 asks what happens when religion becomes a significant force in the public sphere, that is in public forums for the expression of opinion, the exchange of views and debate? Is religion inclined to stifle debate, or can it support democratic participation in decision-making? While such questions cannot be answered with a simple 'yes' or 'no' and always require attention to particular circumstances, an appreciation of the dynamics of religion as discourse and the complex articulation of religion with modernization can enable us to come up with more informed and it is hoped balanced answers. This chapter considers theories of the public sphere and arguments for the decline of discursive democracy in Western societies, with which the growing role of the media is often linked. It also examines the arguments of the philosopher Alasdair MacIntyre that modernity and discursive democracy are fundamentally incompatible. As a case study, it considers the connections between the growth of national television, the rise of the Hindu Right, and the development of religion as a medium of public communication in India (Rajagopal 2001).

Chapter 5 addresses some philosophical – or more precisely 'normative', relating to norms and values – questions raised by the relationship between religion, civil society and the public sphere. It places the concepts of civil society and the public sphere in the context of theories of political liberalism, examining the historical roots of this tradition and the responses to cultural diversity within it of philosophers, including Rawls, Kymlicka and Taylor. It then proposes a model of intercultural communication derived from MacIntyre's work on traditions and epistemological crises. In this context it examines aspects of the treatment of key concepts of modern Western political theory (the state, democracy, law, human rights) in the Muslim world. The final section then seeks to develop an argument for the validity of basic human rights across cultures.

The selection of Britain, Poland, Bosnia, and Egypt as case studies reflects both accident and design. In 1989, when *The Satanic Verses* controversy hit the headlines, I was studying religion and social policy (with an elective in religion and literature) at Newcastle University. I found myself both frustrated and challenged that these disciplinary perspectives did not easily enable me to develop an integrated overall grasp of the situation. Religious studies focused on examining religions discretely, and where it considered their interaction it did so mostly in theological terms, not in terms of their articulation with one another in contemporary societies. Social policy in the 1980s barely considered religion as a significant factor in social relations, focusing instead on race and class, and where it considered religion subsumed it within culture. The interpretation of literature, in my limited acquaintance with it, focused on the interpretation of texts from a variety of 'critical' perspectives rather than on the reception, circulation and use of texts by actual, socially located groups. These observations formed the seeds of my PhD thesis at Leeds University. It examined what light different disciplinary perspectives (the above, plus political philosophy and social theory) shed on *The Satanic Verses* controversy, and how they might be used together to understand the situation better. This work forms the basis of Chapter 6. In broader terms, this chapter provides an example of the relationship between a minority religion and civil society in a secularized, predominantly post-Christian and plural setting.

In 1996 I joined the Open University, and was given the opportunity of taking part in the Religions in Europe Project, which gave me a chance to follow up an earlier interest I had developed in Poland in 1990, when visiting sites associated with the Holocaust. This was the apparent dissonance between two faces of popular Polish Catholicism, one associated, at least in some perceptions, with anti-Semitism, and the other with the pro-democracy and human rights Solidarity movement of the 1980s. When I revisited Poland between 1997 and 1999 I was interested to find out what had happened to the religious enthusiasm for political change evident in the Solidarity movement, how the Catholic Church was adapting to the post-Communist situation, and the consequences for minority religions. This work forms the basis of Chapter 7, and provides an example of the relationship between religion and civil society in a post-Communist setting, where a dominant tradition had been mobilized in the struggle against Communism.

In 2000 I had the opportunity to visit Bosnia as part of a British Academy funded project to examine the relationship between religious belonging and human rights in Central and Eastern Europe. Here I interviewed people involved in non-governmental organizations (NGOs), in the monitoring and implementation of human rights, and in inter-faith reconciliation. Bosnia has become a symbol of religious and ethnic hatred, but this media stereotype masks a complex reality. It is important to tease out the relationship between religion, social integration and social conflict historically, through the conflagration of the early 1990s (and which continued in Kosovo until 1999 and continues, at the time of writing, in Macedonia), and into the postwar reconstruction period. This is the aim of Chapter 8. In general terms, Bosnia provides an example of the relationship between religion and civil society in a post-Communist setting where, in contrast to Poland, in the late 1980s and 1990s religion became mobilized as a divisive social force. In particular, Bosnia has special significance because it represents the first attempt by 'the international community' to deliberately bring about 'democratization', in part by 'building civil society'. Hence it is an important test of how the theory of civil society feeds into policy, and of the adequacy of that theory.

In 2001 I visited Cairo as academic consultant for an Open University educational video on religion and modernization in Egypt. This gave me the opportunity to interview a few of the people (politicians, journalists, professionals, students) who are part of a 'moderate' Islamism increasingly identified by field studies through the 1990s as constituting a major social and political movement and semi-official opposition to the Egyptian government. The movement testifies to the development, especially within the Muslim Brotherhood, of a strategy of long-term Islamization of Egyptian society 'from below' through non-violent and democratic methods. If the movement is true to these methods, then it represents a hugely important phenomenon for understanding the relationship between Islamism and the West in the wake of 11 September 2001. For it suggests that in a Muslim majority society Islam can potentially form a central part of political, social and legal arrangements in a way that may be compatible with civil society and democracy. Egypt is not unique in this respect, for there is also strong evidence that Indonesia, the most populous Muslim society on earth, sustains strong traditions of 'civil Islam', recent instability and the strength of Islamist protest against American bombing of Afghanistan notwithstanding (Hefner 2000). But Egypt perhaps deserves particular attention because of its pivotal role in the Arab world.

The prospect of a democratic Islamism in Egypt stands in stark contrast to many media and even academic presentations of Egyptian Islamism as synonymous with extremism and terrorism, in the wake of events such as the Luxor massacre of tourists in 1993, and of course 11 September 2001. Chapter 9 attempts to portray something of the complexity of Egyptian Islamism, and the articulation between it, the state and civil society. It is important that the present danger does not blind us to this complexity, nor to recognizing the seeds of democratic development where this may at first seem unlikely.

PART I
COMPETING THEORIES

Chapter 1

Rethinking Religion and Modernity

Conventional and Discursive Religion

1. Religion in the Contemporary World: Contradictory Trends?

Most social theories derived from the Enlightenment held that religion would disappear from the face of the earth with the advent of modernity. (Mestrovic 1994 p. 8)

[I]n almost every European country, the twentieth century has seen the power, popularity and presence of religion decline. (Bruce 1999 p. 117)

Egypt's public environment is swamped with the signifiers of religion: on signs, billboards, murals, advertisements, radio and television programs, public events, the covers of books and magazines for sale on every streetcorner and in the style of public dress and grooming. (Starrett 1998 p. 89)

In the 1980s, religion throughout the world was in the forefront of various forms of public collective action, ... often on both sides of every contested issue, itself being both the subject and object of contestation and debate. ... Theories of modernity, theories of modern politics and theories of collective action which systematically ignore this public dimension of modern religion are necessarily incomplete theories. (Casanova 1994 p. 66)

In the face of Europe stands the cancelled world with it cultures and beliefs, wherein all its achievements have been reduced to the completing tools necessary to imitate Europe – most important of which are 'Westernization' and 'Secularization'. ... This is so that the cancelled world can come forward with its accreditation papers to be accepted within 'modernity': And in this cancelled world, wars take place which end up in secular dictatorships which force their masses to take religion lightly and eliminate it from their worlds, if not forcing them in some instances to atheism. All this while whipping these countries into obedience so that they can become dutiful apes obliged to worship: 'Europe'. (Qazim [1986] in Karam 1998 pp. 216–7)

These five quotations give some sense of the breadth of perceptions of and predictions about the role of religion in the contemporary world. Classical social theory widely anticipated the demise of religion, an expectation which seems to have been realized in most of contemporary Europe, according to Bruce. Yet across the Mediterranean, in Egypt, the reverse appears to be the case: although the demise of religion as a factor in public life was widely anticipated here too, since the late 1960s

3

the influence of religion on society appears to have increased to the extent that its presence is visible everywhere in public space. Nor is this a specifically Egyptian or even Islamic phenomenon: as Casanova argues, in the 1980s religion was at the forefront of collective action in many parts of the world (for example Poland, Nicaragua, Iran) and while in the 1990s the tide may have ebbed in some places (for example the religious right in the United States), in others (for example India and the increasing electoral success of the Hindu nationalist BJP – Bharatiya Janata Party (the Indian People's Party)) it has continued to rise. Nor is this resurgence perceived as unconnected with the global processes to be discussed in this book by those who are part of it, as the Egyptian Islamist woman activist quoted here illustrates. Furthermore, such perspectives on these changes sometimes sharply challenge those of social scientists that 'modernity' and 'secularization' describe structural, unintended historical processes, as well as indicating the scale of the challenge to the prospect of a 'global civil society'.

Thus observers and reflective practitioners of religion at the beginning of the twenty-first century face a confusing situation. On the one hand many religious traditions, especially in the advanced industrial societies of the West, continue patterns of decline which can be traced back to the nineteenth century according to many sociologists and historians, as measured by indicators such as attendance at worship and religious belief (Bruce 1996). This is widely seen as part of 'secularization', in Bryan Wilson's classic formulation 'that process by which religious institutions, actions and consciousness, lose their social significance' (Wilson 1982 p. 49). Secularization in turn is understood to be the result of modernization, described by the authors of the World Values Survey[1] as a worldwide process consisting of 'industrialization … urbanization, mass education, occupational specialization, bureaucratization and communications development' (Inglehart 1997 p. 8). And here is the source of the confusion: modernization is held to cause secularization and modernization is a worldwide process. Yet religion is not in decline everywhere.

On the contrary. Rather, there are many signs of both new and continuing vitality amongst religious traditions, ranging from an increasing interest in and spread of New Age beliefs and practices in supposedly secularized societies (Heelas 1996) to the continued growth of historic religions such as Christianity and Islam in Africa and Asia (Gifford 1998). Part of this vitality concerns not only personal belief but also the ongoing and developing public significance of religions. Indeed, during the last three decades it may be argued that there has been a resurgence of religion in the public life of societies as diverse as Iran and the United States (Beyer 1994), Brazil and Poland (Casanova 1994), India and much of sub-Saharan Africa (Everett 1997; Gifford 1998).

Furthermore, it may be argued that religious activity in civil society has played an important role in this resurgence, understanding civil society initially as a realm of social life situated beyond the immediate reach of the state in which networks, organizations and other associations form. Religions have been particularly active in two kinds of situation: first, where the state has retreated or been unable to fulfil basic education and welfare functions, whether through Islamic private voluntary organizations (PVOs) in Egypt (Sullivan 1994), or base ecclesial communities in

Brazil (Nagel 1997) and second, where the state has repressed or undermined the credibility of more overtly political institutions, as in Poland and East Germany in the late Communist period (Kubik 1994; De Gruchy 1995). But, even in democracies with effective state structures, where modernization has been associated with religious decline, religions have continued and even extended their activities in civil society. This is evidenced by examples as diverse as the political mobilization of Evangelical Christianity in the US (Casanova 1994), the increasing self-organization of Muslim groups across Western Europe (Shadid and van Koningsveld, 1996) and the continuing association of religious practice with participation in voluntary work in Britain (Gill 1992).

One aspect of civil society which has been a focus of attention by both analysts and participants has been its connection with recent transitions to democracy. Highly contested and with a long history during much of which it fell into disuse (Keane 1998), the concept of civil society was revived both by opposition movements in Eastern Europe in search of a vocabulary with which to speak about democracy that had not been debased by Communist regimes, and by social and political scientists raiding the archives of social theory in the hope of finding fresh perspectives on the problem of social integration in today's increasingly diverse societies. Some among both groups have, however, become increasingly disenchanted with the term, either as a means of democratic mobilization or as an analytic tool. In Eastern Europe this disillusionment with the democratizing potential of civil society has coincided with a parallel disillusionment with politics generally and also with the churches, or at least their role in public life (Borowik 1997). The same might be said of South America, from where reports of the failure and broken promises of liberation theology may be heard, and even in some parts of the Muslim world, as in Iran where enthusiasm for the Islamic revolution appears to be wearing thin after more than twenty years.

If the identification of civil society with democratization has come increasingly to be questioned, the association of religion in this sphere with democratization must always have looked questionable. For while religious institutions may enable democratic mobilization, both these and more generally the mobilization of national or ethnic identity on the basis of religion can as easily serve as a source of social division (Bosnia, Northern Ireland, Lebanon) as of social integration (Poland, Lithuania, Brazil). Indeed, in none of these cases are these roles mutually exclusive: for example, religious nationalism can lead to discrimination against minorities and hence social division in Poland, while developing inclusive religious identities in Bosnia can lead to improved community relations and hence social integration there. Any understanding of religion in civil society needs to consider this double-edged potential.

Thus, to understand the role of religion in civil society it is important to bear in mind three tensions: between religious resurgence and decline, between civil society as a descriptive and normative concept and between religion as a source of social integration and social division. In this first chapter we shall focus on the first of these tensions.

It is useful to distinguish between two effects of secularization. First, we shall use 'religious vitality' to refer to the extent to which religion is practised. This includes not just traditional observance but what is often today called 'spirituality', meaning beliefs and practices derived from religions or of similar content, but practised independently of the usual channels of religious traditions (for example meditation). Most of the evidence used in scholarly discussion of secularization relates to religious vitality. Second, religion's 'social significance' refers to the influence of religion on other social systems and hence on people's lives as a whole. While these two dimensions may go together, they may not: arguably, it is perfectly possible for rituals to be widely practised, especially domestically, without having much evident impact on wider social life, as Bryan Wilson (1994) argues is the case in Japan. Conversely, a religion which is little practised or practised by few may wield considerable political authority (one could argue for this for the Orthodox church during the recent Yugoslav wars, or, contrastingly, for the Anglican Church in the anti-apartheid struggle in South Africa, which is small as a proportion of the population). Thus, as Wilson (1992 p.199) argues: 'The extent of popular commitment ... do[es] not indicate what significance religion has for the social system. This, I believe, is a much more central aspect of secularization'.

Central to secularization theory's explanation of the decline of religion in Europe (in both senses, vitality and significance) is the process of social differentiation (Tschannen 1991). In this historic process, which can be traced back to the late medieval period, the influence of religion on different spheres of life gradually decreases as the latter become increasingly autonomous. It has been classically expressed by Durkheim (1984 [1893]):

> Originally, it extended to everything; everything social was religious – the two words were synonymous. Then, gradually, political, economic and scientific functions broke free from the religious function, becoming separate entities and taking on a more and more markedly temporal character. God, if we may express it in such a way, from being at first present in every human relationship, has progressively withdrawn. He leaves the world to men and their quarrels. At least, if he continues to rule it, it is from on high and afar off. (p. 119)

Indeed, some contemporary sociologists such as Niklas Luhmann (1982) have argued that differentiation has advanced so far that any form of normative integration – based on shared norms, values and understanding – is unnecessary for the functioning of most modern systems, which are self-sustaining or 'autopoetic'. For example, in the case of the legal system: 'Societal evolution has reached such a high level of differentiation in modern societies that law is an autopoetic system which no longer needs any justification in terms of normative points of view' (Deflem 1996 p. 10).

Clearly, such a development, if correctly identified, has major implications not just for religion but for democracy, a point to which we shall return. For now we can note that the coincidence of differentiation and disenchantment observed by Durkheim does seem to have been the experience of European intellectuals, at least for the last 150 years and it is backed up by a mass of data indicating that the process was not confined to them. For not only did intellectual discourses and scientific and economic practices function as if God were not there, but so too did working people: as populations were uprooted from the countryside and moved to the towns and cities of the Industrial Revolution, church attendances fell and in many cases never recovered. And arguably more decisive than church attendance, the influence of the Church as the moral guardian of the community was decisively broken by the anonymity of city life (Sennett 1994 [1974]). Thus, on this account, the decline of religion is a logical outcome of modernization. Yet differentiation does not appear to lead to disenchantment everywhere. Consider the following observations of the sociologist David Martin (1996a) concerning charismatic and pentecostal Christian groups in contemporary Latin America:[2]

> In Latin America … it is difficult to discern any shift towards rationalization or a diminution in a general presumption concerning the existence of a spiritual world. People seem able to move easily between elements of advanced technological culture and another world infiltrated with healings, exorcisms and providential interventions. There seems no obvious transfer from the strict causality and everyday nature of advanced technology and the inspirited mental furnishings of this personal world. Indeed, the technology subserves this personal world rather than 'vice-versa'. (p. 41)

Mega-cities, satellite television, auto-gridlock and the Internet have all arrived in Latin America, yet God and a whole host of other very active spiritual entities do not seem to have withdrawn from the lifeworld of the people. How can we make sense of the apparently very different impact of modernization processes in different parts of the world? This chapter and the next will try to answer this question. First, we shall examine the historical roots of the theory of secularization, then selected empirical evidence for change in religious vitality and influence in different parts of the world, first quantitative and then qualitiative. Then in Chapter 2 in the light of these findings we shall look again in more detail at the components of secularization theory and consider alternatives to it.

2. Secularization and the Legacy of the Enlightenment

However marginal sociology of religion has become to contemporary social science (Beckford 1989) and whatever the empirical validity of the secularization thesis, the idea of secularization has, either in explicit form as theory, or in more diffuse, implicit form, been highly influential in the development of modern social science and more broadly of the self-understanding of Western societies. As the American-based Spanish sociologist José Casanova (1994) writes:

> The theory of secularization may be the only theory which was able to attain a truly paradigmatic status within modern social sciences. … Indeed, [it] is so intrinsically interwoven with all the theories of the modern world that one cannot discard the theory of secularization without putting into question the entire web, including much of the self-understanding of the social sciences. (pp. 17–18)

In some ways, the effects of this can be seen most clearly in areas of enquiry which do not have the study of religion as their main focus. Thus an examination of scholarship on democratic transformation in Eastern Europe reveals a range of specialist works testifying to the importance of religion in this process, yet mainstream social and political science tends to ignore or explain away the role of religion (Herbert 1999). We shall examine the consequences of this in the context of democratization in Central and Eastern Europe (CEE) in Chapter 2. But first, why should this be? The answer seems to be that many researchers simply assume that religion cannot be of fundamental importance in modern societies (Starrett 1998 p. 245, Milbank 1990 p. 89). Furthermore, such assumptions extend beyond the academic community. A simplified form of the secularization thesis – the view that religion is in decline in the modern world – is simply what many people in the modern West, religious or otherwise and especially Western Europe, take for granted (Wilson 1975 p. 77).

There are historic reasons why this is the case. In the seventeenth century continental Europe experienced bitter and prolonged religious wars. As a result, the political foundations of modern Europe were built on a consensus that religion should not be allowed to become a divisive factor in public life (Stout 1988; Midgely 1989), whether the particular arrangement was the *cuis regio, eius religio* (as the ruler, so the religion) of the treaty of Westphalia (1648), or the secular republicanism of the French Revolution (1789). Furthermore, modernization in Europe occurred over a long period of time, during which institutional religion was often seen as an enemy of modernizing processes. Thus advocates of modern ideas often articulated themselves in opposition to the churches – and especially 'the Church', that is the Roman Catholic Church, which has historically been seen both as the archetypical religion (Durkheim) and as the archetypically anti-modern institution (Weber; Casanova 1994; Mestrovic 1993). However, times change. According to Casanova,

> the Catholic church everywhere has not only accepted the constitutional separation of church and state and the consitutional principle of religious freedom, but also abandoned its traditional attempts either to establish or sponsor official Catholic parties, which could be used to defend and advance the claims of the church. (p. 62)

While our case study of Poland will lead us to question the extent to which Polish Catholicism at least is compatible with modern constitutional democracy, Casanova none the less points to a remarkable historical reversal. However, the anti-modernist stance of the Catholic Church influenced many writers of the seventeenth, eighteenth and nineteenth centuries, from whose ideas Western understandings of the modern world have developed. The seventeenth- and eighteenth-century writers who founded modern political philosophy believed public religion was a potentially divisive force that needed to be contained; we shall examine the consequences of this legacy for contemporary political philosophy in Chapter 4. Most of the nineteenth-century founders of modern sociology added to this the conviction that religion was already declining and would decline further as modernity advanced: Comte, Marx, Durkheim and Weber all held such views (Beckford 1989).

Precisely because of this impressive consensus, it is vital to note that many of the arguments contributing to the 'Enlightenment critique of religion' (ECR; Casanova 1994) were for the most part intellectual rather than empirical: they proceeded from views about the nature of religion rather than from actual studies of religious behaviour. Thus they attacked the truth or moral basis of religion, and because it was believed that such arguments were persuasive, it was held that once people were exposed to them they would stop believing in religion and so religion would die out. The arguments of Marx (religion expresses the suffering of the oppressed, but does not address its cause, which is economic), Comte, who invented the term 'sociology' (religion represents an immature stage of society, to be replaced by the scientific) and Freud (various, but especially God as an invented father figure to compensate for the frailties of earthly fathers), all exemplify this approach.

Contemporary sociologists of religion do not generally make such intellectual arguments against religion. Instead, they are concerned with studying religious behaviour, with observing and trying to measure the impact of religion on societies and with trying to explain their findings. They are not concerned with whether religion is true or not, or with whether it deserves to die out. For example, Bruce (1996) explicitly rejects the view that religion has declined because people have become more sophisticated or better informed, as well as pointing to an important distinction between truth and plausibility: 'It is not the case that religion has declined because people have become better educated and less credulous. ... [W]hether something is true and whether it becomes widely accepted are two very different questions' (p. 38).

In fact, although the growth of scientific understanding and increased educational levels are often linked in popular perception with the decline of religion, contemporary secularization theory sees the undermining of religion as a largely accidental, intended consequence of modernization processes (Bruce 1996), although as we shall see Casanova argues that the ECR does have social consequences under certain conditions. Moreover, the impact of popular forms of Enlightenment arguments that religion ought to decline should not be ignored as a source of assumptions about actual decline, whether among sociologists, or amongst the general population. As we shall see, the fact that Britain has some of the lowest rates of religious belief and participation in the world may also influence perceptions in the British context.

3. Quantitative Evidence of Secularization

(a) Britain

On 28 November 1999 the *Daily Telegraph* announced 'Christianity in crisis as pews empty'. A month later, the same message of the decline of Christianity (at least in Britain) was reinforced in another *Telegraph* headline. This time it was the quality of belief rather than the number of church attenders which was seen to be dropping, as the paper reported the finding of a specially commissioned Gallup poll on the state of Christianity two millennia since the birth of Christ. The paper reports that: 'for millions of self-proclaimed Christians in Britain today, the religion clearly amounts to little more than a well-meaning mish-mash – a haphazard blend of scraps of religious belief together with the simple fact ... of having been born into the Church of England' (28 December 1999 p. 1).

Such findings appear to support the continuing validity of the views of the sociologist Bryan Wilson (1975), who wrote a quarter of a century earlier that: 'To almost everyone ... the secularization process is a self-evident process in contemporary society. Religion is on the wane' (p. 77). However, another article, also published in 1999 and which formed the introduction to a special edition of the journal *Sociology of Religion* devoted to the issue of secularization, states: 'Virtually no empirical research supports the prediction of a societal slide from a peak of sacrality into a valley of secularity' (Swatos and Christiano 1999 p. 216).

How can we explain this contrast? First of all, Britain, along with Scandinavia and North-Western Europe (France and Benelux), are probably the places in the world where evidence for decline in religious vitality is strongest, as measured by church membership, attendance at regular worship and for rites of passage in traditional churches. However, as Gill *et al.* (1998) show in their study of a selection of surveys of religious beliefs in Britain from the 1940s to the 1990s, the process is not one of uniform decline. Taking traditional beliefs first, Gill *at al.* found that belief in God dropped steadily from 79 per cent in the 1940s to 68 per cent in the 1990s (p. 509). Belief in Jesus as the Son of God also dropped steadily from 68 per cent in the 1940s and 1950s to 49 per cent in the 1980s, with belief in God as personal following the same pattern, down from 43 per cent in the 1940s–1950s to 31 per cent in the 1990s. However, belief in God as Spirit or Life Force remained steady through the period, actually increasing slightly from the 1940s to the 1990s, from 38 to 40 per cent. Belief in life after death and the Devil both followed a slightly different pattern, dipping from 49 per cent and 24 per cent respectively in the 1940s–1950s to a low of 37 per cent and 20 per cent in the 1970s, but picking up thereafter to 43 per cent and 26 per cent in the 1990s, perhaps reflecting the shift among church-goers during this period to evangelical, charismatic and pentecostal forms of Christianity which emphasize the supernatural aspects of belief.

In contrast to the overall pattern of decline for traditional beliefs, non-traditional beliefs tend to show stability between the 1970s and 1990s and for longer periods where the data are available (Gill *et al.*1998 p. 513). Thus belief in reincarnation and horoscopes hovered at around 25 per cent from 1970s to the 1990s, while belief in exchanging messages with the dead shows a fairly persistent 14–15 per cent from the 1940s to the present, with a brief dip to 11 per cent in the 1970s, the low-water mark of religious belief generally on these data – and also the period when the secularization thesis enjoyed greatest popularity. Another feature of the data is an increasing polarization between believers and non-believers, reflected in a decrease in agnosticism on matters of traditional belief and an increase in definite disbelief. For example, disbelief in God rose from 10 to 27 per cent between the 1960s and the 1990s and in life after death from 21 to 41 per cent between the 1940s–1950s and the 1990s (p. 509). Disbelief in non-traditional beliefs, while higher than in traditional ones (around 55 per cent for reincarnation, between 70 and 85 per cent for most other items), remained stable. The increase in disbelief in traditional items may reflect the increasing destigmatization of outright disbelief as the association between religion and social conformity declines.

What are we to make of these findings? First, they do not suggest much of a diminution in the propensity of people to believe in the supernatural generally, rather in rates of traditional religious belief, rallying in some areas after the 1970s, together with stability in non-traditional areas. Second, we may note that in its rates of positive disbelief in God and life after death (27 per cent and 41 per cent in the 1990s) Britain appears to be quite exceptional even in European terms: Greeley (1999 p. 190) states that 'in the European countries studies in the International Social Survey Programme ... those who flatly deny both the existence of God and Life after death are generally less than one tenth of the adult population'. This brings us on to consideration of the broader European situation. We opened this chapter with a quotation from Steve Bruce (1999 p. 117), which stated that 'in almost every European country, the twentieth century has seen the power, popularity and presence of religion decline'. And yet study of the literature on secularization in Europe shows that even here consensus on decline in vitality – and most of the quantitative data relate to this – is far from complete.

(b) Western Europe

Rodney Stark (1999) has argued that over the last millennium rates of religious activity in Western Europe have remained remarkably stable, allowing for long-term variations. Stark's evidence for this assertion comes from two sources: first, long-term historical data, which indicate that Northern Europe was never very effectively Christianized, so practice has always been low historically compared with other regions (for example Mediterranean countries). Second, more recent data, for example Iannaccone's (1996) finding that of the European nations he studied, only Britain, East Germany and Slovenia showed evidence of downward trends since 1920 and in the latter cases the onset of decline coincided with the beginning of Communist rule, during which church attendance was heavily penalized. Conversely, in 15 of the 18 nations considered (mostly European) church attendance rates were stable or increased between 1920 and 1990.

These findings conflict with Bruce's European evidence on Northern Europe (1999). Bruce divides these societies into two basic types, those 'where the history of nation-building has left a stable and increasingly prosperous nation-state' and those where this process has been arrested for various reasons. The former have 'largely given up religion', regardless of their religious diversity/homogeneity – Scandinavia, Britain, France, Belgium and Holland are given as examples and statistics are given to demonstrate declining rates of attendance and/or membership in all of these in the last third to quarter of the twentieth century. However, there is 'another Europe': here, as in Ireland or Poland, religion may serve as a repository of national identity and hence religious vitality remains high (88 per cent and 85 per cent respectively attended church at least once month in 1991–3; Inglehart *et al.* 1998). However, religion may not be mobilized in this way and here, according to Bruce, religion will decline as in the case of consolidated nation-states, as a function of modernization in the manner predicted by secularization theory.

Bruce illustrates his argument with reference to the Baltic states. In Lithuania, the Catholic Church became mobilized in the struggle against Soviet power (as it had been in the nineteenth century against Russification) and hence religious vitality remains high: 31 per cent attended church at least once per month in 1996 (Bruce 1996 p. 101). In contrast, in Estonia and Latvia, partly because no one church constituted a substantial majority, the churches did not become mobilized in this way. Hence church attendance rates, as one would expect with fairly high rates of industrialization, are fairly low: only 9 per cent and 16 per cent respectively attended at least once per month in 1996 (p. 102). In brief, Bruce argues that these data illustrate his argument that the social significance of religion declines as a function of modernization, except where it finds work to do other than mediating the natural and supernatural – for example, in providing a focus for national identity.

These data clearly conflict with those of Stark, who found evidence of decline in Northern Europe only in a few cases. How can we account for this difference? In contrast to Stark (1999), whose only source on church attendance in Europe is Iannoccone (1996), Bruce cites different sources for each of these cases. Thus he quotes a French source (Lambert 1994) which states that church attendance, membership and rites of passage have all declined in the postwar era, a Belgian source which shows church attendance to have dropped from 43 to 18 per cent between 1967 and 1990 (van Meerbeck 1995) and a Dutch source which claims that of the 43 per cent who belong to a church, only 36 per cent of Catholics and 43 per cent of Dutch Reformed attended at least once a fortnight in 1991, compared with 71 and 50 per cent from a 58 per cent membership base in 1975 (Decker and Ester 1996).

It is difficult to know why Iannoccone's data differ so much from those collected by Bruce, especially as the study cited by Stark remains unpublished. All things being equal, a range of sources suggesting a common trend provides stronger evidence than a single, dissenting source – but all may not be equal. However, it should be noted that Iannoccone's study refers to a much longer period – 70 rather than 15–25 years. Certainly, part of Stark and Iannoccone's argument elsewhere (1994) is that it is important to consider recent trends in longer-term historical perspective, as the former may be just a temporary blip or part of a long-term cycle. This is an important methodological consideration, although unfortunately the specific interpretation of longer-term trends presented by them is flawed (Hanson 1997). They argue that rates of participation in Christian rites in Northern and Western Europe were always low for several reasons, in particular, Christianity came late (compared with the Mediterranean world), was imposed from above and hence lacked popular support, and medieval Christianity was not much concerned with lay participation or religious knowledge, so there was not a good foundation of these laid for the modern period.

While these are suggestive thoughts, Hanson shows that Stark and Iannoccone's handling of historical data is so poor that their conclusions – in particular that religious participation has not declined during the modern period – cannot be relied upon. For example, all but one of their sixteenth-century sources is English, although they generalize their conclusions to the whole of Europe. Their main source of eighteenth-century data is a description of a single English village in a secondary source. Closer attention to this source reveals that it in fact refers to a late seventeenth-century village and that the low estimate of religious attendance they derive is based on a false reading of the demographic data supplied. Furthermore, they pay little attention to the changing meaning of church attendance over time. Thus Hanson (1997 p. 165) concludes, 'What they have done is to set up an extremely poor argument based on anecdotal, irrelevant or inappropriately applied historical data'.

In fairness, it should be pointed out that Hanson is also critical of Bruce, arguing that his interpretation is simplistic, because of its reliance on statistics and historical anecdote without adequate engagement with non-quantitative data (Hanson 1997 pp. 167–8). However, her criticisms of his handling of empirical data are not so devastating as those made of Stark and Iannoccone. In view of this and the argument for a plurality of sources, it seems reasonable to conclude that the balance of empirical evidence suggests that a decline in traditional religious practice – especially church attendance – did occur in Northern and Western Europe during the last third of the twentieth century. This verdict does not yet take into account the impact of changes in religious practice, or of new forms of religiosity, which we will consider when we look at the American example below.

Davie (2000) provides a rather different perspective on Western European religiosity. First, she relates the decline in institutional participation and traditional indices of religious belief to parallel declines in confidence and participation in public institutions and activities in other spheres – government, electoral processes, trades unions and even sport among them. Soccer, for example, is more watched on television than ever, yet grass-roots participation has fallen. Such trends may presage a crisis in communal life – but more individual patterns of consumption do not necessarily indicate decline in demand for the 'product'. However, there are also counter-trends to individualism: in Sweden regular church attendance is less than 2 per cent, yet more than 80 per cent of adults continue to choose to belong to the Lutheran Church in spite of its recent disestablishment and the cost of having to pay the church tax. Rates of baptism remain high and church weddings are increasing. In Sweden, religion appears to play a continuing role in cultural identity, in locating the individual in relation to a tradition. Davie draws on Hervieu-Léger's idea of religion as 'chain of memory' to interpret this phenomenon and we shall consider the latter's work on the way in which religion in modernity seeps into different spheres of society below (pp. 27 and 36). Davie also points out that the 'vicarious memories' of the Swedish model are precarious: if the basic stories of religious traditions are not transmitted, younger generations may no longer see the point in maintaining the institution, even vicariously and the chain of memory may be broken. This emphasis on the importance of stories in maintaining religious traditions is a theme to which we shall return when we consider Callum Brown's evidence below and signals the importance of qualitative data.

But first we turn to the United States, where in spite of advanced modernization the Western European pattern of decline appears less evident even for traditional religion.

(c) America

Beginning with comparison with Europe, Bruce (1998 p. 227) states: 'Whether one takes church membership, church attendance, the publication of religious materials, the audience for televised religious broadcasts, the USA stands out from the rest of the modern industrialized world, but it does not stand out terribly far'. Yet this is in some ways quite a surprising conclusion, given some of the findings he presents earlier in his book. For example, in the course of explaining why a Christian Right formed in America but not in Britain, he writes: 'Around 40 per cent of Americans are regular churchgoers … Only 10 per cent of the British are churchgoing' (p. 157). This would seem to be quite a striking difference. However, perhaps his point is that American trends in religious belief and practice are in the same direction as elsewhere in advanced industrial societies – that is, generally down. Thus he quotes the findings of the Princeton Religious Research Center's longitudinal study of religious practice, beliefs and attitudes over a fifty-year period, as given by Wade Clark Roof: 'from 1940 to the late 1950s the index rose; but the index plunged during the late 1960s – and during the 1970s and 1980s and well into the 1990s – reaching an all-time low mark over the past half-century in 1993' (Roof 1996 p. 151, cited in Bruce 1998 p. 228).

However, Bruce's interpretation of this as indicating decline in religious involvement in America is challenged by the very source from which he quotes, because of the bias in the survey towards traditional measures of religious belief and practice: 'A close scrutiny of the Princeton Index shows it to be weighted toward traditional belief and commitment … Not included are items that tap into what passes currently as spirituality' (Roof 1996 p. 151). Thus, an important issue is what is being measured as religiosity. In particular, studies that show decline tend to be those weighted to more traditional indicators of belief and commitment. Bruce, like Wilson, tends to attach weight to decline in traditional indices because he sees new, less authoritarian forms of spirituality as symptomatic of secularization. This assessment relates to his understanding of the historic function of religions as providing authoritative institutions, practices and beliefs which make for social cohesion and which less conformist, more individually oriented forms of religion seem less capable of providing. But religion may perform roles other than promoting social cohesion thought provision of an agreed worldview, whether as part of an individual's spiritual quest, or by promoting the public sphere of civil society using particular principles, rather than insisting on conformity. Change of function does not necessarily indicate decline, either in vitality or in social significance.

This can be illustrated by briefly considering recent research on forms of religiosity amongst 'GenXers', a term borrowed from Douglas Copeland's (1991) novel *Generation X* to describe 'the 80 million Americans who were born between 1961 and 1981':

> This is the 'buster' generation, the children of so-called baby boomers. While they are a diverse lot, they also share many common cultural experiences related to advances in technology, the failed marriages of their parents, changes in the structure of the economy and the liberation politics that transpired during their childhood and youth. …

As GenXers seek spiritual experience and religious belonging they have created (and are creating) new religious forms based on their generational experiences, characterized by what I see as significant changes from previous generations. ... First, GenXers evidence a move from written text to narrative and image as a basis for religious belief. ... Second, there is a move ... away from rationalistic, propositional truth claims reliant on the exegesis of written text to truth validated by experience in the religious community. (Flory and Miller 2000 pp. 3 and 245)

This evidence points not only to the importance of generational experience in considering evidence for secularization, but also to shifts in the cultural form of religion (from text to image, from propositional truth to communally validated experience) which are likely to register on conventional measures of religious belief as decline, but may rather indicate only change. This issue points to a central problem with conventional secularization theory – many protagonists do not distinguish between the different public roles that religion can perform, but consider only authoritarian religious institutions, conventional religious thinking (obedience to dogma) and practices (typically church-going, rites of passage) and their attenuated forms. Yet the public spheres of contemporary societies are complex and religions perform a variety of roles within them. In particular, the role of religious discourse is neglected, meaning the way in which religious ways of thinking and representing, untied from authoritative institutions, may none the less capture the public imagination and shape the way issues are discussed. We shall see below that both American and Egyptian public debate on many issues are shaped, indeed in the latter case dominated, not by any one religious ideology or institution, but by a range of competing voices all speaking religious language.

This possibility appears to be missed by nearly all parties in the secularization debate. Certainly, to return to Bruce's use of Roof, the latter does not agree with Bruce that decline in the traditional indices necessarily indicates a general decline in religion; rather that the locus of religious belief and practice is shifting (1996 p. 155), a process which makes longitudinal comparisons problematic. Furthermore, not all longitudinal research supports Bruce's view of a declining trend. On the contrary, Casanova (1994 p. 28) summarizes the position as follows: 'Longitudinal survey research ... shows that there has been no discernible decline of religion in America in this century'. In support of this statement Casanova cites Caplow *et al.* (1983) and Greeley (1989), the former of whom found most indicators of religiosity to have increased in a 'typical' American town since 1924, the latter 'continuity and persistence' across most indicators in surveys conducted since the 1940s (Casanova 1994 p. 243 n. 51). In other words, Bruce and Casanova cite contradicting longitudinal studies of American religiosity. What, then, should we conclude about change in rates of American religiosity? Unlike the Western European case, there is little evidence of decline, but rather the balance of arguments and studies points towards a position of stability with regard to overall participation, combined with diversification in the range of forms of participation.

(d) Within and Beyond 'the West': Islam in the West and the Muslim Majority World

These brief surveys of the Western European and American evidence help us begin
to build a picture of the diversity of religious participation in the contemporary West.
Perhaps more than that, they tell us something about the difficulties of so doing.
When extending such study to areas where Christianity has not been historically
dominant, the difficulties become even greater. As Bruce (1999 p. 197) comments in
relation to the World Values Survey, 'All the quite proper concerns about the wording
of survey questions, the meaning given to them by respondents and the meaning of
their responses are magnified tenfold when researchers try to use a common
instrument across cultures'. For example, the survey asks a question about church
attendance and data are given in relation to Japan. Actually, this increased between
1981 and 1990, from 12 to 14 per cent. But what does this mean? Given the tiny
proportion of Christians in Japan, presumably the question asked referred to some
regularly performed religious ritual, but what is the Shinto or Buddhist equivalent of
church attendance? Koepping, an expert on Japanese culture, argues that the
imported word used to translate 'religion' does not carry the sense of many Shinto
rituals. Furthermore, questions on motivation can also be misleading. When asked
why Shinto rituals are performed, many will answer, 'because everyone else does',
which suggests a low sense of personal belief. Yet when asked what will happen if
such rituals are not performed, many will answer in terms of the catastrophic
consequences the ritual is supposed to ward off. Thus, depending on how one
conducts the dialogue, Japan might seem a highly secularized or a highly inspirited
society. Indeed, the problems of comparability across cultures are such that Casanova
(1994 p. 242) concludes: 'Most attempts I have seen to develop quantitative analyses
of global religious trends appear to be nearly worthless'.

However, this does not mean that such data could not be developed in principle,
at least for those traditions with relative uniformity of practice across cultures. For
example, for Islam, the proportion of people performing the five-times-daily
prayers, of men attending Friday noon prayers and of people fasting for Ramadan
provide workable indicators. Indeed, while it is not possible to build up a
longitudinal study like the Gill *et al.* (1998) analysis for Britain, or the Princeton
index for the United States, some such data already exist in fragmentary form. Thus
Stark (1999 p. 267) provides a brief survey of quantitative data collected in relation
to Islam. Interestingly, he finds a consistent trend: 'Several studies from different
parts of the world suggest that Muslim commitment increases with modernization'.

Further, a study in Java (Tamney 1979) found that 'religious commitment was
positively correlated with education and with occupational prestige', another in
Pakistan (Ahmad 1991) that most 'fundamentalist' leaders are 'highly educated (all
having advanced degrees)' and that their followers are predominantly middle class,
and in Turkey (Mutlu 1996) that the proportion of university students who believed
in heaven and hell increased from 36 per cent in 1978 to 75 per cent in 1991 (Stark
1999 p. 267). We shall also find below that this correlation between educational
achievement, occupational mobility and involvement in the Islamic Trend is
supported by Starrett's study of Egypt (1998). Islam provides a discourse for the

educated middle classes to articulate their hopes and dreams and in some cases a means of practical policy implementation.

In the West, too, there is evidence that Muslim practice is relatively high and may be increasing. Sunier (1995) estimates that roughly 60 per cent of people of Muslim heritage in the Netherlands are practising, Leveau (1988 p. 112) puts the French figure at about two-thirds. Leveau further argues that 'the rigorous interpretation' of Islam amongst 'intellectual believers' may be a 'strategy for coping with French society', a point which would underline Islam's apparent compatibility with modernization. This point is also supported by a study comparing Islam as practised in rural Turkey with practice amongst migrants to a German city (Schiffauer 1988 in Baumann 1999 pp. 73–4). Two characteristics in particular are worth highlighting:

> On the plane of religious choices, villagers collectively agreed on a set canon of rules to be followed by all, while their migrant kin embarked on a far more individual search for truth, hotly debating their allegiances to different Muslim movements. On the plane of self-awareness, ... villagers saw religious obligations as a debt to God that could be made up at any stage before one's death, especially as one grew more pious with age. To the migrants, religious merit appeared as a lifelong commitment to educating one's piety and a constant striving for religious growth. (Baumann 1999 p. 73)

Here, the modern characteristics of individualism, emphasis on personal reasoning and drive for self-improvement all work to reinforce rather than undermine Islamic faith. Such evidence also serves to underline the value of qualitative data, to which we now turn our attention.

While reliable quantitative data for non-Western settings may be in short supply, there is an abundance of qualitative data, mostly produced by anthropologists, which reflect on the relationship between religion and modernization. Such data better address the social significance aspect of secularization because they can capture the impact of religion on other social systems that are difficult to measure quantitively: for example, the political influence of a religious organization, or the impact of its teachings on behaviour. We shall therefore consider three examples of this kind: a study of the impact of mass education in Egypt on the social significance of Islam, the role of narrative in the transmission of faith among British women through the twentieth century; and the public impact of statements by Catholic bishops on public debate in America. Each illustrates the role of discursive religion in contemporary societies. We shall then have some evidence for the impact of religion on other social systems in both a Western and a non-Western setting and be in a position to consider the implications of both kinds of data for the secularization debate.

4. Qualitative Evidence: Three Studies

*(a) Egypt: Gregory Starrett on the Role of State Education in the Islamicization of
          Public Space*

If we are to make sense of [the growth of the Islamic Trend] within the institutional context
of Egyptian society, we cannot dismiss religious concerns as benighted survivals of earlier
social stages, or merely 'inflammations' symptomatic of social pathology and political
strife. Instead, we must see them as perennial questions which persist in an active manner,
adapting and reproducing themselves within and between generations through increasingly
complex interactions with institutions and communications media whose own advent was
supposed to reduce rather than increase the influence of religious ideas in society. (Starrett
1998 p. 91)

In *Putting Islam to Work: Education, Politics and Religious Transformation in Egypt*
(1998) Gregory Starrett takes issue with 'the false assumption that, in the case of
Egypt as in the case of historical development generally, secularism will replace
religion in a global and irreversible evolutionary process' (p. 17). In doing so, he
makes three important points: first, that the same arguments presented by
contemporary academic exponents of secularization are present in popular forms in
the ways the Egyptian élite explains contemporary Islamic resurgence, second, that
such arguments were also used by nineteenth- and twentieth-century colonial
governments and by post-Independence nationalist governments, third, that precisely
these failed arguments have underlain the educational policies of both colonialist and
nationalist governments. As a result of their failure to grasp the dynamic between
religion and modernity, policies designed to curtail the public influence of religion
have in fact had precisely the reverse effect, embedding religious discourse ever
more firmly in the public domain.

How has this situation come about? We shall look much more fully at the broader
situation in Egypt in Chapter 8, but here we shall just follow Starrett's argument quite
closely, which concentrates on the role of education in the process. He traces the
modernization of Egyptian education back to Muhammad Ali's reform of the *kuttabs*
(village schools for religious instruction) in the early nineteenth century, in an attempt
to avoid a repeat of recent humiliations at the hands of Europeans. Ali sought to enable
Egypt to compete with Europe by education, industrialization and improvement of the
military, seeing a necessary causal link from the first to the third of these.
Unfortunately for him, rural peasants also saw the link and were reluctant to send their
children to the *kuttabs* only to have them drafted from there to Ali's technical schools
and hence the miltary: no literacy, no conscription (Starrett 1998 p. 27). However,
reforms effected in 1833 increased the inducements for attendance at these schools
such that rural families could no longer afford to ignore them. So Ali got his literate
and technically educated supply of recruits for the military and civil service.

In another sense, however, Ali's policies failed: British influence in Egypt steadily
increased through the nineteenth century. British colonial administrators built on
Ali's educational legacy, but also brought ideas from Victorian Britain, in particular
the use of religious education to instil the virtues of hard work and obedience to

authority, following the lead of educational reformers such as the Quaker Joseph Lancaster, who argued that 'the Koran [*sic*] might be made, like the Bible, a means of imparting moral truth combined with instructive history' (in Starrett 1998 p. 39).

Although the path was not a straightforward one, the extent to which this strategy was ultimately successful may be gauged by examining the current curriculum in Egyptian primary schools. Starrett (1998 p. 132) quotes from the introduction to a first-grade (ages 5–6) religion textbook (produced for the years 1989–90), which informs teachers that 'religious education … is not material restricted to classrooms, but rather is a complete life-curriculum, including the classroom milieu with all its activities and information and knowledge. It also includes the home environment and society as a whole'. The approach here sets the tone for the rest of the curriculum: as the colonial administrators had hoped, in contemporary public education, Islam has come to be seen as 'the charter for the function of modern society' (ibid. p. 147). Starrett describes this process as the 'functionalization' of religion:

> The functionalization of Egypt's religious tradition meant that the ideas, symbols and behaviors consituting 'true' Islam came to be judged not by their adherence to contemporary popular or high traditions, but by their utility in performing social work, either in furthering programs of social reform or in fulfilling the police functions that Europeans attributed to education as such. (p. 62)

In this curriculum, children learn the Qur'an not in the traditional sequence, but in bite-sized chunks which are thematically grouped (pp. 135–6), often linked to a key moral lesson. There is a developmental sequence programmed into learning, following the same evolutionary logic that Western developmental psychology has built into Western educational systems. This can also be illustrated by considering how teaching about Ramadan, the month of fasting, is structured through the curriculum:

> In the early grades, the meaning and significance of Ramadan is expressed with the formal joy of classroom song and through the ritual fast's place in the life of the family. With time, students begin to learn more about the ritual details of the fast, personal restrictions that are balanced immediately by their beneficial effects on the self and others. Next, fast and feast find their place in the yearly ritual cycle of Islam, their importance matched only by the celebration of sacrifice during the season of pilgrimage. And finally, as the child reaches the age of personal participation, learning about Ramadan becomes learning about individual and social responsibilities. (p. 137)

Throughout the curriculum and indeed more widely in a range of literature, the complementary relationship between Islam and modern science is stressed. Starrett highlights three ways in which this occurs. First, new technologies are used to support the religious system, examples of which include loudspeakers for prayer, audio cassettes of Qur'anic recitation and teaching and using science to calculate the exact times of prayers (p. 139). Second, new technologies are legitimated by Islamic principles: medical technologies, including 'in vitro fertilization, plastic surgery and birth control', may, when 'properly bounded with certain limits … protect or further divine interests by correcting accidental errors or by satisfying other legitimate goals of the individual, family or community' (ibid.). Third, Islamic concepts and practices are presented as being confirmed by modern science, including *wudu* (ritual washing) (ibid.).

Thus far it would seem that the colonial administrators have mostly had it their own way, as their policies were pursued by successive post-Independence governments to the same end of producing a compliant and technically competent workforce. A process of 'internal secularization' would seem to have occurred, in which the religious system has been rationalized and harmonized in line with modern educational and scientific principles. Religion has remained influential in other social systems, but only at the expense of the transformation of its contents to fit the rationalized structure of the modern world system. However, all is not as it seems. First of all, as we saw above with Martin's work on pentecostalism in Latin America, competence in the use of modern technologies does not necessarily entail a decline in belief in supernatural agencies. Rather, people seem perfectly capable of managing to believe both in the spirit world and in science. So also in Egypt:

> [F]unctionalization occurs without the desacralization of the material, so that the process described by Durkheim described earlier in this century as one of the goals of the modern educational system is subverted. Naturalistic and materialistic explanations coexist with supernatural ones, for Muslims perceive the two as noncontradictory. The 'real' reasons for religious practices do not strip off their theological cloaks. Since God is concerned with the welfare of the Muslim community, the presumptions of Islam are not only beneficial, but manifestly rational. (Starrett 1998 p. 153)

Furthermore, as well as creating a workforce fit for service in a modern industrial society, teaching the population to apply Islam to everyday life – or 'putting Islam to work' in the title of Starrett's book – has had other, unforeseen, consequences. One dramatic manifestation is that 'the young men who bomb and shoot tourist buses, government ministers and police tend also to be modern educated, with degrees and diplomas in technical subjects' (p. 199). Such people do not appear to represent the last desperate gasp of a dying traditionalism, but are rather the products of a modern educational system. But how have such acts of terrorism, designed to destabilize the government, been born of an educational process aimed at pacification? Much of the answer has to do with history and politics, especially the defeat by Israel of Egypt and other Arab states in the Six Day War (1967), the perceived failure of secular Arab politics (nationalist and socialist) and the subsequent politicization of Islamic discourse. We shall consider such factors more carefully in relation to Egypt in Chapter 8 below. But for now we can note first that the functionalization of Islamic discourse for opposition political purposes would not have been possible without its prior functionalization for political purposes within the state educational system. Second, and also relevant to our primarily sociological purpose in this chapter, is the role of communications media that were once thought to have a secularizing effect (McLuhan 1975). Thus, in a process that has been paralleled to the European Reformation, mass literacy has freed people to read and interpret the scriptures for themselves (Goldberg 1991 pp. 30 – 32; Starrett 1998 p. 231). As a result, there has been a transfer in authority from the traditional *ulama* (religious scholars) to anyone who can read the scriptures and find the means to disseminate their views, a process greatly enhanced by new technologies:

> This combination of religion and modern education has proved dangerous to the religious establishment and the government that relies on it for legitimacy, because in the world of mass literacy, mass marketing and mass (not to mention international) communication, the exclusive interpretive authority of local, state-based '*ulama* has been permanently broken. Authority is now more a characteristic of products themselves (sermons, lessons, advice, books, magazines, cassette tapes, computer software) than productive processes (apprenticeship, certification, jurisprudential skill). Who the producer is – when that can be determined – is less important than the marketability of what he has to say. (Starrett 1998 pp. 232–3)

It would seem that, contrary to Marshall McLuhan's (1975) view, new technologies do not necessarily undermine religious worldviews. Nor, significantly for our concern with civil society, does an increasing plurality of voices necessarily have a liberalizing or relativizing effect:

> The growth of book publishing in the Arab world resulted in, among other things, at least five different editions of the infamous European anti-Semitic tract 'The Protocols of the Elders of Zion' being available on the streets of Cairo in 1989. The medium is not the only message. (Starrett 1998 p. 93)

New technologies have favoured a revival of ancient Middle Eastern traditions of oral transmission, creating a synergy unanticipated by McLuhan. Historically, the Middle East has been a culture of 'secondary orality': texts have been present for a long time (the Qur'an was recorded in fragmentary form during the life of the Prophet), but the presence of the author or some other authoritative bearer of tradition remained important. The dominance of printed communication media as the voice of the modern state from the late nineteenth century had substantially eroded this tradition; but radio, TV, audio and video recording, as well as some new computer technologies restore something of the dynamic of oral communication and hence 'appear … to restore presence, which for the alternative advantages of record and durability writing systems had moved away from' (Williams 1981 p. 111, cited in Starrett 1998 p. 95).

The means of control have turned into the means of dissent, with the result that the tactic of successive governments to pacify and equip the population for modern industrial life by the inculcation of a rationalized form of Islam through a public educational system (and other authoritative institutions) has seriously misfired: Islam has become embedded in the social system as a central medium of public communication, one which is accessible to a mass public, who can increasingly deploy it for their own diverse ends through an increasing variety of communications media. Yet even this account is too instrumentalized: Islam is not simply 'used', implying some 'real' – or *realpolitik* – motivation behind the manipulation of symbols, images and language. Rather, the Egyptian case is only comprehensible if we allow for the possibility that for the majority of Egyptians Islam is an integral part of the way they make sense of and face practical challenges in their lives. As Reynolds and Tanner (1995), following Geertz (1966), write, '[Religion] is not just a matter of how people cope with the problems of life, but how they conceive of life, which in turn sets the stage from how they cope with it ... religion goes beyond common sense and changes it so that reality is somehow redefined' (pp. 26 – 7). An appreciation of this is often absent in the secularization debate. Starrett shows that many in the Egyptian élite, like Western social scientists, also find it difficult to grasp: he cites examples of secular intellectuals sending their daughters for psychiatric treatment when they start to wear the veil (Starrett 1998 p. 233). And yet it would seem that in Egypt – in spite of policies designed to reduce its influence and the accidental effects of increasing modernization – Islam has not only remained part of the grammar of life, but – through functionalization without disenchantment – has extended and deepened its influence. However, this is not to say that this process is inevitable. We turn next to the British case, where it seems that religion has, on the contrary, lost its discursive power.

(b) Britain: Callum Brown on the Death of Discursive Christianity

In his recent book *The Death of Christian Britain* (2001) Brown challenges the view of conventional secularization theory (summarized in Section 2 above) that Christianity in Britain has been in gradual decline since the beginning of the nineteenth century, in parallel with and as a result of urbanization and industrialization (and hence social differentiation). In fact, the latter processes resulted only in a change in the form of religion – privatization, in the sense of less association with conformity and more with personal conviction. Indeed, Brown argues that the competition between denominations increased religious vitality during the nineteenth century and this vitality largely persisted into the middle of the twentieth. Rather than a slow retreating tide then, the sea of faith was swept away by the cultural cataclysm of the 1960s. Part of his argument is methodological and echoes a point we have already made: to assess the social significance of religion, secularization theorists measure the wrong things. Although one may expect a general correlation between church attendance and the social influence of religion, a far better indication is given by looking at the ways religion influences people's lives and a good way to do this is to look at the texts and artefacts of popular culture and oral history. Hence Brown examined novels, magazines and Christian tracts and conducted interviews across contemporary generations. In particular, he is concerned with the impact of Christian language, morality and narrative on these sources.

At the centre of his argument is the contention that the role of Christian narrative in the construction of the identity of British women was decisively broken by cultural change in the 1960s. This effectively cut the 'chain of memory', to use Hervieu-Léger's term introduced above, and dethroned Christianity from its central role in British culture. The central role of women in the transmission of Christian tradition is traced to the early nineteenth-century 'privatization' of religion, characterized by an emphasis on women as models of piety and in the containment of wayward male behaviour, and on the resultant 'feminization' of spirituality:

Exploration of the role of femininity in piety was never far from the surface in most evangelical literature about men. Religious stories explored the discourse on the feminized nature of the born-again man. In Sydney Watson's *Disloyal* of 1891, Frank Holson was converted by Christian love of his wife and became 'a constant source of wonder to all who knew him': 'His friends in his own wide circle talked of him pityingly behind his back ...and said "Poor Halson! [sic] he's clean gone, don't cher know!" 'Frank was oblivious, having no thought but 'to glorify God among his fellow men': 'His Christianity was a real, robust life; there was nothing namby-pamby about it.' ... In short, the true Christian man had to show restraint which others might show as effeminacy. His main sacrifice would be having to endure the ridicule of his own sex. (Brown 2001 p. 108)

Interestingly, this account of evangelical Christian discourse as feminizing corresponds to contemporary analysis of conversions to pentecostalism in African and Latin America (Lehmann 1996). However, the centrality of the 'virtuous' female role model to Christian tradition in Britain, strongly influenced by evangelicalism, made the tradition itself vulnerable when this role model came under sustained attack in the 1960s. One may, however, ask why it was quite so vulnerable, why a discursive structure that had dominated for 150 years collapsed so suddenly and indeed why, if this is the central cause of secularization, parallel cultural changes in the United States did not signal a parallel collapse.

Brown offers some answers to these questions. In fact, his emphasis on the watershed of the 1960s is slightly misleading because what he shows is that use of Christian discourse to narrate people's lives reduced considerably throughout the twentieth century, leaving only a weakened form in place to withstand the storms of the 1960s. Thus, among male interviewees born in the early twentieth century it is already 'extremely common' to find 'a presence of evangelical polarities and the residue of evangelical narrative structure, but overlain with commentary (ranging from the resentful to the mocking) on illiberal parental attitudes to religion, morality and child discipline' (Brown 2001 p. 181). A generation later (born from the late 1930s) and the influence of evangelical narrative is further reduced; indeed *any* narrative structure is largely absent:

They are of a generation that has not sustained a training in how to express their religiosity. They may even have a sense of religiosity or spirituality, but they are not familiar – like their parents and grandparents – with having to express this. Critically, a very common element is the general absence of the motifs of moral bipolarities (drinking and teetotalism, strict Sundays and the banning of games, strict discipline and naughtiness), as well as the absence of narrative progression that sustained these contrasts. There is indeed a reticence about describing their lives with the same openness as their parents. Constructing a life narrative is less important to them, but equally they do not *conceive* of it as being capable of being rendered in such a format. (Ibid. p. 182)

For the generation born from the mid-1960s in many cases the relationship between religion and personal identity has gone altogether, replaced by a 'stunted' view of religion as church attendance, although Brown notes (but does not expand on) the persistence of a negative link between religion and hypocrisy in this generation. Such a link is perhaps evidence of the continuing power of the 1960s version of 'the

Enlightenment critique of religion', identifying religion with false and imposed morality. Although the testimony of women differs in the sense that the public disavowal of religion was socially taboo and rare until the 1960s, the same gradual distancing from the Victorian advocacy of evangelical morality is evident. Parallel shifts are apparent in autobiography.

On this evidence, although Christian discourses remained publicly influential until they were challenged in the 1960s – mirrored by indicators of religiosity that all start to decline from 1956 and from 1963 'almost enter free fall' (Brown 2001 p. 188) – their common substructure, understood as making sense of individual lives in terms of Christian narrative, was in decay long before that. Unfortunately, Brown does not explain why this is this case, why a structure that had been persuasive for a century, through probably the most dislocating period of industrialization and urbanization, should gradually lose its grip on people's imagination through the twentieth century and suddenly collapse – at least in public influence – when its central model of virtue was attacked by discourses of 'liberation' in the 1960s.

Brown does, however, offer analysis of the contrast with American experience. He desribes 'the same discursive challenge Britain experienced *emerging* in North America in the 1960s, but then not *triumphing* (ibid. p. 197). To explain this he points to the greater resources of American evangelicalism – for example private satellite and cable television – to publicly sustain evangelical discourse. But such means are useless unless the message persuades – as the failure of such channels in Europe testifies (Davie 2000 pp. 24–37). He then argues that America may be experiencing an 'overlap of epistemes' (Foucault's term for 'regimes of knowledge') 'between modernity and postmodernity' (Brown 2001 p. 197). 'Postmodernity' here signals especially 'a collapse of metanarratives', of shared stories for making sense of the world, including the evangelical Christian metanarrative. The problem with this is that in the United States these two putative 'epistemes' do not merely coexist but interpenetrate in evangelical Christianity, undermining the idea of distinctive, qualitatively different 'regimes of knowledge'. Brown here also fails to make a distinction between conservative Christian groups who seek to cut themselves off from mainstream culture and those who seek to penetrate it. These are usually labelled 'fundamentalist' and 'evangelical' respectively in the literature (Smith 1998). But as a series of studies shows – for example some case studies in the 'GenX' religion survey mentioned above – American evangelicalism thrives within – not on the fringes of – popular culture, including youth culture (Flory and Miller 2000, Lyon 2000, Smith 1998).

An intriguing example of this is the current campaign to promote sexual abstinence in American schools, which 'repackages' the traditional discourse on chastity in the idioms of popular culture: virginity bracelets that look like New Age trinkets and slogans like 'Because I have dreams' and 'Don't be a louse, wait for your spouse' (Williams 2001). This places precisely the evangelical role model of feminine virtue attacked in the 1960s at the heart of a government-funded public campaign: 'a young man's desire for sex is strong', one programme says, 'females become aroused less easily and so are in a good position to help' (ibid.). Indeed, American evangelicals demonstrate a similar confident engagement with public culture, while at the same time maintaining a strong sense of being embattled, as Egyptian Islamists, as we shall see below in Chapter 8.

Thus, while not necessarily being entirely convincing, Brown's insightful argument suggests many interesting connections. Like Starrett in relation to Egypt, he demonstrates the importance of discursive religion to an understanding of religion's social significance. Starrett's emphasis on education in sustaining this discursive structure perhaps suggests that closer attention should be paid to this factor in the British context. The Egyptian parallel is also interesting because it suggests that two of our case studies exhibit inverse trends in the public influence of their main religious tradition. As we shall see in more detail in Chapter 8, Islam was largely written off as a political factor in the 1960s. But largely influenced by the crisis in Arab nationalism precipitated by defeat by Israel in 1967, the discursive Islam perpetuated in the schools was put to new use as a political and social identity, as it began to draw on the legacy of those who had mobilized Islam against colonial occupation. In contrast, discursive Christianity's public influence in Britain plummeted in the 1960s. Yet there are also intriguing parallels: the forms of discursive Islam in Egypt in the 1990s in some ways resemble the forms of discursive Christianity that developed in the late eighteenth and early nineteenth centuries in being less tied to traditional legitimating institutions and more characterized by personal conviction. The possible parallel between the centrality of a feminine role model to these discourses is one we shall investigate in Chapter 8.

Looking ahead, discursive religion is hugely important for developing our understanding of religion's relationship to civil society and the public sphere. The kind of discourse sustained by religions is one factor shaping the character of civil society and which may resonate in the public sphere, depending on its social influence. Brown's study makes the connection between discursive religion as a social force and the personal level of religion's ability – or in this case failure – to enable people to make sense of their lives in narrative terms. In this respect it links to the work of Alasdair MacIntyre (1985), who sees the normative disintegration of modern societies as connected with this loss of narrative, to which we shall return. Next we consider our third example, which again highlights the role of religion at a discursive level, but this time examining the influence of Catholic bishops on public discussion of ethical issues in the United States.

(c) America: José Casanova's Deprivatization of Religion Thesis

Casanova argues that the pattern of religious decline common in Western Europe has not generally been replicated elsewhere in the world. He therefore seeks to reformulate the secularization thesis in a way which does justice to both European and non-European evidence. A key part of his argument is that, contrary to the European pattern, as differentiation has progressed in many parts of the world, religion actually re-emerged from the private sphere, a process he calls 'deprivatization'. He defines this as 'a dual interrelated process of repoliticization of the private religious and moral spheres and renormativization of the public economic and political spheres' (1996 p. 359). In other words, religious beliefs cease to be a matter of purely personal preference, but again become the subject of public argument, while concurrently public matters, like the economy and politics, are remoralized, partly by challenges from religious groups. One example he gives of this is the role of the public statements of American Catholic bishops in the 1970s and 1980s on matters as diverse as abortion, electoral politics, international relations and the social impact of economic policies. He argues that through their statements and actions:

> The bishops challenged the claims of the differentiated political and economic spheres that they should be evaluated solely in terms of intrinsic, functionally rational criteria without regard to extraneous moral considerations. Similarly they also challenged liberal individualist claims that morality should be left to the individual moral conscience. (Ibid.)

Two developments were important in enabling the bishops to play this public role. First, transformations initiated by the Vatican II policy of *aggiornomento*, specifically the affirmation of action in the secular realm as 'a constitutive dimension of the church's divine mission' (p. 360) and the acceptance of the modern doctrine of universal human rights, including the religious freedom of the individual. The former gave impetus to the Church's involvement in social transformation (including liberation theology); the latter gave the Church a universal discourse in which to address the world on ethical matters, no longer as a supporter of specifically Roman Catholic interests, but on behalf of all humanity.

Second, local factors. In the United States the transformation of the political and socio-economic fortunes of Catholics from a distrusted, divided community consisting of a small liberal republican élite and defensive ethnic enclaves, to postwar prosperity, social mobility and influence, as well as the focus on the external enemy of Communism, created the conditions in which Catholics had the confidence to implement the message of *aggiornomento* and in which American society was prepared to listen, or at least tolerate. Casanova (1994) summarizes the bishops' contribution to public debate in the following terms:

> What the bishops did was to present the Catholic normative tradition as a basis for public debate. They did not claim to know the answers, a claim which de facto would tend to preclude any public debate, leaving room for only partisan mobilization. In the pastoral letters the bishops only claimed to possess valid normative principles which should help to inform public debate, a debate in which all affected should participate and to which all should have equal access. (p. 204)

Casanova's analysis of the public impact of the Catholic bishops' pastoral letters serves to illustrate the difference between the public sphere of civil society and other public domains. The point of the bishops' statements was not to influence public policy directly (intervention at the level of the state), nor that of political parties (level of political society), but rather to bring the ethical resources of the Catholic tradition to bear on public debate (level of civil society). This distinctive orientation to improved communication rather than specific outcomes is characteristic of civil society, at least on Casanova's normative understanding of the concept. Hence he explicitly rejects assessment of the bishops' impact on policy outcomes, which he agrees was negligible (pp. 201–2) as an appropriate indicator of their success: 'it would be inappropriate, indeed fallacious, to attempt to measure the public relevance of the bishops' public speeches using the criteria of rational strategic action' (p. 202).

However, the volume of public response from all perspectives suggests that the bishops had considerable success in generating debate at the level of civil society, measured not in terms of adoption of their solutions, but of their promotion of tools for a public thinking through of the issues. According to Casanova, the American Catholic example suggests that the best way for religion to maintain its credibility in modern democratic socities is to mobilize non-partisan universalist discourses (such as human rights) in the public sphere of civil society in support of marginalized sections of the population, at the same time as strengthening pastoral and voluntary revivalist activities to support its public voice with social engagement (Casanova 1994 pp. 222–3). In such a situation, a strong public voice for the Church may be one of the few witnesses to the possibilities of human community and solidarity in the face of commercial and administrative pressures.

Whether the reputation for encouraging open debate established by the American bishops in the 1970s and early-mid 1980s will survive the current paedophile priest crisis (2002) is highly questionable. The point for our purposes, however, is that the case demonstrates the capacity of broadly liberal public religion to reassert itself in a western democratic context.

In terms of our concern with the social significance of religion, this example illustrates how discursive religion can be significant for modern societies without mobilizing for or against particular causes, but by improving public communication. Thus it represents a substantial challenge to secularization and modernization theories, for it is evidence of a counter-trend to the central process they describe: social differentiation. Nor is the 'leaking' of religious discourse back into political argument in the case of the bishops an isolated example of 'social de-differentiation' with respect to religion. As Hervieu-Léger (2000) argues:

> The evidence shows [that] the generalized tendency to corral religion [into its own sphere] in no way excludes its presence in areas of social activity outside its control. ... This fluid quality in religious and non-religious processes criss-crossing the frontiers of institutional spheres is all-pervasive. ... religion ... has fragmented across the social spectrum. (p. 109)

Taken together, our three studies of discursive religion illustrate very different yet related trajectories for the interaction between religion and modernization, not least in civil society. In so doing, they have thrown up challenges to the adequacy of the version of secularization theory we have so far presented to account for this relationship. Such evidence forces us to reconsider secularization theory, this time in more depth.

Notes

1   This examined changing social attitudes in 43 societies across the world (Inglehart 1997); see Chapter 2 Section 3 below.

2   Martin examines the spread of evangelicalism – especially of pentecostal groups, which
    now comprise about 70 per cent of a 20-million-strong evangelical constituency, itself
    now some 13 per cent of the population (1996 p. 39). One prominent feature of some of
    these groups is the use of new technologies, in the form of multi-media worship and
    religious radio and television broadcasting.

Chapter 2

Rethinking Secularization

1. Secularization: a Closer Look

(a) Is Secularization One Theory?

The first time the verb 'to secularize' was used in English was to refer to the confiscation of church property by Henry VIII, in the event known as the 'dissolution of the monasteries' in the 1530s. Religion, in some inward and spiritual sense, may or may not be affected by such an event – but the influence of religion on society clearly and demonstrably is, as in this case the Church lost power to the Crown. This remains the primary sense of secularization: at a political level, the separation of ecclesiastical and state power, with the resulting loss of religious authority in the coercive sense. Indeed, this loss of coercive authority is implicit in definitions of the modern nation-state as monopolizing the means of violence (Giddens 1987 p. 121). More broadly, the sociological concept of secularization is concerned with the demonstrable effects of religion; or as Wallis and Bruce (1992 p.11) put it, with the extent to which 'religion makes a difference to the operation and standing of social roles and institutions ... and to the beliefs and actions of individuals'. It is a curious anomaly that, as we have noted, most of the evidence used to argue about secularization does not address this issue, but rather religious vitality. However, it should at once be admitted that there are many diverse formulations of the theory of secularization and one author has even questioned whether it should be regarded as a theory at all, but rather as 'a hodgepodge of loosely employed ideas' (Hadden 1987 p. 598). But as Tschannen (1991) has shown, there is in fact sufficient coherence to the work of a broad range of theorists to describe secularization as a paradigm in the Kuhnian sense (Kuhn 1970).

This means three things: first, 'a paradigm must be grounded in a concrete scientific community' (Tschannen 1991 p. 396). Tschannen shows that such a community existed in the period he studies (1963–c.1990), in the form of key participants in the Conférence Internationale de Sociologie des Religions (CISR). Second, while there may be considerable disagreements, participants 'share a very broad set of assumptions and analytical categories' (ibid. p. 395). Third, these areas of agreement are sufficient to enable development of the paradigm. Tschannen considers seven theorists and from analysis of their work argues for the existence of a paradigm as 'based on a core of three elements: differentiation, rationalization and worldliness' (p. 400).

Rather than rehash Tschannen's painstaking analysis we shall instead consider one influential model of secularization that closely corresponds to Tschannen's core paradigm: the so-called 'orthodox' model developed by Steve Bruce and Roy Wallis

29

(Bruce and Wallis 1992, Bruce 1999). This identifies three elements of modernization as central to secularization, two of which coincide with the core elements of the paradigm[1]: differentiation, societalization and rationalization. For the sake of completeness, we shall also consider 'worldliness', the component of the paradigm which doesn't overlap.

(b) Definitions of Religion

In the introduction we initially defined religions as cultural systems which, through various material forms, stories and rituals, witness to what is believed to be a transcendent reality. We shall pause here to consider briefly issues arising from the question of the definition of religion, because it is possible that confusion over whether religion is in decline or not could arise from confusion as to what religion is. Although this may seem unnecessary, it is not infrequent for scholars of the Middle East, for example, to assert that the rise of political Islam is not a religious revival (for example Tibi 1998), raising a question about the religious status of some of the material considered here. In relation to Bosnia, some scholars have argued that the war was not about religion (for example Ramet 1999), while others have disagreed (for example Sells 1996). And in relation to the secularization debate, some scholars have argued that religion, for example in America, may have retained its outward vitality only as a result of the increasingly this-worldly orientation of it contents, or 'internal secularization' (Wilson 1982). Thus, how one defines religion has crucial implications for one's assessment of its role in contemporary societies.

Scholars (for example Chaves 1994) often divide definitions of religion into two varieties: functional, meaning in terms of what religion does either for individuals or for social systems, and substantive, referring to what religions actually consist of (narratives, symbols, institutions and so on). Durkheim is associated with the functional school, seeing religion as a means of symbolic integration of communities and societies. The function of religion for the collective is primary here. However, more recent scholars have argued that this function is superfluous in today's functionally differentiated societies, whose systems (political, economic, legal and so on) are largely self-sustaining (Luhmann 1982, Beyer 1994). Yet collective symbolization may still be significant at national, ethnic or transnational levels, even if religion does not serve to integrate society at a functional level. Furthermore, religion may take on other functions; making sense of the individual's relationship to nature, society and history, for example, or in relation to other social systems – as in the case of Egyptian education above.

Following Geertz (1966), Greeley (1999 p.190) defines religion as 'a system of narrative metaphors that give purpose to life, that answer questions about tragedy, suffering, death and about happiness and ecstasy'. Like our initial definition, this has both substantive and functional elements: religion *is* 'a system of narrative metaphors' and *it functions* to 'answer questions'. It also intimates some sense of why religion might be compelling. Greeley relates this definition to work on narrative theory and human development, which argues that humans are fundamentally a story-telling species – and hence the importance of 'narrative metaphors':

Turner (1996) ...argues that humans ordinarily cope with a reality through 'parables', that is 'projecting' a story they already know on to an emerging phenomenon that requires explanation. ...Schank (1990) contends that a proper measure of human intelligence is the number and variety of stories a person has at his/her command to explain the phenomena encountered in daily life. Deacon (1997) suggests that humans are a 'symbolizing species' in which the physical brain and the ability to account for reality by symbols co-evolved. (p. 190)

Again, this fits with our emphasis on discursive religion. Such a perspective helps to give a sense of why religions should remain compelling – stories usually told in childhood, not merely recited but made present in symbols, pictures, songs and rituals, help form the religious imagination and become the foundations for later understanding. As Greeley continues:

The stories include powerful religious customs, ceremonies and traditions: when one sits, when one stands, when one does or does not wear a hat, appropriate attitudes during devotion, proper behavior at a funeral or a wedding, familiar hymns and art (the Madonna, for example). While most of these lesser stories might seem trivial to the sociologist, they are in fact the substratum, the infrastructure on which later more formal religious instruction is based. (p. 191)

It is such cultural transmission that modernization processes must undermine if they are to impact on religious vitality. There is certainly evidence that this has occurred in some contexts – the sharp decline in Sunday school attendance in the UK from the early 1960s, for example (Brown 2001) – but it is notable that there is comparatively little discussion of cultural transmission in the secularization literature. It is also true – as we have repeatedly stressed – that religion's political significance is separable from its cultural vitality. None the less, while it remains culturally alive religion is always potentially available as a political discourse. Thus there is a connection between vitality and social significance, but the two should not be conflated. In this context, we turn to consider the 'orthodox' model of secularization.

The Scope of the Theory

Bruce and Wallis (1992) define secularization as follows:

The secularization thesis is a research programme with, at its core, an explanatory model. This model ... asserts that the social significance of religion diminishes in response to the operation of three salient features of modernization ..., namely, (1) social differentiation, (2) societalization and (3) rationalization.

It recognizes, however, that social change is a multiple contingent process and that ideal-typical conditions may not be met. There may be countervailing factors, sometimes generated by the same modernization process. We believe that two such processes, which we call cultural defence and cultural transition, are especially relevant. (pp. 8–9)

We begin with three observations on the form and scope of the thesis as a whole, two very brief and a third somewhat extended, because it has been a point of contention. We shall consider the two 'countervailing factors' that they mention, which also affect its scope. First, the thesis is negative in form. It does not predict that the social significance of religion will change or develop (in various ways), but that it will diminish. This is not necessarily incompatible with various forms of change and development – but the focus of the thesis is not on these, but on decline: overall, religion is predicted to become a less important factor in social life.

Second, the scope of the thesis is extremely broad in the sense that it refers to the social significance of religion as a whole – and it has already been suggested that religion can potentially influence society in many different ways and at different levels. More specifically, few would dispute that in Western societies during the past three hundred years the power of the Christian churches at the level of the state has been dramatically reduced. This does not necessarily imply, however, that religion does not influence society at other levels – as an agent in civil society for example (Casanova 1994; Davie 2000). More generally, there is a concern here that the possibility of the differential impact of change – that influence might increase in some ways and diminish in others – cannot be recognized in a framework that expresses change only in terms of increase or decrease.

Third, the scope of the thesis is extremely broad in a second sense, because modernization, which is seen as the key factor in secularization, is held to be global or near global in its impact (Inglehart 1997). Yet Bruce (1998) seeks to limit its scope by ruling out application beyond 'the West' entirely, a claim that seems to stand in tension with the worldwide scope of modernization:

> In trying to summarize very briefly the impact of modernization on the place and nature of religion, I am referring only to the history of western Europe and to the societies created by migrant Europeans. There is no suggestion that what is offered is a universal template to which all societies must eventually conform. (p. 2)

However, in making modernization the key to religious decline, secularization theorists are opening up the theory to wider application, because modernization has clearly not been confined to Europe and those countries populated by peoples of European descent. It should also be noted that in his caution on this point Bruce appears to differ from Wilson. Complaining that the contributions in the collection edited by Bruce and Wallis focus too narrowly on Christianity, Wilson (1992 p. 195) writes: 'My own usage – and this is perhaps more typically the stance of a sociologist than of a historian – is to adopt a much more encompassing concept of just what constitutes religion: Christianity is regarded as just one species of the genera'.

Furthermore, Bruce's confinement of the theory to 'western Europe and to the societies created by migrant Europeans' oversimplifies the nature of global interaction. Societies were not created by migrant Europeans in isolation, but in 'exchange' – often brutal and always coercive in some sense – with the peoples already inhabiting those territories, who, where they survived the encounter, continue to form part of those societies. Also, one of the other consequences of colonialism is migration of people from areas of colonial influence to Western Europe, so that even this region, so long an exporter of peoples to the 'New World', 'has become a novel experiment in multiple, tiered and mediated multiculturalisms, a supranational community of cultures, subcultures and transcultures inserted differentially into radically different political and cultural traditions' (Modood 1997 p. vi). Thus colonialism and globalization force secularization theory to go global. However, arguments over secularization *have* largely focused on North American and Western European data – and this places limitations on the inferences that should be drawn from those data. None the less, Bruce's qualifications should not disguise the fact that the claims of the secularization thesis are more ambitious than this – indeed, as Wilson argues, the logic of attaching the theory to that of modernization means that it is necessarily global in scope. However, it does allow for some countervailing factors within that global modernization process.

These are the conditions of cultural defence and cultural transition. Bruce (1998) sees these as 'surface' phenomena which may temporarily halt or even reverse the secularizing effects of the 'deep structures' of modernization (that is, differentiation, societalization and rationalization). He describes them as follows:

> Where culture, identity and sense of worth are challenged by a source promoting either an alien religion or rampant secularism and that source is negatively valued, secularization will be inhibited. (p. 25)
> Where identity is threatened in the course of major cultural transitions, religion may provide resources for negotiating such transitions or asserting a new sense of worth. (p. 24)

Cultural defence refers to a situation where religious identity and the institutions which support it become a bulwark against a hostile force. Bruce and Wallis (1992) give the examples of the 'Celtic' areas of mainland Britain – Ireland, Scotland and Wales – where religion is said to form part of a defensive shield against English domination, although Bruce (1999) claims that this role is decreasing. In Northern Ireland, Presbyterian and Catholic identity performs the same role, with no sign of decrease (Inglehart 1997 p. 282).[2] The cultural defence argument is supported by evidence that rates of religious identification, performance and belief remain higher in these areas than in England. The same argument can be used to explain high rates of religiosity in Poland and Lithuania, in relation to Russian domination.

Cultural transition works in a similar way, only the challenge to the group is provided not by a negative external force or factor in society, but rather by the process of cultural change, usually brought about by the migration of the affected group. Religion provides resources for groups to mobilize, as well as a sense of belonging, in the face of what may be an indifferent or hostile receiving society. Examples given are those of Muslims in Britain and of various immigrant communities in the United States. The argument is that once a group is successfully integrated, the organizing and belonging functions of religion are no longer so necessary, so immigrant religiosity will drop to levels of the majority. Bruce and Wallis cite evidence from the United States to support this argument (Brown 1992). If this 'tailing off' effect is not seen, then it can be argued that a situation of cultural transition has transformed into one of cultural defence. Because the role of the migrant community has become problematic in some way, full integration cannot take place and religion remains a cultural defence mechanism against a majority society perceived as hostile.

However, this latter move poses a question that begins to unravel the whole construct. What is the scope of 'culture' here? Does Bruce mean just migrant or ethnic groups? With such groups it is easy to sustain a distinction between 'mainstream' and 'minority' cultures and to talk of eventually integrating the latter into the presumed-to-be secular former. In this way exceptions to secularization are kept safely marginal, even if they persist. But what about American evangelicalism? This is not identified with any migrant or ethnic group, yet its vitality persists (Sections 3(c) and 4(b)). If it is not treated as 'a culture', then the orthodox theory has no explanation to account for it. If it is treated as a culture, or perhaps subculture, then it comes under cultural defence. But then on the one hand the interpenetration of evangelical subculture with youth and popular culture makes the whole idea of a distinct culture difficult to sustain, while on the other hand the persistence and scale of the phenomenon make it difficult to categorize as 'an exception'.

Underlying these difficulties is an inadequate conceptualization of culture. Although Bruce argues that he treats both culture and economics as equally capable of shaping reality, depending on the specific situation (1998 p. 217), neither his statements on cultural defence and cultural transition, nor his relegation of culture to the level of surface structure seem consistent with this argument. By treating religion as something that in modern societies can only temporarily or in exceptional circumstances become socially significant – where identity is threatened by the modernizing agent, or to help cope with cultural transition – the orthodox model of secularization does not allow that religion can actually change public culture – the means of public communication – in ways that do not necessarily disappear when external threats are removed, or difficult circumstances improve. Thus the theory appears to rely on a kind of 'barometric' model of religion as a cultural defence mechanism: religiosity is artificially 'pumped up' as a defence against and way to cope with essentially secular difficulties, but once the latter are resolved, it is assumed that religiosity will drop down again to its 'natural' level. But as Starrett (1998) argues:

> [T]he barometric approach ignores the institutional frameworks and social processes through which culture is created and transmitted. Like other institutions, religious ... ones fill not only a social need, but a social space. They take on a very real life of their own with interests, dynamics and potentials that are only incompletely determined by the intersection of forces that brought them about. (pp. 227–8)

Thus while the concepts of cultural defence and transition are plausible for cases where 'culture' functions as a relatively 'sealed unit', they are inadequate as sole alternatives to decline as a trajectory for religion in modernity as a whole. This is for three main reasons: first, because they cannot explain the persistence of the religion in 'mainstream' culture in modernized societies, second, because they ignore the dynamics of culture and hence cannot explain phenomena arising from cultural change, and third, as we shall see in our critical account of the three core processes of modernization, they ignore other reasons for religious persistence and change.

2. Modernization: Three Core Processes

Modernization is at the heart of secularization theory: it is the deep structure leading to the long-term decline of the social significance of religion. 'Modernization' itself is a complex and contested concept that refers to a range of inter-related processes operating at economic, political, social and cultural levels and originating in Western Europe since the fifteenth century, depending on which development one is concerned with. At an economic level these developments include the expansion of the capitalist system and the spread of industrialization, enhanced in the second Industrial Revolution (from 1850) by the widespread application of scientific knowledge and possibly now entering a new stage,[3] with the emergence of increasingly service-oriented and information-based economies. Politically, they include the emergence of nation-states and the development of bureaucracy to deepen their power, but also the development of representative institutions and concepts of individual rights. At a social level they include the breakdown of face-to-face communities (*Gemeinschaft*) by urbanization and increased mobility, leading to the modern society (*Gesellschaft*) of strangers and *anomie* (social dislocation, experienced as a sense of lostness), but also of unprecedented individual opportunities. The 'orthodox model' of secularization emphasizes three aspects of modernization. In this critical account of the modernization process as envisaged in 'orthodox' secularization theory we continue to consider the criticisms and alternative explanations of other scholars and begin to develop our own alternative.

(a) Differentiation

A central feature of modernization is social differentiation: this is identified by Tschannen (1991 p. 404) as 'absolutely central to all the secularization theories, without exception'. This refers to the increasing division and specialization not only of labour but also of many areas of human activity. Thus society develops into a series of semi-independent systems, each of which has its own specialized language and rules of operation: economic, political, legal, educational and so on. Secularization theory associates this process with the declining social significance of religion: religious institutions gradually lose their grip on different spheres of society. Economics came first with the development of capitalism, which involved the loan of money repaid with interest – the medieval Church had opposed Christian involvement in usury as some Islamic institutions continue to do, because of its tendency to transfer wealth from poor to rich.

In politics, the influence of religion on the state diminished first through the Reformation and then in the formation of nation-states in the late eighteenth and nineteenth centuries, many of which had secular constitutions. These changes were concurrent with industrialization and urbanization, both of which severed ties between religion and production. Then, through the nineteenth and twentieth centuries, religion lost its educational and social influence, as the national and welfare state took over these functions. However, it should be noted that even this core aspect of modernization is not unambivalent in its effects on the social significance of religion. For example, as we have seen, Starrett (1998) argues that the effect of the introduction of a state-run Western-style schooling system in Egypt – indicative of the differentiation of an autonomous educational system, no longer based on religious institutions, as previously – has been to dramatically increase, rather than decrease, the social significance of religion.

Furthermore, although differentiation is a central aspect of secularization theory, not everyone agrees that it is a simple process of specialized systems becoming more and more autonomous. We have already seen both Casanova (1994) and Hervieu-Léger (2000) (Chapter 1 Section 4(c) above) argue that religion in modernity is not confined to a specialized sphere, but rather that 'religion ... has fragmented across the social spectrum' (ibid. p. 109). More broadly, Karl Polanyi argued that 'the industrial revolution produced an economic society (the market economy) that threatened to subsume and reduce autonomous social norms, relationships and institutions' (Cohen and Arato 1992 p. 122). This invasion of social relations by a powerful new form of economic relations produced resistance, 'the self-defence of society', in the form of political revolutions (1848) and labour movements. The German social theorist Jürgen Habermas has developed Polanyi's point, conceptualizing the process of social differentiation as an interaction between 'system' and 'lifeworld'. His account of systems draws strongly on the work of Niklas Luhmann (Rasch 2000). Each subsystem (economic, political, medical, educational and so on) has its own specialist language and rules, but they share a functional orientation and form of reason: instrumental reason. Instrumental reason is closely linked to its corresponding form of action:

> [Instrumental] [a]ction is described as the self-interested behaviour of individuals in an objectivated world, that is, one in which objects and other individuals are related in terms of their possible manipulation. The rationality of action is correspondingly conceptualized as the efficient linking of actions-seen-as-means to the attainment of goals. (White 1988 p. 10)

Treating people and things in this way means you can achieve goals much more efficiently. But there are costs. First, as we noted in Chapter 1 Section 2, Luhmann has pointed to the decoupling of systems like law from normative legitimization, and Habermas (1996) is particularly keen to contest this. Second, treating the environment as a resource to be exploited has arguably led to environmental damage (Beyer 1994). Third, the Holocaust was made possible by the industrial apparatus of mass death and arguably not just by sheer processing capacity, but because of the corrosive effects of action at a distance on human moral response (Bauman 1989).

For Habermas, the common concern here is the damage caused by the decoupling of systems from the social fabric of everyday life. He calls the latter the 'lifeworld', 'the reservoir of implicitly known traditions, the background assumptions that are embedded in language and culture by individuals in everyday life' (Cohen and Arato 1992 pp. 427–8). Lifeworlds share a different form of reason, communicative reason, which is oriented to interpersonal understanding. For Habermas, what has gone wrong with modernization is that the growth of instrumental reason/action has outstripped the growth of communicative reason/action, so that systems have come to dominate lifeworlds, a process he describes as the 'colonization of the lifeworld'.

However, whereas Polanyi (and many other critics of modernity) focused on the damage caused by the dominance of systems, Habermas's account recognizes the benefits as well as the costs of systems, for example in providing steering mechanisms which coordinate action in increasingly complex societies/polities. What is needed to counteract the dominance of the economic system is not a reactive bolstering of the political system, as in state socialism, or some attempt at de-differentiation, whether putting the ownership of the means of production in the hands of the workers, as in classical Marxism, or by the creation of small-scale communities of virtue at odds with modernity (MacIntyre 1985). Rather, what is needed is the strengthening of communicative reason/action, and the societal space where this can happen is civil society, conceived of as the 'institutionalized framework of a modern lifeworld stabilized by fundamental rights' (Cohen and Arato 1992 p. 440).

We shall return to and develop this concept of civil society in Chapter 3, but for now it is important to note that whereas secularization theory tends to treat social differentiation as if it (a) can be taken for granted, (b) is neutral in its effects, and (c) reduces the social significance of religion, none of these is necessarily true. Rather, (a) differentiation has been accompanied by de-differentiation, especially (but not only) the invasion of social by economic systems; (b) the effects of this have been far from neutral (for example, at least in part, global warming, the Holocaust); and (c) the development of specialized modern systems (for example education in Egypt) can sometimes increase the social significance of religion.

Neither, however, is Habermas's development of the theory of social differentiation in terms of system and lifeworld unproblematic when it comes to the theorization of the role of religion in this process. Rather, in his major theoretical work (1987) and as we noted above, Habermas reads modernization as a process of 'the linguistification of the sacred', whereby the integration of society through religious ritual is gradually replaced by integration through discussion leading to rational agreement. Here is a modern version of the Enlightenment critique of religion, whereby unreasonable religion is replaced by reasonable secularism. For now, we shall note just two problems with this. First, like other Western Europeans, Habermas too closely identifies religion with its role of state legitimization in the history of Western Europe. Religion can in fact perform many other roles, including precisely that 'moral-practical rationalization' of the lifeworld that Habermas seeks as a counter to its colonization by systems (Casanova 1994 p. 233). The reasoned public discussion of ethical issues promoted by the American bishops is an example of this (see Chapter 1 Section 4(c)). Indeed, Habermas seems to be beginning to realize the positive contribution of religion to this process (Habermas 1997).

Second, Habermas over-rationalizes social integration, which takes place not only through rational discussion but through a whole range of communications media through rational and non-rational means. Religion's contribution to this process need not be restricted to the generation of irrational 'communal effervescence' created through ritual (Mellor and Shilling 1995) or to highly rationalized Habermasian discussion. Rather, like most of the rest of communication, religious communication is a mixture of cognitive, emotional, practical and aesthetic content. None the less,

Habermas's theory will play an important role in our interpretation of the interaction between religion, civil society and the public sphere in modern societies.

(b) Societalization

The second feature of modernization associated with secularization is 'societalization': this refers to the break-up of small communities as a result of rural-urban migration and changing work patterns, following the various phases of industrialization. The argument is that religion was an integral part of village life, celebrating the rhythm of the seasons and marking the stages of life. Religion served to knit together the small community. But modern urban life breaks up these small communities and hence the social significance of religion is diminished. In contrast, modern societies are integrated through a variety of other means, especially through the growth of systems, including the bureaucratic supervision of the state, processes of production and consumer markets. Such complex societies, it is argued, do not rely on shared beliefs for social cohesion; rather, impersonal rational systems provide social integration. As a result religion loses its influence on public life: it becomes privatized and, so the orthodox theory runs, without compulsion it ceases to matter at all for many individuals.

However, as with differentiation, while it is helpful to understand some evidence, as a general account of the process of societalization this will not do. First, it ignores the non-instrumentally rational factors shaping the emergence of modern societies. One of the biggest of these was the development of nationalist ideologies, which are not rational systems but 'quasi-religions' consisting of symbols, beliefs and stories (Baumann 1999 p. 42). We shall return to the importance of the relationship with nationalism for understanding religion's role in civil society in Chapter 3, but for now we should note that societalization is not just a consequence of developments in communication and production, but as much of developments in culture, of which religion, like nationalism, was (and remains) very much a part. Second, the impact of structural changes such as urbanization and industrialization on religion varies. While it might have decimated Anglican practice when workers moved from rural Lancashire and Cheshire to Manchester and Liverpool in nineteenth-century England, this appears not to happen when Turkish Muslims move from rural Anatolia to German industrial cities like Stuttgart and Düsseldorf in the late twentieth century, as Baumann (1999) summarizes Schiffauer's (1988) article:

> On the plane of ritual, villagers' experience stressed the ancient communal character of all households participating in the same ceremonies in the life and seasonal cycles. In German cities, the rituals became conscious affirmations of a religious order, as opposed to the secular order in which migrants now found themselves. On the plane of political ideas, villagers professed some sympathy with applying Islamic law (*sheriat*), but they felt none of the great hopes that migrants could attach to an Islamic reform of the law. (p. 73)

Combined with the characteristics of greater internalization and intellectualization of religion noted above (Chapter 1 Section 3(c)), this evidence suggests that religious traditions can adapt successfully to societalization processes. Nor can these changes be dismissed as the special case of 'cultural transition', as Bruce's orthodox model might suggest, for the same processes of adaptation take place when rural-urban migration occurs within a state, as from rural to urban Egypt (Starrett 1998). Nor can they be dismissed as Muslim exceptionalism, for they are also observable amongst Christian populations in Latin America (Martin 1996a) and amongst Hindu populations in India (Rao 2000). But why should nineteenth-century European and late twentieth-century global effects of modernization on religion diverge so sharply?

Briefly, two reasons might be suggested. First, the impact of choice may vary according to the social function of religion. For orthodox secularization theory, a belief is strongest when it is universally shared (Bruce 1996). Disagreement and diversification within a tradition presages its decline and a line can be drawn in Western European history from Christendom through the Reformation to the proliferation of Nonconformist groups, continuing to the present. But it may be that whether diversification coincides with decline or not depends on the social role of religion within a society. If religion is associated with legitimization of the state, such fracturing of the sacred canopy (Berger and Luckmann 1967) may presage decline. But where, if we use Habermas's terminology, the political subsystem unburdens religion of some of its coordinating functions, religion is 'freed up' to do other things in civil society. Depending on local and global market conditions, religion may prosper in this marketplace of ideas. This appears to have happened in America (Martin 1996b) and to be happening now in places as diverse as Latin America (ibid.), India (Rajagopal 2001) and Egypt (Starrett 1998).

This is also essentially Casanova's explanation of the difference between the Western European experience of modernization's impact on religion and that of the rest of the world, except he adds an additional explanation as to why the association with the state proved so costly in the Western European case. The strong connection between churches and authoritarian regimes in Western Europe during the early modern period generated the anti-religious discourses described by Casanova as 'the Enlightenment critique of religion' (1994; Chapter 1 Section 2). Where religion resisted modernization these discourses took root and religion suffered; where religion did not support tyranny they lacked plausibility and their influence was limited. This may also explain why these discourses have had relatively little impact in the non-Western world, except through the agency of Marxism (as in China), itself a version of 'the Enlightenment critique of religion'. As we shall argue in more detail in Chapter 3, where modernization is perceived as imposed by an external source (as in colonization), such critiques of indigenous religious traditions (and even adopted ones) are unlikely to be widely persuasive.

Second, whether religion becomes important as a medium of general social communication may depend on the timing of structural modernization. If urbanization – with its spatial separation of urban workers from their rural backgrounds – occurs at a time when transport and communication are expensive and both media (dominated by print) and access to media (expensive, élite controlled, limited worker literacy) are limited, then kinship networks and consequently cultural traditions (like religion) are likely to be severely disrupted. This appears to have happened in nineteenth-century Europe; although revisionist accounts like Brown's question this (2001; see Chapter 1 Section 4(b)). However, if urbanization occurs at a time of relatively cheap instant communication, proliferating media and much improved transportation, kinship links may be greatly extended over space and cultural traditions successfully transmitted (and transformed), and this appears to have happened in Egypt, India and Latin America, as well as among migrants to Western Europe. Furthermore, under conditions of scarcity urbanization may increase rather than reduce people's reliance on kinship networks, again favouring cultural transmission – another Egyptian example, Singerman's (1995) study of family, politics and networks in urban Cairo, illustrates the point.

Following Van der Veer *et al.* (1997), Baumann (1999 p. 155) describes the processes through which cultural traditions have been transmitted and transformed through global migration as 'long-distance familism, political or religious transnationalism and cross-diasporic exchange'. A striking example of long-distance familism and religious transnationalism is provided by the rapid global-spread stories of milk consumption by Ganesh statues amongst the Hindu diaspora in 1997 (Beckerlegge 2001). This example also shows how mastery of new technology is quite compatible with an enchanted view of the world – a social reality contrary to the third pillar of secularization theory: rationalization.

(c) Rationalization

The third feature of modernization associated with secularization is 'rationalization'. Whereas differentiation and societalization concern social processes, rationalization concerns the way people think and, as a result, how they act. Rationalization in orthodox secularization theory refers to the process by which, in everyday life, naturalistic, physical explanations gradually displace explanations that refer to supernatural agencies. Thus disease is no longer caused by curses or demons, but by germs, immune failure and genetic mutation. Note that it is not being argued that 'science replaces religion' on an intellectual level. Rather, the criteria by which rationalized explanations come to replace supernatural ones are those of practical usefulness. For example, in many cases, understanding that disease is caused by germs enables one to take effective preventive or reactive action: washing surgical instruments to avoid passing on infection, or taking penicillin to kill bacteria. In other words, such explanations are 'technically efficient': they enable us to do specific things more effectively. Hence Bruce and Wallis (1992 p. 14) describe rationalization as 'the pursuit of technically efficient means of securing this-worldly ends'.

However, this view can be challenged in several ways. First, our account of Habermas has already shown that there is more to reason than the technical or instrumental. Reason is also communicative and the role of religion in reproducing social systems through communicative action is one reason why religious systems may prove more resistant to instrumental rationalization than the orthodox account suggests. Second, there is strong empirical evidence that this is the case. As we argued above (Section 2) Martin (1996b) has shown that Latin American pentecostal groups have no apparent difficulty in combining living with advanced technology and intense belief in supernatural entities which forcefully affect their everyday lives. Nor does this appear to be a peculiarly Latin American phenomenon – Rao (2000) reports a similar concurrence in urban India, Koepping (2000) in Japan and Starrett (1998) a rather differently constructed but functionally similar cohabitation of scientific rationality and supernatural belief among educated Egyptians.

It is worth looking a bit more closely at how this 'mental cohabitation' of inspirited and rationalistic worldviews works in practice, if only because the idea of religion-science conflict is so firmly entrenched in Western European cultural traditions. Below is part of a transcript of an interview with Ursula Rao, an anthropologist who conducted fieldwork in a city in Northern India in the 1990s. Rao was interested in 'trying to understand how people who believe in rational thinking defend their belief in the gods and in divine intervention in this world' (in Herbert 2001c). One aspect of her study focused on an employee of the State Bank of India, Bogwa Sahab, who as well as being a computer specialist also claimed to receive revelations from the goddess (*deva*). In this following passage, Rao recalls Sahab's explanation of his experience of the goddess in terms of skill/knowledge rather than belief/faith. One widespread aspect of Hindu belief is the close identification of an image of a deity (*murti*) with the presence of that deity. Rao's question here is trying to access how Sahab reconciled this understanding with his scientific-rational worldview:

> Showing him a picture of the goddess I asked him, 'what do you think, is this the goddess or is this a picture of the goddess?' and he told me 'See, belief is like a skill. It's a skill that opens to you ... one particular world of knowledge'. For he would not understand religion actually in terms of belief but in terms of knowledge, seeing that there's one particular way of learning which can open this world of knowledge and he compared it to reading. He said, 'if you know a script [alphabet] you can read the signs and you can understand the power of the text. Now if you don't know the script you throw the paper away because it doesn't talk to you. The same way is with the goddess, she is represented in a statue or in a picture, or she comes to you in a dream. But you need to be able to read her signs so you have to acquire this skill of reading and then you know that she's there. It's not a question any more of your believing or not believing, but it's a question of you learning to read the signs, to enter this particular world of knowledge. So it's not really different from chemistry, where you see something happening, something turning from blue to red and then give an end result because you have the background knowledge to explain what is happening here.' (Ibid.)

By narrating his experience of the goddess in terms of perception rather than belief Sahab harmonizes it with his scientific worldview. Rao found the same phenomenon when she asked people about the 'milk miracle' of 1997, when people in India and across the Hindu diaspora reported that statues of the god Ganesh 'drank' milk: 'Those people who believed that really a miracle had happened, they would explain it in terms of an experiment and not in terms of a belief. They would never ask you "Do you *believe* what happened?", but they would ask you, "Did you *see* what happened?"' (ibid.). The prestige in which science is held and a view of it as quite compatible with religion is also evident in the following extract from a letter from an Indian viewer of a televised version of the *Ramayana*: 'My spontaneous reaction is that the language of the dialogues is most scientific, most expressive, most soothing, most natural and has achieved the task of directly entering the heart' (in Rajagopal 2001 p. 137).

One way of understanding these accounts is in terms of discourse analysis, meaning in this context a way of analysing speech or writing in terms of people's practical intentions and the kinds of rhetorical repertoires they have available to them. In terms of the social reproduction of knowledge the key question is not whether something is true or not, but whether it works. Scientific discourse has prestige in India (as elsewhere) and it has probably shaped the way that people talk about their religious experience, but many Indians seem to be able to find ways of talking about and living with the effects of science and religion without experiencing a conflict between them. The rationalization component of the orthodox secularization thesis claims that as people begin to use scientific-rational discourses to interpret the world, this will gradually displace religious discourses. In many contexts, this is not happening. In summary, where the motivation to break the religion-state hegemony that made the Enlightenment critique of religion plausible in Western Europe is absent (Casanova 1994; see above, subsection (b) on 'Societalization'), people find practical ways to reconcile scientific-rational and religious discourses. In such contexts religious discourses are transformed by this process without losing their supernatural element.

(d) Worldliness

Wordliness is the third core element of the secularization paradigm identified by Tschannen, but it does not form an explicit part of the Bruce and Wallis model. Luckmann (1987) argues that the modernization process causes the religion to become more oriented to 'this-worldly' concerns: examples might include the denominational churches becoming more concerned with social and political issues and new religious movements (NRMs) with personal improvement, so that Transcendental Meditation (TM) markets itself not as a religion but as a technique which leads to a more productive life. This appears to be similar to what Wilson (1992) calls 'internal secularization', defined by Chaves (1994 p. 757) as 'the process by which religious organizations undergo internal development towards conformity with the secular world'.

Unlike the three characteristics of modernization in the 'orthodox model', 'worldliness' refers to an effect rather than a set of clearly identified causes producing an effect, which seems a good analytical reason to exclude it from our core model. A further problem with it is that it presumes that religion was historically less concerned with this-worldly ends than with more 'spiritual' matters. But this is a contentious claim and probably itself the outcome of intellectual snobbery and the privatization process it purports to explain. Popular religion has always been concerned with this-worldly ends; the point, however, is the means through which they are sought. Many healings and exorcisms of Latin American pentecostalism and the miracles of popular Hinduism testify to the continued vitality of the pursuit of this-worldly ends through supernatural means, as does the 'prosperity gospel' and the 'chanting for change' of Nichiren Buddhism.

Thus a concern with 'worldliness' does not presage the decline of religion. But what if the practices of a religion become indistinguishable from those of a secular organization, except for an 'overlay' of religious language, as cynics might argue of the increasing focus of liberal Christian groups on social and political issues? However, in this case the ends sought are frequently justified by reference to a theological framework – indeed the ultimate ends sought are not improvements in social conditions or political freedom (though these may be the intermediate ends), but rather justice, which for many traditions is identified with the will of God. Thus the 'worldliness' construct seems to say more about the model of religion of the observer than about the process of religious change in modernity.

Both in our presentation of quantitative and qualitative evidence of religion in modernity and in our discussion of secularization theory we have voiced not only criticisms of the orthodox model, but alternative ways of understanding religious change. The next section introduces a couple of new perspectives and develops alternatives thus far only partially outlined, before seeking to consolidate our rethinking of secularization in the conclusion.

3. Alternatives to and Perspectives on Secularization Theory

(a) Rational Choice Theory

One recent challenge to secularization theory has come from a group of American sociologists who argue that modernization in itself is irrelevant for religious vitality; rather, rates of religious belief and practice follow cycles over long periods of time (hundreds of years) and are largely determined by market conditions. This 'supply-side' explanation of religious change is based on rational choice theory (RCT). RCT argues that variations in the level of practice of religions can be understood in the same way as levels of consumption of other kinds of goods. Thus it is argued that the degree to which demand for religion is present depends, as with other goods, on the richness and diversity of products available in the marketplace: the more and better choice, the more demand is likely to be stimulated. Hence religion has done well in America, where lack of a state monopoly and the presence of church-state separation has meant that a range of religious products competing on a level playing field has been available from the start, that is, from Independence (1779). It is for this reason, Finke and Stark (1992) have argued, that American church membership has steadily increased from the end of the eighteenth century to the present day. By contrast, in Western Europe, where state churches fought hard to maintain a religious monopoly and choice was restricted, religious demand has been lower.

There are, however, a number of good reasons for being sceptical of the claims of exponents of RCT. First, empirical evidence: one clear difference between RCT and secularization theory is that RCT predicts that a large number of religious competitors each with a small market share will increase competitiveness and hence boost religious vitality. In contrast, secularization theory predicts that the reduction in shared beliefs attendant on fragmentation of worldview will reduce religious vitality. Both Bruce in Europe (1999), and Olson in America (1998), have shown that neither large-scale nor detailed local studies support the predictions of RCT. Second, as we saw in Section 3(b) above, some of the central studies which have been used to support RCT (for example Finke and Stark 1992) have been shown to be methodologically flawed (Hanson 1997). Third, there are concerns about the 'ecological validity' of RCT – that is, whether the simple, individualistically oriented theory translates well into complex areas of social life where factors such as altruism and group solidarity come into play. Thus, for example, RCT has been found to be a poor predictor of political behaviour, such as voting patterns (Dryzeck 1995). While, as Greeley (1999) argues, RCT can in principle take into account a range of factors, the resemblance to a classic market situation – and hence the predictive validity of the model – appears to diminish in proportion to such complexity.

Some critics have sought to attack RCT's practitioners but rescue the market metaphor. For example, Hervieu-Léger (2000 pp. 163–4) argues that when originally used by Berger and Luckmann (1967), 'The metaphor of the symbolic market was in no sense meant to imply that the production and consumption of religious signs relate literally to highly problematic laws governing the production and consumption of goods and services'. Rather it referred to the reduction in barriers to moving between traditions, which 'pushed up competitiveness between the dominant purveyors of meaning' (ibid.). And indeed there is evidence to suggest that many people in affluent societies are behaving more as consumers in their approach to religion, as we shall see in the next section (Bowman 1999). Under such circumstances one would expect RCT to have greater applicability. Thus it is not necessary to see secularization theory and RCT as mutually exclusive rivals; rather, the motivational factors highlighted by RCT may play a role in explaining the religious choices made by people in some situations, against the broader backdrop of modernization. Furthermore, as we have seen, dissociation from a state monopoly does seem to have a positive effect on religious vitality in many cases, but for different reasons to those highlighted by RCT theorists (Casanova 1994; above, section 2 (b) on 'Societalization').

(b) Postmodernization Theory

Another perspective on the contemporary diversification of religious fortunes is Richard Inglehart's (1997) 'postmodernization' or 'postmaterialist culture' theory. The term 'postmodern' is used in many ways, but especially to indicate forms of culture that reject the supposed modern emphasis on order, rationality, cultural and political convergence on a common modernity and, in philosophical terms, epistemological foundationalism: the attempt to find universal and incontrovertible foundations for knowledge (Bauman 1993). This includes increased scepticism towards what Lyotard (1986) calls 'metanarratives', large stories based around the idea of a common truth or quest for truth (for example science, religion, progress). Contrary to some portrayals, Lyotard does not say science is 'just a story' like any other; rather he carefully distinguishes between the very different forms of legitimation of different discourses. A clear account of this is given in Lash (1990 pp. 90–97). However, our concern here is not with epistemology but with confidence in major institutions and discourses, especially in advanced industrial societies. Although it may be argued that these counter-tendencies were always present in modernity, the loss of confidence among cultural élites in these elements of modernity and their widespread dissemination, was arguably characteristic of the late twentieth century. We have already come across some empirical evidence for this: Davie (2000) points out that decline in participation and confidence in major religious institutions is paralleled in other spheres (for example political), while Brown (2001) has demonstrated the declining hold of religious narrative on moral identity formation in Britain.

Inglehart's empirical base derives from the World Values Surveys (1981 and 1991), a comparative study of 43 societies from across the world. His interpretation draws on secularization theory, but departs decisively from it. Using these data, Inglehart seeks to relate modernization processes to cultural change, including religious change, on a global scale. The data need to be treated with some caution, because of the very real problems of comparison across cultures. None the less, for making comparisons across a wide range of societies and especially for introducing a concept of postmodernization that maps cultural change on to clear economic and attitudinal correlates, it is an important contribution to the current debate.

Inglehart argues that modernization theory as expounded by secularization theorists is roughly correct for one phase of modernization, but that it fails to capture changes that occur as populations in advanced industrial societies reach a point where increases in material wealth no longer convert into perceptions of an increase in quality of life (1997 p. 106). At this stage, when their sense of security is no longer increased simply by having more, people start to look around for other things to improve their quality of life: environmental, health and spiritual issues are among these. At this stage, one sees a shift from 'materialist values' to what he terms 'postmaterialist values':

> The term 'Postmaterialist' denotes a set of goals that are emphasized after people have attained material security and because they have attained material security. ... The emergence of postmaterialism does not reflect a reversal of polarities but a change of priorities: Postmaterialists do not place a negative value on economic and physical security – they value it positively, like everyone else; but, unlike materialists, they give even higher priority to self-expression and to quality of life. (p. 35)

Inglehart calls this process 'postmodernization', seeing the various features associated with cultural postmodernism – a revalorization of tradition, a renewed emphasis on culture, a decline in 'metanarratives' (certainty-giving stories), whether of science, religion or the nation – as consequences of this fundamental shift in survival strategies, enabled by the success of modernization. Modernization was successful in achieving economic growth and hence drastically reduced mortality rates; but at a cost in terms of quality of life. Increases in growth no longer translated into large increases in life expectancy. Hence:

Postmodernization represents a shift in survival strategies, from maximizing economic growth to maximizing survival and well-being. ... [N]o strategy is optimal for all conditions. Modernization ... probably also increased psychological stress. ... Postmodernization, on the other hand, has a mildly negative linkage with economic growth, but a strong positive linkage with subjective well-being. With the transition from Modernization to Postmodernization, the trajectory of change seems to have shifted from maximizing economic growth to maximizing the quality of life. (p. 106)

Such a context, Inglehart argues, is barren ground for traditional authoritarian religions, which continue to decline, but also for other authority-oriented institutions, including those which assumed a central role in modernity, such as political parties, the scientific establishment and the state:

This new trajectory shifts authority away from both religion and the state to the individual, with an increasing focus on individual concerns such as friends and leisure. Postmodernization de-emphasizes all kinds of authority, whether religious or secular, allowing for a much wider range for individual autonomy in the pursuit of individual well-being. (pp. 74–5)

This account also sheds light on why rationalization – the extension of instrumental rationality into more and more spheres of life – also seems limited in its penetration of the lifeworld. This is so even in advanced industrial societies like those of Europe, where conditions conducive to disenchantment have historically been present – i.e. powerful and authoritarian religious institutions and widespread dissemination of Enlightenment critiques of religion. Rationalization is limited because:

[I]nstrumental rationality gained an exaggerated prominence during the rise of industrialization, but today ... a growing segment of society is concluding that the price is too high. Rationality, science, technology and authority are here to stay; but their relative priority and their authority amongst mass publics are declining. (p. 23)

Such conditions, he suggests, may be fertile ground for newer forms or styles of religion and 'spirituality', such as the New Age, new religious movements and new styles of traditional religions. As evidence for this Inglehart cites the finding that in 18 of 21 countries there was an increase in the number of people saying that they 'often' think about the meaning and purpose of life (p. 286). Conversely, such conditions are bad news for traditional forms of religion. However, this would seem to ignore the adaptive capacity of the latter. As we have seen Casanova (1994) argue in relation to Roman Catholicism, even the most archetypically authoritarian of religious traditions can reinvent themselves for the anti-authoritarian 'network society' (Castells 1996), in this case through its post-Vatican II emphasis on civil and political freedoms, human rights and the spiritual value of life. However, Inglehart does not consider this latter possibility, and in general his findings are more persuasive for the liberal than illiberal elements of postmodern culture.

Inglehart's work suggests that the emergence of 'spiritualities' disembedded from their traditional contexts is one of the features of the religious landscape when the authority structures of historic religions break down under the influence of societal differentiation, conditions of material surplus enable individuals to pursue their own religious quests, and global communication creates a global market in religious goods. As Bowman (1992) has pointed out, personal religiosity has always been highly eclectic and deviated from official versions, but:

> The big differences nowadays [in postmaterialist contexts] can be seen in individuals' freedom to talk openly about their beliefs, in the perception that there is not one version of 'Truth', the notion of serial spirituality or 'singular, serial and multiple seeking strategies' (Sutcliffe 1997) and in the range and availability of materials for the individual collage. (Bowman 1999 p. 182)

Inglehart also offers an explanation of what he terms 'a global trend toward fundamentalism' – referring to the rise of the Religious Right in the US, the BJP in India and Islamic fundamentalism as examples of this phenomenon. Unfortunately, Inglehart does not define fundamentalism, but seems to use the term to refer to conservative religious traditions with an authoritarian orientation.

He sees the increasing activity of such groups as due to three distinct factors. The first is a vocal rearguard action in advanced industrial societies by groups who hold traditional religious values. As we have seen, in these societies security is high and because of this, numbers in such groups are dwindling. This means that those that remain feel threatened, become increasingly vocal and hence contribute to the media perception of their strength. The second is that there are genuinely popular movements in developing societies where 'insecurity is pervasive' because of difficult social and economic conditions (Inglehart 1997 p. 281). The third set of conditions supportive of fundamentalism he associates specifically with Islam in Arab countries, where oil wealth has enabled a transition directly from pre-modern, traditional conditions to postmodern conditions, at least as defined in terms of material security.

This is an interesting account, but it is problematic in a number of ways. In the case of first-world fundamentalists, it is not clear why such groups do not perceive the benefits of material security and hence liberalize in the first place, without getting into the vicious circle described. The account ignores the fact that while first-world societies may be affluent overall, disparities of wealth are increasing and the world has become a threatening place in other ways: increasing diversity may itself be perceived as a threat. However, more damagingly, such psychological explanations of the rise of fundamentalism run into difficulties when cases are examined in detail, because it is often not those groups that are most vulnerable who express a 'fundamentalist reaction'.

The Egyptian case illustrates the point. Egypt lacks oil wealth and hence better fits the second group than the third, with poor economic conditions getting worse: per capita income declined between 1988 and 1996 and the gap between rich and poor grew (Boyle and Sheen 1997 p. 26). If Inglehart's thesis that security and traditional values are inversely related is correct, then one would expect (assuming the identity of traditional values and fundamentalism) fundamentalism to be strongest among the most insecure. However, this appears not to be the case. It is not the rural poor, but the educated – often to university level – and mobile who tend to join Islamist groups. Furthermore, this composition also calls into question the connection between fundamentalism and traditional values, for the education of such people 'constitutes extensive contact with Western institutions' (Starrett 1998 p. 225). Indeed, as we have already suggested, 'fundamentalism' in Egypt is not best understood as a traditional reaction against modernization, but rather as a modern project involving the functionalization and extension of religious discourse into every corner of modern life – beating the panoptical state at its own game.

So, as an explanation of the Egyptian case, Inglehart's account appears flawed in at least two crucial ways: it wrongly explains adherence to traditional religious values in terms of lack of material security; and it wrongly characterizes Islamic fundamentalism as a traditional form of religion. There are further problems too: in particular, by taking the nation-state as his unit of analysis, Inglehart ignores differences within nations. Yet theories of globalization argue that increased worldwide communication means that connections between segments within societies can often be as or more significant than national boundaries (Castells 1996). Furthermore, we have already noted the likely significance of the very different ways modernization has been mediated to different societies.

In conclusion, Inglehart's account of the re-enchantment of parts of populations of advanced industrial societies is rather more persuasive than his account of the 'rise of fundamentalism', although elements of both are useful in building an overall picure of the relationship between religion, modernization and, in view of his account, postmodernization. Given the problems with Inglehart's account of fundamentalism, we now turn to consider the use of this term and an influential theory that has been developed to account for this purported phenomenon, a theory that also turns on the relationship between religion and modernization.

(c) The Construct of Fundamentalism and Modernity's Relation to Politicized Religions

Many scholars have objected to the use of the term 'fundamentalism', especially in a cross-cultural context (Esposito 1992; Karam 1997). They argue that it carries negative, stereotypical connotations and misleadingly carries understandings from its origins as a label for developments in the American Protestant Christian tradition that are inappropriate for understanding phenomena in other traditions (Esposito 1992 p. 8). Such scholars also note that it is rejected by those it is used to describe, especially Muslim groups (Karam 1997 p. 162) and, when used as a blanket term to cover a very diverse range of religio-political phenomena, wrongly implies 'a monolithic threat that does not exist' (Esposito 1992 p. 8). The concept of fundamentalism, such critics argue, is an influential but basically misleading way to represent the contemporary revival in public forms of Islam.

However, this does not mean that the term fundamentalist should be dismissed out of hand. One major international comparative project, the Fundamentalism Project of the American Academy of Arts and Sciences, employed an interdisciplinary approach and drew on scholars with expertise in different geographical areas. It concluded that there is an identifiable cluster of features characteristic of certain contemporary religious groups found across cultures and traditions and which therefore justifies use of the term 'fundamentalist' (Marty and Appleby 1991).

Marty and Appleby, directors of the Fundamentalist Project, argue for a 'family resemblance' understanding of fundamentalism, in which not all movements will share all or even any one characteristic with every other, but each will have several characteristics (1991 p. 816). Amongst these characteristics they include the following key features:

1. religion is made an exclusive basis for communal and personal identity (p. 817);
2. religious truth is depicted as indivisible, for example scripture cannot contain contradictions or errors (p. 818);
3. 'a selective retrieval of doctrines, beliefs and practices from a sacred past … accompanied in the new religious portfolio by unprecedented claims and doctrinal innovation' (p. 835);
4. an idealist version of history, in which history is seen as planned by God or otherwise predetermined and they see themselves as actors in this history (p. 819);
5. strict and exclusive boundaries are constructed to enable them to maintain such views (p. 821);
6. a utopian vision of society in which they aim to replace the existing structures of state and society with their own, understood to be based on a divine blueprint (p. 824).

This understanding is used by Tibi (1998) to discuss Islamic groups in the Middle East, and this region will be used as a test case of the theory's cross-cultural validity. He emphasizes three of these features: an idealist interpretation of history, a utopian vision of society as derived from divine law and the selective reinterpretation of traditional doctrines (pp. 13–14). He further seeks to locate the emergence of 'non-Western fundamentalism' in a global, post-cold-war context, arguing that contemporary forms of fundamentalism are unique among post-colonial movements in that they not only seek political emancipation from European domination, but also rebel against Western culture and values:

> [W]e are even now witnessing a simultaneity of structural globalization and national and international cultural fragmentation … The political articulation of non-Western fundamentalism is peculiar in that it assumes the shape of a revolt against the West. But unlike the anti-colonial revolt it is not simply a political upheaval, for it is directed against Western norms and values as well. (p. 3, 179)

Tibi makes an important point here: whereas anti-colonial movements and post-colonial governments tended to seek to replace colonial governments with forms of home rule based on Western ideologies – republican, democratic, nationalistic, Marxist and so on – the rejection or substantial modification of these ideologies by contemporary movements which deploy religious discourses is striking.

Thus Marty and Appleby's understanding of fundamentalism and Tibi's development of the concept provide a suggestive framework for cross-cultural comparison. However, the framework can be misleading if used to interpret particular situations without looking at the local detail. For example, Marty and Appleby (1991) describe the fundamentalist interaction with modernity in the following terms:

> Coupled with ... envy and resentment of modernity is a shrewd exploitation of its processes and instrumentalities. (p. 827) ...Not only do fundamentalists draw upon modern organizational methods and structures; they also benefited from the encouragement or direct support of colonial powers and later took advantage of the openness of secular democracies. (p. 828)

Applied to the Middle East, this is a gross misrepresentation of the postwar period, in which authoritarian states have repeatedly refused democratic participation in government and brutally suppressed opposition groups. Both government and opposition have made use of modern technologies and methods, so the characterization of religiously based opposition movements as distinctive in this respect is also misleading.

Another example where a general theory of fundamentalism can be misleading (when used to interpret the situation in the Muslim world) is the psychological 'explanation' of the politicization of religion, as we saw with Inglehart above. Marty and Appleby quote with approval the view that 'fundamentalism represents "a delayed reaction to the psychological heritage of European colonial rule"' (Lawrence 1989 p. 100, in Marty and Appleby 1991 p. 814). However, while this psychological explanation of a siege mentality may make sense in contexts where numbers of believers are declining, it seems less persuasive in situations where movements are growing rapidly both in numbers and influence. Furthermore, as Moaddel (1996 pp. 330 – 31) points out, the century or more gap between significant European incursion and the rise of fundamentalism in the 1970s surely casts doubt on such an explanation.

A more plausible immediate explanation of the religious form of opposition movements lies in governments' own attempts to intervene in cultural production – and specifically to use religion to legitimize state power. We saw this with Egyptian education following Starrett (1998) in Chapter 1 and Moaddel (1996) argues similarly in relation to Syria and Iran. It was this that led to opposition mobilization on a religious basis. The problem is that Marty and Appleby's analysis stresses the defensive psychological reaction of fundamentalists while ignoring the threat of state power which makes such a reaction comprehensible, indeed, rational. Hence, as a 'one-size-fits-all' explanation it is extremely misleading.

More broadly, any dichotomy between so-called 'fundamentalism', and Islam as a religion and ethics quite separate from politics, is overly simplistic when applied to the Middle East. Rather, there is a continuum of attitudes between secularist and fundamentalist positions, with the majority falling somewhere between the two and all but the secularist extreme influenced to a greater or lesser extent by religious discourse. As Dalacoura (1998 p. 130) writes of Egypt, 'Secularism and Islamic fundamentalism are minority positions in Egypt in the 1990s'. In Egypt, public debate *has* become increasingly polarized (Flores 1997), but use of the term 'fundamentalist' does not get us very far in understanding the situation and indeed seems likely only to increase polarization . Therefore we shall avoid use of the term in the main narrative, but recognize that it is widely used, and explain what different authors mean by it when we come across it.

The term 'Islamist' (*Islami* in Arabic) is sometimes used to describe politically active forms of Islam and this will also be used here. It is useful because it links the ideas of groups in political opposition in Egypt and elsewhere with groups who have achieved power in other countries (for example Iran, Sudan and, briefly, in the mid-1990s, Turkey) and are therefore no longer 'opposition groups'. Although the Islamist movements in these countries are very different, certain ideas, such as that of an 'Islamic state' and the call to 'implement *sharia*', unite them. Ghadbian (1997) offers the following definition of Islamism:

> All individuals and groups seeking to change their societies by deriving their ideology from Islam. While these groups and individuals differ in methods, approaches, styles and [on] substantive issues, they agree on the positive worth of Islam and the relevance of its basic concepts and values to the contemporary world. They want to shift the frame of reference in the public realm to one in which Islam, in its varying interpretations, is a major shaping force. (p. 59)

In contrast to 'fundamentalist', which is a term 'totally rejected by its supposed adherents', 'Islamist' is a term 'which many Islamist activists themselves often identify' (Karam 1997 p. 162). Karam gives the example of one 'young middle-ranking activist of the Egyptian Muslim Brotherhood', who said, 'It gives me a source of pride and satisfaction to be referred to as an Islamist [*Islami* in Arabic]. All I seek is to see Islam implemented' (ibid.).

Like secularization theory, general theories of fundamentalism assume that religion can only articulate with modernization in defensive (fundamentalist) or aquiescent (liberal) modes. In the first case belief in the supernatural is sustained, but at the expense of conflict with modernizing elements in society. In the second case it is gradually abandoned. These two responses may account for a significant amount of data, but they do not exhaust the options, and distort those cases they fit when applied exclusively. Rather, we need to be open to the possibility of religion adapting in a range of ways to modernization and postmodernization processes, including, as we saw in the Egyptian case in Chapter 1, that of functionalization without disenchantment. Here, structural modernization is embraced, but supernaturalism sustained.

(d) Casanova's Post-Secularization Thesis

We have already seen that Casanova (1996) argues that religion in modernity sometimes deprivatizes (the American Catholic bishops, Chapter 1 Section 4(c)) and that religious decline only follows from modernization *if* religion is closely allied to the state *and* versions of the Enlightenment critique of religion (ECR) become widespread (1994; Chapter 1, Section 2). Using these arguments and a study of American Protestantism and Catholicism in America, Brazil, Spain and Poland,

Casanova (1994) argues that most formulations of the secularization thesis have wrongly conflated three related but distinct processes:

1. The differentiation of modern societies into semi-autonomous spheres, involving the freeing of secular spheres from religious institutions and norms.
2. The decline of religious beliefs and practices.
3. The marginalization of religion into a privatized sphere.

In brief, he argues that (1) is correct, but that (2) and (3) only follow in the presence of a church-state alliance and the dissemination of the ECR. If, on the contrary, religions learn to embrace differentiation, indicated by support for democracy and acceptance of a new role as one voice amongst many in the public sphere, they can prosper. Hence it is not modernization but 'the historic attempt to preserve and prolong Christendom in every nation-state and thus to resist modern functional differentiation that nearly destroyed the churches in Europe' (ibid. p. 29). As a counter-example of the renaissance of public religions in the late twentieth century, Casanova considers Spain: 'Spain has not only joined the European Community but has also apparently adopted the general European pattern of secularization' (p. 90). In spite of the efforts of reforming Catholics, from the dissociation of the Church from the Franco regime to the contributions of Catholic activists to the democratic opposition and the development of civil society and through to the Church's role in national reconcilation, the Church had for too long been associated with the 'caesaropapist' path of alliance with reactionary political power. Thus under contemporary democratic conditions the Church has been unable to articulate its voice in public debates in a way which effectively transcends that history:

> On some of the occasions when the catholic church joined Spanish public debates, its participation remained largely ineffective, among other reasons because it was unable to frame its discourse in such a way that it could not easily be dismissed as a conservative partisan critique of the Socialist government or as an empty traditionalist critique of modern secular culture. (Ibid. p. 90)

Deprivatization in Spain, then, has been largely unsuccessful. But Casanova also examines three other cases during the same period: first, Poland, where the role of Catholicism in support of the Solidarity movement led to the eventual transition to democratic government, second, Brazil, where the Church's opposition to the national security government and 'trickle-down' economics, as well as the development of the People's Church and base ecclesial communities, contributed to the transformation of Brazilian society and the return of democracy, and third, American Protestant evangelicals and the rise of the Christian Right. In each case he finds striking evidence of deprivatization. How does he explain this pattern?

We have already discussed the impact of the Vatican II policy of *aggiornomento* for Catholicism and the specific factors affecting Catholics in postwar America, and we shall return to the case of American Protestantism. But for now we can note that Casanova also points to an important additional general factor: the development of communication technologies which enabled the creation of a transnational civil society. This was particularly important in Poland and elsewhere in Eastern Europe in undermining the legitimacy of Communist regimes. Examples of religion using these technologies, especially television, to maximize the impact of their symbolic media, include open-air papal masses displaying Solidarity banners, Solidarity rallies displaying crucifixes, and candle-lit peace vigils in predominantly Protesant East Germany. Concerning this creation of a transnational civil society Casanova (1996) claims:

> When human rights and the internal affairs of sovereign states become everybody's business, being constantly monitored by governments, by the mass media and by governmental and nongovernmental organizations and when global public opinion and the United Nations no longer respect the principle of non-interference in the internal affairs of sovereign states, it becomes ever more difficult for absolutist rulers to erect Berlin walls or protect their frontiers from an ever-expanding civil society. (p. 363)

However, an apparent limitation on Casanova's argument as a general one is the restriction to predominantly Catholic (and entirely Christian) examples. How are Casanova's arguments borne out in relation to other traditions?

In particular, in Muslim majority societies Islamic groups do not appear to need to restrict their activities to civil society in order to attract popular support. Rather, Islam has increased its influence on the state not only in countries where there has been an Islamic revolution (Iran, Sudan), but also through the 'Islamization' of law, in Egypt, Pakistan, Nigeria and elsewhere. Outside the Arab world, Islamist political parties have achieved success in local and national elections across the Muslim world (Therborn 1997) and their limitation in the Arab world is largely the result of exclusion from democratic participation by governments (Ayubi 1991). The faltering prosperity and political insecurity of many of these societies of course suggests explanations of religious mobilization along the lines of Bruce's categories of cultural defence and cultural transition and Inglehart's argument from insecurity.

But while these may have some validity, as we have seen in the Egyptian case at least, these face some difficulties. This is both because they predict mobilization of the wrong groups and because they fail to capture the way in which religion functions as a cultural system – not just to fill social space but to transform its meaning. A further possibility is that just as the Enlightenment critique of religion fails to find purchase in societies without a history of a 'caesaropapist' alliance between religious and political authorities (for example America, Brazil), so in societies where religion has a long history of a supportive relationship with state authorities, continuous involvement in the legal sphere, and is not associated with social conflict (for example most areas of the Sunni Muslim world), the role of religion at the levels of the state and political society is viewed differently than in predominantly Christian and post-Christian cultures.

The continuing role of *sharia* law and courts alongside secular state legal systems into the twentieth century in most cases and in many cases continuously, may well be a significant factor here. For with the exception of India, where the rise of the BJP is perhaps best interpreted as a nationalist movement seeking to privilege a particular religious group, it is difficult to think of a non-Muslim example where ambitions by groups mobilized on a religious basis at the level of political society and the state attract such extensive popular support. This is not to say that such support goes uncontested, and certainly there are important arguments about the validity of ideas like the 'implementation' of *sharia* and 'Islamic state', which we shall consider in Chapter 5. Furthermore, there is evidence that religion is limited in its ability to operate at a systemic level in some cases: Beyer (1994) interprets Iran's economic difficulties in this light, although the role of international sanctions and war with Iraq are clearly also important factors.

In the case of conservative American Protestantism, Casanova to a large extent shares Bruce's assessment that as a political force at the level of party politics (political society) and hence (or otherwise, through direct lobbying and so on) the state, the impact of the New Christian Right has been limited and its prospects of success are not great. This is because its potential support base is too small (not more than 20 per cent of the electorate) and too divided, and because the opposition which its formation mobilized proved (and is likely to continue to prove) more organized and effective (1994 pp. 157–66). However, this is a different matter to its potential impact at the level of civil society. Following Neuhaus (1984), Casanova argues that participation in the public sphere of civil society poses a dilemma for the fundamentalist wing of conservative Protestantism, because public mobilization is based on private, subcultural conviction and argument developed on the basis of a narrow range of unchallengeable assumptions. Such mobilization in sufficient numbers can achieve electoral success, runs the argument, but as soon as it is exposed to either the muddied compromises of practical politics or the glare of 'public reason', that is, to those who do not share its presuppositions, fundamentalism faces in the first case a crisis of conscience and in the second case a crisis of plausibility (Casanova 1994 pp. 165–6). Casanova further argues that those conservative Protestants who are prepared to make practical political compromises have the best prospects of success but that in doing so they will cease to be fundamentalists. Such an interpretation would fit with the distinction between fundamentalists and evangelicals developed above (Smith 1998).

As far as the role of religion in civil society is concerned, the reliance of Casanova's argument on a concept of public reason is important. It is also contested. For example, MacIntyre (1985) has argued that modern ethical discourse should be seen as a series of incommensurable fragments of traditions between which rational resolution is impossible, raising questions about any concept of 'public reason' or even the possibility of genuine consensus in contemporary societies. We shall consider MacIntyre's arguments further in Chapter 3. From another perspective, a range of studies on public communication has problematized the concept of public reason and the public sphere of civil society as the location of its exercise and we shall also examine these in Chapter 3. Both perspectives pose challenges to Casanova's notion of civil society and there are further problems that we shall begin to consider now.

The first point to note is the apparent inconsistency between Casanova's acceptance of structural differentiation and his argument for deprivatization. As we noted above, deprivatization involves religion 'seeping' into other spheres. Casanova deals with this by constructing a clear barrier to restrict such 'seepage'; religion can flow into civil society, but it must not penetrate political society or the state. But this description raises an important question about the nature of Casanova's 'barrier': is it normative (based on the idea that religion should be restricted to civil society) or descriptive (based on observation of compatibility in practice)? The answer would seem to be both: he argues that religion should restrict itself to civil society because it would be undemocratic not to; and that where it fails or refuses to do so it loses popularity because the ECR comes into play against it. And yet it is not clear that 'seepage' can be easily confined to the public sphere of civil society. As Asad (1999) comments:

> [Religion] is not indifferent to debates about how the economy should be run, which scientific projects should be publicly funded, or what the broader aims of national education system should be. The legitimate entry of religion into these debates results in the creation of modern 'hybrids': the principle of structural differentiation, according to which religion, economy, education and science are located in autonomous social spaces, no longer holds. (p. 179)

Such 'hybridity' or 'seepage' becomes apparent in conflicts between the open democratic ethos of the public sphere of civil society and the absolutist ethical aspects of religious traditions. Casanova (1996) shows awareness of this tension when he writes of the widespread Catholic disobedience to the Church's teaching on sexual morality, especially contraception, which he argues can be justified by the principles of Vatican II:

> Implicitly at least, by their ecclesiastical disobedience in combination with their expressed unwillingness to leave the church, indeed through their refusal to consider that by obeying the church hierarchy they are breaking communion with the church, Catholics are saying that they have internalized the teachings of the second Vatican Council in a way in which the Council fathers may not have envisaged when they proclaimed the doctrine of freedom of conscience and when they defined the church as the people of God. (p. 368)

Yet it is not clear that he fully acknowledges the difficulties this tension causes, both in this and other cases of deprivatization, difficulties which may threaten the Church's success in establishing itself as a significant and respected voice in the public sphere of civil society. Consider, for example, the Church's use of undemocratic political strategies in Poland in the early 1990s in relation to abortion, the constitution and religious education (Gilarek 1999; below, Chapter 7). The crunch comes when the Church is faced with a choice between commitment to participative, deliberative democracy and the strategically best way to defend its sacred principles. For example, in the case of an issue like abortion, should the Church prioritize its commitment to deliberative democracy by supporting a referendum and arguing its case in the public sphere (at the risk of losing), or by trying to influence the government directly? The American bishops notwithstanding, the Church's instinct may, in many cases, be for the latter (as we shall see in Chapter

7 below, it was in Poland). Furthermore, it is not clear that this instinct is out of line with Catholic teaching: the conciliar documents of Vatican II do not unambiguously require a subordination of all aspects of the common good to the principles of participative, deliberative democracy. Casanova (1996) states that:

> If the bishops [in the United States] through their public intervention have now asserted their 'right and competence' to intervene in public affairs, at least implicitly they also have come to recognize the public's right to judge their speech in accordance with the universalistic criteria of open, rational debate, which at least ideally govern the public sphere. (p. 369)

Our analysis suggests two problems with this statement. First, it is not clear that the bishops would be able to accept such a statement explicitly formulated, because it implies a dissolution of the authority of tradition and of their role as bearers of that tradition. This in turn suggests that the legitimate role of both authority and tradition in modernity stands in need of some further consideration than Casanova provides. Furthermore, the possibility of public debate approximating to this ideal needs critical assessment.

Given its central role in his argument, Casanova's concept of civil society, including the 'transnational' variety, remains insufficiently developed. In particular, his presentation does not seem to consider that the globalization and multiplication of media which enable this transnationalization can as often be accused of inhibiting public debate by oversimplification, domination by commercial interests and corruption by powerful interest groups, as of creating the participatory democratic forum he seems to envisage (Mayhew 1997). Casanova acknowledges his debt to Habermas, but neglects Habermas's account of the decline of the bourgeois public sphere in the nineteenth century, raising as it does the difficulties of open, public rational discussion amongst diverse participants and in contexts shaped by commercial and other interests (Habermas 1989).

Considering the contemporary context, Castells (1996) has argued that 'the information society' is characterized by new patterns of exclusion as well as unprecedented opportunities. We shall consider his account more fully below in Chapter 4, because it has particular relevance for how the ideal of communication in the public sphere works out in the reality of contemporary global developments. But in the context of alternatives to secularization theory, we can note that Castells sees religiously based communal mobilization as a significant form of resistance to dominant globalizing forces (1997a). Similarly, in a major consideration of the impact of theories of globalization on religion, Beyer (1994) comes to the conclusion that religion, by virtue of being difficult to confine to any one sphere of differentiated societies (the seepage phenomenon we have noted), provides significant resources for resistance to dominant systems. He considers in particular the case of religiously inspired environmental activism, but also warns of the limits to the functionalization of religions in providing alternative modes of operation for systems, using the example of Iran's economic problems.

In the next chapter we shall consider how contemporary civil society and the public sphere are best to be understood and how religion is to be seen in relation to them, in the light of the criticisms we have made of Casanova. But first let us summarize where our investigation of the relationship between religion and modernization in Chapters 1 and 2 has brought us.

4. Conclusion

In Chapter 1 we began with the idea of secularization as the most influential and comprehensive theory of the relationship between religion and modernization, yet challenged by the apparent diversity of the fortunes of religion in different parts of the contemporary world. We considered the entwining of the idea of secularization with modern notions of progress, for example in the development of the various forms of the Enlightenment critique of religion in response to church-state relations and religious conflict in early modern Europe. While sociologists have sought to differentiate such critiques from their models of the effects of structural modernization, the assumptions among social analysts in Western societies that religion in modernity will and should decline remain both influential and conjoined. We shall see further evidence of this in Chapter 3 when considering accounts of democratization in Eastern Europe. We also noted that two distinct elements tended to be conflated in secularization theory: religious vitality and significance, both of which are in turn multifaceted phenomena. We then found that the quantitative evidence on vitality tended to confirm our initial impression of the diversity of religion's fortunes in the modern world. However, a pattern began to be discernible, with decline evident in Western Europe but apparently much less so in America and perhaps even the reverse in Latin America and the Muslim world. This impression was confirmed by considering qualitative evidence from Egypt, Britain and America, which also suggested dimensions of religion's social significance not readily accessed either in quantitative studies of religious belief and behaviour or of institutions: the role of religion as discourse and symbol. This discursive religion is often less anchored in traditional authoritative institutions than has historically been the case, and is suggestive of the diverse roles religion can play in contemporary civil societies.

In Chapter 2 we then turned to review secularization theory in more detail in the light of the evidence we had gathered. Having decided that the theory constitutes a paradigm and clarified our definition of religion, we noted some parameters and limitations of the theory – specifically, its universal scope and one-dimensionality. We then considered the three core processes common to many versions of the theory: social differentiation, societalization and rationalization. We concluded that although there is strong evidence for differentiation and societalization the former is conceptually problematic, because it is also accompanied by various forms of 'seepage' between systems. These include especially the seepage of economic interests into other spheres (Polanyi), but also the deprivatization of religion (Casanova). Furthermore, these processes are not unambiguous in their effects on religious traditions. Indeed, they may enhance as well as diminish the social significance of religion, with examples of the former being the functionalization of Islam within Egyptian educational (and, as we shall see further in Chapter 9), health, welfare, legal and political systems.

Such examples cannot be readily reduced to the cultural defence/transition exceptions of orthodox secularization theory, for they illustrate transformations in the role of religious discourse not envisaged in such theory and suggest successful mutation of system-lifeworld articulation rather than temporary defence of the lifeworld, to use Habermas's terms. Furthermore, secularization theory tends to ignore the negative consequences of differentiation. While Habermas theorizes this in terms of colonization of the lifeworld by systems, he wrongly precludes religion from a role in the lifeworld's communicative rationalization and hence more than merely its temporary defence. In the case of rationalization, it simply appears to be the case that disenchantment does not always follow rationalization of the lifeworld and it may be rather that a specific conjunction of religion-state relations is required for it to do so.

The alternatives to secularization theory we then considered further enabled us to enrich our account of religion-modernity interactions. Rational choice theory (RCT) is limited as a total model, but useful for understanding behaviour when conditions approximate to the market ideal. Inglehart's postmodernization theory helps make sense of both the fact and form of some of the re-enchantment of culture in affluent societies. Marty and Appleby's theory of fundamentalism sheds some light on cases where conservative religions react defensively to structural modernization, but in many cases they do not, adapting rather than retreating, as both evangelical Christians (Smith 1998; above, Chapter 1) and the growth of diverse Islamisms suggest. The simple reductionist psychological models used by both this theory and RCT are particularly unhelpful. Casnova's deprivatization of religion thesis is far more helpful, especially in its differentiation between three spheres of public life (civil and political society and the state), enabling a much more nuanced understanding of the public role of religions. Yet Casanova's conflation of the empirical and normative limitation of religion's compatibility with modernity to civil society is arguably inadequate to Islamic examples and perhaps also to other non-Western traditions (including Christian Orthodoxy) and his concepts of civil society and the public sphere need further critical investigation and development.

What then is our final verdict on the religion-modernity relation? Modernization tends to weaken the power of traditional religious institutions because of the diversification of channels and forms of communication in modernity. Arguably – and we shall consider further evidence for this below – this is so even in what might be described as the hardest cases of religious revival – where religious ideology becomes a medium of popular protest in contrast to discredited regimes associated with secularist policies. Here, traditional religious institutions may be revived by governments seeking to increase their legitimacy (as with Al-Azhar in Egypt) or reintroduced in radically new forms (as with the government by clerics in Iran). But in both cases, while these institutions are undoubtedly more influential than under previous nationalist administrations, they are ill equipped to compete with the multiplication of opinion generated by modern education systems and communications media. However, these media do not necessarily have a secularizing effect. Rather, religion as discourse can become the central medium of public communication. And even in cases where religion does not become the dominant language of protest – as in Latin America for example, where liberation theology's mobilizing success was limited – religious discourses and practices can still thrive alongside advanced technology, mass literacy and urbanization. Thus in both cases, and to borrow Foucault's (1991 [1977]) metaphor derived from the French Revolution, cutting off the head of the king does not destroy power but disperses it more widely through the system. Indeed, it may even intensify its disciplinary effects. So with religion, whose modern discursive power may even exceed its traditional institutionalized power. However, as this comparison suggests, potency is no guarantee of a positive relation to democratization and it is to this we turn next, first in relation to civil society (Chapter 3) and then the public sphere (Chapter 4).

Notes

1   Interestingly, neither Bruce and Wallis (1992) nor Bruce (1999) refer to Tschannen's work.
2   Inglehart's evidence also shows increased church attendance and proportion of people saying 'God is important in their lives' in the Republic of Ireland between 1981 and 1990 (1997 pp. 282 – 3).
3   Sometimes called 'postmodernization'. See Inglehart (1997) and Section 3(6) below.

Chapter 3

Rethinking Civil Society

Civil society is that part of social life which lies beyond the immediate reach of the state and which ... must exist for a democratic state to flower. It is the society of households, family networks, civic and religious organizations and communities that are bound to each other primarily by shared histories, collective memories and cultural norms of reciprocity. (Douglass and Friedmann 1998 p. 2)

It is a very serious mistake and it certainly historically and methodologically naive, to assume that the category [of civil society] simply and perfectly clearly represents some determinate reality existing 'out there'. (Tester 1992 p. 124)

When the intellectuals of Eastern Europe came to power, they thought they could have it all – enlightenment, capitalism and democracy itself. The practical task of social reconstruction makes these social ideals difficult for intellectuals to sustain. The utopian ideology they bring to their task, however, reduces even further the possibility of success. ... In the good bad old days, opposition intellectuals coined the term 'real socialism' to dramatize how socialism in practice departed from the dream. It is time to start talking about 'real civil society'. (Alexander 1990, in Alexander 1998 p. 2)

1. Civil Society: a Contested Concept

Chapter 2 has argued that Casanova's reformulation of the secularization thesis is a productive one for expanding its explanatory power and indeed enables progression from a theory of religious decline in modernity to one of change and diversification. Furthermore, Casanova identifies religion in the public sphere of civil society both as important for understanding contemporary religion itself and as a force resisting the domination of social life by the functional imperatives of state and market – resisting, in Habermas's terms, the colonization of the lifeworld (Casanova 1994 p. 229). Thus civil society can be seen as vital to the success of democracy.

Yet difficulties were also identified with Casanova's concept of civil society and the quotations above suggest further problems. The first quotation is useful because it specifies the kind of social institutions associated with civil society; but it is inadequate because while the importance (indeed necessity) of civil society for democracy is stated, the question of how civil society is supposed to produce its democratizing effects is not addressed. This is a common problem; as Keith Tester (1992 p. 128) comments on John Keane's work (which will be considered further below), all too often 'It is simply asserted that civil society involves democratic pressures; the connection is never really deconstructed or interrogated'. Therefore, a critical theory of civil society will need to examine this connection. A related problem is that, as with Casanova, the concept often tends to include a utopian element, which means that civil society is more than a description of 'what's actually there' beyond the state; it is an ideal of what *ought* to be there. According to Seligman (1992), since the early modern period the idea of civil society has been laden with hopes for its civilizing, democratizing and socially integrating influence. It is this normative content which gives the concept of civil society rhetorical power when mobilized against a repressive state (Havel 1987) and also its critical edge when used as an ideal-type with which actually existing arrangements can be compared (Keane 1998 p. 37). But such a normative concept can also be a hindrance to analysis, obscuring complex relationships. As Therborn (1997 p. 45) observes, 'its strongly normative character makes the concept little apt for analytical purposes. Indeed, its application to the empirical world usually tends to veil a number of social and political features, turning the concept into false ideology'.

To illustrate his point, Therborn considers the example of the mobilization of opposition to the Communist government in Poland in 1976–89, usually hailed as a triumph of civil society. He argues that the uneasy alliance of groups opposing the government – workers seeking to maintain food subsidies, the Catholic Church, socialist dissidents – had little to do with the normative concept of civil society as either containing or supporting public discussion. In fact, there was little public discussion of major issues, such as the country's long-term economic problems. In the event, the economic policy adopted by the first Solidarity government was formulated by a small team of economists and implemented without public consultation. Thus by imposing a normative blueprint on a complex social and political reality the concept of civil society serves to conceal more than reveal. The problem here seems to be that a normative concept of civil society ties together in apparently necessary relationships what sceptics argue are better seen as many contingent factors. In this case it is assumed that a collection of interests ranged against the state generates inclusive discussions, and also that when civil society groups enter the political arena they automatically take their discursive ethos with them. But, as we shall see further in Chapter 7, symbolic unity in opposition to the state did not generate an effective public sphere, and transition to power may alter the ethos of opposition groups.

On the other hand, this does not mean that the development and activity of associations between the individual and the state cannot lead to an effective public sphere of discussion, or that civil society cannot nurture habits that transfer into political life. Rather, a critical theory of civil society will want to establish how and why the actual networks and institutions of civil society lead to democratizing outcomes, rather than abandon the concept altogether. One way to begin to develop such a concept is to make a distinction between empirical and normative civil society, seeing the task of a critical theory of civil society as to investigate the conditions under which the first becomes the second, to use studies of the first to refine the second, and studies of the second to critique the first.

As Therborn's argument and the second quotation suggest, the attempt to 'apply' utopian visions of civil society in post-Communist Eastern Europe has to some extent discredited the current concept, calling for its development to articulate more persuasively with harsh economic, political and social conditions. This chapter seeks to develop such a concept. In particular, it seeks to bring together both the 'insider' perspective of political philosophy and the 'outsider' perspective of sociology, transferring the argument made in the following quotation by Habermas (1996) from law to civil society:

> Without the view of law as an empirical action system, philosophical concepts remain empty. However, in so far as the sociology of law insists on an objectivating view from the outside ... sociological perception falls into the opposite danger of remaining blind. (p. 66)

This approach will be further developed in Chapter 4 in relation to the closely related concept of the public sphere. Although the distinction between civil society and the public sphere wasn't (and isn't) always clear, there is some consensus that the associations which form civil society in some way feed into the public sphere, thus differentiating the two concepts. Thus Habermas describes civil society as 'composed of more or less spontaneously emergent associations that, attuned to how social problems resonate in the private spheres, distil and transmit such reactions in amplified form to the public sphere' (ibid. p. 367).

A critical theory of civil society will therefore want to ask what kind of associations these are, how they emerge and interact with each other and other institutions, and how they 'distil and transmit' reactions from the private to the public spheres. It will also want to go beyond theoretical concerns to ask how civil society might serve to integrate the very diverse groupings found in today's societies – including for example anti-globalization protestors, Islamists, gay rights activists and anti-vivisectionists. Acknowledging the challenges presented by this diversity, it will be argued that the concept none the less remains useful. In particular, many of the criticisms levelled at it can be met by three strategies: first, as above, by distinguishing between two contemporary uses, empirical and normative, second, by situating civil society in the broader context of a theory of democratization, since civil society alone cannot produce democracy, and third, following Alexander (1998), by making a distinction between the meaning of the term in different historical phases. We now turn to consider this second step.

2. Civil Society and Democratization

Theories of democratization seek to understand the factors influencing the emergence and success of the formal properties of modern democracy in particular societies. Minimally, these formal properties are universal adult suffrage, representation through the elected candidates of freely formed political parties, and the rule of law implemented by an independent judiciary. Many would also include mechanisms for the protection of human rights. Such theories are increasingly inclined to attribute a role in democratization to civil society. However, this does not mean that civil society alone can produce democracy. For example, the former East

Germany boasted a dense network of civil society organizations, in line with Northern European norms and in excess of those found in Southern European societies (Therborn 1997 p. 47). Yet this was one of the more repressive Communist regimes. In fact, one may even argue that the very density of networks of civic association facilitated the police state, for it was via these networks that informants worked. Moreover, informants did so without necessarily compromising the autonomy or purposes of such organizations (Spülbeck 1996). The same dense civil networks can work against democratization by enabling the surveillance state.

Thus, what seems to be important is a balance between civil society, other parts of society and the state. Writing in an Indonesian context, Hefner (2000 p. 215) argues, 'The process depends not just on formal elections and constitutions but on a delicate balance between society and the state'. He thus identifies three crucial elements: first a tier of civic organization 'characterized by voluntarism, independent associations and a balance of powers between state and society as well as among civil organizations themselves', second, 'a public culture that draws on those separate experiences to promote universal habits of participation and tolerance' (ibid.) – in the terms we have used here, civil society and the public sphere, and third, the role of the state: 'The Indonesian example ... makes clear, ... these two developments come to nothing if they are not reinforced by a third above and beyond society: the creation of a civilized and self-limiting state' (ibid.).

Indeed, it may be argued that across the Muslim world it is the character of the post-colonial state that has posed the greatest obstacle to the development of democracy, rather than, for example, Islamic culture or even Islamist groups. Later in this chapter we shall argue specifically that Islamic culture is not incompatible with civil society, and pursue the argument that the state is a central problem for democratization in relation to Egypt in Chapter 9 below.[1] But for now the salient point to note is that Hefner proposes three elements as crucial for democratization: civil society, public culture and the state.

Yet while the state is important to democratic outcomes, it is sometimes possible for civil society to develop some autonomy and play a democratizing role even under an oppressive state. Eastern Europe under Communism provides some notable examples, but that of Turkey is also instructive, for two main reasons: first, because this is a Muslim majority society in which Islamic groups form a considerable part of empirical civil society, and second, because it shows the difficulties of attempts at social engineering in civil society: Turkey provides a striking example of state-sponsored civil society running out of control and turning against an oppressive state.

Following the *coup* of 1981, Turkey's military government encouraged the growth of Islamic groups to counter the perceived threat of Communism. It has been argued that such groups tend to replicate the patterns of state authoritarianism in their organizational structures and hence lack the 'horizontal' component taken to be characteristic of civil society (Antov and Nash 1999). None the less, there is substantial evidence that they perform a democratizing function in encouraging alternative perspectives and providing public milieux for discussion and dispute (White 1996). Such milieux include women's groups, student groups and a proliferation of media activity. In such contexts discussion may be constrained by norms viewed as oppressive in a Western setting, studies suggest a developing diversity which belies stereotypes of Islamic revivalism. For example, Özdalga shows in her study of women students in Islamic movements that individuals manage to combine traditional approaches to arranged marriage, feminist attitudes to the role of women in work and leadership, and revivalist Islamic attitudes to dress and public morality. Thus in Turkish society, the relation of Islam to democratization is complex, but should not be dismissed:

> some positive contributions are presently in the making within the press and other media (large variety of publishing houses, newspapers, magazines and TV channels) in education (private schools of high quality …) among women of different social standing (study circles, door-knocking campaigns, maternal and other forms of social support) and in party politics (effective grass-roots organizations). Those who close their eyes to the dynamic and pluralistic aspects of the Islamic movement and focus only on its negative, communitarian aspects, contribute indirectly to the formation of impediments to a viable civil society. (Özdalga 1997 p. 83)

Taking these two examples together, it seems that the 'spontaneity' of civil society organizations does not mean that they will necessarily be effective in developing the public sphere (East Germany); but neither is the initial relationship with the state definitive (Turkey). In one case spontaneous associations fail to mobilize against an oppressive state, while in another state-sponsored organizations generate vociferous opposition and public milieux for discussion.

It is also important to recognize the roles of other parts of society in contributing to democratization. Stepan and Linz (1996) do so in their comparative study of the conditions of democratic transition and consolidation in Southern and post-Communist Europe and South America. They suggest that five factors are of critical importance to democratization: a 'free and lively civil society'; a stable, uncontested territorial state with an effective bureaucracy; respect for the rule of law; political society; and economic society. Political society here refers to 'mechanisms such as political parties and interparty alliances, elections and electoral rules, political leaders and legislatures' (Keane 1998 p. 48). Economic society refers to a 'mixed system of legally crafted and regulated non-state forms of property, production, exchange and consumption' (p. 49). At each level the crucial element is the presence of institutions able to guarantee the 'integrity' – that is the diversity and autonomy – of each sphere from state or other monopolistic control. Linz and Stepan also stress the importance of the form of pre-democratic regime and of contingencies like the timing of the onset of democratic revolutions and prudent leadership (pp. 46 – 7).

Stepan and Linz's model shows features of each of the three types of theory of democratization outlined by Potter *et al.* (1997), in their major comparative study of democracy from the eighteenth to the late twentieth centuries. These types of theory are modernization, élite and structural theories. In brief, modernization theories of democratization hold that once a certain level of development (principally economic) is achieved, democratization will come about. Linz and Stepan give less attention to economic development *per se* than to the conditions for the development of a regulated market economy and also stress the importance of political society. In this they reflect Potter *et al.*'s criticisms of overly deterministic economic models. For example, Lewis argues that while 'It was the more socially and economically developed countries in Eastern Europe that democratised more rapidly, it is nevertheless difficult to identify any "modernization theory" that actually explains this' (Lewis in Potter *et al.*, 1997 p. 414). Furthermore, only weak correlations between levels of social and economic development and democratization are found outside elsewhere in the world and during other periods of history.

Transition theories argue that the actions of political élites at key moments or crises best explain democratization, and Stepan and Linz's emphasis on the role of leadership coincides with this. Again, Lewis finds more evidence in CEE than elsewhere to support this view (Potter *et al.* 1997 pp. 418–9), while stressing that under conditions of globalization international events play a larger role than either of these models permits, based, as with much political and sociological theory, around the analytic unit of the nation-state. We shall develop this point further when we examine the concept of transnational civil society below.

Structural theory emphasizes the importance of social, economic and political developments over a long period of time, and Stepan and Linz's emphasis on the stability of the territorial state through time, as well as on the development of political and economic society, fits well with this. It is possible to argue that structural theory provides a more nuanced version of modernization theory, emphasizing the diversity of interacting factors in varying historical and cultural circumstances, rather than the linear trajectory with its possibly ethnocentric assumptions underlying unreformed modernization theory. As with Stepan and Linz, this can be usefully combined with élite theory to help understand why, given long-term historical conditions, democratic transitions occur at particular times.

In summary, democratization appears to depend on civil, economic and political society and especially on the development of cultures of social trust allowing for freedom of development within these spheres, a key symptom of which is respect for the rule of law. Without agreement on the basic political unit of the state, the development of such trust is extremely difficult. International factors also play a growing role in a global information economy, and the role of political actors at moments of crisis is likely to be influential. Civil society, then, is just one factor in the process of democratization. Disillusionment with civil society as failing to 'deliver democratization' may in part be due to the failure to recognize this multifactorial and multiple contingent process.

From these models, it is clear that civil society is not a sufficient condition to bring about democratization, but the question remains as to whether it is a necessary one. Can élites (national or international) bring about democratization 'from above', if they can secure the legal framework of political, economic and civil society, and are prepared to invest in stimulating activity in these areas? In other words, how far does democratization need to spring up from the grass roots? As the Turkish example suggests, social engineering is not a precise science and such schemes can backfire. We shall pursue this question more fully with specific reference to Bosnia in Chapter 8.[2]

A further relevant question to ask of theories of democratization is, what kind of cultural variation can be accommodated within the scope of democracy? The Turkish sociologist Serif Mardin begins by answering 'the question of whether the ideals of democracy and civil society are generalisable to the the Muslim world' with the response that 'civil society is a Western dream, a historical aspiration' (Mardin 1995 p. 278). However, by the end of his answer Mardin has modified this relativist position. Aspects of the pluricentric social organization that underpinned the historic development of civil society in the West have also appeared elsewhere in the world as part of the modernization process, including in Muslim societies (Mardin in Hefner 2000 p. 214).

None the less, while Mardin argues that 'many modern Muslim states are beginning to acquire a skeleton of institutions' similar to the West's, he cautions that Western and Muslim 'dreams' have not converged, because Muslim societies have inherited a 'collective memory of a total culture which once provided a "civilized" life of a tone different from that of the West' (ibid. p. 290). According to Mardin, this was a culture oriented to collective faithfulness to divine revelation, not to autonomy and self-determination that are typical of post-Enlightenment Western culture. Hefner takes issue with Mardin's conclusion, arguing that the Indonesian example shows Mardin's portrayal of Muslim cultural orientation to be 'too textual and too unitary' (2000 p. 214). Rather, 'the social imagination of Muslim Indonesians ... has been filled with disparate dreams' (p. 215). The development of democracy in Indonesia, however, indicates that the disparate dreams have resulted in the striking of a different balance between democratic values to those prevalent in contemporary Western societies. For example, there is a greater emphasis on public morality. But this, Hefner (2000) argues, does not necessarily make such societies any less democratic:

> The practice of democracy requires a balance among its core values and that balance inevitably varies over time and place. ... Liberal philosophers might see this variation as a fatal flaw, wondering how democracy can flourish if the social achievement of freedom, equality and tolerance is not everywhere the same. But because it depends on a culture larger than itself, democracy is not one structure but many related and various forms. Not everything can be relative, of course; certain core values remain the same. But the sameness is one of family resemblance rather than mechanical reproduction.
>
> Inasmuch as variation of this sort exists in the West, we should not be surprised to see that democratization in the Muslim world will strike its own balance among values. Like Western civic democracies not long ago, Muslim democrats may prefer a stronger commitment to public moral education than contemporary Western liberals do. But this variation is not a deviation from the democratic plan, but proof of its contextual realization. (pp. 216–7)

If a critical theory of civil society is concerned to understand the relationship of civil society to democratization, then it will be important of discern what the 'core values' mentioned by Hefner are, in order to determine the limits of the cultural variability of democracy. Perhaps it is not possible to work these limits out precisely in advance of encountering particular examples, but this is certainly a question we shall need to ask as we look at the role of religion in civil society in different cultural (indeed, multicultural) contexts. We shall also address it in this chapter when we consider Islam's compatibility with civil society in the context of Gellner's theory, the consequences of multiculturalism for the theory of civil society, and in Chapter 5 when examining challenges to the universality of human rights articulated by Muslim critics.

But before moving on from theories of democratization, it is important to note some disconcerting parallels between theories of democratization and secularization. Both are designed to explain the impact of structural modernization[3] on a social sphere – that of political and religious life respectively. Neither purports to advocate the process it describes, but only to investigate the circumstances under which it occurs. Both theories claim to explain particular rather than general change – religious decline and democratization, rather than religious and political change in general. Yet in both cases there is some ambiguity among proponents as to whether they are in fact explaining a universal evolutionary (if uneven) process. There can also be a blurred connection between explanation and advocacy, especially with democratization, as, in the West at least, democratization is regarded as a universal good and becomes an explicit policy goal – in Bosnia, for example and perhaps in Afghanistan. In contrast, not since 1989 (except perhaps in China) has social secularization been an explicit policy goal.

These parallels should be enough to alert us to the potentially imperialistic tendencies of both theories. We have already seen that the impact of modernization on religion is better described in terms of diversification and change rather than convergence and if the world's religions have neither converged, nor convergently disappeared, we should be alert to parallel phenomena in the political field. The question of the legitimate diversity not just of the cultural forms of democracy but of democracy itself needs to be addressed, and we shall approach this in the context of a discussion on culture and human rights in Chapter 5 below. Given their common link with modernization theory, we also need to be alert to the kind of account of religion's social manifestation that democratization theories presuppose. For this purpose we now turn to their application to Central and Eastern Europe.

3. Religion and Civil Society in the Fall of Communism: a Challenge to Secularization Assumptions in Social and Political Theory

The previous section introduced David Potter *et al.*'s (1997) volume *Democratization* as a major historical and comparative study of the process in the nineteenth and twentieth centuries. Here the volume serves as an example of the neglect of religion in mainstream studies of democratization, and as a way into describing some of the roles religion can play in contemporary empirical civil societies. In the Potter volume religion receives brief consideration in three contexts: first, in relation to Muslim societies, second, as a factor in societal cleavage, and third, in passing as a factor in participation in the Polish general election of 1991. In the first two cases religion is seen as a negative factor in democratization (the Islamic case will be discussed further below). In the third it is seen as positive, but in neither the second nor the third case is any exposition of the substantive content of religious traditions given, nor it is argued why this should relate either positively or negatively to democratization. In the third, Polish, case, religious practice and local church organization are mentioned as positive factors in electoral participation, but no discussion of why religious tradition might play this role is considered – it is simply mentioned as a rather puzzling and specific institutional factor. In short, religion receives little attention. This, is understandable if religion is not important, but in fact other scholars contest this. Thus, Patrick Michel (1992) writes in an Eastern European context:

> Religion made a significant contribution to the long process whereby Eastern Europe emerged from communism. (p. 339)

Jan Kubik (1994) states specifically of Poland:

> All opposition groups recognized Catholic Christianity as the highest moral authority and constructed their discourses on its foundation. (p. 103)

And Cornelia Heins (1994) argues in an East German context that:

> Neither punishment nor scorn, atheism nor new rituals, … could stop the democratising influence of the church, which since 1957 the SED[4] had called the 'last organized enemy'. (p. 212)

The complete lack of recognition of these arguments in Potter *et al.* (1997) suggests that the authors operated on a fairly robust assumption that religion could not be of any great political significance and could therefore be safely ignored.

In other cases religion may be considered as contributing to the process of democratization, but the substantive content of religion is ignored, on the assumption that the accidental location of religion in a particular society provides sufficient explanation of its involvement – this might be termed the 'empty vessel' approach. Sometimes such approaches make an explicit commitment to secularization theory, for example Węcławowicz's (1996) survey of religion in Poland, which states: 'If the imposed communist system, together with urbanization and industrialization, created the first phase of secularization of Polish society, the last years of transformation to democracy could be treated as a second phase of secularization' (p. 112).

We shall begin our response to this argument by outlining four ways in which religion contributed to the development of civil society in the late Communist period in CEE, and which therefore suggests that neglect and the empty vessel approach are mistaken. First, religion contributed to the development of civil society by providing an institutional space in otherwise totalitarian societies within which it was possible to organize various forms of opposition to the communist state. An example here is the role of Lutheran Churches in the German Democratic Republic (GDR) (Pollack 1995 p. 102; Cantrell and Kemp 1993, 1995), where large demonstrations originating on church premises were organized in Leipzig, Berlin and elsewhere.

However, the East German case also provides a strong counter-example to any general thesis of CEE religious revival, as falling membership and attendance seem to be a well-established postwar pattern, reversed only briefly, in terms of attendance in contexts associated with political protest, in the late Communist period. This is supported by evidence that citizens' movements increasingly organized independently of the Church once public space opened up (Pollack 1995 pp. 103–4). But even here, the fact that the Church was in a position to provide such space in the first place requires explanation and should not be treated as accidental. For example, the fact that the Church was one institution that the ruling SED found impossible to absorb within the state's monopoly on public life may be connected to the content of religious tradition. In this case, the Lutheran doctrine of the two kingdoms is the culturally specific form of the general Christian perspective that pronounces judgement (however deferred) on the existing political order and hence can form the basis of social criticism (Krusche 1994; Burgess 1997).

Second, religion provided a symbolic resource, or fund of collective memories, which were mobilized to oppose or subvert state-imposed Communist ideologies. An example here is the role of Christian symbolism in the opposition movements in Poland. Jan Kubik has described the Pope's visit on 8 May 1979 in these terms and the subsequent impact of Catholicism on the symbols and imagery of Solidarity (Kubik 1994 pp. 129–238). In this role religion permeates the symbolic structure through which political reality is interpreted. Once a crude positivism is rejected and it is accepted that we can only understand social reality through narratives and symbols, there is no reason to relegate religion to the status of dependent variable in this context.

Third, religion functioned as an institutional and ideological connection with an international order, which stretched beyond both the state and the Communist bloc. This is particularly evident in the case of the Catholic Church in Poland, but also relevant to the East German case where links between Lutheran churches East and West persisted despite their organizational separation in 1968 and blossomed into peace movements on both sides of the Iron Curtain (De Gruchy 1995 pp. 193–205). In the case of the Churches, such claims are not merely international but purport to transcend time, linking past and future in an eschatological narrative re-enacted at each Mass and of which Pope John Paul II's open-air Masses in Poland provide powerful examples.

Fourth, religion functioned as an intellectual force from which opposition thinking and identities could be self-consciously constructed. Here one can point to the influence of Catholic intellectuals on KOR, the Workers' Defence Committee in Poland, or on the members of Charter 77 in Czechoslovakia (Luxmoore and Babiuch 1995a and 1995b). Even where intellectual engagement does not result in conversion in a conventional sense, it may be argued that aspects of religious thought were not merely accidentally related to but substantially constitutive of opposition thought. The Czech leader Vaclav Havel provides a possible example of this, for there is both external evidence of the influence of Catholic intellectuals on the group which produced Charter 77, and internal evidence in Havel's writings on the influence of the Catholic tradition of natural law.

For example, Havel (1987) opposes moral relativism in the name of 'perennial' values (p. 137). He further states that these values are not entirely effaced by their systematic neglect, but rather; 'Under the orderly surface of the life of lies ...

slumbers the hidden sphere of life in its real aims, of hidden openness to truth' (pp. 57–8). He contends that opposition action required a belief in the intrinsic value of standing up for the truth, a belief antithetical to the instrumental approach to life decisions implicit in utilitarian or rational choice theories, arguing that 'It is difficult to imagine a reasonable person embarking on such a course merely because he or she reckons that sacrifice today will bring reward tomorrow' (p. 62). Indeed, Havel directly invokes metaphysical reasoning in his legitimization of opposition political action:

> It [the world] owes its internal coherence to something like a 'pre-speculative' assumption that the world functions and is generally possible at all only because there is something beyond its horizon, something beyond or above it that might escape our understanding or grasp, but, just for that reason, firmly grounds this world, bestows upon it its order and measure and is the hidden source of all the rules, customs, commandments, prohibitions and norms that hold within it. (p. 137)

Regardless of the philosophical merits of this position and of the subsequent disillusionment with ethical concepts of civil society that we have noted, such ideas were socially significant in so far as they influenced Havel, who became politically influential in the Velvet Revolution and democratization of Czechoslovakia. As we have seen, transition theories emphasize the role of political élites and in the absence of widespread long-standing popular protest movements except in Poland, these assumed a particularly important role in the initial democratic transformation of CEE. Furthermore, there is some evidence that in Poland and the Czech Republic at least, religious thought had a substantial impact on these élites in the late Communist period (Suggate 1992, Walters 1993). But it is also possible to argue that the Churches functioned as networks for the transmission of élite ideas to the masses, which in turn enabled opposition mobilization (Casanova 1994 p. 232).

However, in spite of this counter-evidence, assumptions about the insignificance of religion in modern social and political processes are often present in theories of civil society. In part, the problem is that the concept of civil society was developed by early modern writers (for example Locke, Ferguson, Hobbes) who were concerned about how societies would hold together under newly emerging modern conditions in which traditional sources of authority – including religion – were losing their grip. Civil society – arising out of voluntary relationships between people – was seen as an important part of the solution. Religion, at least the predominant forms of Christianity in its early modern setting, especially Roman Catholicism – with its traditional hierarchical notions of authority – was conceived from the beginning in opposition to civil society. As we have seen, more recent formulations have included religious organizations as part of civil society (especially in America), once the relationship between religion and the state has been broken. But while religion has been reincorporated at a substantive level within theories of civil society, assumptions about the nature of religion inherited from the founding fathers of the concept persist, rendering this reincorporation problematic. With this in mind we turn to consider the history of the concept of civil society, and we shall revisit the normative issues raised here in Chapter 5.

4. A Brief History of the Concept of Civil Society

[T]he great French sociologist Alexis de Tocqueville concluded that congregational Christianity was a vital element in the democratic culture of early-nineteeth century America. De Tocqueville understood that the American separation of church and state took government out of the business of coercing conformity, but it did not take religion out of public life. The arrangement re-located religion not so much to the private musings of isolated individuals but to a civil sphere of voluntary association and public debate. The result was not religion's decline but an extraordinary efflorescence characterized by vigorous denominational competition and continual public argument. (Hefner 2000 p. 9)

In perhaps the most comprehensive account of the development of the concept of civil society, Cohen and Arato (1992) trace the origins of the concept from Aristotle's *politike koinonia* (political community) through the Roman translation *societas civilis*, to the medieval city-state (pp. 84–6). But the modern history of the concept begins with Hobbes (1588–1679), Locke (1632–1704) and Montesquieu (1689–1755). Assessing the work of these thinkers, Keith Tester (1992 p. 13) argues that the modern idea of civil society 'is best interpreted as a social and historical category by which those who have lost, or have been denied, any faith in the natural artifice attempt to explain, confirm and renaturalize ... their social condition'.

Thus the idea of civil society was first articulated in competition with this 'natural artifice', the idea of a natural stable hierarchy of social order sanctioned by God (Locke). Indeed, 'social' order is anachronistic, since in pre-modern society the human world was seen as continuous with the natural world as part of creation. The early moderns instituted 'the social' as an artificial human construction defined in opposition to the natural world, against which the social construction of civilization had to be guarded (Hobbes). Part of the undermining of the natural artifice – a process precipitated by the growth of commerce undermining the power of the nobility and by urbanization and early industrialization – was the problem of 'the stranger'. This refers to unregulated social interaction with so many diverse others that they could not be contained by familiarity or rigid categorization. Tester therefore describes the imagination of civil society as the alchemical synthesis of sameness from difference, or of homogeneity from heterogeneity.

Thus the early modern concept was introduced by these opponents of their respective *anciens régimes* in the late seventeenth and eighteenth centuries. These thinkers were convinced of the bankruptcy of the old patriarchal order of authority, but unsure how society could avoid degenerating into chaos without it (Tester 1992). One solution was to reinvest the monarch's authority in the state, but this still needed to be legitimated from the bottom up (Hobbes, Rousseau). Thus 'horizontal networks of interdependencies' (Habermas) or 'relations of symmetric reciprocity' (Tester) took centre stage in their theorizing. However, their deconstruction of patriarchy only went so far. The 'horizontal networks' they saw replacing the old hierarchies were composed of men like themselves – they did not include women or the lower orders. This patriarchal and elitist construction of the early modern concept of civil society raised doubts about its contemporary relevance. Furthermore, the universality of the civil society they imagined was in some ways bounded by the nation-state. And as Enlightenment thinkers, it is also not surprising that their accounts of civil society tended to incorporate some version of the Enlightenment critique of religion, which Chapter 1 showed to be problematic as a factual account of religion in modernity.

Not all of these thinkers, however, were hostile to religion, or saw it as a dangerous divisive force to be contained. Visiting America in the 1830s, de Tocqueville was one of the last users of the idea in this early modern sense of 'an inclusive, umbrella-like concept referring to a plethora of institutions outside the state' (Alexander 1998 p. 3). Freed from the ties of state, de Tocqueville saw religion as a vital contributor to American democracy. This first broad and idealistic use of civil society is described by Alexander as the first phase of the modern theory of civil society (CSI). It was to brought to an end by the decisive intervention of Karl Marx.

No sooner had de Tocqueville completed the second volume of *Democracy in America* (1840) than Karl Marx began a series of writings (1842–45) that were to reduce the scope of civil society and link it to capitalist domination in a way that virtually put the concept out of circulation for a century (Abercrombie *et al.* 1994 p. 429; Alexander 1998 pp. 4–5). For Marx, 'Not only is civil society now simply a field of play of egotistical, purely private interests, but it is now treated as a superstructure, a legal and political arena produced as camouflage for the domination of commodities and the capitalist class' (ibid. p. 429). This marks the beginning of the second historical phase (CSII) identified by Alexander (1998 pp. 4–6), but Marx's deconstruction of civil society as a reification of particular interests (in Marx's case, class) can also be seen as setting the pattern for subsequent critiques of CSI, including those of its recent revival. For example, shortly before his death in 1984, Michel Foucault criticized the concept of civil society in relation to Poland in a manner similar to Therborn (1997), described at the beginning of this chapter: 'when one assimilates the powerful social movement that has just traversed that country to a revolt of civil society against state, one misunderstands the complexity and multiplicity of the confrontations' (Foucault 1988 p. 167). For Foucault, civil society obscures the complexity of social and political relations in a particular dualistic kind of way: 'it's ... never exempt from a sort of Manichaeism that afflicts the notion of "state" with a pejorative connotation while idealizing "society" as a good, living, warm whole' (pp. 167–8).

Indeed, although Foucault explicitly addresses the concept of civil society only rarely, much of his intellectual endeavour was concerned to show how much of modern social and political science and theory had misunderstood the notion of power as centralized in the state. Instead, Foucault sees power as far more diffuse and pervasive, vested in the intellectual 'disciplines' which seek to objectify knowledge (1992); in the 'disciplinary' practices of modern medical and welfare systems (especially asylums and prisons, 1991) and in the reflexive construction of the self as the subject of sexuality (1979). Foucault's work, then, suggests that rather than a free space for the jostling of diverse associations and groupings giving rise to a public sphere in which a free exchange of views can occur, the reality of civil society is a complex network of power relations, with power being exercised not only through individuals and institutions, but through disciplinary discourses and practices.

Rather more straightforwardly, recent critics of international donors seeking to build 'civil society' in Bosnia (Chandler 1998) or Africa (Hearn 2000), argue that such efforts tend to reflect donor priorities rather than engaging effectively with the grass roots. Thus the role of civil society in channelling private or 'lifeworld' concerns into the public sphere is blocked or distorted. As this explanation indicates, this criticism can be accommodated within a critical model of civil society and shows one of the ways in which empirical civil society can fail to match the promise of the normative concept. Foucault's criticisms can also be accommodated; there is no problem is arguing that empirical civil society is embedded in the kind of power relations Foucault describes, nor in analysing these in Foucauldian terms. As we have said, the contingency of normative civil society does not preclude its possibility. Furthermore, many of the criticisms aimed at the concept of civil society refer to an uncritical use of CSI, rather than to a critical deployment of the concept.

Before its revival in the last two decades of the twentieth century, perhaps the most influential formulation of civil society had been that of Antonio Gramsci (1891–1937). Gramsci's work forms part of a Western European re-examination of Marxist thought and especially the role of culture, which comes to be seen as more than mere superstructure. This understanding has been influential from Japan in the 1960s to Central America in the 1990s (Keane 1998 pp. 12–14). Gramsci saw civil society as ambivalent: on the one hand it was the means by which the state secured authority through consent rather then coercion, but on the other hand it was also potentially the site of most effective resistance to the state. This is because where the state is entrenched in institutions and the minds of the population through a developed civil society, it cannot be moved by frontal assault – hence the failure of revolutions other than the Russian, where civil society was not well developed, during Gramsci's lifetime. However, the 'trenches' of civil society are also potentially sites of resistance to the vested interests which control the state – places where the proleteriat can reflexively deconstruct the 'second nature' of existing arrangements (Tester 1992 pp. 140–43). Gramsci's understanding may now be seen to have been superseded because the proleteriat is no longer the global force it once was (Keane 1998 pp. 16–18). But his insight into the ambivalence of civil society – that it could become the site of resistance to a repressive state as well as the means of entrenchment of the state – was to be revived in Eastern Europe in the 1980s.

The revival of CSI in Eastern Europe in the 1980s, followed by its rapid worldwide dissemination to the Middle East (Therborn 1997), Africa (Hearn 2000), China (Strand 1990) and South America (Hudick 1999), gave new impetus to the concept, which became a powerful source of mobilization against repressive states. The idea of the spontaneous self-organization of society also appealed in a Western context in which the limits of state intervention, especially of the welfare state, seemed to be increasingly exposed. But the difficulties of post-Communist reconstruction (Skapska 1997), the limitations of Western strategies to promote civil society in developing societies (Hearn 2000) and the problems of applying the concept cross-culturally (Hann 1996), together with criticisms of the CSII kind, have left many disillusioned with the concept. However, Alexander (1998) argues that as well as disillusionment these challenges have also led to the emergence of the refined concept 'CSIII', 'more precise and more specific than the all-inclusive umbrella idea of CSI, more general and inclusivist than the narrowly reductionist association of CSII' (p. 6).

Alexander's own proposed definition of CSIII is as follows:

> Civil society should be conceived ... as a solidary sphere in which a certain kind of universalising community comes gradually to be defined and to a certain degree enforced. To the degree that this solidary community exists, it is exhibited by 'public opinion', possesses its own cultural codes and narratives in democratic idiom, is patterned by a set of peculiar institutions, most notably legal and journalistic ones and is visible in historically distinctive sets of interactional practices like civility, equality, criticism and respect. This kind of community can never exist as such; it can only exist 'to one degree or another'. (Ibid. p. 7)

Alexander's concept represents an improvement on the vague breadth and confusion of normative and empirical elements in CSI: his normative concept recognizes the contingency of the democratizing effects of empirical civil society. It also overcomes the negative narrowness of CSII, pointing to the potential modes through which civil society can exercise its democratic effects. However, it conflates civil society with the public sphere, which we have argued are better kept analytically distinct: civil society organizations channel private opinion into the public sphere, they do not constitute the latter. His ascription of institutions to civil society is also problematic. Journalistic institutions are appropriately located in civil society (although they would not be if the state controlled the media), but law is more problematic, as at one level it is clearly a function of state, even though it needs legitimization from civil society. Alexander's definition then, is best seen as one of several recent attempts to refine the concept of civil society in response to the kind of criticisms the current renaissance of the concept has stimulated. In Section 7 we shall consider further examples of contemporary critical developments of the concept, but first we consider some of the factors shaping 'real' or empirical civil society in the contemporary world. Thus in Section 5 we tackle the question of the relation of Islam to civil society and in Section 6 the relationship between civil society, national cultures and cultural diversity.

5. Islam and Civil Society

Islam is perhaps the prime example of a religious tradition that is widely considered in the West to be in tension if not outright conflict with the normative tradition of civil society (Halliday 1996), and contemporary perceptions are now further shaped by the events of 11 September 2001. It is therefore more important than ever to consider the evidence for these perceptions of incompatibility. This section will take the form of a critique of the most fully articulated case to date for incompatibility. In his influential *Conditions of Liberty: Civil Society and its Rivals*, the late Ernest Gellner claimed that Islam is fundamentally unsecularizable and concludes from this that Islam is also incompatible with civil society, both normatively and empirically

(1994 p. 15). Gellner understands secularization as the declining social significance of religion – 'in industrial or industrializing societies religion loses much of its erstwhile hold over men and society' (ibid.). While religion remains socially significant, argues Gellner, the development of individual autonomy is constrained. This in turn constrains the development of civil society because, as Özdalga (1997 p. 74) explains, 'Individuals, who are not able to act independently of the community of believers, cannot become the building-stones of the kind of intermediary organizations on which civil society is built'.

This section challenges each stage of Gellner's argument and hence its polarizing consequences. First, we shall argue that Gellner neglects the different ways in which modernity has been mediated to different regions and hence the consequences of this for modern institutional forms and discourses such as civil society. Second, we shall argue that Muslims have generated a range of responses to the discourses of democracy, civil society and human rights. This contradicts the simplistic integralist position – the view that Islam insists that all aspects of life should directly governed by its unchanging precepts – that Gellner attributes to Islam. Third, we shall argue that the historical model on which Gellner bases his argument applies only to a minority of historic Muslim societies and that the historically predominant model of Muslim society has been characterized by institutional differentiation. Fourth and finally, we shall argue that in practice in many parts of the Muslim world today Islam has proven itself capable of mobilization as a public discourse without stifling but rather contributing to democratic pluralism.

First, then, the impact of modernity on a region as a whole may be a key factor in shaping the reception and cultural embedding of modern ideas such as civil society. This account of different historic routes to modernity complements the discussion of the theory of modernization in Chapter 2, which stressed the complexity of the process and the diversity of its impacts. Therborn (1997) outlines four routes to modernity. First, the Western and Central European route in which both modernity and anti-modern movements were an internal development; second, the route of the New Worlds in the Americas and Australasia, areas where European settlers came to constitute a majority of the population and where opposition to modernity was principally perceived to lie in the Old, European, World; third, the Colonial Zone, where modernity arrived from outside and resistance to it was domestic and suppressed, but where those of non-European origin none the less continued to constitute a majority of the population, for whom 'everyday life … kept its own laws and customs, though often rigidified by colonial intervention or "indirect rule"'(ibid. p. 50); and fourth, countries characterized by 'Externally Induced Modernization', selectively imported by a ruling élite never over-run but pressured by European and American imperial powers, of which he gives China, Japan, Iran, the Ottoman Empire/Turkey and the North African states most resistant to colonialism as examples.

Most Muslim societies fall into the third or fourth category. In such contexts:

> The key actor [in modernization] is … a modernizing part of the ruling body, trying to adapt both the state and society to external challenge and threat. Cleavage patterns tend to run both between modern and anti-modern parts of the élite and between the former and anti-

modernists among the people, with the latter sometimes winning, as in Afghanistan and Iran. In this complex pattern of conflicts and alliances, ... the meaning of popular rights is ambiguous, not seldom rejected by (large parts) of the people as anti-traditional. (p. 51)

Under these conditions, one might anticipate ambivalent attitudes to modern discourses, including civil society: certainly this has occurred with other modern discourses such as democracy and human rights. Indeed, normatively, Muslims have in fact taken up a full range of positions on the compatibility or incompatibility of the relationship between Islam and both democracy and human rights. Thus Goddard (1999) outlines four positions on the relations between Islam and democracy, ranging from the view that democracy is anathema to Islam through to the view that democracy is essential for Islam. Similarly, Halliday (1996) outlines five positions that Muslims have taken up on human rights, again ranging from full compatibility through to outright rejection (we shall discuss these further in Chapter 5). Each position within both spectra seeks to justify itself in relation to the Qur'an and Sunna, the primary textual sources of Islamic law.

This contemporary ideological pluralism corresponds to the diversity of historical forms of Muslim society. For example, Ira Lapidus (1992) argues that whereas Gellner, working principally from North African examples, sees just one Islamic blueprint for society, two have in fact been present from a very early stage of Middle Eastern history, with Gellner's model historically the less influential:

> The Middle Eastern Islamic heritage provides not one but two basic constellations of historical society, two golden ages, two paradigms, each of which has generated its own repertoire of political institutions and political theory. The first is the society integrated in all dimensions, political, social and moral, under the aegis of Islam. The prototype is the unification of Arabia under the leadership of the Prophet Muhammad in the seventh century ... The second historical paradigm is the imperial Islamic society built not on Arabian or tribal templates but on the differentiated structures of previous Islamic societies ... By the Eleventh century Middle Eastern states and religious communities were highly differentiated ... Thus, despite the common statement that Islam is a total way of life defining political as well as social and family matters, most Muslim societies ... were in fact built around separate institutions of state and religion. (1992 pp. 14–15)

Thus the Western history of social differentiation is not the only one, and historically most Muslim societies have been socially differentiated. Yet Gellner the sociologist does not simply argue that Islam is normatively resistant to differentiation. Rather, he argues that this normative orientation coincides with structural features that render Islam 'secularization-resistant' (1994 p. 14). Drawing on North African examples, Gellner characterizes Muslim history until modernity as a cyclical process driven by relations between two versions of Islam: an urban, scripturalist, 'High' version and a rural, ritualistic, ecstatic and saint-mediated 'Low' version. The High version is prone to laxity and pragmatic compromise over time, but at just such times it has been reinvigorated by the zeal of discontented followers of the Low version who appropriate the ideals of 'High' Islam and are powered by *asabiyya* (energy of tribal groups). But modernity broke this cycle:

Come the modern world however – imposed by extraneous forces rather than produced
indigenously – and the new balance of power, favouring the urban centre against rural
communities, causes central faith to prevail and we are left with a successful Ummah at
long last. This is the mystery of the secularization-resistant nature of Islam ... (Ibid.).

The centralized state, asserting its authority over rural areas and destroying tribal
society, is able to sustain the reforming zeal of High Islam. Both versions of High
Islam are compatible with instrumental aspects of modernity – industrialization,
urbanization and so on – and hence increasingly displace the popular saint-led Low
Islam throughout an increasingly urbanized society, except for Westernized élites.
Furthermore, it is the puritanical version of High Islam that triumphs over the lax
variant because only the latter has genuine local appeal (ibid. p. 23).

However, while this account helps to explain the popularity of Islam in some,
especially North African, societies, it remains limited. First, it is limited in
geographical and cultural scope, because as we have seen (following Lapidus) it does
not fit societies where imperial Islam has long predominated and the influence of
tribal groups has remained marginal (for example Ottoman and Mughal lands).
Second, it neglects the central historical factors that have shaped the emergence of
modern political Islam – namely the crisis in nationalist ideologies and the failure of
both socialist and capitalist development models in many parts of the Muslim world
(Ayubi 1991; Binder 1988). Third, it flies in the face of the fact that where Islamic
groups have been permitted to enter the democratic process as political parties, they
have shown themselves both willing and able to follow democratic procedures. As
Ibrahim (1997a) comments:

> Beyond the Arab world, Islamists have regularly run for elections in Pakistan, Bangladesh
> and Turkey since the 1980s. In Indonesia, Malaysia and the Islamic republics of the former
> Soviet Union, Islamists have peacefully been engaging in local and municipal politics ...
> It is important to note that in three of the biggest Muslim countries (Pakistan, Bangladesh
> and Turkey) women have recently been elected to the top executive office in the land ...
> The important thing in all these cases is that Islamic parties have accepted the rules of the
> democratic game and are playing it peaceably and in an orderly manner. (p. 41)

As we have already seen in the Turkish context (Özdalga 1997), such observations
at the macro-political level are complemented at the micro-sociological level.
Furthermore, other discourses dependent on strong individuation – such as human
rights – have also taken firm root in many Muslim societies, such that, in spite of the
ambivalence associated with them, they now form part of the terms of public debate.
This is illustrated by Dwyer's conversations with intellectuals about human rights in
Tunisia, Morocco and Egypt, many of whom were active in human rights
organizations. Indeed, the range and persistence of such organizations, in spite of the
difficult conditions in which they operate, is itself refutation of Gellner's thesis. But
more than this, Dwyer (1991) shows the extent to which human rights discourse,
contested and polysemous as it is, has penetrated contemporary Middle Eastern
societies. As he concludes:

> Few Middle Easterners I spoke to seem ready to dismiss the idea from their cultural repertoire: they may challenge its foundations, or its provenance, or the content given it by specific groups, but the concept itself has come to constitute a symbol of great power. (p. 192)

Thus Gellner essentializes connections between Islam, civil society and democratization which are in fact contingent. Islam is not necessarily incompatible normatively or practically with structural differentiation and many Muslim societies in practice support both diverse civil societies and democracy, even though and unsurprisingly given the manner of their reception of modernity, these discourses are contested and viewed with ambivalence. Furthermore, it is important that the problematic reception of these discourses in the Muslim world is not viewed against their presumed-to-be unproblematic acceptance in the West. Here too the articulation of these concepts is problematic (Lanham and Forsyth 1994). In the next section we examine the implications of discourses of nationalism and multiculturalism for religion and civil society.

6. Civil Society, National Cultures and Multiculturalism

> Today's multiculturalism is no longer concerned with the 'folk cultures' of white people flocking to cities run by other white people who despised them and often wanted them out again. The present day challenge, both political and theoretical, is about three other concerns. The points of the multicultural triangle are about nationality as culture, ethnicity as culture and religion as culture. (Baumann 1999 p. 84)

As Baumann's statement indicates, the cultural diversity of the lifeworlds from which empirical civil societies coalesce is no longer the consequence of the impact of rural-urban migration and subsequent class stratification that formed the background to classical social theory in the nineteenth century. Rather, global migration patterns have produced new challenges. This section discusses the significance of national cultures for the formation of civil societies and the implications of this for religion. Civil societies, on the whole, are formed within national cultures. What are the consequences of this?

Given the universalistic orientation of normative civil society and the particularist focus of nationality, this question has received surprisingly little attention in the civil society literature (Cohen and Arato 1992; Keane 1998). In part this may be because, as Seligman argues, the process of nation formation in Western Europe (and the United States) led to the formation of national identities that were relatively universalistic in orientation and therefore not perceived as in conflict with the normative orientation of civil society (1998a pp. 160–64). According to Seligman, this 'successful' process of national integration, in which national identity 'crystallized' out of different ethnic groups, was a result of a long process of 'prior consolidation of administrative, legal and cultural institutions' (p. 161). This led to an empirical civil society in which diversity was only a matter of 'interest':

In the West the voluntary organizations of civil society are interest groups; they are organized for the pursuit of mutual interest on the institutional level (of what Habermas would call strategic action). Their interaction with other groups is defined by this instrumental rational orientation (and the terms of membership within the group are likewise so defined). They do not posit (or indeed represent) an alternative moral vision to that of society at large. They do not as such undermine or threaten the overriding definitions of membership and participation in collective life. They are themselves predicated on the definition of public space as one of instrumental action between autonomously constituted individual moral agents. (pp. 163–4)

However, as a picture of actual civil society in the West, this is highly questionable. With MacIntyre (1985), we may want to question whether Western societies share any moral vision. But even if one reduces the claim for homogeneity from a shared moral vision to agreement on basic principles combined with an agreement to disagree on substantive issues (the liberal distinction between 'the right' and 'the good'), consensus even on basic principles is lacking. Thus studies on attitudes to human rights have shown that:

> many Americans do *not* hold attitudes compatible with international standards on civil and political rights, much less on economic and social rights. … Paradoxically, rights have been practised in the democratic West despite intolerant and authoritarian views on the part of many citizens. (Lanham and Forsythe 1994 p. 246)

The arrival and embedding of significant numbers from non-Western societies has further underlined the fact that empirical civil society contains groups with diverse moral visions. Thus differences between groups within national societies cannot be reduced to differences of interest. National cultures have not performed the integrating role envisaged by Seligman. Thus they are likely to be perceived as particular and biased by minority cultural groups, and the gap between national culture and the universalistic orientation of normative civil society remains an important and problematic one.

This problem becomes even more acute in regions where the nation state preceded cultural and institutional nation-building, for example in Eastern Europe. As György Csepeli, a Hungarian analyst of nationalism and ethnicity in Eastern Europe writes, 'The concept of the nation came before the establishment of proper national institutions and the emerging national ideology therefore had to refer more actively to elements of the ethnocentric heritage such as descent, cultural values and norms' (Csepeli 1991 p. 328, in Seligman 1992 p. 162). The less integrated the national culture, the stronger the appeal to ethnocentric norms. If this is true in Eastern Europe it is likely to be far more so in other parts of the world, where projects of national unification are even more recent, for example in Africa and much of the Muslim world. And the greater the ethnocentric basis of national ideology, the greater the tensions between this and the universalistic orientation of normative civil society. In response to this, since the late 1980s political philosophers have attempted to find ways of reconciling ethnic and national difference with liberal philosophy, as part of an effort to integrate diverse ethnic and national groups within civil society at a normative level. In Chapter 5 we shall examine their efforts. Here, we shall try to develop a picture of the significance of national culture for civil society formation, drawing on Baumann's (1999) portrayal of three Western European national civic cultures and especially the French case.

Baumann gives as an example of the strongly secularist character of French national civic culture the decree issued by the Minister of Education to directors of state schools in response to the *foulard* ('headscarf') affair in the early 1990s. This controversy concerned Muslim schoolgirls who wore headscarves to school and ran into trouble with school authorities and ultimately the Ministry of Education. Below, the minister explains the reasons for his ban on the wearing of such Muslim scarves:

> In France, the national project and the republican project have conjoined with each other around a certain idea of citizenship. This French idea of the nation and the Republic will by its nature respect all convictions, in particular those of religion, politics and cultural traditions. But it excludes the explosion of the nation into separate communities, indifferent to each other and considering only their own rules and laws and engaged in simple co-existence. The nation is not only a collection of citizens pursuing individual rights. It is a community of destiny. This ideal is pursued first and foremost in schools. This laicist and national ideal is the very substance of the school of the Republic and the foundation of its duty towards civic education. That is why it is impossible to accept the presence and proliferation of signs which are so [ostentatious][5] that their signification is precisely to separate certain students from the rules of the communal life of the school. These signs are in themselves elements of proselytism, the more so as they are accompanied by a questioning of certain courses or disciplines, as they jeopardise the security of students, or they lead to disturbances in the common life of the institution. (Bayrou 1994, translation by Baumann, in Baumann 1999 pp. 49–50)

This is a classic statement of the privatization of religion: religion is fine as long as it is a matter of private conviction, not public life. More strongly, Baumann paraphrases the minister's phrase '[France] is a community of destiny' with 'France is a religion' (p. 50). In other words, this implicit model of privatization is one in which the socially integrating function performed by religion is now performed by the ideology of nationalism, whose guardian is the secular state.

Thus Baumann argues that French civic culture is dominated by a state-sponsored and fairly intolerant form of civil religion. The integrating and legitimizing functions of religion in the *ancien régime* have, in a fairly direct sense, been taken over by the secular state that prescribes and polices civic culture. Civil religious elements are found in all civic cultures, but their presence in the French case is particularly striking because of the state's insistence on its secular character. Baumann contrasts this with German civic culture, which he characterizes as peculiarly responsive to international judgement on its democratic credentials and as unusually deferent to expert opinion. He also contrasts French with British civic culture, which he sees as peculiar in the extent to which it recognizes, indeed he would argue exacerbates, even creates, ethnic difference. We shall return to the last point, but first consider his comparison of the three:

> While experts in Britain are expected to be on tap, their colleagues in Germany are always on top.

If German civic culture puts a prize on individual morals, its French counterpart seeks its strength in universal and anonymous competition regulated by an absolute equality of rules. The font of all liberty is equality and the shared faith in reason as such. While each minority in Britain may fight for its own particular deal, all minorities in France are expected to share this common faith in a centralist and antiparticularist cult of one metareligious rationality. The French revolutionaries turned the cathedral of Paris into a Temple of Reason and the French state élites have kept reinventing this civil religion of One Reason for All. It is as if in the French Republic, which replaced dynastic absolutism with the absolute value of citizenship, had declared ethnic and religious loyalties illegal for all time. (Ibid. p. 48)

In terms of the general formation of empirical civil societies, such differences in national civic cultures are bound to have an important influence, especially for religious groups. However, Baumann's particular descriptions are not definitive – for example in view of our case study of Britain in Chapter 6 it is worth noting that his categorization of Britain as an extreme case of recognizing/promoting communal separatism is challenged by other studies. Thus in a study of the social and political integration of migrants that focused on citizenship and welfare systems, Soysal (1994) argues that there are three basic forms of 'incorporation regime'. These are liberal (integration mostly through labour markets, for example Switzerland), statist (for example France) and corporatist (through corporate bodies other than the state, for example the Netherlands). Rather than an extreme example of corporatism, Soysal sees Britain as a mixture of corporatist and liberal types.

Thus one's characterization of national civic cultures depends on the kind of analysis underlying one's account: in Baumann's case the structuring of competition for state resources, especially at local authority level; in Soysal's case the means through which the state seeks to integrate migrant populations. I have argued elsewhere (Herbert 2000) that recognition by the state of forms of collective identity is perhaps best measured by considering a range of ways in which such identities are used as a basis to distribute power or allocate resources. Recognition of group religious identity can take various forms, including representation on local and national government consultative bodies, public funding for religiously based schools, the distribution of welfare resources and the collection of national and local statistics. In the Netherlands recognition takes place in all of these cases (though to varying extents according to locality), in Britain in some and in France in none.[6] In each case these differences reflect historic developments: in the Netherlands the 'pillar system', which provided a communally based method of institutionalizing equal treatment between Catholics and Protestants; in France the legacy of the Revolution and anti-clericalism; in Britain the adaptation of colonial practices and a strong tradition of local government.

Baumann also provides important evidence that in allocating resources on a corporatist basis, local and national states not only recognize but actually shape or even create religious identities as political identities, in a process he describes as 'community competition in the political field' (1999 p. 123). Based on his fieldwork in Southall, West London, an Asian majority area (Baumann 1996), he later comments:

In Southall ... the fact that public resources are, as the word goes, targeted at cultural communities leads to a political scene in which the common good is seen as a competition of any one community with [every] other community. ... In the process, every minority has to struggle against all others and each of them becomes a community of disappointment and suspicion that complains that some other community is getting a better deal while the common good gets nowhere. (1999 p. 124)

This competition rewards groups for identifying communally on a religious or ethnic basis, potentially exacerbating and even creating divisions. It exerts a powerful influence on the way individuals associate and hence on the formation of empirical civil society. However, it also needs to be considered against the counter-example of international donors in Bosnia who, by stipulating multi-ethnicity as a prerequisite for funding, have created a dichotomy between well-funded NGOs with shallow grass-roots participation and impoverished 'nationalist' groups whose sense of isolation is reinforced (see Chapter 7; Chandler 1998). Both deliberate social engineering and the accidental consequences of state intervention are important factors in the formation of civil society. Furthermore, Baumann's exposure of the 'communifying' effects of the 'recognition' of religious and ethnic groups provides an important background against which to consider the efforts of political philosophers to offer a normative framework for conducting the 'politics of recognition'; see below, Chapter 5.

We have now considered a range of factors that influence the construction of civil society: the mode of modernization, historic patterns of religion-state relations and nation-building; and the policies of local authorities, states and trans-state actors. We have also pointed to what might be described as a process of cultural diversification of democratization as democratic forms and norms spread to societies culturally distant from their historic Euro-American origins. Let us now consider how theories of civil society have responded to these developments.

7. Contemporary Critical Development of the Concept of Civil Society

John Keane (1998) uses the category of ideal-type (German *Idealtyp*) to describe the concept of civil society. He defines civil society as 'an ideal-typical category that describes and envisages a complex dynamic ensemble of legally protected non-governmental institutions (NGIs) that tend to be non-violent, self-organizing, self-reflexive and permanently in tension with each other and the states that frame, construct and enable their activities' (p. 6). An ideal-type acts as a model with which actually existing arrangements can be compared. Other examples include Troeltsh's ideal-types of church and sect, later enriched by the concept of denomination, which has shaped the sociological study of religious groups. An ideal-type gives the observer some idea of what is being looked at before it is seen: it shapes the interpretation of reality. In this sense it functions rather like a hypothesis – it directs enquiry. But whereas in an experimental setting a hypothesis is open to disconfirmation, an ideal-type is less prone to correction. If reality can be made to look at all like the ideal-type, it will tend to remain as an interpretative framework unless a better or more influential framework is available. However, a process of iteration can go on whereby the ideal-type is itself modified in response to observation. None the less there is a tendency for an ideal-type with a long tradition and well embedded in popular usage to prove resistant to modification. This provides another perspective on the problem of normative concepts we have already discussed and responded to by proposing a normative-empirical distinction in the use of the concept of civil society.

Keane describes three uses of civil society in the current literature, first, in the analysis of actually existing arrangements. He gives the example of research in China which has looked for associations and organizations analagous to those associated with civil society in Western contexts, partly in order to discover whether the preconditions for the development of democracy exist (1998 pp. 37 – 41). In this context, Liu and Wang (1988) argue that there has historically been no analogue of the free individual as a bearer of rights in Chinese tradition, and no idea of society as a collective independent of the state. Furthermore, although there is a long history of protest against injustice and hence of a distinction between the government and the governed, no clear distinction between public and private spheres developed. Thus 'the meaning of terms like *guan* (official), *gong* (public) and *si* (private) remained both indistinct and ambiguous' (Keane 1998 p. 38).

However, other researchers have argued that there has been a significant tradition of societal self-organization against the incursions of warlords and the state. They point to the development in Beijing by the 1920s of a dense network of private associations (inns, clubs, guilds, brothels, temples and parks) giving rise to public spheres of controversy (Strand 1990, in Keane 1998 p. 39). Indeed, they compare these to the London coffee houses and Parisian salons of Habermas's bourgeois public sphere, to be discussed further in the next chapter. But for our purposes here, the Chinese example serves to illustrate how a process of iteration between the construct of civil society and actually existing arrangements sheds light on both. On the other hand, approaching the Chinese example with a model derived from Western examples may lead to a misconstrual of the former. Thus the example helps us to see some of the risks and possibilities of deploying the concept of civil society in cross-cultural analysis.

Second, Keane shows that civil society can be used to calculate political strategy in order to achieve some predefined or assumed good. Keane uses Thomas Paine's revolutionary pamphlet *Common Sense*, which advises on the best tactics for challenging despotic power by 'building the earthworks of civil society' as a historic example (1998 p. 41). This use corresponds to CSI. The third use of civil society Keane delineates – although he finds few examples of it in the literature – is to legitimize the concept in cross-cultural usage; 'that is, to highlight the ethical superiority of a politically guaranteed civil society compared with other types of regime' (ibid. p. 37). Here Keane's argument connects with the point made at the end of Section 2 about the legitimacy of cultural variation in the form of democracy and indeed the cross-cultural legitimation of democracy itself. Keane argues that too many users and theorists assume the moral superiority of civil society, whereas within and especially beyond Western cultural boundaries the concept needs reasoned advocacy. He therefore develops his own position.

Following Hegel, he points to the historical contingency of civil society – and hence its vulnerability and the need to actively sustain it. This serves as a defence against accusations that civil society is an abstract ideal, but seems more of a rallying call to defend the concept and examine more closely the conditions of its production and maintenance, than an argument designed to convince the sceptic. His second argument is a post-foundationalist one. This means that the view that social and political arrangements cannot be justified by arguments able to command universal agreement supported by appeal (foundations), but only to particular, contingent circumstances (MacIntyre 1985; below p. 109f.). It thus rejects the transcendental approach (following Kant) to philosophical argument (Rorty 1982). Keane's argument justifies civil society pragmatically because it provides the best conditions under which a diversity of forms of life can flourish. However, the difficulty comes in persuading those who do not think that diversity is, in itself, a good thing. Keane's answer to this, following Rorty, seems to be that such criticism can only be articulated from within civil society, hence presupposes that which is opposed. To engage in such criticism is self-contradictory:

> Paradoxically, the post-foundationalist argument that I am trying to develop insists that the meaning and ethical significance of civil society at any given time and place can be asserted and/or contested as such only within a sociopolitical framework marked by the separation of civil and state institutions, whose power to shape the lives of citizens is subject permanently to mechanisms that enable disputation, accountability and representation. (Keane 1998 p. 56)

At one level, this is plainly wrong. It is quite possible, for example, for a conservative Iranian *mullah* to argue that civil society as practised in the West leads to the corruption of morals and is therefore undesirable. To do so from Iran, would be to criticize civil society from a location clearly not marked by a separation of civil and state mechanisms. Present global conditions mean that public argument isn't bounded by national societies. However, this very point can be used to argue for the existence of a transnational civil society which enables such criticisms to be articulated. At the transnational level, then, Keane's argument can be sustained. But a further objection remains: advocates of civil society are often keen not just to defend but to export the concept and not just at the transnational level, but within national societies. Therefore any justification that limits its scope to a particular societal community is inadequate. Any post-foundational theory for the normative justification of civil society needs to explain why civil society should be attractive to those not already convinced of its benefits – an issue of no small significance when considering, for example, the future of political arrangements in Afghanistan. We shall pursue this issue in Chapter 5, but here focus just on Keane's argument.

A further defence of civil society offered by Keane (1998 p. 51) is that all empirical civil societies to date have thrown up challenges about the nature of society: 'all hitherto existing and present-day civil societies contain powerful countertrends that ensure society has no fixed and immutable meanings'. This ability for society to question itself can be seen as a spur to continual societal self-improvement and in a social evolutionary sense as an adaptive feature. However, as Mardin's reflections on Islamic and Western cultural orientations suggest, not all cultures regard social criticism so highly. As indicated, we shall return to these normative issues in Chapter 5. First, however, we shall address the issue more pragmatically: part of Keane's problem here may be that his understanding of civil society is too tied to a particular cultural context and hence the problem of cross-cultural legitimization. In this context, the political anthropologist Chris Hann (1996 p. 20) argues that 'Instead of searching for the replication of one particular western model around the world, we should … be prepared to understand civil society to refer more loosely to the moral community, to the problems of accountability, trust and co-operation that all groups face'. Thus, in recognition of the diversity of ways in which trust and cooperation develop in different societies, he argues that a functional definition of civil society should replace the predominant structural-normative definition, that civil society should not be 'defined negatively, in opposition to the state, but positively in the context of the ideas and practices through which co-operation and trust are established in social life'.

Does this solve the problem? Partly. Hann is right to insist that we should be open to the variety of ways in which the relationships of trust and practices of cooperation that enable community and political society form and function. It is arrogant and foolish to seek everywhere the replication of Western European and American practices, for example. Hann's redefinition also opens up space for a fresh appreciation of the contribution of religion to the sustaining of trust and co-operation. However, a problem arises when one asks specific questions about who is cooperating with and trusting whom, for not all trust and cooperative relationships are generalizable in the way Western civil society models tend to assume. Thus not all local practices which establish trust and cooperation between local people welcome strangers as equals and few have established cultures of equality between the sexes. Some, as in many post-Communist societies, are formed on the basis of covert networks that, however justifiable under conditions of oppressive government and insidious propaganda that created a culture of deceit and stealth, are not conducive to the practice of open democratic relations.

In structural terms, then, global interconnection challenges the way local practices have developed to sustain trust and co-operation and those cultures that have a long history of democratic citizenship may have something to offer those more recently exposed, as well as lessons to learn. Indeed, Hann recognizes the possibility of this two-way exchange when he points to the double meaning of his title, *Civil Society: Challenging Western Models*. However, he does not consider the problems arising from the varying specificity of trust relationships and which serves to distinguish between Western concepts of civil society oriented towards a generalized concept of trust and the more widespread concept of trust as locally based. This is not to say that non-Western cultures have lacked a concept of universal moral responsibility – they have not – but this responsibility has tended to be hierarchically ordered, in accordance with the social stratification of pre-modern societies. In John Hall's rather pejorative terms, pre-modern civility was structured within and between 'social cages' (1998). It is the rise of discourses of equality and citizenship, with the change from functionally stratified to functionally differentiated societies, which has given rise to the modern concept of generalized trust.

Adam Seligman describes this distinction between generalized and local or hierarchy-dependent trust as one between 'trust' and 'faith'. Thus Seligman defines 'trust' as 'an unconditional principle of generalized exchange unique to modern forms of social organization' (1997 p. 171), developed to fill the 'gaps' between role expectations as these diversified in modern societies. Here trust, underpinned ideologically by belief in humanity's natural universal qualities, gradually replaces faith, understood as divinely sanctioned confidence in role expectations based on divine *fiat* (p. 44). However, because trust is based on the same Enlightenment assumptions about human nature and communities as normative civil society (CSI), when these cease to hold good, differences can no longer be negotiated by appeal to common understandings in a shared lifeworld. Instead they can only be contained through instrumental systems of control: here Seligman points to the increasing use of speech codes, litigation and physical violence in American public life (1998a pp. 4–5, 10, 13). Thus we shift from a medieval world of stable roles, hierarchically organized and legitimated by faith, first to a modern world of horizontal trust relationships and then to a late/postmodern world in which roles and boundaries must once again be codified and policed in the absence of consensus. This latter context also sets the scene for the emergence of identity politics.

The central phase of this account – the growth of generalized trust – can be challenged from a feminist perspective by arguing that the oppression and exclusion of women and other groups persisted and even intensified during this period (Calhoun 1993). But Seligman does not deny this; rather his intention is to chart the emergence and decline of the modern concept of trust. Yet the neglect of this 'underside of modernity' as an ongoing feature, rather than a late/post modern re-emergence, may none the less distort his presentations. Indeed, Foucault's argument that from the beginning modernity was marked by an intensification of disciplinary and surveillance practices provides an important counter-narrative to the 'modernity as emancipation' trajectory followed by Seligman and implicit in many constructs of civil society. This is especially important when considering his accounts of faith and faith-based organizations.

Seligman's image of faith springs from the Western tradition of political philosophy, which stresses features specific to the post-medieval Christian setting from which it grew. Galtung (1994) emphasizes two features of this tradition. The first is, 'verticality', meaning that authority for forms of interpersonal relationship tends to be conceptualized as descending 'from above', initially from God and later from the state, as opposed to growing 'horizontally' out of existing habits and customs. Thus while the idea of formal equality between all citizens was absent from all pre-modern societies, European societies were distinctive in the strength of their vertical patterns of legitimization. This relates to their second distinctive feature, a tendency towards individualization: if society is imaged as a net, this tradition sees individuals as existing in the 'knots' at the intersection between strands, in contrast to other cultural formations, in which individuals are also seen as in the 'net':

> Imagine a hunter-gatherer or pastoral-nomadic community with people woven together in structures that take the shape of rights and duties. ... the more densely the net is spun, the more difficult or meaningless it will be to detach the individual from the network. Individuals are in the *net* as well as the *knot*. (Ibid. p. 6)

Of course, Seligman is not concerned with hunter-gatherers and individualization is part of the modernizing process as systems and roles differentiate. But at least initially we need to leave open the possibility that different cultural formations may respond to this process in different ways. Certainly, religious traditions have very different starting-points and different strands exist even within Western traditions:

> Individualising Judaism/Christianity/Islam with a transcendental god emphasizes the knots, the union-oriented Hinduism/Buddhism with a more immanent god-concept the nets. Transcendental religions endow human beings with individual souls which can attain union with god. Immanent religions depend less on that concept, which is rejected out of hand in radical Buddhism. But occidental religions also have immanent, net-oriented, collectivist aspects. ... God also speaks through the people. And the whole tradition of democracy took shape and is still taking shape. (Galtung 1994 pp. 6–7)

We have seen that Seligman's characterization of faith as a vertical relationship in contrast to horizontal relationships of trust seems to preclude the possibility that faith could promote trust. But Galtung's challenge to this vertical construction of faith opens up other possibilities. One that will be pursued here is that religious traditions, including some quite conservative ones, may actually promote civility, in the sense of respect for individuals, recognition of other communities and determination to solve differences through reasoned negotiation. In this way they may promote a general sense of trust in others in society, in the modern, generalized sense. This is not to say that faith cannot also lead to the opposite of civility: as the legitimization of ethnic cleansing in the former Yugoslavia, not least by Serbian Orthodox religious discourse illustrates and as we shall discuss further below in Chapter 6 (Sells 1996). But this disparity of evidence argues for a careful analysis of each situation, not for an *a priori* rejection of faith as a possible contributor to trust and civility.

Seligman's differentiation of faith and trust enables us to plug a gap in Hann's conceptualization of civil society as the 'ideas and practices through which trust and cooperation develop'. It enables us to specify that the type of trust needed to promote cooperation in modern plural societies is the modern, generalized, kind. Our critique of Seligman further enables us to see that religions should not be ruled out as possible sources for the promotion of this generalized trust. This point closely mirrors our argument (following Casanova) against Habermas in Chapter 1 that religions should not be ruled out as agents of communicative rationalization. In terms of developing a critical theory of civil society, the concept of generalized trust and its genesis from the diverse organizations and practices of empirical civil society enables us to see how such diverse groupings might work together to create a participatory public culture. However, something more than generalized trust is also needed to promote participation in the public sphere.

Political philosophers such as William Galston (1991) have argued that civic virtues are needed to sustain public life in liberal societies and lists independence, social responsibility, tolerance, law-abidingness, loyalty and courage among them. Contrary to the 'orthodoxy' that 'the liberal-republican polity requires no more than the proper configuration of rational self-interest', he amasses a range of evidence to suggest that the cultivation of virtue is essential for its maintenance and that this was also the assumption of earlier generations of political philosophers:

> Nathan Tarcov concludes that 'instead of a narrowly calculating selfishness, Locke teaches a set of moral virtues that make men able to respect themselves and be useful to one another both in public and in private life.' Ronald Terchek extends this thesis to Adam Smith and John Stuart Mill, who he interprets as recommending 'the cultivation of those habits which turned us towards the practice of virtue.' (Ibid. p. 215)

Will Kymlicka (1989) has reassessed the value of cultural membership for the liberal tradition, part of which is the role of cultural communities in the formation of character. Taking the two streams of argument together, we can begin to see an appreciation of the role of cultural communities for the formation of civic virtues emerging in contemporary liberal philosophy. Alasdair MacIntyre (1985) has developed this argument further and can help a critical theory of civil society to specify how the diverse groupings of civil society sustain a participative public culture by cultivating virtue as well as creating generalized trust.

8. Virtue, Community and Civil Society

Outside theological circles where it has enjoyed some popularity and influence (Milbank 1990, Fergusson 1998), MacIntyre's work is perhaps most closely associated with a nostalgic and communitarian critique of modern society. Thus it has been argued that MacIntyre fails to recognize both the achievements of liberalism and the complexities of modern socially differentiated societies (Poole 1991; Stout 1988). However, behind the rhetoric of communitarian isolationism, MacIntyre offers a sociological and philosophical analysis that can provide the basis for an understanding of the relationship between religious organizations (and other groups with a distinctive ethos) and the formation of civil society. He does so by developing an account of the relationship between what he terms 'practices', virtues and their social context and consequences.

By practice MacIntyre (1985) means:

> any coherent and complex form of socially established human activity through which goods internal to that form of activity are realized in the course of trying to achieve those standards of excellence which are appropriate to and partially constitutive of, that form of activity, with the result that human powers to achieve excellence and human conceptions of the ends and goods involved, are systematically extended. (p. 187)

Thus practices are complex social activities involving technical skills which systematically realize and develop goods internal to the activity. MacIntyre gives examples as diverse as chess, football and natural sciences, also arguing that creating and sustaining human communities ('households, cities, nations' (p. 188)) was widely understood as a practice in the ancient and medieval worlds. We suggest that a modern equivalent of this understanding might be revived today in response to the failure of 'hidden hand' theories of social integration. MacIntyre initially defines a virtue as 'an acquired human quality the possession and exercise of which tends to enable us to achieve those goods which are internal to practices and the lack of which effectively presents us from achieving any such goods' (p. 191). Thus virtues refer to certain learned consistencies of attitude or behaviour which enable the achievement of goods internal to practices: MacIntyre cites justice, courage and honesty as examples (ibid. p. 191). For MacIntyre, such generalized dispositions can only be developed through the discipline involved in submission to and immersion in a 'practice'.

A key characteristic of practices is that excellence in a particular practice is pursued for its own sake; for the pleasure or satisfaction derived from the practice itself rather than any external form of reward. They are thus oriented to 'internal goods'. By contrast, 'external goods' lie beyond and bear no intrinsic relation to an activity, such as working to earn money or performing to attract praise. For MacIntyre modernity is dominated by external goods, which are corrosive of practices; thus football and opera have become multi-million-pound businesses, creating tremendous pressures on participants to divert attention from internal to external goods; the same could be said of the increased administrative burdens on teachers or health professionals.

However, although practices are prone to corrosion by instrumental systems (i.e. those developed to serve the interests of external goods), practices remain important for systems to be sustained – indeed systems are parasitic on the practices they corrode. Thus while emphasis on external goods may lead to professional fouls in football and drug-taking in athletics, notions of fair play and standards of excellence intrinsic to those sports persist. MacIntyre does not deny the validity of external goods altogether; indeed he accepts the vital role they play in maintaining institutions necessary to sustain practices (p. 196). But it is when external goods predominate that practices are corroded and virtues collapse. It is clear that MacIntyre sees the pursuit of practices as demanding:

> goods can only be achieved by subordinating ourselves within the practice in our relationship to other practitioners. We have to recognize what is due to whom; we have to be prepared to take whatever self-endangering risks are demanded along the way; and we have to be prepared to listen carefully to what we are told about our inadequacies and to reply with the same carefulness for the facts. (p. 191)

In this process virtues such as respect for others, courage, humility and perseverance are learned. In what kind of civil society groupings are such virtues cultivated? MacIntyre takes the view that in modern societies practices persist only in compromised form and on a small scale, divorced from the major institutions and dominant discourses. This is because 'the tradition of the virtues is at variance with central features of the modern economic order and especially its individualism, its acquisitiveness and the elevation of the values of the market to a central social place' (p. 254). Hence his turn to small communities, survivals of communal practice consistent with a tradition of the virtues, as potential sites for its regeneration. In particular, in an American context he mentions 'some Orthodox Christians and Jews', Irish Catholics and black and white Protestant groups from America's South (p. 252). It is noticeable for our purposes in examining the relationship between religion and civil society that the communities of virtue MacIntyre mentions are religious.

In a British context both Jonathan Sacks from a Jewish perspective (1991, 2001) and Robin Gill from a Christian perspective (1992, 1999) have argued that religious communities play a significant role in cultivating virtue and generating social capital for civil society. Brown's description of discursive Christianity and Starrett's of discursive Islam (Chapter 1) give a further indication of how this process might work. Thus the moral narratives that inform people's self-understanding and motivation are in part formed by their religious upbringing or education – Gill in particular highlights the role of liturgy in this moral formation process (1992). So we can envisage a process through which religious groups might nurture civil society. But does any kind of hard evidence for this exist?

Gill's recent work (1999) attempts to demonstrate the effects of this process empirically by examining British social attitude surveys to see if church-going (or a history of church-going) makes any quantifiable difference to moral attitudes, expressions of altruism and participation in PVOs (private voluntary organizations). The last is of particular interest for our purposes, because if evidence for it were found, this would suggest the significance of religious participation for wider involvement in the community. Using British Household Panel Survey data (1995), Gill found a statistically significant correlation between participation in voluntary service groups (VSGs) and church-going. Thus 27 per cent of members of VSGs were weekly church-goers (compared with 11 per cent of the total sample), 42 per cent attended church at least monthly (compared with 18 per cent) and only one-third reported they never attended church (compared with two-thirds of the total) (1999 pp. 106–7). Furthermore, the forms of voluntary activity most closely related to membership of a religious group were services, residents'/tenants', women's, political party, pensioners' and trade union groups, precisely those most related to community advocacy and participation. In contrast, sports and social group membership was least closely related to religious group membership – although, as we have seen, MacIntyre's work suggests the former should not be ruled out as sites for the cultivation of virtue (1985 pp. 107–8).

Gill argues that in spite of such evidence – and a range of parallel studies, some in Western European countries and Australia – religious belonging is not ascribed the same kind of significance in mainstream sociological analyses as other variables:

In almost any other area of sociology a variable which tested so consistently significant (for example gender or social class) would be taken very seriously as an independent variable. In less technical language, it would simply be assumed that it is a key factor in shaping the values held by an individual. ... the more regularly individuals go to church the more likely they are to share and practise distinctively Christian virtues. While these virtues are not absent from the broader society, they are found disproportionately amongst churchgoers and especially amongst the most regular churchgoers. (1999 p. 200)

Thus Gill provides evidence that regular church-going cultivates Christian virtues which correlate with the civic virtues discussed by Galston and MacIntyre and which translate into increased participation in the more community-building-oriented parts of the voluntary sector. The neglect of this evidence by mainstream sociology is consistent with our evidence of parallel neglect of religion's involvement in democratization in Eastern Europe amongst mainstream political scientists, and arguably further demonstrates the influence of secularization assumptions on social scientific analyses. In terms of developing a theory of religion's relation to civil society, it suggests that religious organizations foster the kind of participatory citizenship on which an active civil society depends.

However, Gill cautions that while in Britain, with some variations, participation in civic-oriented PVOs is fairly evenly spread across denominations, American evidence suggests that some theological orientations are much less likely to lead members to wider social engagement (1999 p. 120). Thus in Britain Anglicans are more likely to be involved in political parties and environmental groups than Catholics, but Catholics are more likely to be involved in trade unions, while participation in VSGs is fairly evenly spread across Anglican, Catholic and free churches (ibid. p. 110). But in America, while the connection between church membership and involvement in civic-oriented PVOs is high for all Catholic groups and some Protestants, the connection is much weaker for certain conservative Protestant groups (Wilson and Janoski 1995 p. 137). Although it is not clear whether the categories used correspond, this difference would seem to fit with the evangelical/fundamentalist distinction developed by Smith (1998) and noted in Chapter 1. Thus fundamentalists are suspicious of wider social engagement, while evangelicals (and others to the 'left' of them) see society as an arena for redemptive action and therefore promote engagement in various forms of social action beyond specifically proselytizing activities among their members.

Such evidence is suggestive of the way in which all but the most inward-looking of religious groups can contribute to the development of civil society. Yet MacIntyre's analysis also raises the question of whether modern social organization corrodes virtues to the extent that no truly civilized civil society can ever emerge under prevailing modern conditions – dominance of the market and so on. Translated to the public sphere, MacIntyre raises the possibility that the diverse social groupings of modern societies lack sufficient shared understanding to make the kind of debate envisaged in the concept of a normative public sphere possible. In the next chapter we shall consider this challenge.

For now, let us consider further elements that can help us to develop our understanding of the dynamics of religion and civil society. Cohen and Arato's (1992) reconstruction of the concept of civil society provides two such elements. First, following Habermas, they conceptualize civil society as 'the institutionalization of the lifeworld'. Therefore, civil society organizations are not just aggregations of private individuals clustering together, but they are doing so in ways that reflect the cultural contexts in which they are formed, including discursive and institutional religion. Second, they argue that civil society is the institutionalization of the lifeworld *stabilized by basic rights*. The discourse of rights here provides a way of structuring the range of forms of institutionalization of the lifeworld arising from the diversity of culture and of normatively countering authoritarian tendencies within culture, society and state. However, this places a great deal of weight on the concept of rights, yet both the articulation of rights with culture and the epistemological basis of rights are problematic, and we shall need to address these issues in Chapter 5.

Conclusion

In summary, the understanding of civil society developed here takes as its starting-point the kind of social institutions associated with the concept in Western societies in many definitions: for example, 'the society of households, family networks, civic and religious organizations and communities that are bound to each other primarily by shared histories, collective memories and cultural norms of reciprocity' (Douglass and Friedmann 1998 p. 2). Following Hann, however, it was proposed that cross-culturally it is necessary to be open to the possibility of functional equivalents of such institutions in other cultural contexts, the functions sought being the generation of trust in the generalized modern sense (following Seligman) and the promotion of civic virtues (following MacIntyre). Civil society alone, however, does not produce democratization (for example East Germany), which also requires legally regulated economic and political societies and an effective and self-limiting state. Yet civil society can sometimes promote democratization in spite of an authoritarian state. However, where this occurs, formation aspects of the civil society organization formed are likely to mirror an oppressive regime (for example Turkey and as we shall see further below, Poland and Egypt).

Civil society is prone to reification, as Marx first pointed out and therefore we introduced the distinction between normative and empirical civil society to preserve the tension between ideal-type and actuality. Cohen and Arato's definition of civil society as the institutionalization of the lifeworld embedded in basic rights helps to remind us of the cultural construction of civil societies and of its role in mediating between the individual and the state. The mention of rights also reminds us of the enterprise of the normative justification of civil society and we considered Keane's attempt at this and shall continue this project further in Chapter 5 in the fuller context of a discussion of the liberal tradition. Thus we have now outlined some elements of a critical theory of civil society and begun to examine the articulation between religion and civil society. The next chapter will undertake the same process for the concept of the public sphere, as well as the transnational dimension of civil society, which needs to be considered in the context of globalization.

Notes

1   We have already noted something of the character of the Egyptian state in Chapter 1.
2   This brief characterization should not be taken to indicate that there is no 'indigenous' basis for civil society in Bosnia, as we shall see.
3   That is, industrialization, urbanization, occupation and role specialization, nation-state formation; later, revolutions in communications technologies.
4   Sozialistische Einheitspartei Deutschlands (De Gruchy 1995 p. 290).
5   I have substituted 'ostentatious' for 'ostensive' here, as I believe this better conveys the sense of the original.
6   However, controversially, questions on ethnicity were included for the first time in 1999 in the French national census, though only for a 1:50 sample. See Marshalls (1998 p. 56).

Chapter 4

Rethinking the Public Sphere

One of the promises of modernity is that a free public can settle divisive issues through mutual persuasion. (Mayhew 1997 p. 12)

What matters at this stage is the construction of local forms of community within which civility and the intellectual and moral life can be sustained through the new dark ages which are already upon us. ... We are waiting not for Godot, but for another – doubtless very different – St. Benedict. (MacIntyre 1985 p. 263)

1. Introduction

This chapter seeks to develop the concept of the public sphere and its articulation with religion. It begins by considering different stories of the genesis of the public sphere – secular and religious. It then argues that the concept of a unitary public sphere is no longer viable and needs to be replaced by an account of multiple, intersecting and contesting public spheres, whose inter-relation is problematic. It also argues that the political and historical character of the public sphere in different contexts needs to be more fully recognized, in particular in accounting for the articulation of religious and post-religious elements, and of national and cultural identities.

We then consider a radical attack on the very possibility of a modern public sphere (and indeed a modern normative civil society) by the philosopher/social critic Alasdair MacIntyre. MacIntyre argues that the citizens of modern societies simply do not share enough in common to have the kind of debate that the idea of the public sphere implies. The whole model of democratic legitimacy flowing from the twin sources of local political representation and the discursive (in Habermas's sense) formation of public opinion in the public sphere is confounded from the start by an epistemological diversity that makes resolution of difference through rational discussion impossible. Or, to put it another way, that recalls Callum Brown's analysis of the 'death of Christian Britain' in Chapter 1, modern individuals can no longer articulate coherent moral stories about themselves, largely as a result of the decline of the social influence of religious narratives. For MacIntyre, this individual incoherence is intrinsically related both to social disintegration and to modern political and economic systems. However, it is argued that while MacIntyre provides important insights into contemporary cultural and religious diversity, he moves too quickly from a fundamentally sound analysis of the causes of serious disagreement to the impossibility of reasoned exchange as the basis for social coexistence.

We have already had reason to criticize Casanova's account for focusing on the democratizing potential of the public sphere supported by transnational civil society while neglecting the possible costs of this global development. We shall examine these costs further using the work of Manuel Castells as providing the best synthesized account of the conditions of global public communication. This completes our preliminary examination of the empirical existence and theories used to explain religion's articulation with civil society and the public sphere. We then turn in Chapter 5 to the issue of the normative justification of the ideals of these areas.

2. The Genesis of the Modern Public Sphere

We have seen above that theories of civil society and democratization have tended to incorporate both assumptions from the Enlightenment critique of religion and from the conflated theory of secularization, such that religious decline and privatization are assumed to be bound up with societal differentiation. However, both Casanova's Catholic examples and the Muslim examples considered in arguing against Gellner suggest that such connections are contingent and religion can retain a public role in civil society under conditions of continuing differentiation, whether in Brazil or Turkey. It should not come as a surprise, then, that the role of religion appears to have been marginalized in conventional accounts of the genesis of the public sphere. We now extend our critique of the account of religion in democratization and civil society to the public sphere.

According to Habermas (1989 [1962]), the public sphere is a space in which matters of public significance can be discussed by individuals in their private capacities and in which the outcome should, in principle, be decided by the quality of argument alone. He identifies the historical emergence of this ideal with the coffee-houses, salons and table societies of late eighteenth- and early nineteenth-century London, Paris and Frankfurt, but with ancient precedent in the brief history of rule by householder assembly (democracy) in the Athenian city-state (Habermas 1989 [1962], Arendt 1972). It is important to note that he sees this ideal as only ever partly realized and thus sets up the same tension between the normative and empirical public sphere as we have seen in the case of civil society. However, a number of scholars have challenged this account, including some that attribute a key role to religious groups. Mayhew, for example, argues that while Weber traced the origins of the secular economic ethic to the doctrine of predestination, he neglected the parallel religious origins of the secular idea of a free-speaking community. Mayhew traces the origins of the ideal of the public sphere to the 'Protestant renewal of the doctrine of "Communion of Saints" in post-Reformation and especially Puritan, religious thought (1997 p. 157). This emphasized the communion of saints as a living community, free speech as necessary for the communication of the Spirit and rightly guided deliberation as the best way to determine the truth. Thus he argues that 'Public space did not initially emerge in London's eighteenth century coffee houses, as Habermas seems to suppose, but in the intellectual circles of radical seventeenth century ministers whose writings exhibit self-conscious awareness of their public creating roles' (p. 161).

In fact, we do not need to choose between two rival explanations: both developments were important for the genesis of the public sphere. Indeed, a range of precedents can be discerned across culture and history, including many religious examples. In *Christianity and Democracy* (1995) De Gruchy places the developments traced by Mayhew in a broader and longer historical perspective, tracing a tradition of free-speaking assembly from Anglo-Saxon Christianity through the Reformation, to the New England Covenant and nineteenth-century British Nonconformity. Nor is this development confined to the Anglo-Saxon world, as Van der Veer illustrates in his intriguing paper on the development of the public sphere in nineteenth-century Britain and India (1999).

Van der Veer strongly challenges the connection made by political philosophers from Mill to Habermas to Charles Taylor, between secularism and the development of free milieux for public discussion. In South India, demands for state neutrality specifically arose from religious groups, Christian and Hindu. Christian missionaries feared that the East India Company planned to create an established Hindu religion, or 'Hindu Raj', fears aroused by the government of Madras's takeover of the running of Hindu temples in 1817 (Frykenburg 1997 p. 90; Van der Veer 1999 p. 19). It was these groups that first demanded a free public sphere, demands later added to by Hindu voluntary revivalist societies in the 1820s formed in reaction to Christian missionary activism (Van der Veer 1999 p. 23). Together, these groups forced the government to adopt a new policy of 'non-interference', eventually made into law in 1863 (p. 20). Thus 'this dialectic of aggressive missionization and Hindu resistance created a public sphere in South India which does not at all evoke the image of a "secular atmosphere" (ibid.). In a comparative context, Van der Veer comments that 'it is remarkable to see that both in the American colony and in the Indian colony it is the Christian dissenters which try to erect "a wall of separation" between church and state' (p. 21). Following Mayhew, one might add that it was the conviction that truth will ultimately triumph in unconstrained public discourse which led them to do so. In India, the shift of the state to a more neutral role in relation to religion through the nineteenth century – instead of trying to influence public religion through existing patronage networks – did not lead to religious decline. Neither did a parallel though less marked development in Britain – especially the enfranchisement of Nonconformists in the 1830s. Rather, in both cases, a vigorous voluntary religious sector developed. In Casanova's terms, the locus of public religious activity in both societies moved from the public sphere of state to the public sphere of civil society:

> The separation of church and state as a sign of secularity did not result in a secular society in Britain or in India, but initiated a shift in the location of religion in society from being part of the state to being part of a newly emerging public sphere. (Van der Veer 1999 p. 23)

Van der Veer's analysis moves beyond Mayhew and De Gruchy in claiming not only that religion was involved in the genesis of the public sphere at the level of ideas (through the secularization of a religious concept – Mayhew), or through historic precedent (De Gruchy), but also that *under modern conditions* it was the activity of religious groups that carved out a public sphere in opposition to the state, forcing the state to become more secular in the process. This is precisely the opposite of the self-image of the Enlightenment critics of religion and their current heirs in political philosophy (Midgely 1989; Stout 1988). This account provides evidence against secular stereotypes of religion as intrinsically antagonistic to free speech. In this context we turn to consider contemporary accounts of the public sphere.

3. Models of the Contemporary Public Sphere

In his influential early account of the genesis of the modern public sphere, Habermas (1989 [1962]) argued that the ideal was only ever met even approximately in practice when participation in it was restricted. Thus the coffee houses, salons and table societies of late eighteenth- and early nineteenth-century London, Paris and Frankfurt respectively limited involvement to a section of predominantly male bourgeois society. What, then, of the public sphere in which the boundaries of the public have been continually expanded and fractured, by increasing inclusiveness, diversity and an explosion in the media of communication? And what of the contentious distinction between public and private, of the culturally contingent limits on public discussion imposed by bourgeois society? We have already seen that religion has challenged the place assigned to it in the private sphere by liberal theory, but this is only part of a broader struggle to redefine the limits and contents of publicness, not least in relation to labour, gender and sexuality. In this context, feminists have questioned the notion of a unitary public sphere and we shall ask if it is accurate or helpful to view the public sphere as a unitary entity governed by the rules of rational discourse. Such questions and issues have led to the development of several models of the contemporary public sphere.

Seyla Benhabib (1992a) outlines three variants. The first, following Arendt, looks back to the Greek *polis*, envisaging public space as an agonistic arena of competition for the display of excellence and sees argument over the public good as part of this competition. Arendt relentlessly criticizes 'the rise of the social' – societal differentiation resulting in the emergence of the economic market and the family from the 'shadowy realm of the household' into the public sphere. At first sight this might seem contradictory: how does differentiation result in increased interaction between the spheres? Arendt's argument resembles that of Polanyi and Habermas (Chapter 2), because differentiation is seen to involve a concurrent process of de-differentiation whereby economic interests penetrate other spheres – the colonization of the lifeworld, in Habermas's terms. For Arendt, this expansion of the economic sphere – with its model of the maximizing self-interested individual – has been at the expense of universal, common concerns, which she sees as properly political. Thus Arendt's can be seen as an élitist model of the public sphere, but for the reason that to allow wider participation and the penetration of economic interests would corrupt its orientation to the common good and tarnish the quality of argument which it can sustain. In this sense her argument resembles that of Schmitt (1985): mass participation destroys the quality of political life (Tester 1992; Cohen and Arato 1992). Thus Benhabib (1992a) sees Arendt as implicitly opposed to political universalism:

> If the agonistic political space of the *polis* was only possible because large groups of human beings – like women, slaves, children, laborers, noncitizen residents and all non-Greeks – were excluded from it while they made possible through their labor for the daily necessities of life that 'leisure for politics' that the few enjoyed, then is the critique of the rise of the social, which was accompanied by the emancipation of these groups from the 'shadowy interior of the household' and by their entry into public life, also a critique of political universalism as such? (p. 75)

Or, to turn the criticism on its head, are attempts to revive the ideal of the public sphere bound to collapse into nostalgic élitism? Benhabib argues that Arendt's understanding of the public sphere, while not simply élitist nostalgia, is none the less incompatible with modern ideals of universal political participation and structural conditions of societal differentiation. The pluralization and continuing expansion of 'the public' means that the conditions of moral and political homogeneity necessary for Arendt's 'vying for excellence amongst peers' (1992a p. 79) no longer exist. But it is not only the membership of the public that enlarges and diversifies, but also the content of public conversation: '[W]hen freedom emerges from action in concert, there can be no agenda to *predefine* the topic of public conversation, the struggle over what gets included in the public agenda is itself a struggle for justice and freedom. (ibid. p. 79). This argument is also at the root of Benhabib's objection to a second model of public space – the liberal one. For this operates with predefined categories of the right and the good and public and private which, she argues, both in fact are and in principle should be, the subject of political argument. 'The right' here refers to principles of justice and a supposedly universal order that are properly matters of public deliberation, 'the good' to ethics which are taken to be particular and matters of personal, private choice. Benhabib asks, 'who is to decide which is which?' and answers:

> The liberal theorist ... assumes that the primary groups [in] the conversation ... already know that a particular problem is a moral, religious or aesthetic issue, as opposed to an issue of distributive justice or public policy. ... Take, however, issues like abortion, pornography and domestic violence. What kinds of issues are they? Are they questions of justice or the good life? The distinction between [these] ... cannot be decided by some moral geometry. Rather, it is the very process of unconstrained public dialogue that will help us define the nature of the issues we are debating. (1992a pp. 82–3)

The same, one might argue, applies to religion. The standard liberal position assumes a universal, neutral standpoint from which such judgements can be made (we shall return to recent developments on this point in Chapter 5). But such a position is always liable to sociological deconstruction. Part of the problem is that liberalism models the public sphere too closely on judicial relations. There is a social need for the law to be seen as impartial within a society – even if from a comparative cultural or historical perspective it can clearly be seen to embody particular, local values. But to limit the public sphere in this way is to foreclose the possibilities of social change through the medium of talk. Benhabib gives the example of health in the workplace, where issues once construed as 'trade secrets' and defined as private have, through the efforts of labour movements, become matters of public concern and eventually public policy (ibid. pp. 83–4).

Benhabib then turns her attention to the third model of the public sphere, that of Habermas in his writings following his initial historical account of the emergence of the ideal of the public sphere (1989 [1962]). For Habermas, 'Public space ... is viewed democratically as the creation of procedures whereby those affected by general social norms and collective political decision [that is, presumably, everyone] can have a say in their formulation, stipulation and adoption' (1993 p. 87).

So far the position is little different from that of liberalism, which also insists on democratic legitimization, but generally places less emphasis on participation in deliberation and on the social and political conditions which make this possible. However, for Habermas public dialogue is not constrained by an untenable construct of 'neutrality', but rather by a model of 'practical discourse'. This is a process that enables the 'redemption of normative claims to validity' (Habermas 1990 p. 103), that is, for testing whether claims about norms (moral, legal, political and so on) raised in a particular public context are justifiable. Although the context for engaging in practical discourse is always a particular normative disagreement, practical discourse operates under the constraints of the 'ideal speech situation' in which

> each participant must have an equal chance to initiate and to continue communication; each must have an equal chance to make assertions, recommendations and explanations; all must have equal chances to address their wishes, desires, feelings; and finally, within dialogue, speakers must be free to thematize those power relations that in ordinary contexts would constrain the wholly free articulation of opinions and positions. (Benhabib 1992a p. 89)

Habermas maintains that such a procedure is compatible with a distinction between the right and the good – defining the distinction as between that on which consensus is possible in principle (that is, 'the right') and that on which it isn't ('the good'). In contrast, Benhabib argues that such a radically open procedure 'undermines the substantive distinctions between justice and the good life, public matters of norms as opposed to private matters of value, public interests versus private needs' (ibid. p. 89). Habermas objects to Benhabib's conflation of the sociological distinction between public and private with the philosophical distinction between right and good (1992a p. 105). However, it is not clear how this helps his case of proposing that the latter distinction is beyond discursive reformulation. Therefore, we may follow Benhabib in accepting Habermas's radical ideal of the public sphere expressed in the procedure of practical discourse as providing a useful model, but also in rejecting his attempt to pre-determine the boundaries of the right and the good in advance of actual dialogue. We also follow her in rejecting his unitary ('undifferentiated') model of the public sphere, because 'there may be as many publics as there are controversial general debates about the validity of norms. Democratization in contemporary societies can be viewed as the increase in and growth of autonomous public spheres among participants' (1992 p. 87).

Nancy Fraser takes up Benhabib's argument for a critical model of the public sphere, contending that societies in which inequalities exist between social groups need 'subaltern counterpublics' (1992 p. 123) to counter the hegemony of dominant groups in mainstream public spheres. She argues that 'revisionist historiography ... records that members of subordinated social groups – women, workers, peoples of colour and gays and lesbians – have repeatedly found it advantageous to constitute alternative publics' (ibid.). Furthermore, such groups not only make up alternative publics but also affect mainstream discussions and may thus come to change the terms of public debate in general. The same may also be said of religious groups. For example, Asad (1991) writes in the context of Muslims in Britain:

> if the adherents of a religion enter the public sphere, can their entry leave the pre-existing discursive structure intact? The public sphere is not an empty space for carrying out debates. It is constituted by the sensibilities – memories and aspirations, fears and hopes, of speakers and listeners – and also by the way they exist (and are made to exist) for each other. Thus the introduction of new discourses may result in the disruption of established assumptions structuring debates in the public sphere. More strongly they may *have* to disrupt existing assumptions in order to be heard. (p. 181)

We shall consider these comments further in the context of *The Satanic Verses* controversy below in Chapter 6. For now, we simply note that in debating the public sphere it is important not to lose sight of the fact that public spheres are constituted by encounters between real people in real (or virtual) spaces. Returning to Fraser, we note that she goes further than arguing that the benefits of multiple publics are restricted to conditions of structural inequality, however ubiquitous these might be. Rather, the cultural embeddedness of institutions and practices which constitute public spheres inevitably make them more hospitable to some modes of expression than to others (1992 p. 126). A plurality of public spheres is therefore to be favoured in principle. It is also important to note that the example of counter-publics (women, labour, environmentalist and so on) shows that multiple public spheres are not islands, but articulate with wider and more influential publics.

Further support for a model of multiple public spheres comes from Keane (1998). Keane identifies three phases in the development of modern ideas on the public sphere. The first is during the struggle against despotic rule in early modern Europe and closely coincides with the modern mobilization of the idea of civil society. The second, closely identified with a German intellectual tradition stretching from Weber to Arendt and Habermas, criticizes the effects of the dominance of commodity consumption and production on civil life in the name of a public sphere. The third identifies the public sphere with public service broadcasting. Each idealizes a unified public sphere that can only be sustained by excluding participants or ignoring inequalities in abilities and opportunities to engage in public discourse. We have considered examples of the first two models and the public service model also fails both because it is limited as a means of public participation and because it has become untenable in an era in which distinctions between public and private broadcasting are breaking down. This breakdown stems from the increasing intrusion of the market into public broadcasting and because 'market-led media are subject to a a long-term process of self-politicization, in the sense that they are able to address matters of concern to citizens capable of distinguishing between market "hype" and public controversies' (Keane 1998 p. 175). Accordingly Keane concurs with Benhabib and Fraser that 'a theory of civil society and public life that clings dogmatically to the vision of a unified public sphere in which "public opinion" and the "public interest" are defined is a chimera – and that for the sake of democracy it should now be jettisioned' (p. 189). Keane therefore distinguishes between three levels of public sphere – micro, meso and macro. The 'micro-public sphere' designates arenas of debate with numbers of participants ranging from a few to thousands and from new social movements that challenge dominant modes of distribution and interpretation of information through to more conventional formations such as 'the discussion circle, the publishing house, the church, the clinic, the political chat over a drink with friends' (p. 172). Keane also includes children's video games that encourage children not just to play within the rules of the game but to actively engage in the shaping of their virtual environment. The 'meso-public sphere' comprises large-circulation newspapers and national broadcast media, including the proliferation of television talk shows which encourage debate on controversial issues such as 'teenage sex, pregnancy and child abuse' (p. 175). The 'macro-public sphere' is distinguished from the meso-public sphere by its regional (for example EU) or global reach. It comprises on the one hand multinational communications firms specializing in one-way communication – a generalization complicated by audience interactivity – and on the other hand the bi/multidirectional communication forms of the Internet and other electronic media, with their potential for the development of 'cyberdemocracy'.

As Keane's examples suggest, such levels of public sphere, while clearly able to represent or sustain certain forms of debate, are very different from Habermas's ideal of practical discourse. Indeed, Benhabib shows considerably more scepticism than Keane about the potential of new media to sustain public debate, seeing instead (in the tradition of Arendt and Habermas) a decline in the quality of and possibilities for public discussion:

> In existing Western democracies, under the impact of the mass media, growth of corporatization and of business-like political associations … the public sphere of democratic legitimacy has shrunk. … The autonomous citizen, whose reasoned judgement and participation was the *sine qua non* of the public sphere, has been transformed into the 'citizen consumer' of packaged images and messages or the 'electronic mail target' of large lobbying groups and organizations. (Benhabib 1992a p. 93)

The conditions of interaction between this shrinking public sphere and the growth of multiple publics need to be examined. Furthermore, if the number of public spheres is to grow, then the interaction between them also needs to be considered. For this, we must focus our account of the articulation of religion and modernization (Chapters 1 and 2) specifically on the issue of public communication. For this purpose, after sketching some perspectives on globalization, we shall outline Castells's argument in his trilogy *The Information Age: Economy, Society and*

Culture (1996–7). This will enable us to reflect critically on Casanova's optimistic but perhaps idealistic account of transnational civil society introduced in Chapter 2.

4. Globalization and the Rise of the Network Society: Prospects for Transnational Civil Society and Public Spheres

Globalization refers to the process of parts of the world being drawn closer together through improved communications, increased economic exchange, political interdependence and cultural interaction, so that it comes to be conceived as an interconnected whole. However, especially with respect to the cultural sphere, increased interaction does not necessarily lead to convergence. As Tibi (1998) has argued, we may have a global economy and there are signs of the emergence of a global polity, or at least of aspects of transnational governance, although nation-states remain fundamental aspects of the world system. But in spite of the global dissemination of some cultural forms, it is at the level of culture and not least religion, that global integration seems to be most fiercely resisted.

As Beyer (1994) points out, different social and political theorists have highlighted different aspects of the globalization process (pp. 14–44). Thus Wallerstein (1979) emphasizes the incorporation of ever more local and regional economies into the capitalist world system, Meyer (1980) stresses the role of nation-states in conditioning the functioning of that economy, and Robertson (1990) the social and cultural consequences of and resistance to globalizing forces, particularly in terms of the *Gemeinschaft/Gesellschaft* (local community/modern society) dichotomy of classic sociological theory. Luhmann (1982), as we have already seen, focuses on the tendency towards differentiation which becomes paradoxical in the context of globalization, such that even as systems become more closely integrated, so their increasing functional specialization means that they can operate without overt reference to one another. Writing after Beyer, Castells adds a further dimension to the globalization debate through the concept of the 'network society'. For Castells, the integration of new information technologies into modern societies is leading to radical transformations of their economic, social and political organization and cultural forms, creating new social cleavages and enabling the emergence of new identities (1996, 1997a, 1997b).

As we noted in Chapter 2, Casanova's account of the deprivatization of religion depends in part on the democratizing power of transnational civil society. We are now in a position to critically evaluate this concept in the light of theories of globalization. We shall proceed by first examining the idea which seems to have most influenced Casanova, then by considering this in the light of a more detailed exposition of Castells' work and that of other theorists as relevant. Although Casanova does not develop his own account in detail, he refers to Lipschutz's concept (1992). In contrast to dominant conceptions in international relations of a global order based on anarchy or self-help (between states) Lipschutz sees global civil society as 'the conscious association of actors, in physically separated locations, who link themselves together in networks for particular political and social purposes' (p. 393). Such an arrangement, he claims, acts in parallel with and increasingly influences both the dominant political and economic international orders. In a reversal of Habermas's fear of the colonization of the lifeworld by the instrumental rationality of the market, Lipschutz sees the development of a 'norm-governed social system' as facilitated by the global diffusion of consumer culture: 'it is the very homogeneity and pervasiveness of this consumer culture – and its extension to institutionalized politics as an historical process – that has opened up a political space for the revival of civil society' (p. 392). Lipschutz also connects this development to the empowerment of non-state organizations in the face of the inability of states to cope with the costs of economic globalization. The latter include economic restructuring leading to social dislocation and unemployment and lower taxes leading to tightening welfare budgets – whether imposed by the World Bank on debtor nations or self-imposed by the governments of Western democracies. He also connects it to the growth of new social and political identities challenging the state-dominated world order – in a similar way to Castells (1997a – below p. 106). Like other analysts of new social movements (NSMs) (which he sees as one part of broader networks of action and knowledge constituting global civil society), he refers to examples such as human rights, environment and development organizations, as well as to transnational connections between indigenous peoples. As well as being factually transnational, such groupings are also ideologically so – thus Lipschutz refers to 'a growing element of global consciousness in the way members of global civil society act' (p. 399).

Lipschutz sees the ideas and modes of production of liberalism (individualism, including human rights and consumerism) as increasingly becoming the global 'operating system' at the level of culture and as undermining identities based on national states. However, since liberalism fails to provide a sufficient 'anchor for identity', new forms of collective identity, sometimes local or regional, sometimes cosmopolitan (where nationality does not simply map on to territory), are being created (ibid. p. 414). Of course within Europe, since Lipschutz wrote, the former Yugoslavia has shown that where nationality fails to map on to territory civil war can also be the result. His identification of the new global operating system with liberalism should also alert us to Benhabib's criticism of the liberal public sphere as predefining the scope of publicity in the interests of dominant groups. It should also remind us of Tibi's argument, amply attested by many of the examples we have considered, that cultural diversification is as much the outcome of globalization as cultural convergence. Lipschutz gives credibility to Benhabib's criticism when he identifies the rise of 'powerful people' – those with access to and knowledge to activate new information systems – as the key agents in the challenge to the global order of nation-states:

> If the threat to the material base is not immediate, but emerges over the longer term, it is likely that structures of reproduction and legitimation will be challeneged by those who are slowly becoming aware of this crisis as a result of their training and relationship to the state, that is the intelligentsia, the educated and the 'powerful people'. (p. 418)

However, there is a danger here that cyberdemocracy will provide participation for the global information élite at the expense of excluding of the rest of 'unwired' global society. Furthermore, the same global infrastructure also facilitates global criminality – from internet porn to cocaine trafficking. A further cause for concern is the quality of communication in global civil society. As Lipschutz admits in relation to the powerful medium of television, 'The high cost of television time means that only those with ample media budgets are able to get their views across and whatever passes for analysis is usually compressed into sound bites or two-minute visuals' (p. 412).

The problems and prospects for such developments are placed in a wider perspective by Castells (1996). New information technologies have created a new international division of labour: high-value informational labour, high-volume lower-cost labour, producers of raw materials and the devalued 'redundant producers' (p. 147 n. 13). The location of labour does not coincide with countries, but rather 'with networks and flows, using the technological infrastructure of the informational economy' (ibid.), with the result that even marginalized national economies have connections with high-value networks, while powerful economies have redundant producers in their population – a 'Fourth World' (Castells 1997b). Thus for economic purposes location in a particular nation-state becomes a less significant indicator of wealth than the individual's relation to the global economy. The growing influence of transnational flows of capital is one factor undermining national sovereignty, although nations remain significant actors (1997a p. 107). One aspect of these flows is the growth of transnational criminal activity, resulting in a proliferating global criminal economy, which brings its own harvest of misery (1997b pp. 166–205) and is especially relevant in the post-Communist world.

The functional differentiation across societies highlighted by Luhmann is also important, since this feature creates difficulties both for centralized forms of legitimization, religious or otherwise, and for political intervention (concentrated at the national level) in economic processes (concentrated at the regional and global level). This in turn reduces the possibility of political participation in economic affairs. We have seen (Chapter 2) challenges to Luhmann's argument on the grounds that it underplays these costs of social differentiation, ignores elements of resistance to the process and neglects the de-differentiation processes that accompany it. But no critics dispute that differentiation combined with de-differentiation in the form of economic invasion of other spheres makes political control of systems and political participation more rather than less difficult, the promise of 'cyberdemocracy' and 'transnational civil society' notwithstanding.

Castells (1997a) shows how this cumulative political participative deficit is reflected in increasing disillusionment with conventional politics in democractic societies, indicated by expressions of dissatisfaction with political leaders and declining participation in national and local elections (pp. 342–9). However, he identifies three counter-trends that are of relevance to attempts to reconstruct civil society and develop public spheres of discussion. First, he argues that there are significant attempts to revitalize the local state through citizen participation and the use of new technologies. In this context he refers to citizen consultation and local self-management schemes in Holland and Brazil (p. 350). Second, he refers to the potential of cyberdemocracy, although he also warns that there are dangers. Should cyberspace become a key forum for citizen participation, this could indeed recreate Athenian democracy, including the empowering of the privileged few, in global terms, and excluding the overwhelming majority. He also points out that 'the volatility of the medium could induce an accentuation of "show politics" ... on-line politics could push the individualization of politics and of society, to a point where integration, consensus and institution building would become dangerously difficult to reach' (p. 351). Castells argues that in traditional politics in the US the Internet still functions mostly as a one-way communication system, as political parties develop ever tighter control over their members' interactions with the media. Rather it is in the realm of 'symbolic politics' and in the 'issue-oriented' mobilization that electronic communication is likely to have the most impact (p. 352). These forms of mobilization for 'non-political' causes, electronically mediated or otherwise, are likely to have a significant impact on the future shape of democracy. Examples of organizations working in this way include Greenpeace, Oxfam and Amnesty International, each of which campaigns around a cluster of issues and strives to avoid political partisanship in the conventional sense, yet aims to influence political actors through symbolic non-violent action and grassroots mobilization. Castells argues that such groups 'seem to win increasing legitimacy in all societies and to condition the rules and outcomes of formal political competition. They re-legitimize the concern with public affairs in people's minds and lives' (p. 353). Yet in doing so they 'bypass formal politics and [hence] may undermine even further the institutions of democracy' (p. 352).

Castells also touches on questions relevant to civil society and the public sphere in his analysis of identity politics, of which he identifies three kinds: legitimizing identities; resistance identities; and project identities. The first arises from the dominant institutions of society and is associated with civil society in the Gramscian sense of ambivalent institutions intermediate between the citizen and the state, capable of acting both as the defences of the state and as sites of mobilization for the proletariat. Like Keane, Castells dismisses civil society in this sense as a focus of resistance to the dominant forces of globalization, because the proletariat is no longer the force it was, and because some of the traditional intermediary institutions (for example traditional churches in Western Europe, trade unions) are in decline. Instead, he proposes that the main source of challenge to dominant forms of globalization in the information society will come from communally organized resistance identities and project identities. In our broader definition, these too can be seen as part of both empirical and normative civil society. He sees resistance identity-based groups as expressions of 'the exclusion of the excluders by the excluded. That is, the building of defensive identity in terms of dominant institutions/ideologies, reversing the value of judgement while reinforcing the boundary' (1997a p. 9). Certain forms of nationalism, religious fundamentalism (oriented to protecting a cultural enclave) and queer culture are examples of this form of resistance. A second form of identity that articulates a different form of resistance is 'project identity'. This attempts to challenge the dominant terms of globalization, especially the dominance of the functional logics of the differentiated spheres. Castells's conception of project identity draws on French sociologist Alain Touraine's (1985) and Habermas's (1987) work on new social movements (NSMs). NSMs are seen as harbingers of new forms of emancipatory social action under conditions of intensified globalization. They are distinctive because, in contrast to traditional opposition movements associated with civil society, they challenge 'the meaning and value of the social system as whole' rather than the distribution of goods within it (Beckford 1989 p. 144). Furthermore, they do so by shifting more and more from the 'political' form of collective action to a cultural ground. Such a shift is particularly important for understanding the potential forms of interaction of religion with modern social systems, for the holistic orientation of religious systems makes them well suited to articulate this kind of challenge. This complements the argument of Beyer (1994 and above Chapter 2) that religions' holistic perspectives enhance their ability to respond to the residual problems of the global system. This account situates this potential in the context of a general shift to culture as the site of political contestation. Castells (1997a) points to some manifestations of 'project identity', including religious and secular examples:

> [T]he building of identity is a project of a different life, perhaps on the basis of an oppressed identity, but expanding toward the transformation of society as the prolongation of this project of identity, as in the ... example of a post-patriarchal society, liberating men, women and children, through the realization of women's identity. Or, in a very different perspective, the final reconciliation of all human beings as believers, brothers and sisters, under the guidance of God's law, be it Allah or Jesus, as a result of the religious conversion of the godless, anti-family, materialist societies, otherwise unable to fulfil human needs and God's design. (p.10)

Thus Castells assigns a significant role to religion as a source of communal identity in contemporary societies, alongside nationalism, ethnicity, feminism and environmentalism, and to these 'project identities' (in the sense of projected towards to the transformation of society) as sources of resistance to the dominant global systems.

So what is the appropriate balance between Lipschutz's optimism and the criticisms of the new global public spheres that result from transnational networks and organizations implied by the work of Castells and others? The extension, multiplication and commercialization of public spheres does not seem entirely to attenuate, fragment or swamp the ideal of open, participative public communication. Indeed, Castells's theory suggests that religion will be among the leading idioms used to articulate resistance to the dominant terms of globalization. However, he is unsure how successful these project identities will be (1997a p. 67). In this context we turn to consider the critique of the public sphere implied in the work of MacIntyre.

5. MacIntyre and the Possibility of a Modern Public Sphere

MacIntyre questions the very possibility of a public sphere in modern societies. The basis for his critique of the prospect of contemporary civil societies giving rise to a democratic and participatory public sphere is qualitatively different to others we have encountered. These include the early Habermas's view that the late eighteenth-century bourgeois public sphere collapsed because of the intrusion of class and commercial interests, and Seligman's parallel view that contemporary societies are so diverse that differences can no longer be negotiated by appeal to common understandings in a shared lifeworld, but only through instrumental systems. MacIntyre's position is different because for him it is not diversity itself (cultural, religious or linguistic), nor the intrusion of class or commercial interests (though the latter are significant), that undermines public communication, but rather the shattered substructure of moral discourse. In short, MacIntyre argues, if I read him correctly, that because we can no longer make sense of our own moral lives we can no longer engage in a civil way with those of others.

In Chapter 3 we introduced MacIntyre's work as providing conceptual resources for thinking about how civil society organizations can contribute to democratization by the development of virtues and communities of virtue. We also noted, however, that MacIntyre holds that modern societies are antithetical to the cultivation of virtue because of the domination of external goods (the colonization of the lifeworld, in Habermas's terms). Here we shall consider the counterpart to that argument, which is that modern moral discourse has developed in such a way as to deprive 'moderns' – I believe here MacIntyre means most of the inhabitants of the modern West – of the ability to construct coherent moral narratives. As evidence for this process, consider Brown's (2001) work on the declining influence of Christian narrative in Britain (Chapter 1 above). For MacIntyre (1985) this collapse of narrative undermines our social competencies:

> We enter human society with one or more imputed characters – roles into which we have been drafted – and we have to learn what they are in order to be able to understand how others respond to us and how our responses to them are apt to be construed. … Deprive children of stories and you leave them unscripted, anxious stutterers in their actions as in their words. (p. 216)

Most significantly for our purposes, it may be argued that the inability to construct moral narratives undermines our ability to communicate rationally with others whose way of life differs from our own. To understand his argument more fully it is useful to compare the form of ethics MacIntyre espouses (virtue ethics) with that of more dominant contemporary approaches. Contemporary ethical theories are of three main types: consequentialist, deontological, and virtue ethics. In some ways these approaches are so different that one may question whether they are theories of the same thing at all (Baron *et al.* 1997). This can be seen by contrasting their approaches to questions of justice in policy or institutional arrangements. Characteristically, the consequentialist asks whether the *consequences* of a policy or set of arrangements are just, the deontologist whether the *principles* informing them are just and the virtue ethicist whether this is the kind of policy or arrangement which a just *agent* (individual, community or society) would produce. However, the contrast between these three approaches does not mean that they are mutually exclusive in practice – practical moral discourse is likely to contain elements of each. But their differences do point to underlying and deep seated disagreements between advocates of each approach.

In contrast to virtue ethics' agent-centredness, the other approaches share an abstract individualism that neglects the complex web of life of which 'principles' and 'consequences' form only a part. Thus one may argue that virtue ethics should logically lead to a consideration of social and cultural processes, although in practice this has not generally been the case. Indeed a counter-accusation is rather that virtue ethics has failed to engage with specific policy issues to the same extent as alternative approaches. This may be partly because its focus is on the broad development of character rather than particular situations, but is probably also partly because of its intellectual isolation (Baron *et al.* p. 175). However, there are deeper reasons why both virtue ethicists and deontologists tend to step back from immediate policy issues.

First, there is scepticism about the consequentialist assumption that it is possible accurately to predict the consequences of actions in complex social settings, an assumption that the consequentialist shares with the positivist social-scientific methodologies which tend to inform policy studies. One such example is rational choice theory (RCT; above, Chapter 2), which holds that individual agents will behave so as to maximize their own advantage. At first sight, RCT may appear agent-centred like virtue ethics, because its self-description proceeds from the supposed action of agents. However, it is more accurately described as consequentialist, as it proceeds from an *assumption* about the action of agents, rather than making this the subject of *critical investigation*, as in virtue ethics. Thus its emphasis is on the prediction and measurement of consequences, given certain assumptions about the way people generally behave. This approach has found it difficult to make sense of complex social behaviour, because this is influenced by factors other than narrow self-interest, for example group solidarity and processes of negotiation and discussion (Dryzeck 1995 pp. 111–5).

Second, consequentialism lacks substantive moral content. For example RCT provides no critical judgement on the maximizing behaviour of individuals, while utilitarianism, which transfers the assumption of maximizing behaviour from the individual to society, provides no critical interrogation of its maxim 'the greatest happiness of the greatest number'. Rather, such principles have to be imported from elsewhere, usually from deontology. For example, 'bottom-loaded utilitarianism' imports the concept of rights from deontology to qualify the utilitarian maxim 'the greatest happiness of the greatest number' with the statement 'provided certain minimum rights of individuals are protected'. Thus consequentialism is parasitic on other traditions for substantive moral judgements. Yet its major source for these judgements, deontology, has come to seem increasingly questionable, as the search for incontrovertible foundations for moral principles continues to prove elusive (MacIntyre 1985).

MacInytre explains both the failure of this search for foundations in modern moral philosophy and of public discourse in modern societies as a consequence of the abandonment (in theory and social practice respectively) of a teleology of human nature. Teleology means 'explanation by design or purpose' and such an account of humanity is central both to the Aristotelian conception of virtue ethics to which MacIntyre subscribes and to religious traditions. (Indeed, MacIntyre sees the Jewish, Christian and Islamic as deriving from Aristotle). In Chapter 3 we introduced MacIntyre's sense of 'practice' as a social activity dedicated to the pursuit of internal goods and which leads to the development of virtues. Part of the Aristotelian conception of the goods for which practices are pursued is that goods are never pursued entirely for their own sake. Rather, each good is pursued for the sake of another good and so on, so that all goods can ultimately be arranged within a hierarchy whose summit would be *the* good, (MacIntyre 1967a p. 59). Aristotle does not attempt to specify what the supreme good is, nor to choose between the various candidates available to him; rather what is important is the assumption of a supreme good as the *telos* of ethical life; indeed of life as a whole. Thus practices and virtues may be understood as linked teleologically to a hierarchy of goods. MacIntyre's scheme may therefore be represented thus:

practices – virtues – unity of an individual life – moral community
– tradition of enquiry – supreme good

Of course, in religious traditions attempts are made to articulate the supreme good, or revelations of it are believed to have been received. But MacIntyre argues that the assumption of (or belief in) such a supreme good is not peculiar to religious belief but is constitutive of rational enquiry as such (1988 pp. 134–6). Basing the practice of ethics on an unspecified *telos* may seen unreasonable at first, but MacIntyre invites us to consider the parallel of the practice of modern natural science:

> From a standpoint outside of any established scientific community, on the basis of data uncharacterized in terms of any established theory, there are and can be no sufficiently good reasons to suppose in respect of any particular subject matter of enquiry, let alone in respect of nature as such, that there is one true fundamental explanatory theory. Only for the inhabitants of such a community, who possess some established theory or sets of theories and who have so far characterized the data in terms of them, can the question be put: In the light of the norms of evaluation which we now possess, which of the presently competing overall theories is the best, or can we conceive of a better? That there is a true theory to be found is a presupposition of the ongoing activity of the scientific community; that there is a supreme good for human beings is a presupposition of the ongoing activity of the *polis*. (p. 134)

Thus MacIntyre argues that an unfounded assumption of the underlying unity of being is necessary to support a rational ethics, just as it underpins a rational science. However, modern forms of moral philosophy (for example consequentialism, deontology) have abandoned the teleological structure of Aristotelian ethics on which medieval (Christian, Jewish and Islamic) ethics relied. These ethical systems had a threefold moral structure: '[U]ntutored human-nature-as-it-happens-to-be, human-nature-as-it-could-be-if-it-realized-its-*telos* and the precepts of rational ethics as the means for the transition from one to the other' (1985 p. 53). But the effect of emptying reason of its teleological content was to uncouple the three components of this account and displace the second component, leaving a twofold scheme of humanity-as-it-is and the need for a rational ethics to police this condition. Thus the Enlightenment project is to provide a rational basis for such ethics, but without the crucial teleological middle term which made sense of its ancestors' formulations, it is doomed to fail (pp. 54–5).

Thus ethics needs an account of the moral development of human beings in terms of substantive virtues and their relation to society. Without such an account, moral philosophy and more significantly modern forms of moral discourse derived from it, are reduced to calculation devoid of substantive values (consequentialism), or an assertion of principles that cannot be justified in relation to an account of human nature or society (deontology). The consequence of the latter, which MacIntyre sees as a key failure of the Enlightenment project, is a prevailing belief in the 'irreducible plurality of values', which enters the sociological tradition as 'an insistent and central Weberian theme' (1985 p. 109). In this context, the government of modern societies becomes a matter of containing plurality behind a mask of 'effective' management and bureaucracy, precisely the diagnosis of Seligman.

What are we to make of this critique? MacIntyre's account of the transformation of the modern moral discourses that have accompanied modern structural transformations provides an important insight into some contemporary confrontations – for example between liberals and some Muslims over the publication of *The Satanic Verses*, as we shall see below in Chapter 6. It is important to note in this context that MacIntyre sees the abandoning of the teleological form of ethics as a contingent rather than a necessary consequence of modernization, and hence doesn't reduce such conflicts to a pre-modern/modern confrontation in which the latter must inevitably triumph. MacIntyre's understanding of the relationship between socio-cultural context and moral discourse is also important for helping us to envisage how understanding between people from quite different traditions might be achieved, as I shall argue in Chapter 5.

However, whether MacIntyre's characterization of contemporary moral discourse implies the impossibility of a modern public sphere is doubtful. Just as Habermas overestimates the importance of a rather restricted sense of rationality to public discourse, so MacIntyre overestimates the importance of underlying epistemological coherence, if the purpose of public discourse is the achievement of practical compromise based on an always incomplete but partly overlapping mutual understanding. It is true that MacIntyre points to a problem not just with modern moral philosophy but with modern society, because dominant modern systems are oriented to external goods and hence corrode practices, as we saw in Chapter 3. But this points to the difficulty rather than the impossibility of a modern public sphere. We shall pursue the idea of how 'overlapping mutual understanding' might be achieved in Chapter 5, first through a critical examination of Rawls's (1993) idea of an 'overlapping consensus', then by developing MacIntyre's idea of communication between traditions. First, however, having decided that the possibility of a modern public sphere remains open we turn to consider what kind of public sphere is practically possible. In the next section we consider a recent example of the emergence of a national public sphere in India, involving both new communications media (television) and a central role for religion (Hinduism). Then in Section 7 we shall consider suggestions for practical strategies to democratize public spheres.

6. Rajagopal on a Televised Religious Epic and the Public Sphere in India

Rajagopal (2001) recounts the development of the Indian public brought about by the creation of a national television audience in the late 1980s, followed rapidly by the arrival of satellite television and the dismantling of state controls by 1992. In particular, he examines the relationship between the serialization (in a mammoth 78 episodes) of the Hindu epic the *Ramayana* from January 1987 to September 1990 and the rise to power of the BJP (Bharatiya Janata Party) in the early to mid-1990s, achieving a consistent period in office from March 1998 (ibid. pp. 326, 275). The study sheds light on the impact of the introduction of new media 'before the rationalization of politics and the "disenchantment of society" (p. 7). Indeed, the serial vividly illustrates the practical compatibility of religious devotion and advanced technology: 'In my house, my grandmother would not eat before she watched it, just as she would not eat before her daily worship. And granny would take off her slippers and bow to Ram-ji before watching with great absorption' (respondent in ibid. p. 138). Thus considering this example will bring together our focus on the diverse impact of modernization on religion in Chapters 1 and 2 with that on civil society and the public sphere. We shall focus specifically on the issues relating to the development of multiple public spheres and the role of discursive religion within them.

Rajagopal (2001) describes the Indian situation as characterized by:

> split publics … residing across distinct language strata, media and socio-cultural domains [especially as constituted by the audience of the different newspapers and radio stations]. … The introduction of a new system of representation, in this case television, set up new circuits of exchange across a split public, thereby casting the existing terms of translation and the status of the bourgeois public sphere itself, into crisis. (p. 148)

The serial was the first to reach a mass audience and in doing so it brought together diverse publics. It offered a model of a past golden age in which 'authoritarianism' and 'complete mutual recognition between rulers and subjects' were miraculously combined (p. 149). It led to a 'crisis' in the status of the 'bourgeois' public sphere because, by presenting a religiously legitimized alternative to India's secular republic, it exposed the narrowness of the social base on which state secularism rested: 'If secularism had been declared by state fiat, the power of new communications brought home the fact that secularism existed, willy-nilly, as largely the sign and exercise of membership in a cultural élite' (ibid.). The serial was authorized by the Congress Party and broadcast on state television in spite of official secularism in an attempt to improve the party's popularity by presenting the image of a harmonious India. But instead the epic exposed fractures in contemporary society in the mirror of a mythical past and thus created an opportunity for Hindu nationalists. The BJP was able to capitalize on the nostalgic appeal to an idealized past by contrasting it with present disorder and intimating the possibility of its revival and thus created a fragile coalition across a public deeply divided by caste and regional differences. They were inadvertently supported in this by the commericalization of Hindu symbols and discourse triggered by the series and the follow-up *Mahabarata*, which reached an even wider audience (ibid., p. 375).

While critics may write off these events as opportunistic and cynical manipulation of religious enthusiasm by nationalist politicians, such criticisms ignore the widening of participation in politics that resulted. They also make the secularist error of assuming that the political mobilization of religious discourse can always be deconstructed to reveal 'real' secular motives (Milbank 1990 pp. 101–45). However, as we saw in the case of Egypt, such a perspective fails to recognize the dynamics of culture and that religion's entry into political discourse alters the public sphere itself (Starrett 1998; Asad 1999). On the issue of increased political participation, one can point to two distinct phenomena. The first is the rise to positions of political power previously unreached by individuals of low or *dalit* (untouchable)[1] caste background (Mendelson and Vicziany 1998 p. 203; Dalrymple 1999 p. 10). For the new Hindu nationalism is populist and pan-Hindu, not Brahminically dominated (that is, by the traditional priestly caste). Although this process is complex and also owes much to the rise of an independent *dalit*-based political movement, such a change cannot be attributed simply to government positive discrimination in favour of scheduled castes in education and employment. Decades of this had not produced the change in composition of political leaders, especially in the North. Second, political campaigning now actively seeks to engage with a much wider constituency across the electorate (Rajagopal 2001 p. 279).

Yet arguably the price to pay for this participation has been increased 'confusion' (ibid.) in political life and a lowering of the quality of public discussion. On the specific question of political violence, although Rajagopal reports some appalling incidents connected to the rise of the BJP, he also argues that 'the level of communal violence under a BJP government has been lower than that under Congress' (p. 280). On the deterioration of political debate, what has happened in India seems similar to the parallel impact of television on politics in America. This has involved more commercially oriented campaigns focusing on simple and emotive messages communicable by the televisual media and shallower support for political parties leading to intensified competition for floating voters (Mayhew 1997). The main difference, however, is that the induction into the televisual age has been accompanied by an increased circulation of religious discourse and symbols, a phenomenon that Rajagopal argues is likely to outlast the perhaps temporary success of the BJP, whose support is based on a fragile coalition of deeply divided groups. Thus he concludes:

> Even in the absence of Hindu nationalist domination then, we may have in India a
> Hinduized visual regime, evidenced for example in commodity consumption in daily life,
> acting as a kind of lower-order claim than national identity and continuing to have force in

politics, albeit of a more dispersed, subtle and less confrontational kind, in a kind of capacitance effect whereby social energy may be accumulated and stored [like electric charge] via allegiance to such images, to be put to use at some future moment, though in ways that would be hard to predict. (2001 p. 283)

Thus contemporary empirical public spheres are a long way from the Habermasian 'ideal speech situation'; yet they can become more inclusive than the bourgeois public sphere on which Habermas modelled his ideal concept ever was. In this situation, what is needed are practical ways to make contemporary public spheres more able to sustain and develop reasoned discussion. It is to such suggestions that we turn next.

7. On Democratizing Empirical Public Spheres

Leon Mayhew (1997) offers an account of the 'New Public' of multimedia and professional communication which seeks to chart a course between an idealized picture of public discourse that risks irrelevance to social analysis and a realism that reduces the public sphere to the strategic action of power politics. Although his focus is on political communication, predominantly in America, is narrower than civil society or the public sphere, his rehabilitation of rhetoric and concept of 'forums for the redemption of rhetorical tokens' is highly relevant to our concerns. Against Habermas he seeks to rehabilitate rhetoric as a social practice which can enhance participation: 'Rhetoric is not merely the instrumental, not just a way of tricking your opponents with a flow of words, but a means of entering public life. Rhetoric integrates culture and eloquence by providing life enhancing vocabularies for social participation' (1997 p. 35). Rhetoric serves as a kind of shorthand because time, resources and space for argument are limited. As such, rhetoric relies on trust, trust that behind rhetorical 'tokens' lie arguments which could redeemed if necessary. Inflated rhetoric, based on unrealistic claims which cannot be redeemed, undermines such trust and leads to disillusionment with political institutions, decline in participation, apathy and resentment. To counter this problem, public forums for the redemption of rhetorical tokens are needed: 'From a sociological standpoint, the public sphere does not depend on the unrealistic notion that rhetoric can be banished in favor of fully rational discourse on all issues at all times, but on the institutionalization of forums for the redemption of rhetorical tokens' (p. 15). Mayhew identifies several features of the New Public that serve to dissociate public deliberation from the structure of social life. These include the use of dissociated symbols which bear only weak ties to issues of public policy, techniques such as 'narrowcasting', or targeting influential groups and avoiding wider public debate, 'spin', in the sense of 'strategic rhetorical devices to avoid answering questions directly' and plain one-sided communication (p. 237). They also include the commercialization of political campaigning, the cost of television access, the compression of messages in this medium and the use of negative campaigning. Bearing in mind our earlier discussions, the differentiation of public space and the fragmentation of audiences must also be considered, even though the same trends simultaneously enhance the possibility the presentation of diverse perspectives.

As counter-trends, Mayhew identifies a variety of 'deliberative forums for communicative redemption' (ibid. p. 256) which have developed in America – milieux where the rhetorical tokens of civic leaders can be redeemed. He distinguishes 'forums', where more than one standpoint is represented, from 'platforms', where a single position dominates. He further distinguishes between diffuse, third-party and citizen forums and between moderated or indirect and direct debate. Diffuse forums provide a good opportunity for broad participation, but the lack of constraints makes it easy for leaders to evade demands for the redemption of tokens. Third-party forums are organized by independent groups and tend to be characterized by an opportunity for different sides to present their views, together with critical comment by a third party. Standard newspaper articles often follow this format. Citizen forums enable the general public to quiz leaders, and have multiplied with the proliferation of talk shows in recent years. The fact that the questioners are not known to the public arguably facilitates concentration on the quality of argument rather than the prestige of the antagonist, but many talk shows narrowcast to a particular constituency or focus on issues of little relevance to public policy. Indirect debate interposes a third-party questioner between antagonists, typified by American presidential debates. Direct debate is favoured by most of the American public but resisted by candidates, presumably because indirect debate means they can avoid persistent awkward questions from actual antagonists.

Mayhew also mentions the work of organizations like the Harwood Group and National Issues Forum, which aim to foster effective citizenship by providing training in public deliberation. But while such groups show that people are keen to reconnect with public issues and work together, there is little evidence that such groups are effective in reconnecting larger forums in the political system. However, as we have already indicated, Castells's (1997a p. 50) report of work in cities in Brazil and Holland provides some evidence of what can be achieved at this level through citizen consultation and local self-management schemes that make use of electronic communications media.

Again in an American context, Barber (1998) recommends actions that could be taken to improve public communication and participation. In addition to ideas we have already discussed, he highlights: the need to recreate and develop new forms of public space lost with the spread of shopping malls and fear of inner city violence; 'domesticating and democratizing' production and consumption and hence addressing some of the economic routes of disenfranchisement; encouraging voluntary work; and cultivating participation in the arts and humanities. While some trends he addresses (for example malls and gated communities) have gone further in America than in Europe, they are also of broader relevance – the trend of the middle classes to insulate themselves from the poor of their own society is a widespread if not universal phenomenon.

How does religion articulate with these problems and proposals? One of the strengths of some traditional religious groupings as a social forum – for example the parish – has been that they bring together a range of people who would have little to do with each other otherwise in increasingly differentiated societies. Yet with the shift of religion towards a more voluntary basis as part of the differentiation process has been to weaken this mixing effect. For example, in an American context Farnsley (2000) points to the flaw in government plans to channel aid to inner-city areas via local churches because the congregations of these churches are often no longer local residents. As in the rest of life, many Americans have become religious commuters. Certainly, religions in civil society are not in a position to address major economic and political causes of global disenfranchisement in an independent capacity, which is why these important issues have not been a major focal point of discussion here. Yet religions can and do spearhead campaigns on specific issues, for example the Jubilee campaign for Third World debt relief led by evangelical Christian churches in Britain. We have already seen (following Gill 1999, in Chapter 3) that British churches make a disproportionate contribution to the civic-oriented voluntary sector. Nor does the decreasing relationship between religious affiliation and locality or the increasing connection between religion and identity mean that all the strength of religion in cutting across social barriers has been dissipated. As Beyer (1992) concludes in the context of religion and environmental activism:

> The characteristic disadvantages of religion vis-à-vis other systems, rooted as they are in the very nature of religious communication [that is, lack of specialization and instrumental orientation], point to a different, more indirect way of making its influence felt in global society. ... [R]eligion can offer significant organizational, ideological and motivational resources which primarily religious, but also non-religious, people can use to conceptualize 'residual' problems and mobilize to deal with them. (p. 13)

8. Conclusion

The first two chapters sought to develop an understanding of the relationship between the global process of modernization and religion, against the background of the increasingly challenged view (secularization) that the advance of the former corrodes the vitality and social significance of the latter. It was argued that in the absence of a close identification between the state, ruling élites and religion, religion seems in most cases well able to adapt to modernization, although its characteristic social forms and relationship to social systems change. In particular, religion as discourse comes to predominate over religious institutions, and religions either functionalize within or operate at the interstices of dominant functional systems. The latter position in particular enables religions to form the ideological basis of social movements critical of dominant modes of globalization.

This sketch of the possible configurations of religion in modernity then formed the basis for discussion of how religion might be thought to function within modern civil societies and public spheres. To develop this discussion, however, it was necessary to develop an understanding of these constructs themselves, since they are hotly contested concepts. A distinction was made between normative and empirical concepts to facilitate their use in the analysis of particular cases, the need for openness to cultural variations was stressed, and both concepts were located in the context of a larger theory of democratization. In particular in this chapter the idea of multiple public spheres was developed and potentials and pitfalls for public communication in globalizing societies was assessed. This was then developed first with particular reference to the creation of a national public in India through the televisual dissemination of a religious epic, and then to ideas and efforts to revive and develop public spheres in the United States.

However, we have not yet addressed directly the cross-cultural legitimation of the normative concepts of civil society, the public sphere, or indeed democracy, beyond their use as analytic comparative tools. Yet the very idea of a liberal society to which these concepts refer is a contested one in the contemporary world. It is therefore to the normative justification of these concepts that the next chapter is devoted. In order to develop the argument in a cross-cultural context we shall, in addition to developing general arguments, describe and analyse relevant debates and socio-political arrangements in Muslim majority societies. Thus as well as advancing a normative argument, the chapter will provide some substantive background relevant to Muslim communities in each of the case studies in Part II of the book, but most especially to Egypt, the only Muslim majority society considered.

Note

1 For a discussion of the difficulties of terminology in referring to these groups see Mendelson and Vicziany (1998 pp. 2–5).

Chapter 5

Rethinking Liberalism and Rights

[T]he problem of political liberalism is: how is it possible that there may exist over time a stable and just society of free and equal citizens profoundly divided by reasonable religious, philosophical and moral doctrines? (Rawls 1993 p. xxv)

Political liberalism ... is indivisible. It will either prevail worldwide, or it will have to be defended by non-discursive action. (Binder 1988 p. 1)

To believe one can deal with issues of rights while neglecting religion is to lose power to deal with most human beings. To believe one can deal with them from some supposed neutral point above the religious fray, for example in the name of some secular Enlightened republicanism, is to show unawareness that the religions of the world regard Enlightenment reasoners to be one more set of competitors on the religious scene. (Marty, in Witte and van der Vyver 1996 p. 15)

1. Introduction

If religion is playing new roles in modern, globalizing societies, operating in dispersed form as discourse cut loose from traditional sources of authority, what implications does this have for traditions of political philosophy based on a model of church-state relations derived from early modern Europe? The vision outlined by John Rawls in the first quotation specifies political liberalism in the form of a quest – a never-ending quest to find the social and political arrangements that will best support and help to create the kind of society Rawls describes. This vision grew from the religious strife of early modern Europe, but in contexts where descent from European societies is not claimed, or is in some way problematic, it may have very different cultural resonances.

How applicable are liberal political traditions in other cultural contexts, for example in Muslim majority societies, given their association with colonial history and contemporary geo-political relations? In view of such considerations, is it possible, in the way that we have argued that civil society and the public sphere need be reconceptualized to reflect a diversity of societies and their interconnection, that the political philosophy that provides the normative underpinning for these concepts should also be reformulated? In particular, the discourse of human rights is central to liberalism but does not go unchallenged, especially in the Muslim world and in non-Muslim Asian societies (Mayer 1995). It is therefore important that human rights discourse is both articulated and legitimated within non-Western cultural milieux, including religious discourses, as the third quotation indicates.

This chapter begins by examining how liberal thinkers have argued that contemporary societies should respond to the presence of public religion, at a time when their populations are becoming increasingly religiously diverse and global interaction more intense. It should be noted that the kind of diversity these predominantly American and Canadian thinkers envisage is one in which the majority is presumed to be liberal and the challenge of diversity springs from illiberal (or at least non-liberal) minorities. These include indigenous groups (Inuit, Native Americans), long-established communities (Amish, Haredim and so on) and recent immigrants (for example orthodox Muslims). They do not address contexts where liberalism is a minority tradition.

However, the work of Leonard Binder, author of the second quotation above, is an important exception to this. He takes as the focus of his study 'the major states of the Middle East', Muslim majority societies where liberalism is a minority tradition and seeks to examine the case that can be made for the promotion of political liberalism here. He argues that 'we live in a single world of meaning and experience and that recognition of this … unity is the foundation of political liberalism' (p. 20). On this basis he attacks the appropriation of the critique of orientalism by experts in development studies to justify cultural relativism: the view that 'culture areas are unique and therefore beyond the reach of any general paradigm' (ibid. p. 21). Taken to its logical conclusion, such a position would preclude the advocacy of human rights across 'cultural areas'. For this reason the final part of this chapter is concerned to develop a concept of human rights that can engage with cultural diversity yet upholds the universality of basic rights, in accordance with our concept of civil society as stabilized by these.

Of particular relevance to our concern with Islam and civil society is Binder's view that the weakness of secular ideologies means that the only realistic prospect for the advancement of political liberalism in this region is an Islamic liberalism. He therefore sets out to map the contours of such a hybrid, seeking its roots in Islamic political thought, including that of Abd al-Raziq, Sayyid Qutb, Tariq al-Bishri and Zaki Nagib Mahmud. Readers with an acquaintance with these thinkers may well be surprised at the inclusion of Qutb, whose work has also been the inspiration of the political violence of the most militant Islamists. None the less, Binder argues that Qutb's 'central themes of aesthetics and consciousness indicate that it is anything but a scripturalist reflex' and hence 'may be helpful in altering the popular conception of the balance between scriptural and nonscriptural elements in Islam' (p. 20).

While we support Binder's raising of the question of political liberalism in the Islamic Middle East, welcome his challenge to relativism in area studies and find his reading of Islamic political thought provocative and productive, we follow a different strategy here, one that is more consistent with our focus on empirical civil society and seeks to support this. Therefore, after considering the arguments concerning cultural diversity within Western liberalism, we address the Muslim majority context in the following way. First, we describe differences between Muslim liberals and Islamists over the scope of *sharia* (Islamic law), *ijtihad* (new interpretation) and the form of government legitimized by Islam, especially the idea of an Islamic state and *shura* (consultation) as the basis for democracy. We then examine the diversity of

Muslim normative perspectives on human rights and seek to develop an argument for their universality. This focus on human rights is justified on two grounds. First, the normative concept of civil society developed requires that the institutionalization of the lifeworld that forms it is stabilized by basic rights, and we seek to give this a normative grounding. Second, concern about Islam and civil society in the West focuses on issues of human rights, so this relationship is crucial for assessing the prospects for an Islamic civil society.

2. Liberalism, Religion and the Return to 'Classical Liberalism'

The reason for the centrality of liberalism to this chapter on the normative justification of cross-cultural conceptions of civil society is its promise to provide just and rational means by which people of diverse commitments can peaceably live together as equals. For this reason, advocates of liberalism have claimed that it is *the* form of political philosophy that, if consistently applied, will yield the most tolerant social and political arrangements. Furthermore, it claims to be a pragmatic philosophy, so that, unlike various religious philosophies which might claim to be most tolerant if certain ideal conditions are met, liberalism recognizes in its most basis formulation the diversity of human opinion and therefore claims to be realistically applicable. Hence, as Chaplin (1993 p. 32) writes, 'Liberal pronouncements lead us to expect that liberalism will generally be more tolerant than any other theory'. The aim of this section is to assess this claim. Liberalism developed alongside structural modernization (urbanization, industrialization, collapse of traditional social stratification), conditions which now apply worldwide. Arguably, this historic genesis gives it an advantage over rival normative claims to structure the integration of diverse groups within modern societies. For example, some Muslims have claimed that an Islamic system which gives Christian and Jewish peoples the status of *ahl al-dhimma* ('protected subjects') would be superior in practice to liberal arrangements: 'I state that we [the Islamists] will never treat the Christians and Jews … in the same way as their governments treat the Muslim minorities in the homelands where they are in the majority' (Zainab al-Ghazali, leader of the Muslim Sisters in Egypt, quoted in Ayubi 1991 p. 53). Indeed, it may rightly be claimed that in the Middle Ages the Ottoman Empire provided a more tolerant system than that of medieval Christendom, judged by the treatment of religious minorities in each (ibid. pp. 52–3). However, in the Ottoman *millet* system that was the major historical institutionalization of this system, Jews and Christians had a protected but subordinate status. This was not a system of equal citizenship. Hence:

> The problem is, of course, that non-Muslim groups living in modern Muslim societies may not find sufficient reassurance in a formula that was superior several centuries ago. … This formula, which was so noble in the Middle Ages, does not seem compatible with the egalitarian achievements of the latter part of the twentieth century (p. 52).

Furthermore, al-Ghazali engages in a denial of history when she implies that historic religious minorities in Muslim majority societies in some sense belong to the governments of Christian and Jewish majority societies. As Fahd al-Fanik, a Jordanian Christian responds, 'we do not accept belonging to a foreigner since we are pure established Arabs (*aqhah*) who lived here before the Islamic conquest' (p. 53).

Indeed, some Muslim scholars have argued from within Islamic jurisprudence (*fiqh*) for recognition of the full citizenship of non-Muslims (p. 52) and these arguments are important for the development of a rights-supportive culture in Muslim majority contexts. But the fact remains that liberalism is the political philosophy that has made equality between citizens, individual liberty and tolerance of diversity most central to its project. Furthermore, it is not a coincidence that the liberal tradition first emerged in early modern Western Europe, but this is not because there is anything inherently tolerant about the Western tradition. Rather, as was argued in Chapter 2, it was here that modern functional systems first eroded the social stratification systems of previous world empires, with the result that collective difference could no longer be resolved by social stratification, as it was in the Ottoman *millet* system or in medieval Christendom. Another solution was needed. Yet as differentiation and globalization develop, including new trends towards de-differentiation and the re-emergence of public religions, the liberal solution is showing signs of strain. One particularly problematic area is that of religion, whose location in the social system has diversified since the early formulations of liberalism.

The idea that religion, if allowed to predominate in the political arena, is prone to disrupt civic peace, was a basic tenet of the liberal tradition. Indeed, it has been argued that the European nation state was created as a solution to religious conflict: 'liberalism was born out of religious conflict and the attempt to tame it by accommodating it within the nation state. The case for religious toleration was central to its development' (Lukes 1991 p. 17). This idea is often repeated in contemporary liberal texts and could even be described as a major feature of the sacred landscape of liberalism (Asad 1993, 1999). Mary Midgely (1989) tells the story:

> For a long time, Catholics and Protestants shared the view that only one of their creeds could survive. This meant that one had to destroy the other and they differed only on which one it should be. … Certain people, however, such as Montaigne and Locke, saw a possibility of approaching the problem differently, so that this kind of question would not arise. They proposed finding a way to view this disagreement as a normal one, containable within the scope of a decent human life. Their work made it possible for toleration to be developed without the fearful sense of betrayal which it had seemed at first to involve. (p. 242)

Jeffrey Stout (1989) expands on this narrative by contrasting theological vocabularies with the new secular ones, in terms of their ability to handle disputes concerning the common good:

> Might it be that theology got into trouble with the intellectuals largely because it was unable to provide a vocabulary for debating and deciding matters pertaining to the common good without resort to violence? Could it be that the distinctive vocabularies of modern politics and ethics – the languages of human rights, of Benthamite utility, of respect for persons and so on – owe their existence in part to a complicated history of attempts to minimise the unhappy consequences of religious conflict? (p. 222)

These new secular vocabularies sought to overcome the divisiveness of religious vocabularies through the means of the universal human subject, the management of human interests through the mechanism of the market and the discipline of the sovereign nation-state. However, for classical liberalism this did not imply the exclusion of religion from public life. Rather, at least in the British and American (as opposed to French) contexts, religion was seen as the foundation of personal morality, so that it is appropriate for the state to ensure that this foundation is maintained in good order.

Thus Galston (1991) argues that classical liberal theories recognized the importance of a foundation of moral consensus rooted in shared culture and were prepared to take steps to safeguard it when it appeared to be threatened (pp. 259–63). Public religion played an important part in this shared culture. Examining Locke's arguments for religious toleration, Galston finds that Locke was opposed to coercion in religion, but not to persuasive public discourse on religious matters and certainly not on moral matters. Locke believed that while religious knowledge could only be verified eschatologically – no human court could decide – rational knowledge of morality was possible. Hence for Locke toleration did not mean the inviolability of the individual conscience; civic peace was of paramount importance. On this basis Galston argues that 'conceptions of … the social role of religion can be defined which are at once faithful to liberal principles and far more hospitable to moral and religious traditionalism than is the understanding that dominates contemporary liberal theory' (p. 241). However, the classical liberal understanding of religion and society was not to last. Gray (1986) sees the origins of a more contemporary liberal attitude to religion and culture in J. S. Mill. With Mill, the range of matters held to be beyond rational arbitration extends from the religious to the moral sphere: hence the state comes to be seen less as a guardian of public morality and more as a morally neutral arbitrator between conflicting parties. This claim to neutrality, together with the competence to enforce its will through the state, leads to the claim that liberalism provides the most effective guarantee of toleration, in both religious and moral matters. However, the importance of culture in sustaining morality is still recognized by Mill. It is only with the discrediting of conceptions of collective cultural difference after the Second World War that this recognition ceases (Kymlicka 1995 pp. 57–8). Thus the attenuation of the idea that religion and other forms of sociality and shared culture play an important role in the maintenance of morality has been a gradual and, in its advanced form, comparatively recent development in liberalism.

Thus, in a contemporary context in which the viability, universality and neutrality of liberalism have all been challenged, some liberal thinkers have dug back into liberal tradition and sought to revive a more realistic if less ambitious liberal project from liberalism's classical phase, one more attuned to the diversity of contemporary Western public cultures (Gray 1986; Galston 1991). However, there are some difficulties with this proposal. Classical liberalism was patriarchal, bestowing rights upon men rather than humanity and presuming a particular patriarchal household pattern in common with traditional forms of religion. Furthermore, as Dorrien (1990 p. 3) argues, in classical liberalism property rights were given priority over rights to democratic self-government. Is it possible selectively to retrieve the classical liberal project without these less palatable features? Perhaps, but there is another problem. If religion was allowed a greater role in classical models of liberalism, it was Western Christianity which was seen as the archetypal form of religion in this period. In what sense can public religion be understood to undergird public morality when the forms of public religion are radically diverse?

As we have seen, reasonable answers have been given to this question. Gill (1992), for example, argues that the form of Christianity, Judaism and Islam as worshipping communities based around an ethic of care for others provides such an undergirding. Sacks (1990) and Küng (1991) argue along similar lines for a broad coalition of people of faith. These arguments are fine from an empirical perspective – in Chapter 3 we used them to suggest how such 'communities of virtue' can support civil society and considered ways that their social influence (or lack of it) can be assessed. But if we are looking for a common normative argument for public morality, working from common premises to agreed conclusions, such arguments face the problem that a section of secular opinion simply rejects the idea of the necessity of any kind of religious basis for public morality. Perhaps, then, it is not possible to have a common normative argument for public morality in this sense. We saw in Chapter 3 how the French state's attempts to construct one, 'France is a community of destiny', do not reflect the empirical diversity of French society.

But another possibility is a post-foundational structure of argumentation that allows that starting with different premises people may arrive at common conclusions. As we saw in Chapter 4, MacIntyre provides a framework for seeing how such a process can be conceived without sliding into relativism. But here we shall focus first on John Rawls, whose developing position is indicative of the transformation – and difficulties facing – the contemporary liberal tradition.

3. John Rawls: from Comprehensive to Political Liberalism

Just as Chapter 3 showed the difficulties of returning to the seventeenth- and eighteenth-century concept of civil society under contemporary conditions of social differentiation, so we have seen that a return to classical liberalism is not a straightforward solution to problems of public religion and cultural diversity in contemporary societies. However, the notion that a public role for religion is not necessarily alien to liberal tradition is a welcome insight in contexts where more militantly secular forms of liberalism and illiberal forms of public religion tend to receive most attention. Rawls represents an alternative and influential liberal trajectory, though one that has changed direction over the years, shifting from a comprehensive and universalist conception to a political one tied to democratic culture, in which the concept of autonomy takes centre stage, as it does for other modern liberal theorists (Kymlicka 1995; Raz 1986). As we shall see below, Charles Taylor's turn to the collectivist strain in the counter-Enlightenment tradition of modernity represents a third possible development of the liberal tradition.

In the 1980s and 1990s North American political philosophy increasingly engaged with issues of cultural diversity (Rawls 1993; Kymlicka 1995; Galston

1991). Through dialogue with Habermas, the scope of this debate has extended theoretically to engage with continental European critical theory, and politically and culturally with Western European issues, such as the controversy over political asylum in Germany (Habermas 1993; Habermas in Taylor 1994). In this debate, one of the key issues addressed has been the limits of toleration of illiberal minorities in liberal societies. Although the focus of this debate is on ethnicity and culture, it also has relevance for the public recognition of religion and for the integration of public religion in contemporary societies. This is partly because the description 'illiberal minority' might be said to fit the situation of some religious groups in North America and Western Europe and partly because, as we have seen, religion may become the focus of the mobilization of ethnic or cultural identity.

This new awareness of cultural difference has coincided with an attack within Western philosophy on foundationalism, as we saw with MacIntyre's diagnosis of the 'failure of the Enlightenment project' in Chapter 3. Whether as a result of recognition of cultural diversity or philosophical attack, Rawls has backed down on claims of liberalism's universal validity. Thus in *A Theory of Justice* (1973) he sought to justify liberalism on universal rational grounds, but by 1985 he had abandoned this attempt:

> By contrast with liberalism as a comprehensive moral doctrine, justice as fairness tries to present a conception of political justice rooted in the basic intuitive ideas found in the public culture of a constitutional democracy. We conjecture that these ideas are likely to be affirmed by each of the comprehensive moral doctrines influential in a reasonably just democratic society. Thus justice as fairness seeks to identify the kernel of an overlapping consensus, that is, the shared intuitive ideas which when worked up into a political conception of justice turn out to be sufficient to underwrite a just constitutional regime. This is the most we can expect, nor do we need more. (1985 pp. 246–7)

In other words, like Richard Rorty (1979, 1982), Rawls shifts the justification of liberalism to a 'communitarian' ground (its validity is restricted to a specific community), that of existing consensus in 'reasonably just democratic societies'. Another part of the development of Rawls's argument is a reduction in the scope of the liberalism he seeks to defend. Whereas previously he had seen liberalism as *the* comprehensive moral doctrine of 'the well-ordered society', he now recognizes it to be just one among many possible comprehensive doctrines present:

> The serious problem I have in mind concerns the unrealistic idea of a well-ordered society as it appears in *Theory*. An essential feature of a well-ordered society associated with justice as fairness is that all citizens endorse this conception on the basis of what I now call a comprehensive philosophical doctrine. ... Now the serious problem is this. A modern democratic society is characterized not simply by a pluralism of comprehensive religious, philosophical and moral doctrines but by a pluralism of incompatible yet reasonable comprehensive doctrines. No one of these doctrines is affirmed by citizens generally. (1993 p. xxi)

Therefore, instead of developing this comprehensive doctrine, he seeks to develop a political liberalism that deliberately restricts itself in scope to the political arena, leaving aside metaphysical questions (pp. xxvi – xxviii). Such a political conception of 'justice as fairness' does not, according to Rawls, seek to continue 'the Enlightenment project' of justifying morality on universal rational grounds (MacIntyre 1985 pp. 36–78; Rawls 1993 p. xviii). Hence he throws down the gauntlet to those like MacIntyre who reject liberalism as the outgrowth of this project.

It will be argued here that Rawls's recognition that there is a range of 'reasonable comprehensive doctrines' is welcome, permitting religious and secular traditions to be recognized as equal participants in a rational conversation, as well as recognizing that agreement secured on such a basis is likely to be more stable than that imposed from a secularist perspective (Rawls 1985 p. 250). However, it will also be contended that the basis on which he argues that these perspectives will come together in an overlapping consensus to support the principles of political liberalism – and specifically the concept of 'justice as fairness' – is inadequate. Instead, a stronger argument needs to – and can – be made for something like Rawls's political liberalism. By 'something like' we mean a method of differentiating between comprehensive and political conceptions of the good, which seeks on this basis ways of developing sufficient consensus on the latter to enable peaceful coexistence between people profoundly divided by the former. How might such an argument proceed?

First, negatively, the idea of pre-existing consensus within 'well-ordered societies' on a political conception of the good will be shown to fail with respect both to agreement within Western constitutional democracies and to sustaining any kind of a categorial division between these and non-Western societies. It therefore needs to be replaced. Second, it will be argued that its replacement is important, because liberalism both as a philosophy and as a set of institutions developed specifically to deal with the problems of pluralism has an important contribution to make to enabling peaceful coexistence in today's globally interconnected and culturally fractured world. Third, fortunately, such an argument is in fact available and will be developed from MacIntyre's theory of the interaction between traditions of enquiry. Let us begin by outlining some key features of Rawls's position.

Rawls (1993) tells a similar story to Midgely, Stout and Gray above in stressing the origins of liberalism as a response to endemic religious strife in early modern Europe (pp. xxi-xxv). He contrasts ancient Greek civic religion with medieval Christianity (he means Catholicism) and the post-Reformation Catholic and Protestant Churches, arguing that is the character of the latter which gave rise to the modern problem of justice: 'What the ancient world did not know of was the clash between salvationist, creedal and expansionist religions. That is a phenomenon new to historical experience, a possibility realized by the Reformation (p. xxv). However, this is a very parochial view. For example, salvationist, creedal and expansionist religions had already confronted one another in the Middle East and across North Africa since the eighth century, when Islam first expanded beyond the Arabian Peninsula into what had previously been Byzantine territory. They did so again during the Crusades. Rather, what is distinctive about the modern problem of justice is that modern functional systems have eroded the social stratification systems of previous world empires, with the result that collective difference can no longer be resolved by stratification, as in the Ottoman *millet* system. Rawls's treatment of this issue suggests that his position is likely to have difficulty accommodating the need to negotiate an overlapping consensus on an intercultural basis.

In describing comprehensive liberalism, Rawls explains how Hume and Kant, as key founders of the liberal tradition, sought to 'establish a basis of moral knowledge independent of ecclesiastical authority and available to the ordinary and conscientious person' (p. xxvi). To do so, they sought to answer three basic questions:

> Is the knowledge or awareness of how we are to act directly accessible only to some, or to a few (the clergy, say), or is it accessible to every person who is normally reasonable and conscientious?
>
> Again, is the moral order required of us derived from an external source, say from an order of values in God's intellect, or does it arise in some way from human nature itself (either from reason, feeling or a combination of both), together with the requirements of our living together in society?
>
> Finally, we must be persuaded or compelled to bring ourselves into line with the requirements of our duties and obligations by some external motivation, say, by divine sanctions or by those of the state; or are we so constituted that we have in our nature sufficient motives to lead us to act as we ought without the need of external threats and inducements? (pp. xxvi-xxvii)

Comprehensive liberalism opts for some form of the second alternative in each case. Given the way that religion is positioned in these dichotomies, it is clear that any advocacy of religion as an important basis for public morality is likely to meet with opposition from advocates of a comprehensive liberalism. However, it should also be noted that the diversity of religion and in particular the diverse impact of modernization processes on religious traditions, means that religious responses to these questions are by no means exclusively of the former kind.

Many advocates of political Islam, for example, are emphatic in their rejection of the authority of the *ulema* and insist that each individual is capable of understanding the Qur'an for themselves. We have seen that contemporary Catholicism also positively encourages post-conventional moral reasoning, which requires the individual to think for themselves rather than blindly submit to tradition (Casanova 1994). Furthermore, in the Christian tradition, natural theology has long insisted that moral knowledge is part of both human nature and the natural order and this has its historic parallel in Islam in the tradition of the Mutazilites. In contemporary Islam, broadly 'liberal' exegetes hold that the Qur'an and *sunna* (traditions about the Prophet) do not legislate in detail, but rather that both specific laws and the form of government are matters for the community to decide upon according to circumstance. Such views are not easily categorized as either the first or second kind of answer to the second question.

Regarding the third question, in dialogue or polemic with Christians, Muslims often make the point that Islam does not emphasize the fallen nature of humanity, but rather holds that the individual is capable of following the 'straight path'. In other words, human nature can provide sufficient motives to enable us to act as we should. Christians may respond that while salvation requires the grace of God and human striving is insufficient, this is not the same as external compulsion to conform, but rather, on the contrary, requires an inner transformation. It is true that the Christian tradition, like the Islamic tradition, has sanctioned the use of external coercion to prevent vice, but recognition of this should not be allowed to negate the importance of inner motivation. It is also the case that issues such as the *hadd* penalties (punishments for certain crimes specified in the Qur'an) support the view that Islam is best characterized by the first response to the third question. None the less, the complexity of religious responses to these questions reinforces the view that contemporary religions cannot be straightforwardly characterized as authoritarian, in contrast to comprehensive liberalism's tolerant individualism.

Political liberalism, however, does not hold that comprehensive liberalism should prevail in contemporary societies. Instead, it aims to be impartial with respect to comprehensive doctrines, arguing only that the second form of answer should prevail in the political sphere (Rawls 1993 pp. xxvii–xxviii). Rawls's sense of 'political' here is a broad one, incorporating the state, political society and civil society. It is particularly concerned with the process of 'public justification': 'The aim of political liberalism is to uncover the conditions of the possibility of a reasonable public basis of justification on fundamental political questions' (p. xix). In this respect, it resembles Habermas's normative concept of the public sphere (Chapter 4). This being the case, the same problem arises as for the Habermasian public sphere described above – for as Benhabib (1992b) has shown with respect to gender and Asad (1999 p. 181) with respect to religion, the boundaries and nature of 'publicness' are continually subject to contestation and change. How, then, does Rawls propose to construct the public sphere in such a way as to exclude the influence of comprehensive doctrines? Rawls (1985) legitimates his political conception of liberalism using the idea of an overlapping consensus: individuals and communities may affirm the concept on a range of grounds, that is, with reference to different comprehensive doctrines (p. 250).

The particular political conception of liberalism that Rawls argues can be supported by an overlapping consensus in well-ordered or democratic societies is one of 'justice as fairness'. Of what does this consist? The 'overarching fundamental intuitive idea' of justice as fairness is 'that of a society as a fair system of cooperation between free and equal persons' (p. 231). This is held to be 'one of the basic intuitive ideas … implicit in the public culture of a democratic society' (ibid.). The idea of justice as fairness further proposes 'two principles of justice to serve as guidelines on how basic institutions are to realize the values of liberty and equality' (p. 227). Rawls presents these as a framework within which to adjudicate between two competing tendencies in the democratic tradition. The first, following Locke, stresses individual liberties, the second, following Rousseau, the virtues of political participation. These principles are:

1. Each person has an equal right to a fully adequate scheme of equal rights and basic liberties, which scheme is compatible with a similar scheme for all.
2. Social and economic inequalities are to satisfy two conditions: first, they must be attached to the offices and positions open to all under conditions of fair equality of opportunity; and second, they must be to the greatest benefit of the least advantaged members of society. (ibid.)

Rawls further asserts that this consensus is supported by all reasonable comprehensive doctrines in a democratic society (p. 250) and assumes that supporters of such doctrines will consent to exclude aspects of their visions of the good 'surplus' to justice as fairness from the public arena (p. 231).

However, there are at least three fundamental problems with his position. First, we shall argue that empirical evidence does not support Rawls's assertion of a consensus in favour of this conception of justice as fairness, even if public institutions in some societies do embody its values. Second, this might not be such a problem if Rawls could provide good reasons why supporters of comprehensive doctrines should accept their exclusion from the public sphere. However, as we shall see (following Kymlicka 1995), he does not. Third, even this would not matter so much if he offered a conceptual framework that could explain how such a consensus might be developed. However, he does not. Instead, he writes of the philosopher's role as being to 'collect such settled convictions such as the belief in religious toleration and the rejection of slavery and [to] try to organize the basic ideas and principles implicit in these convictions into a coherent conception of justice' (1985 p. 228). But in the absence of a pre-existing consensus, more is required than this: rather there is a need for public forums for deliberation (and hence consideration of the articulation between civil society and public spheres discussed in Chapters 3 and 4). There is also a need for a means of conceiving of the articulation of competing comprehensive theories, adherents of which may in practice not be easily persuaded to accept the private/public division that political liberalism requires.

Let us consider some relevant empirical evidence. First, as we noted in Chapter 3, even in societies with what might be described as advanced democratic cultures, such as the United States, Lanham and Forsythe (1994 pp. 245–6) argue that empirical studies show that 'many Americans do *not* hold attitudes compatible with international standards on civil and political rights, much less on economic and social rights'. Second, in the case of Eastern Europe, the increasing incorporation of Eastern European nations into the institutional frameworks of Western Europe and the liberal character of these institutions – in economic, political and civil terms – suggests that perhaps such a consensus might be thought to exist. Yet studies by anthropologists (Hann 1996, 1997) concerning civil society in these contexts raises doubts about this conclusion. Even a supposedly liberal institution such as the European Court of Human Rights (ECHR) recognizes that Europe lacks 'a uniform conception of the significance of religion in society' (*Otto-Preminger-Institut vs Austria* 1994 para. 56; Evans 1997), suggesting further caution on this point. Third, the latter judgement widens the scope of this reservation beyond Eastern Europe to Western Europe, since it was issued in relation to Austria. This point is reinforced by the Court's case law on Greece, which clearly shows that a communitarian conception of religion predominates and that this has by and large been supported by the Court (ibid.).

There therefore seems to be a disparity between the character of institutions and the attitudes of many citizens in Europe and America, and even doubts about the liberal character of some institutions, such as the ECHR. All this raises doubts about political philosophers' description of these societies as 'liberal' in any simple sense consistent with political liberalism and thus unsettles the philosophers' role as the collector of 'settled convictions'. The disparity between aspects of liberal institutions and popular opinion widens as we extend the scope of enquiry to the Middle East. Here there are deep fissures separating political élites responsible for crafting and maintaining political institutions, the developing middle classes and the mass of the poor (Arkhoun 1994).

None the less, Arab governments are signatory to international human rights agreements and human rights organizations have grass-roots movements in many Arab countries (Mayer 1995, Dwyer 1991). As we shall see, there is also a substantial body of opinion among Muslims both within and beyond the Muslim majority world that can appropriately be described as liberal (Ayubi 1991, Tibi 1998, Arkhoun 1994). Furthermore, we have already noted that there is evidence of vigorous public debate in some Muslim majority societies (for example Turkey, Indonesia, Egypt, Tunisia).

Taken together with the evidence presented relating to America and Europe, such evidence suggests that the liberal/illiberal distinction does not coincide conveniently either with nation-state or confessional boundaries. From this perspective, Western and Muslim majority societies are better seen within a common analytic framework, each characterized by varying relations between élite political attitudes, their institutional expression, the views of the majority of the populace and those of extremist groups who seek to impose their will by violence. Rawls provides no way of seeing how an overlapping consensus might emerge from this kind of diversity of opinion. Do other liberal theorists?

4. Kymlicka and Taylor: Cultural Membership and the Politics of Recognition

We begin with consideration of two further criticisms of Rawls's position by other liberal theorists. First, Kymlicka (1995) points to another problem with the idea of an overlapping consensus as the basis for political liberalism. He argues that Rawls's proposal that adherents to comprehensive doctrines other than liberalism will accept liberalism in the public sphere and consent to leave their doctrines at home, so to speak, is not just politically unrealistic but conceptually flawed. Given the centrality of individual autonomy to both comprehensive and political liberalism and the plain rejection of autonomy in the private sphere by some minority groups in America, Rawls faces a problem: 'The problem is to explain why anyone would accept the ideal of autonomy in political contexts unless they also accepted it more generally' (Kymlicka 1995 p. 160). Kymlicka uses legal cases involving two North American historic religious minorities (Hutterites and Amish) to argue that groups who reject autonomy in private life also tend to reject it in public contexts (pp. 161–2). Indeed, they do so for good reasons, since Kymlicka argues that the practice of autonomy is indivisible: 'Accepting the value of autonomy for political purposes enables its exercise in private life, an implication that will only be favoured by those who endorse autonomy as a general value' (p. 162). Thus the idea of autonomy in the public sphere is not likely to arise from a lifeworld that rejects it as a personal value, because autonomy in the private sphere and autonomy in the public sphere are both logically and socially related.

Second, Fitzmaurice (1993) criticizes Rawls's concepts of primary and secondary goods, which have undergone development between *A Theory of Justice* (1973) and *Political Liberalism* (1993). Initially, Rawls held that 'primary goods' are: 'goods which it is supposedly rational to want whatever one wants, because they provide the instrumentally necessary conditions for the achievement of any determinate conception of the good whatsoever and are equally useful in the pursuit of all' (Fitzmaurice 1993 p. 55). Examples include freedom of action and equality of opportunity. However, as Nagel (1978) has argued, such goods are not equally useful for the realization of all particular conceptions of the good. In particular, traditional, religiously based societies may fear that such 'goods' erode their sense of the common good. Thus increased individual choice may be seen to weaken extended family structures. For example, the Western practice of caring for the elderly in specialized institutions away from the family is frequently seen in Muslim majority societies as a clear example of the corruption of Western societies. The rationality presupposed by Rawls's theory is therefore that of a particular economic system and culture.

In the face of these kinds of criticisms Rawls has altered his justification of primary goods. As Fitzmaurice argues:

> He now acknowledges that the goodness of the primary goods derives not from their constituting the universal means to desire fulfilment, but from the fact that they provide the conditions under which the individual may form a conception of the good independently. (1993 p. 56)

In other words, for Rawls, the ability to choose one's conception of the good is the highest good; autonomy becomes the most highly valued virtue in Rawls's scheme. This, he further acknowledges, is a culturally specific value. Conversely, any system in which a conception of the good is substantially provided, or revealed, is excluded. Yet this retreat into cultural relativism does nothing to address the problem of groups both within and beyond Western societies who subscribe to the view that certain collective goods are more important than some aspects of individual autonomy.

Kymlicka's response to this is to argue that in order to form a conception of the good at all one must already be securely grounded in a societal culture (1995 pp. 82–93). Such societal cultures are the primary means of transmission of ways of understanding which enable us to comprehend our environment and our relationship to it and hence 'Understanding ... cultural narratives is a precondition of making intelligent judgements about how to live our lives' (1995 p. 83). Kymlicka also argues that some goods must be pursued collectively in order to be pursued at all. Since making intelligent judgements about how to live one's life requires that one be part of a culture, cultural membership is one of them. Thus although Rawls denies that cultural membership is a primary good, Kymlicka argues that this position is inconsistent. If autonomy is central to liberalism and autonomy depends on cultural membership, then cultural membership must be a primary good.

The implications of this are considerable: Kymlicka argues that recognition of cultural membership means that it deserves protection and support by the state, in the form of measures such as 'the public funding of schools, language rights, veto powers [and even] the re-drawing of political boundaries' (p. 155). Recognition of collective rights such as these may be a way of empowering individuals within cultural minority communities to exercise their autonomy, as well as drawing cultural minorities into a common discourse of rights, of which their collective rights are a recognized part. This therefore represents Kymlicka's response not only to problems in Rawls's account of primary goods, but also to the problem of the indivisibility of autonomy and to the problem of forming an overlapping consensus.

Thus Kymlicka moves decisively beyond Rawls. He not only recognizes that adherents of a variety of comprehensive doctrines other than liberalism can participate in rational debate about the terms of social cooperation, but also that there is a connection between cultural rootedness and the ability to exercise autonomy, and hence participate in such a debate. Habermas (1994a) makes a similar point when he writes: 'A correctly understood theory of rights requires a politics of recognition that *protects the integrity of the individual in the life contexts in which his or her identity is formed'* (p. 113, emphasis added). Such statements can help us to see how public reasoning to achieve an overlapping consensus might be reconceived as the articulation of diverse traditions of enquiry, including religious traditions, a concept we shall develop in our account of MacIntyre's work below.

Like Kymlicka, Charles Taylor (1994) also argues that cultural membership should be recognized as a primary good. Taylor's argument is developed as part of a much broader thesis on the way in which demands for recognition of cultural membership have come to be articulated in Western societies, seeking a historical explanation of the thesis that 'our identity is partly shaped by recognition or its absence, often by the misrecognition of others and so a person or group of people can suffer real damage, real distortion, if the people or society around them mirror back to them a demeaning or contemptible picture of themselves' (p. 25). He traces the origins of this concept of recognition to the breakdown of hierarchical relationships with the advent of modernity. The need for recognition of one's identity is not unique to modernity, but modernity has created conditions – in particular, differentiation and globalization – in which recognition is more likely to fail and thus it becomes a problem. Indeed, such recognition may then become a psychological need, on top of the need identified by Kymlicka for some kind of coherent cultural tradition within which choices become comprehensible.

Taylor extends the consequences of recognizing cultural membership as a primary good, arguing that such recognition implies a duty to ensure the survival of the culture within which choices are made:

> Where Kymlicka's interesting argument fails to recapture the actual demands made by the groups concerned – say Indian bands in Canada, or French-speaking Canadians – is with respect to their goal of survival. Kymlicka's reasoning is valid (perhaps) for *existing* people who find themselves trapped within a culture under pressure and can flourish within it or not at all. But it doesn't justify measures designed to ensure survival through indefinite

future generations. For the populations concerned, however, that is what is at stake. We need only think of the historical resonance of 'la survivance' among French Canadians. (p. 41, n. 16)

This imperative to cultural survival may clash with some individual rights to uniform treatment. Taylor argues that a liberal society should not abandon the fundamental rights enshrined in the liberal tradition – 'rights to life, liberty, due process, free speech, free practice of religion and so on' – in order to ensure cultural survival (p. 59). But in recent times, the list of 'liberties' has been greatly expanded by the process of constitutional review and these additional rights and freedoms *are* up for negotiation. Thus Taylor's model depends on a distinction between fundamental liberties and those that are important but revocable if public policy provides an adequate reason for doing so. In the case in question the 'adequate reason' is cultural survival: 'They [that is, forms of liberalism that recognize collective goals] are willing to weigh the importance of certain forms of uniform treatment against the importance of cultural survival and sometimes opt in favour of the latter' (p. 61). However, Taylor's argument here is rejected by Habermas (1994a), who voices an important criticism:

> The ecological perspective on species conservation cannot be transferred to cultures. Cultural heritages and the forms of life articulated in them normally reproduce themselves by convincing those whose personality structures they shape, that is, by motivating them to appropriate productively and continue the traditions. The constitutional state can make this hermeneutic achievement of cultural reproduction of life-worlds possible, but cannot guarantee it. (p. 130)

Taylor is also criticized by the anthropologist Baumann (1999 and above, Chapter 3), who argues that culture is essentialized and reified by Taylor: 'Multicultural society is not a patchwork of five or ten fixed cultural identities, but an elastic web of crosscutting and always mutually situational identifications' (p. 118). Of course, their different perceptions may in part mirror the different contexts in relation to which their ideas are formed, for example Kymlicka's Inuit who may well live in isolated cultural communities, in contrast to the urban cosmopolitan context on which Baumann reflects. Yet Baumann's point is well made and points to a tension between what observers of culture tend to see (culture as process) and what bearers of cultural identities tend to feel (culture as roots).

Thus, while there seems to be an emerging consensus amongst liberals of the importance of culture to self-formation, this consensus has its limitations and disintegrates further if pushed beyond the boundaries of professional philosophers. For while it maybe agreed that where a distinctive culture (including religion) forms part of a person's background that certain special measures may be justified to support the maintenance of that culture, there are none the less disagreements as to how far this should extend, especially in view of the malleability of culture in many contexts. None the less, the basic point remains that Rawls, Kymlicka, Taylor and Galston all begin to shift the liberal tradition towards a recognition of its own traditionality, a move endorsed also by Baumann, if I read him correctly. They thus move towards a position from which liberals can enter into negotiation with non-liberals, recognizing that both parties have a territory to defend, rather than assuming the neutrality of liberalism.

The following section seeks to build on this insight by developing an understanding of how such traditions with quite different concepts and values (the post-foundationalist condition described in Section 1) can arrive at shared understandings (the overlapping consensus). Indeed, it sets out to show that they can do so without the need for one tradition to absorb the other (assimilation), or conceding that there is no rational way to reach agreement (relativism), or claiming to discover some universal foundation (foundationalism).

Before proceeding, however, we need to consider some objections that can be made to MacIntyre's concept of tradition on which the argument relies, and to our use of it. In particular, the charge of reification is one that can be made, especially against the way in which we shall develop MacIntyre's concept in the next section. For MacIntyre develops an ideal-type of tradition which privileges intellectual enquiry but situates it firmly within culture. We suggest retaining this sense of the importance of locating intellectual enquiry within culture while applying the concept to cultural traditions that fail to meet MacIntyre's rather strict definition of what constitutes a tradition. There are thus two dangers: an over-differentiation of what is in fact a highly mixed cultural milieu, marshalling contemporary cultures into MacIntyre-style traditions or 'social cages', and then exaggerating the internal coherence of these traditions to conform to MacIntyre's ideal-type.

However, it is argued that the dangers of reification can be overcome by making a distinction between normative and empirical traditions, recognizing that reality is always more messy than the ideal-type. Furthermore, especially when considering religious traditions, which tend to see sustaining a coherent intellectual tradition as part of their core identity, it is suggested that the concept can shed particular light on intercultural encounters. Relevant examples are the integration of religious minorities within the civil societies of plural democracies and the encounter of liberal and Islamic ideas within the civil societies of Muslim majority cultures, few of which are currently democratic. MacIntyre's account of interaction between traditions suggests the possibility of meaningful exchange and mutual learning without compromising integrity.

It should be stressed that we are not offering a common syncretizing substantive theory which, if everyone subscribed to it, would end all conflict. Rather, its aim is meta-ethical rather than ethical – to show how shared reasoned agreement might be reached between rival traditions of enquiry, rather than to pre-empt the conclusion of discussions that have hardly begun.

5. MacIntyre on Traditions of Enquiry in Interaction

The main traditions on which MacIntyre has worked are 'traditions of meta-ethical reasoning which take as their subject ... the practical moral tradition of particular societies' (Turner 1990 p. 178). This emphasis on practical moral tradition is significant in challenging the distinction between facts and values embedded in much philosophical and social scientific discourse. Thus the 'facts' of minority cultures, including social organization (for example *biraderi, jati*) or material products (for example saris, *halal* food) are not neatly separable from 'values' or moral traditions; rather, practices enact convictions. For MacIntyre, the scope of tradition is not confined to practical moral discourse; instead, tradition is a holistic term that embraces all aspects of cultural production, from agriculture to music to metaphysics.

Thus MacIntyre (1985) develops a concept of 'traditioned reason':

> all reasoning takes place within the context of some traditional mode of thought, transcending through criticism and invention the limitations of what had hitherto been reasoned in that tradition; this is as true of modern physics as medieval logic. Moreover when a tradition is in good order it is always partially constituted by an argument about the goods the pursuit of which gives to that tradition its particular point and purpose. (pp. 221–2)

MacIntyre sees three recurrent phases in the normal life of a tradition (1988 p. 355). In the first, stable, phase the tradition is sustained without major challenges (though healthy tradition is always partially constituted by debate about the particular goods which give the tradition its purpose). The second phase is characterized by crisis; challenges internal or external to the tradition threaten its coherence and viability, established authorities are called into question – this is called an 'epistemological crisis' (1977 p. 455). The third phase is resolution of the crisis, which is achieved by satisfying three criteria (1988 p. 362). The reformulated tradition must: (i) be able to explain the reason for the crisis, (ii) show how it has resolved the conflict which caused the crisis and (iii) demonstrate that it can do this while retaining substantive continuity with the original tradition: '[s]ome core of shared belief, constitutive of allegiance to the tradition, must survive the rupture' (p. 356). An explanation or insight (or other cultural product) originating outside the tradition may become part of the transformed tradition as part of the process of resolving an epistemological crisis.

MacIntyre proposes that traditions develop in particular historical circumstances the practical rationalities that they develop in response to particular needs do not conform to some common extra-traditional standard; however, common principles of logic apply in each case.[1] Therefore, when two historic traditions interact, it is possible that participants in each can come to recognize that participants in the other tradition are reflecting on the same issues, defining 'the same' not by some external, universal standard, but by standards internal to the tradition in which the participant already stands, and by reference to common rules of logic (1988 p. 358).

MacIntyre's model cannot guarantee resolution between traditions, for it offers no standard external to particular traditions to which to appeal (beyond the presumption of the unity of truth discussed in Chapter 4, Section 5). Such standards can, we have already seen, always be exposed as some particular standard writ large. But, unlike the radical incommensurability of most postmodern positions that effectively abandon public space in favour of personal assertion, MacIntyre provides a way of making sense of interactions between traditions. Such sense is not guaranteed, but MacIntyre shows us how it can happen.

Interaction between traditions occurs by a process of 'translation'; a process MacIntyre describes as learning 'a second first language' (pp. 370–87). Such a process does not presuppose a common reality to which we can have direct access; rather the only realities to which we can have access are tradition-embodied languages. The language of each tradition cannot be understood by an outsider except by coming to grasp the grammar of that language, a grammar not reducible to linguistic rules, but constructed in relation to the totality of the culture of the tradition.

On such a model it is possible for participants in traditions which begin from quite different practical rationalities – incommensurable foundations – to come to recognize that another tradition is not only addressing common issues, but may be able to propose solutions to problems not available within their own tradition:

> When they have understood the beliefs of the alien tradition they may find themselves compelled to recognize that within this tradition it is possible to construct from the concepts and theories peculiar to it what they were unable to provide from within their own conceptual and theoretical resources, a cogent and illuminating explanation – cogent and illuminating, that is, by their own standards – of why their own intellectual tradition was unable to solve its own problems or restore its coherence. (p. 364)

In this way traditions may develop commonalities – shared conceptions, shared practices – at certain points, while remaining quite different at other points. Thus this model provides a way of thinking about how differences between traditions might be resolved while each tradition retains its integrity; indeed, each tradition retains its integrity precisely by drawing on the resources of another tradition.

The very fact that as a part of this process a tradition must come to recognize the inadequacy of its own position to date and to accept defeat in respect of truth by another tradition, refutes relativist and perspectivist challenges, for on those accounts such self-criticism is not possible (pp. 364–5). To this the relativist may reply that it may be possible for traditions to coexist for long periods without precipitating epistemological crises for one another, such that the relativist account would, under those conditions, be accurate. However, conceding this point does nothing to damage the account of traditions in interaction advanced. Here, MacIntyre's riposte that relativists must advance their claims from within a particular tradition seems correct, but not entirely relevant (p. 367). A better argument would seem to be that the cases in which the relativist argument can be held to apply must in any case, under modern conditions of globalization, be relatively few.

As we indicated above, the model has significant problems that become apparent when one tries to reconstruct social reality in its terms, of which we shall develop two. First, to reiterate, it becomes difficult to see how the intellectual coherence attributed to traditions matches the reality of either religious or cultural traditions in highly differentiated societies, or even in traditional societies, given the historic diversity of religious traditions. Second, it seems to assume a symmetry of power between traditions, whereas relationships between immigrants and host societies, for example, are likely to be radically asymmetrical, as the language analogy suggests. However, while traditions may be far more piecemeal than MacIntyre appears to allow, the model enables us to make sense of the holistic aspirations of some religious traditions and their coherence may be reinterpreted on an individual, psychological level as a narrative framework which helps one to make sense of the world, and which is partly shared by others. Furthermore, while power is unequally shared, the model gives us a way of thinking about how immigrant religions and cultures can become sources of resistance to dominant ideologies and values. It also urges the basic beliefs and values of society into the public sphere, to justify and renew themselves.

In this context, we turn to consider the interaction between liberal and Muslim discourses on socio-political arrangements in the Muslim majority world. This has three purposes: first, to help make sense of and to complement the more empirical focus on the role of Islam in civil society in the case studies in Part II, second, to indicate the kind of context with which political liberalism needs to engage if it is to be advocated in Muslim majority societies and third, to examine whether the 'traditions in interaction' model we have developed from MacIntyre is in fact helpful in understanding these kinds of situations. In particular, in Section 8 we shall advance a case for the normative justification of basic rights that builds on the understanding developed here.

6. Arguments over Islam's Public Role

Except for a small minority of secularists, all groups in the Muslim majority world generally agree that Islam has and should have some sort of public role concerned with the promotion and even regulation of public morality: in this sense, Islamic liberalism differs from its Western counterpart (Curzmann 1998). The question, then, is what kind of public role? On one side of the debate, liberal Muslims argue that 'Islam is indeed a religion of collective morals [and hence public] … but there is very little in it that is specifically political – that is, there is very little in the original Islamic sources on how to form states, run governments and manage organizations' (Ayubi 1991 p. 4). On the other side, many Islamists (*Islāmi* in Arabic) seek the establishment of an 'Islamic state', although there is much debate on what is meant by this. Perhaps the term is best defined as Muslims who seek the extension of the influence of Islam in all areas of life: personal, and economic, and in civil and political society, and the state. Modern disagreement among Muslims on the issue of Islam's public role can be traced to two publications in Egypt in the 1920s, which followed the end of the Ottoman Empire and the dissolution of the *caliphate*. In traditional Sunni Islam, the *caliph* is the successor to Muhammad as leader of the Muslim community. The longest surviving claim to this title was the Ottoman one, abolished by Attaturk and his secular nationalist movement in 1924, following the dissolution of the Ottoman Empire after its defeat in the First World War. This event triggered a re-thinking of Islamic political theology, centred in Egypt.

The two key books in this debate were Rashid Rida's *The Caliphate and the Great Imamate* (Tibi 1998 p. 150)[2] and 'Ali 'Abd al-Raziq's *Islam and the Basis of Government* (1925 ibid.). The first of these argues for *din wa dawla* (unity of religion and state) and has become a major source for political Islam, influencing the early Muslim Brotherhood, which as we have seen was founded in 1928. In contrast al-Raziq, the sheikh of al-Azhar, argued that the concept of unity of state and religion has no basis in the primary sources of Islam. It should be noted that neither work is traditional Sunni political theology, because both abandon the institution of the caliphate. Al-Raziq argued for a separation of religion and politics, although he thought that religion should retain a role in maintaining public morality. Many political Islamists, following Rida, also see the destruction of the caliphate as the work of a colonial conspiracy against Islam (Tibi 1998 p. 158); but whether they do or not, the restoration of the caliphate is not central to their plans: 'If political rule, first, is based on the *shari'a* of God and, second, is accepted by the Muslims, then the form matters little' (Jarisha and Zaibaq 1978 p. 201, translated in Tibi 1998 p. 154). Instead, they seek the establishment of an Islamic state, using the slogan *din wa dawla* (unity of religion and state). This is a rhetorically unifying slogan that hides many differences of opinion on what an Islamic state should involve, and on its relationship to civil society, democracy and human rights. Thus the debate begun by Rida and al-Raziq continues today: for example, in the late 1980s, another al-Azhar professor, Muhammad Sa'id al-'Ashmawi, published *Political Islam*, in which 'he insisted that Islam was, from the beginning, an apolitical religion concerned solely with spiritual and ethical guidance' (Flores 1997 p. 83). Responding in a pair of articles and echoing Rida, the Islamist Fahmi Huwaydi contended that 'the political and legislative character of Islam [are] its main distinctive feature' (ibid.).

So contemporary debates over the public role of Islam stem from the crisis caused by the dissolution of the caliphate, and broadly divide Sunni Muslims into two camps. Islamists argue for a central place for Islam at all levels of public life: state, political society and civil society. In contrast, those advocates of 'official Islam' sympathetic to the government (for example some of the professors and sheikhs of al-Azhar) have generally argued that Islam should be kept out of political society. The proper public role of Islam is to support a general public ethos and to influence the character of the state, as well as civil society in support of the family, welfare and Islamic values. A third position, liberal Islam, to which many Muslim scholars working in the West belong, limits the role of Islam to public morality in civil society.

Underlying arguments over the Islamic state is a basic disagreement about how to read the sacred texts of Islam. A key question here is: do the Qur'an and *hadith*[3] actually authorize any particular form of government? This is important because if legitimization for a particular form of government can be found in Islamic sacred texts, then Islamists have a powerful normative argument for the creation of such a government. However, liberals argue that the Qur'an has very little to say on the matter. Thus, while there are approximately 200 verses in the Qur'an of a broadly legislative character – commanding or prohibiting specific actions and in some cases specifying punishments – these fall far short of a full legislative programme. Hence, as we shall see, the problem with the call to 'implement *sharia*'. Furthermore, the Qur'an contains no directions about the kind of political system through which laws should be enacted or enforced. Hence liberal Muslims ask: 'If Islam was meant to be a political order, then why does the Qur'an leave this issue without further clarification?' (al-Najjar in Tibi 1998 p. 166). Thus in spite of their insistence on an Islamic mandate for a specific form of government, Islamist writers are unable to spell out in detail what this would involve (Tibi 1998 p. 161; Ayubi 1991). Therefore, liberal Muslims tend to conclude that Islam requires no particular form of government or political order, but rather provides at most a political ethic for governance, which is compatible in practice with many forms of government. As we shall see below, in Egypt at least, moderate Islamists' quest for an Islamic order, seems to come close to this position, thus indicating the range of meanings attached to the idea of an Islamic state (Abdo 2000).

However, Islamists also tend to argue that something more *can* be said – government should be defined in terms of the implementation of *sharia* (Tibi 1998 p. 169). Two hundred verses can provide a great deal of guidance, and then there is the expansive *Sunna* (traditions of the Prophet). This brings us to the issue of the contested concept of *sharia*, usually translated as 'Islamic law'. Liberals tend to point out that the original meaning of *sharia* is a way or path rather than a law:

> Islamic law is not a code. This is why the frequently heard call for its implementation is meaningless, most particularly when calls are made for the application of *shari'a* – this last term does not designate law, but is a general term designating good order, much like *nomos*[4] or *dharma*.[5](Al-Azmeh 1993 p. 12)
>
> [T]he *shari'a* was neither revealed at once nor has existed as an abstract issue. It was always related to existing realities. ... Without taking into consideration these reality-related origins ... while pleading that it be implemented, we will be dealing with theoretical and logical concerns contradictory to the spirit of Islam. (Al-Ashwami in Tibi 1998 p. 171)

Islamists counter that the Qur'an does, none the less, prohibit certain acts and even specify certain penalties for particular crimes (for example amputation of the hand for theft, flogging for fornication). One complication here is that the distinction between *sharia* ('way' or 'law') and *fiqh* ('jurisprudence', meaning 'legal theory') tends to become blurred in contemporary debate. *Fiqh* is a body of commentary that developed over a period of several hundred years. While it has provided the basis for the interpretation of *sharia* in many different settings, it has never been applied in a uniform or consistent way (see Tibi 1998 p. 188). In this way it differs from a legal code in the modern Western sense. Thus:

> Today, when ... some ... call for the implementation of shari'a, what they really have in mind is the implementation of the jurisprudence formulated by the early jurists. This jurisprudence has now been extracted from its historical and political context and endowed with everlasting, essentialist qualities. The point is thus overlooked that this jurisprudence was in the first place a human improvization meant to address certain political and social issues in a certain historical, geographical and social context. (Ayubi 1991 p. 2)

There is, therefore, an important question as to whether *sharia* is the kind of thing that can simply 'be implemented'. To answer this, it seems that important questions of interpretation need to be addressed. Some method is needed for carefully comparing the meaning of a text in its original context with its possible meanings in the present. Unfortunately, the rhetoric of Islamists often seems to imply an attempt to 'translate' the text directly into the present, without attention to the historical and cultural gap between the present and the context in which the text was produced: 'Muslim scripturalism seldom addresses the issue of meaning, that is, what believers within a certain historical context derive from the text they read' (Tibi 1998 p. 208). Similar problems are found with another important Islamist concept, that of *shura* (consultation), used to legitimize democracy. This illustrates both the potential and problems of trying to use the *Qur'an* to support a particular modern system of governance. As we have noted, there is a division amongst political Islamists on the issue of democracy. Among the founding generation of Islamists there was considerable resistance to the concept (for example Mawdudi and Qutb; see Tibi 1998 p. 177; Ghadbian 1997 p. 72). However, the dominant position now is to lay claim to it and seek to support it on Islamic grounds by developing the Qur'anic concept of *shura*. The textual basis for this is limited, as the term occurs in only two passages in the Qur'an. Of these:

> The first honors '[those] who avoid gross sins and indecencies and, when angered, are willing to forgive, [those] who obey their Lord, attend to their prayers and "conduct their affairs by mutual consent".' (Qur'an: Surat *al-Shura*, 42/37–8). The second passage is in the sura of *'Imran:* 'Take counsel with them in the conduct of affairs' (Qur'an: *'Imran,* 3/159). Historically, this precept conjures the pre-Islamic system of intertribal consultation among leaders of ethnic groups. (Tibi 1998 p. 174)

The primary reference of the first passage seems to be the principle of consultation in personal conduct, while that of the second to consultation among tribal leaders or elders. On this basis it may reasonably be argued that the practice of consultation is characteristic of Islamic morality, on both a personal and collective level, and that it is therefore appropriate to extend this principle to political governance in modern societies. This is a reasonable argument and indicates the potential to develop liberal interpretations of Islam. But it is often also extended to claim democracy as an Islamic invention and to arguing that *shura* offers the ultimate form of democracy. These are much more problematic claims – indeed arguably in the first case untenable. However, in their favour one might argue that it is important to seek as broad a cultural base of cultural legitimization for democracy as possible, and that Western forms should not be presumed to be historically prior or superior.

But they also point to a deeper problem with Islamist interpretation, which is the tendency to insist that there is only one valid reading of a text. For the fact that *shura* did not originally have the full sense of modern democracy implies that while a political extension of the concept may be one valid interpretation, it is not the only legitimate reading. Indeed, this reading arguably only becomes possible in a context in which modern democracy already exists: the early sources of Islam legitimate only limited forms of consultation, in matters of personal conduct and among leaders. Thus Islamists exaggerate when they claim: 'Islam protects the individual from tyranny no less then any of the most developed modern constructions' (Abu-Zaid-Fahmi in Tibi 1998 p. 175). As we shall see in the case of human rights, it is important to face differences between systems squarely, rather than seek false harmonization.

Another important term in political Islamist discourse is *umma*, understood as the entirety of the Islamic community. Because this is not territorially limited, it is sometimes understood as an implicit critique of the restrictive territorial boundaries of the nation-state. However, as Ayubi (1991) argues, 'neither in the Qur'an itself nor in subsequent writings was this term given such an unequivocally religious connotation' (p. 3). Instead, it carries the sense of 'a people', rather than a religious community. Thus a pattern begins to emerge in the development of these political Islamist concepts: an Islamic state, the application of *sharia*, *shura* and *umma*. Each is contentious, but Islamists tend not to acknowledge the legitimacy of alternative readings, especially those that reduce *sharia* to personal ethics.

However, much of the Islamists' insistence on the implementation of *sharia* and resistance to debate about what exactly this may involve is due to the confrontational environment within which their claims are articulated. As we shall see below in the case of Egypt, Islamist groups often have to operate underground and under constant fear of state harassment and arrest. It is also important that fiery Islamist rhetoric is considered in the context of the broader life and work of Islamist groups. As we shall see in Chapter 9, social Islam's welfare role is a far more pervasive aspect of ordinary Egyptians' lives than political Islam. Furthermore, while the above concepts may be problematic, Islamists also have at their disposal tools for the reinterpretation of tradition.

The most prominent of these is *ijtihad* (new interpretation). Traditional scholarly consensus had restricted this open form of reinterpreation, but both Islamic liberals and Islamists have revived it. One interesting example of its relatively recent application is the debate about freedom of religion that the Human Rights League of Tunisia held when seeking to develop a human rights charter that could be agreed with all members of the organization – from secularists to Islamists – during the late 1980s (Dwyer 1991). In their initial draft the League's committee opted to strengthen Article 18 from the Universal Declaration of Human Rights (UDHR) on freedom to change religion, adopting the following wording. The original UDHR Article 18 is given first:

> Everyone has the right to freedom of thought, conscience and religion: this includes freedom to change his religion or belief, either alone or in community with others, to manifest his belief in teaching, practice, worship and observance. (UDHR in Dwyer 1991 p. 236)

> Everyone has the right to freedom of thought, conscience and religion; this includes the right to change one's religion or belief or his interpretation (*ijtihad*) of it and the freedom to express this by teaching or practice and to publicize and to observe it, either alone or in community with others, upon the condition of respecting the rights of others. (LTDH draft, ibid. p. 172)

Three main changes are made. First, the right to individual interpretation is made explicit, so that individuals expressing unorthodox opinions cannot find themselves accused of apostasy. Second, the right to publicize such changed beliefs is made explicit, to safeguard freedom of speech. Third, a condition is added: respect for the rights of others, so that controversial opinions should not be stated in a provocative or insulting manner. Such conditions might help to make the new freedoms more palatable to conservative opinion in Tunisia, but may also be seen encouraging an ethos of responsibility in an open and free public sphere[6]. Let us consider the first of these modifications in a little more detail. Charfi explains:

> You know, here in Tunisia we are very attached to the notion of interpretation or *ijtihad*. We have introduced important new *ijtihads* here in Tunisia as when, for example, we abolished polygamy. And logically, in order to guarantee freedom of *ijtihad* you have to, in effect, suppress punishment for apostasy. Why? Because if you suggest an *ijtihad* that goes against establishment thinking and if your right to express and argue for your *ijtihad* isn't guaranteed, you may be accused of apostasy. (Charfi, in Dwyer 1991 p. 176)

In particular, the execution of Muhammad Taha for apostasy in Sudan in January 1985 was uppermost in the minds of the charter writers (p. 177). This kind of formulation suggests how a way might be found to reconcile a system which has *sharia* as its principal legal basis with modern conceptions of freedom of speech. Such a development, however, raises wider questions concerning the relationship between Islam and human rights, an issue at the heart of the relationship between Islam and normative civil society. It is to these that we now turn. First, we shall consider the diversity of Muslim perspectives on the relationship between Islam and human rights, then develop a more general thesis on the relationship between human rights, culture and modernization.

7. Muslim Responses to Human Rights

> To those who argue that attaining full human rights is a universal human aspiration, others may respond that the notion of human rights is simply a product of one particular civilization's history ... many Middle Easterners have ideas about human rights that ... must be understood in the context of the sustained engagement between the Middle East and the West going back to the time of Muslim penetration into Spain and Europe in the eighth century, through the Crusades of the eleventh century and beyond and into the more recent colonial and post-colonial periods. This context has forged complex, many-tiered, starkly ambivalent and often actively hostile attitudes in many Middle Easterners towards Western traditions, Western forces and Westerners themselves. The idea of 'human rights', closely associated with the West over the last few decades, is prey to the same complexity. (Dwyer 1991 pp. 1–2)

This history means that Muslim attitudes to the West and ideas associated with the West, including human rights, have become complex. One response to this complexity is to deny the relevance of Western experience to Muslim-majority societies: 'The democratic system prevailing in the world does not suit us in the region ... Islam is our social and political law. It is a complete constitution of social and economic laws and a system of government and justice' (King Fahd of Saudi Arabia in *International Herald Tribune* 15 March 1992; in Halliday 1996 p. 138).

In this statement King Fahd is representative of Muslims who argue that the historically and culturally specific origin of human rights discourse limits the scope of its applicability. Islamic systems are simply different to Western ones, they work for Arabs, and so there is no reason to try to impose Western systems like human rights on Arab countries. Such a position may be further supported by arguing that the negative consequences of Western freedoms – materialism and sexual immorality for example – are incompatible with Islam. Aspects of equality between the sexes may be challenged on these grounds, arguing that a complementary rather than an equal relationship between the sexes – as encoded, for example, in Islamic inheritance laws – is a better model for a just society. Such an argument may be described as *particularist*: it defends the denial of the relevance of human rights discourse in a different cultural setting (Halliday 1996).

Halliday dismisses such an argument as an example of the 'fallacy of origin: the fact that a set of ideas was produced in one particular context says little about their subsequent authenticity' (p. 158). Perhaps a better argument is that modern developments such as globalization and the growth of the state impinge on everyone's lives, so that particularism is now only ever a partial defence, for particular cultures always exists in tension with the universalism of various global systems.

A second argument that human rights provisions are already contained in the Qur'an and these are in themselves sufficient to safeguard human dignity – hence no further supplementation, such as a secular conception of human rights, is needed. Halliday (1996 p. 136) describes such as a position as *assimilationist*: the principles of human rights are already respected in Islam, so concerns related to human rights can be assimilated within existing Islamic frameworks. Dalacoura (1998) quotes a statement from former Iranian President Rafsanjani, which exemplifies this position:

> That which the international community is trying to draw up nowadays has been under discussion in Islam for a long time and in the Islamic country of Iran, many of the individual and social rights from which Muslims have benefited also hold good for [religious] minorities; a clear example of this is the presence of deputies representing those minorities in the *Majlis* [representative assembly] with the same rights as deputies of the Islamic *ummah*. (*Summary of World Broadcasts* 1174 A/6 11 Sept 1991; quoted in Dalacoura 1998 pp. 54–5)

The clue to the problem here lies in the word 'many' – religious minorities in Iran do enjoy 'many' rights, including those of political representation referred to, but these are not the same as those enjoyed by Muslims and therefore they are not equal as citizens, as the UDHR demands. Rather, the position of recognized religious minorities in Iran is a modern version of the traditional Islamic policy towards recognized minorities, which provides them with a recognized but subordinate status. While this may have been enlightened in comparison with medieval European arrangements, it falls short of modern human rights standards. Furthermore, it falls far short of religious liberty, for groups which are not recognized have no such protection.

Another case is the various laws relating to women. For example, women inherit half the amount due to men (their responsibilities are also different) and in certain situations two female witnesses are considered equivalent to one male witness. At least at a literal level, these laws are plainly in contradiction of modern human rights principles, even if various forms of *ijtihad* might be able to find a deeper compatibility. Thus such an assimilationist position refuses to recognize real differences between modern human rights and traditional Islamic systems.

A related position is *appropriation* (Halliday 1996), which can be seen as a more aggressive version of the same position. Here it is argued not only that *sharia* provides fully for human rights, but also that its provision is superior to Western formulations. This position is represented by the various Islamic declarations of human rights, for example the 1981 Universal Islamic Declaration of Human Rights (UIDHR) and the 1990 Cairo Declaration of Human Rights (see Mumms, ed. 2001). For example, the UIDHR, produced in 1981 by the London-based, Saudi-backed, Islamic Council, states, 'Islam gave to mankind an ideal code of human rights fourteen centuries ago' (in Dalacoura 1998 p. 50), thus implying that all other formulations are less than ideal. In this document, all rights specified are described as 'subject to the Law', that is, *sharia*, for example 'no one shall be exposed to injury or death, except under the authority of law' (Article 1, ibid.), thus ignoring any possible conflict between the *hadd* penalties (amputation for theft, flogging for adultery and so on) and international understandings of 'cruel and degrading treatment'.

The Cairo Declaration (CDHR) has greater significance than the UIDHR, as it has been endorsed by the foreign ministers of the Organization of the Islamic Conference, to which 'all Muslim countries belong' (Mayer 1994 p. 327). Mayer provides a detailed discussion of this document. Article 1 states: 'Human beings are equal in terms of basic human dignity and basic obligations and responsibilities, without any discrimination on the grounds of race, colour, language, sex, religious belief, political affiliation or social considerations' (p. 329). Mayer describes this article as 'typical of the evasiveness in the formulations often seen in Islamic human rights schemes' (ibid.): it looks at first sight like a guarantee of equality, but in fact it substitutes the concept of dignity for those of rights and freedoms and hence specifies no entitlement, in contrast to the corresponding Article (2) in the UDHR: '[e]veryone is entitled to all the rights and freedoms set forth in this Declaration, without distinction of any kind' (p. 330). Considering the consequences for women – Article 6 of the Cairo document provides that woman is equal to man in human dignity, not rights – Mayer argues:

> In a human rights scheme that purports to follow a religious law that, as traditionally interpreted and applied, has reinforced patriarchy and denied women equality, invocations of women's 'dignity' or equality in 'dignity' in lieu of rights are not likely to provide legal grounds for challenging ingrained patterns of discrimination. (pp. 330–31)

However, not all assessments of the Cairo document are so negative. While admitting the apologetic function and regretting the lack of critical historical engagement with the text, Islamic reformer Arkhoun (1994) none the less argues:

> The great virtue of this declaration is that it expresses the convictions, modes of thought and demands that contemporary Muslims are coming to embrace. ... to cloak such precious rights as religious freedom, freedom of association, freedom of thought and freedom of travel in the full authority of the Islamic tradition is not a negligible phenomenon. (p. 107)

Thus such documents can be seen as a step on the way towards the critical integration of Islam and human rights, opening up a process of intercultural dialogue which has been largely neglected. Islamic liberals have been at the forefront of this, although there is a frequent problem that rather than seeking a critical integration there is instead (as with assimilationism but in reverse) a liberalized presentation of Islamic tradition that ignores 'hard cases' (Weeramantry 1988). Such positions might be called 'liberal harmonizing', emphasizing the positive relationships between Islamic and human rights traditions, but neglecting their differences.

However, other liberal Muslims do seek to face such differences head on. Such Islamic liberals, of the 'confrontationalist' variety, openly face up to differences between *sharia* and human rights, arguing that the terms of integration of contemporary society are so different to pre-modern forms – in particular the political supremacy of Islam can no longer be presumed – that substantial reinterpretation of the tradition is required. They may also combine support for a secular conception with an argument that this has been too narrowly defined, and hence that distinctive Islamic perspectives – as well as those of other religions and cultures – are necessary for a truly universal conception of human rights. Such arguments complement those of some Western critics of a static Western conception of human rights (Galtung 1994).

An example of such a confrontationalist liberal approach is the work of the Sudanese scholar An-Na'im. Educated in law at Khartoum, Cambridge and Edinburgh universities (Curzmann 1998), An-Na'im was forced to flee Sudan after translating the controversial work of Muhammad Taha, who was executed as an apostate by the Sudanese authorities in 1985 (Dalacoura 1998 p. 61). Controversy over Taha's work centres on the distinction he makes between Meccan and Medinan *surahs*, arguing that those verses revealed post-*hijra* (after Muhammad and his followers migrated to Medina, where the first Islamic political community was established) reflect the needs of the early political community and are not intended as everlasting law. An-Na'im accepts and develops this distinction and on this basis challenges even commands which are clearly stated in the Qur'an, such as the *hadd* penalties. An-Na'im has been head of Africa Watch, a human rights organization based in Washington DC and currently (2000) teaches at Emory University. An-Na'im (1998) states clearly:

> Unless the basis of modern Islamic law is shifted away from those texts of the Qur'an and *sunnah* of the Medina stage, which constituted the foundations of the construction of the *shari'a*, there is no way of avoiding a drastic and serious violation of universal standards of human rights. ... We be must prepared to set aside clear and definitive texts of the Qur'an and *sunnah* as having served their transitional purpose and implement those texts of the Meccan stage which were previously inappropriate for practical application, but are now the only way to proceed. (p. 234)

The significance of setting aside the 'clear and definitive texts of the Qur'an and *sunnah*' is that An-Na'im moves clearly beyond the limits of traditional interpretation, including *ijtihad*, which is bound by such texts.

An-Na'im does not insist that his particular methodology – rejecting Medinan in favour of Meccan *surahs*, thus reversing the traditional method of abrogation – is the only way to reform Islamic law. What he does insist on are three points: first, that such drastic reform is necessary, because *sharia* can no longer function as the public law of Islam, second, that the cultural legitimation of human rights discourse in an Islamic idiom is crucial for human rights implementation (1992 p. 21) and third, that the rejection of *sharia* does not necessitate the rejection of Islamic public law – hence he does not privatize Islam.

Other reformers have suggested alternative, less radical, methodologies. The Tunisian reformer Talbi distinguishes between the Qur'an and Sunnah, disputing the provenance of some of the latter and arguing that although all Muslims are bound by the Qur'an's basic teachings, Muslim traditional theology, for historical reasons, does not always reflect the spirit of the Qur'an (Talbi 1998). The feminist scholar Fatima Mernissi (1988) adopts a similar approach. It is important to note that while the direction in which such scholars take their arguments does involve radical departures, the fundamental method of assessing the authenticity of the traditions from the vast range available is entirely consistent with traditional practice. It is An-Na'im who is distinctive – and indeed for many orthodox Muslims apostate – in effectively undermining the authority of the Medinan *surahs* of the Qur'an itself (for example Tamimi in Herbert 2001b).

These approaches demonstrate that Muslim scholars are attempting to construct forms of Islamic practice which are compatible with human rights principles, and that such constructions are not necessarily a contradiction in terms. However, Muslim liberals face an uphill struggle in the contemporary Middle East, given the history of authoritarian government and of Islamist responses to this, as we shall see in the case of Egypt. None the less, it is important to recognize the extent of the cultural penetration of rights discourse within these societies, as Kevin Dwyer (1991) does in his anthropological study of rights talk and organizations across the Middle East. Indeed, Dwyer concludes:

> Few Middle Easterners I spoke to seem ready to dismiss the idea from their cultural repertoire: they may challenge its foundations, or its provenance, or the content given it by specific groups, but the concept itself has come to to constitute a symbol of great power. (p. 217)

At this point we shall broaden the argument still further, having surveyed the diversity of Muslim opinion on the articulation between Islam and human rights, to ask what the relationship of human rights is to culture in general. The impetus to do so relates back to the first part of this chapter, where we considered the crisis in liberalism's claims to universality. We have seen that liberal theorists such as Rawls have retreated from a comprehensive liberalism and restricted the claims of political liberalism to societies where those claims are already at least implicit in settled cultural convictions. We have argued that this retreat within supposed cultural boundaries is empirically problematic (such a consensus is absent in Western societies), politically inadequate (because it abandons liberal minorities) and philosophically flawed (because the normative claims of liberalism, democracy, civil society, human rights and so on are not culturally restricted). Using MacIntyre

(1985), we therefore sought instead to develop an understanding from which intercultural dialogue can develop without sliding into either relativism or cultural imperialism. Here we seek to ask if it is possible to build on this understanding to arrive at some kind of interculturally valid agreement on basic human rights.

Whether this kind of agreement is possible affects the whole way in which the issue of culture and human rights (and hence religion and human rights) is approached. For if human rights are universal in some sense, then opponents of this position are simply wrong and advocates are justified in trying to enforce their implementation, even if this risks conflict with cultural traditions. However, if universality can not be justified, neither can enforcement. Following the discussion gives us the opportunity to examine the articulation between the ideal concept of human rights and the discourse of human rights deployed in different cultural conditions and hence to make a contribution to bridging the gaps between political philosophy, social theory and empirical study that we have identified. Furthermore, since we have argued that normative civil society needs to be embedded in basic rights, this gives us the opportunity to think about what this might mean in cross-cultural articulation. According to the method we have developed, any intercultural validity claims must be redeemed in intercultural public spheres. The following argument is therefore merely a proposal in search of such intercultural redemption, at a time when human rights discourse in both increasingly mobilized and increasingly contested in intercultural communication.

8. Are Human Rights Universal? Culture, Religion, Modernity and the Genesis of Rights

The human rights activist and Islamic scholar An-Na'im makes the following observation on the question of whether the Qur'anic prescription of amputation as a penalty for theft is a case of 'cruel, inhuman or degrading treatment or punishment':[7]

> From a secular or humanist point of view inflicting such a severe permanent punishment for any offense, especially for theft, is obviously cruel and inhuman and probably degrading. This may well be the private intuitive reaction of many educated modernized Muslims. However, to the vast majority of Muslims, the matter is settled by the categorical will of God as expressed in the Qur'an and, as such, is not open to question by human beings. ...
>
> Thus, in all Muslim societies, the possibility of human judgement regarding the appropriateness or cruelty of a punishment is simply out of the question. Furthermore, this belief is supported by what Muslims accept as rational arguments. From the religious point of view, human life does not end at death, ... In the next, *eternal* life, every human being will stand judgement and suffer the consequences of his or her actions in this life. A religiously sanctioned punishment, however, will absolve an offender from punishment in the next life because God will not punish twice for the same offense. ... To people who hold this belief, however severe the Qur'anic punishment may appear to be, it is in fact extremely lenient and merciful in comparison to what the offender will suffer in the next life should the religious punishment not be enforced in this life. (1992 p. 35)

This passage raises in acute form the issue of the role of culture in relation to human rights: according to An-Na'im, the majority of Muslims simply perceive the human condition differently to their secular counterparts, and therefore their understanding of what constitutes 'cruel, inhuman or degrading treatment or punishment' is different. Both Muslim and secular reactions, however, are equally rational responses to reality as differently perceived. In an increasingly interconnected world, how might we respond to such continuing cultural differences?

Two issues are central to the relationship between rights and culture. The first is the role of culture in the implementation of rights. This can be dealt with quite quickly: it is clear that we see articulation with local cultures as essential for human rights to be implemented. In many places across the world human rights agreements entered into by states lack instruments of enforcement; even when they are incorporated into domestic legislation enforcement remains problematic. Even in the Council of Europe area, which has the most developed regional and national mechanisms, it is difficult for the international community and domestic legal systems to secure implementation (Janis 1997). The cultural embedding of human rights is therefore crucial to secure their implementation. Second, what is the role of culture in the origination of rights? Are rights things that exist in some universal sense, above and beyond culture, or are rights the product of culture and therefore limited in their cross-cultural validity? Or, as we shall argue, are rights universal in the sense of implicit in some sense within cultures? It is on this question that we shall focus here.

We shall begin by considering arguments for the universality of human rights in the Western legal and philosophical traditions. These approaches to justifying human rights have tended to downplay or deny the role of culture. One important reason for this is that conceding that culture plays a role in the genesis of rights has been seen as the path to relativism, the view that any moral stance is as good (or bad) as any other. If relativism is accepted, it is argued, on what grounds can cruelty or tyranny be opposed? In the Muslim world, such opposition can be made in the name of God, but in the West there has been a tendency to divorce religion from the justification of public morality. Thus although religions may contribute to supporting public morality, the latter must, it is argued, rest on another basis. This is partly because the prevalence of religious plurality, agnosticism and atheism means that there is no shared basis of religion from which such an understanding could derive. It is also partly because of the history of involvement of religion in social conflict in the West, a history that is further embodied in Western intellectual traditions, as we have seen.

So what arguments have been made to support the legitimacy of rights independent of culture? Broadly, there are two influential positions: 'positivist' and 'naturalist'. The former is typical of legal approaches, the latter of philosophical ones. Their main features are:

> The positivists consider the content of human rights to be determined by texts agreed upon by states and embodied in valid treaties, or determined by obligatory state practice attaining the status of binding international custom. The naturalists, on the other hand, regard the content of human rights as principally based upon immutable values that endow standards and norms with a universal validity. In neither ... instance does culture enter into

the deliberative process of interpreting the meaning [or] justifying the applicability ... of human rights. (Falk 1992 p. 44)

The positivist argument has some merit in enabling governments and non-state agencies to draw attention to the obligations that governments have already undertaken to observe. But they tell us nothing about the ethical validity or authority of human rights concepts, only that these have been approved by proper legal procedures. Hence when, as in the Muslim Middle East, the validity of human rights discourse is called into question on the grounds of its historical origins or cultural specificity, the positivist argument provides no counter-argument in kind. This leaves us with the naturalist argument.

Within the West, naturalist arguments have been called into question in recent years. MacIntyre (1985) has summarized some of the counter-arguments. First, an empirical one derived from the observation of history: if human rights are universal, one might expect to find some evidence of their recognition in different times and cultures. Yet

there is no expression in any ancient or medieval language correctly translated by our expression 'a right' until near the close of the middle ages: the concept lacks any means of expression in Hebrew, Greek, Latin or *Arabic*, classical or medieval, before about 1400, let alone in old English, or in Japanese until as late as the mid nineteenth century. (p. 69, emphasis added)

However, while the absence of rights thinking before the modern period may give us pause for thought, it is not decisive. For rights could still be seen as always having existed, only waiting to be discovered. Thus the fact that bacteria went unrecognized until their discovery in the mid-nineteenth century, does not mean that they didn't exist until Pasteur discovered them under his microscope. None the less, this empirical historical and cultural difference does raise difficulties for notions of self-evidence and intuition with respect to rights. Unfortunately for the naturalist case, most arguments presented in its favour have tended to appeal to these concepts (MacIntyre 1985 pp. 69–70). In the contemporary context, it seems sufficient for living people simply to deny that they have such intuitions or find the concept of rights self-evident, for this kind of naturalist case to fall apart. And if the concept of human rights is not already articulated in particular cultural systems, it seems unreasonable to expect its immediate implementation.

However, it will be argued here that the weakness of these particular naturalist arguments does not imply that the concept of human rights as universal needs to be abandoned, nor even that the naturalist case is entirely without merit. First, something of the naturalist argument can be rescued by considering the basic, biological needs of human beings. Differing metaphysical frames might challenge the priority accorded these needs, for example whether amputation constitutes 'cruel or inhuman treatment' in rival (in this case) Islamic and secular worldviews. But the satisfaction of many such needs (for food and shelter, and for protection from arbitrary attack and experience of pain) may be agreed across cultures, and may be articulated in terms of rights (the right to food, shelter and so on). However, this 'bottom-up' biological approach does not get us very far: political and civil rights cannot be articulated biologically, but are essential to the modern concept of human rights.

A further possible development of the 'naturalist' approach (that human rights are in some sense universally present 'out there') is to extend it into the cultural sphere. Thus rights may be thought of as deriving from the social properties of cultural systems, which require development to be expressed as rights in the modern sense, but can none the less be regarded as implicit.[8] Thus the mutual recognition accorded to individuals in cultures x, y and z may be articulated in terms of rights: of wives to material support from their husbands, of children to support from their parents (and vice versa later in the life-cycle), of strangers to hospitality from the community and so on.

However, the specifying of these rights illustrates two properties that distinguish these networks of mutual obligation from modern systems of rights. First, they are generally two-way, so that giving or receiving entails entitlements and obligations. In contrast, although the connection between rights and responsibilities is often stressed, a distinctive characteristic of modern human rights is that individuals are entitled to at least some of them regardless of whether they have honoured their responsibilities or not: in this sense, they are held to be 'inviolable'. Second, they are often not equal obligations, but rather reciprocal obligations based on different roles in the social system. Thus masters owe certain dues to slaves, husbands to wives and elders to children and vice versa, but these dues are not the same. Reciprocal rights are compatible with a stratified society (as most pre-modern societies were), equal rights are not. Thus the idea of equality which is so prominent in modern concepts of human rights is absent.

None the less, it may still be argued that these networks of mutual obligation have the germ of the idea of human rights and hence, given appropriate educational or developmental opportunities, provide a basis for the development of a rights-supportive culture. Furthermore, they may also open up new perspectives on the Western concept of human rights. For example, as we saw in Chapter 3 Section 7, Galtung (1994) argues that the Western view emphasizes features specific to the post-medieval Christian setting from which it grew, at the expense of other features which may be equally important for protecting individuals and communities from harm. In particular, the individualistic orientation of Western perspectives discriminates against groups whose greatest political asset may be their ability to organize collectively, for example indigenous and immigrant groups, including religious groups:

> Human rights become individual rights to the extent that individuals are the ... units to which ... norms are related and in which they are ultimately fulfilled. This excludes collective rights such as peoples' rights and other group rights. Women, age-groups, indigenous peoples, ancient peoples, non-Western cultures pocketed inside Western societies are such groups, at the bottom of society often engaged in efforts to imitate the state subjugating them ...they are in need of human rights protection to preserve and enhance their group characteristics, not only as individuals in a given social structure. ... The individualizing prospect of human rights deprives these underprivileged groups of their major political asset: mobilization and organized struggle as a group. (ibid. p. 16)

The denial of political representation to Islamists by many governments in the Middle East and of collective recognition as Muslims to Muslim minorities in many parts of Europe (for example France (Herbert 2000) and Bulgaria (Eminov 1997)) is precisely this kind of deprivation in practice. In fact, as we have seen in Section 4, there have been recent efforts to recognize philosophically something like a collective right to cultural survival in the face of the plight of many indigenous peoples and this contested development has its parallel in international human rights agreements:

> An emergent right of cultural survival and flourishment within international law is signalled by the United Nations charter [articles 13, 55, 57 and 73 affirm 'cultural cooperation and development as among the purposes of the UN'], article 27 of the Civil and Political Rights Covenant [recognizes 'the right of members of ethnic, religious or cultural minorities ... to enjoy their own culture, to profess and practise their own religion [and] to enjoy their own language'], the Convention Against Genocide [defines genocide as 'acts committed with intent to destroy ... a national, ethnic, racial or religious group'] and the UNESCO Declaration of Principles of Cultural Co-operation [affirms 'a right and duty of all peoples to protect and develop cultures throughout human kind']. (Anaya 1995 p. 325).

However, in spite of the prominence of religion in these statements, there is a difficulty in their interpretation with respect to religion that arises from the ambiguous nature of the concept of religion in international law. The problem is that on the one hand, religion is seen as a voluntary activity, hence the right of people to choose and change their religion is made central. But on the other hand, religion is seen as an integral part of culture that defines their identity at a fundamental level. The more religion is seen as something which can be easily changed (or abandoned), the less it is seen as really essential to people's lives and vice versa. The predominance of the former (choice-based) view in international law means that religious minorities are unlikely to benefit from protection designed to ensure the cultural survival of a people.

Thus we have seen that looking for the seeds of human rights in different cultural systems seems to provide some basis for asserting their universality and can also expand our understanding of what those rights entail. However, we need to consider some objections to this first argument. Is it still a 'naturalist argument'? For it derives from cultural, not biological, systems. Yet if human beings are by nature social animals and cultural systems the product of human sociality, one could still argue that it remains a naturalist argument. This is because it derives not from some contingent feature of a particular culture, but rather from the basic properties of human sociality that make particular cultural formations possible. But more importantly, wherever one draws the culture/nature line, the purpose of the naturalist argument is to preserve the universality of human rights and that is precisely what this argument seeks to do.

However, this defence raises a further objection: why should participants in a range of non-Western cultures where the modern concept of human rights remains potential rather than actual wish to have this potential developed, wish to be educated in the Western ways that have brought so much destruction to their cultures? The answer to this lies in their very incorporation into the world system. We have argued that the state is the main threat to human rights in most Muslim societies (as we shall see further below with Egypt) and more generally that the modern state has brought a whole new set of threats to individuals. Human rights are a moral language uniquely designed to cope with this threat, specifying the individual's rights with respect to the powers of the state that are unique to modernity and reaching out beyond the state to an international sense of obligation that transcends state boundaries.

Indeed, the developing discourse of human rights responds not only to the emergence of the state system, but also to the unprecedented interaction between peoples brought about by international migration, urbanization and communication, which has created a world of strangers in which traditional, communally based and culturally specific systems of mutual obligation struggle to retain their binding force. While we argued in Chapters 1 and 2 that developments in cheap and accessible communication technologies sometimes preserve these bonds more than was once thought possible, this is turn provides a further argument for rights – to defend dissenting individuals and groups from resurgent forms of communal identity.

In terms of our model of intercultural communication, the onset of modernization and the development of the world system (including states) precipitated the epistemological crisis that led to the development of human rights discourse in the West, the first area affected, because previous moral discourses were unable to counter the new threat to the individual posed by the state and to older moral discourses by differentiation. However, in the process the teleological conception of humanity that had underpinned previous discourses was jettisoned, depriving these new discourses of the coherence that enables intercultural communication. In the Muslim world the same impingement of the world system affects (and has long affected) non-Western societies, and our argument is that the solution offered by human rights discourse to protect the individual both created and threatened by the world system may also be a solution here, not in terms dictated by the West but in terms of their own cultural and moral traditions. The retention within non-Western cultures of teleological concepts of ethics that can link the abstract modern individual to the lifeworld suggests that this exchange need not be one-way.

So perhaps the strongest case for rights is not a top down one derived from abstract principles, but rather a bottom-up one derived from a combination of biological needs, the properties of cultural systems and the history of their emergence as a way of protecting the individual from the growing powers of the state, an experience that has now become global. From this perspective, the language of rights is a useful, indeed vital, invention for the prevention of cruelty and suffering in modern contexts. Civil and political rights play a crucial role in defending the interests of individuals against the incursions of states and of trans-state actors ranging from multinational corporations to radical Islamist groups. Human rights discourse thus becomes universally applicable by virtue of the empirical universality of the modern nation-state and the modern world system. Equally, however, the universality of the modern concept of human rights may be challenged through the examination of non-Western cultural formations. Such comparison reveals, for example, an individualist bias that discriminates against some groups whose best chance of political mobilization is on a group basis, especially indigenous groups, but also in some cases religious groups.

Thus while the effects of globalization are felt everywhere in the modern world, states articulate with very different cultural systems. Indeed, it may be argued that while economic and political systems have become more interconnected and convergent, cultural systems have become more fragmented and divergent (Tibi 1998 pp. 82–113). This may be a reaction to the convergence of other systems, as culture becomes the only way to articulate difference in the modern world system. In these circumstances, the need to articulate rights through culture becomes, as we have seen, both imperative and intensely problematic: that is, imperative to defend the rights of individuals against the problematic products of the world system, including incursions of the state and of culturally based communal groups.

Conclusion

We have argued that the problems in the cross-cultural legitimization of liberal ideas such as civil society, the public sphere and human rights are best addressed through a model of intercultural communication derived from MacIntyre, a model that can articulate between recent developments in liberal thinking on cultural diversity and Muslim responses to liberal ideas and institutions. We have further argued that in spite of the failure of transcendental arguments, the idea of basic rights as underpinning the institutionalization of civil society can be supported drawing on a combination of biological, cultural and historical arguments.

The discussion of liberal responses to cultural diversity complements the more empirical focus on the issues raised by *The Satanic Verses* controversy and the relationship between Muslims, civil society and the public sphere in Britain in the next chapter. The discussion of arguments concerning the public role of Islam and Islamic responses to human rights is of relevance to three of the four case studies in Part II where Muslim groups feature: Britain, Bosnia and Egypt. It is of most direct relevance to Egypt, where Muslims are a large majority. Chapter 9 will complement the normative discussion here with an empirical focus on Egypt, examining the development of an Islamic 'parallel society' and the relationship between women, Islamisms and the state in this context. The aim is to bring the fruits of recent fieldwork to bear on the dichotomies within which the role of Islam in Egyptian society is frequently described. Perhaps here, in places, is the empirical basis for the Islamic liberalism that Binder, with whose work we opened this chapter, seeks. The two Central and Eastern European case studies are poised intriguingly between the supposed 'extremes' of majority presumed-to-be liberal Britain, and majority Muslim (presumed not to be liberal) Egypt. Clearly, the post-Communist region has its own shared legacy and disparate histories. But it is hoped that bringing critical theories of religion and modernization, civil society and the public sphere to bear on these cases will provide a mutually illuminating perspective both on these theories and on the cases themselves. It is to this examination of the role of religion in civil society in Britain, Poland, Bosnia and Egypt that we now turn.

Notes

1   For example in 'Rationality and the Explanation of Action' (1971). He affirms this
    position in *Whose Justice? Which Rationality?*: 'All the traditions with which we have
    been concerned agree in according a certain authority to logic both in their theory and in
    their practice. Were it not so, their adherents would be unable to disagree in the way in
    which they do' (1988 p. 351).
2   For more on Rida see Kerr, M. *Islamic Reform: The Political and Legal Theories of
    Muhammad Abduh and Rashid Rida* (Berkeley: University of California Press 1966).
3   'Traditions', that is, about the Prophet and his followers. Only those traditions concerning
    the Prophet himself (the *sunna*) are an authoritative source of *sharia*. The four sources of
    sharia most widely accepted in Sunni Islam are the Qur'an, *sunna*, *'ijma* (consensus, that
    is, of the scholarly community) and *qiyas* (analogical reasoning). *Ijtihad* (independent
    reasoning) has always also been accepted by *Shia* Muslims and is also now accepted by
    most Islamic modernists, that is, both the Islamists and the liberals under discussion here.
4   *Nomos* – Greek for 'custom' or 'tradition'.
5   *Dharma* – the Hindu term for divine/social order.
6   Looking forward to Chapter 6, it is perhaps worth considering whether a charter like this
    might have prevented the kind of controversy that blew up over Salman Rushdie's novel
    The Satanic Verses in Britain and elsewhere in 1988–89. The initial request of British
    Muslim leaders concerned at the representation of the Prophet was for the novel to be
    reissued with an explanation that the book is a work of fiction that does not accurately
    portray early Islamic history (Samad 1992 p. 514).
7   From Article 7 of the International Covenant on Civil and Political Rights (An-Na'im
    1992 p. 30).
8   Habermas (1987) has constructed a complex theory about the mutual moral obligations
    implicit in the basic structure of human communication. However, as a universal basis for
    modern human rights this falls prey to the same weakness as the simpler naturalist
    argument presented here: two specific features of modern rights systems – equal rights for
    all and the idea that rights precede obligations – cannot be justified on either basis
    (Bauman 1993 pp. 220–1 n. 30).

PART II
CASE STUDIES

Chapter 6

After *The Satanic Verses*

Muslims, Civil Society and the Public Sphere in Britain

Question: What is the opposite of faith? Not disbelief. Too final, certain, closed. Itself a kind of belief. (Rushdie 1988 p. 62)

The events following the publication of Salman Rushdie's *The Satanic Verses* highlight the fundamental obstruction to the further development of society. Belief, that is the dogmatic rejection of reason and the acceptance of ideas on the basis of 'faith' alone, provides man with a box to hide from the realities of life. Belief, be it religious or political, has been the major cause of war, conflict and disunity. ... To build a better society and a better world we must be prepared to question and to reason; belief obstructs the path towards achievement of this ultimate aim. (Letter to the *Independent*, cited in D'Costa 1990 pp. 425–6)

When characters in a novel are burned to death (or vilified), we are reminded that it is, after all, 'only a story'. And yet a literalist response doesn't seem equally convincing to us when we are told that the book burned is, after all, 'only paper and ink'. The liberal expressions of outrage at this symbolic act – no less than the anger of South Asian Muslims at the publication of the book – deserve to be more fully explored than they have been, so that we can understand the sacred geography of secular culture better than we now do. (Asad 1990 p. 258)

1. Introduction

The controversy that erupted after the British publication of Salman Rushdie's *The Satanic Verses* in September 1988 contains many of the elements we have emphasized as characteristic of the global development of religions in the late twentieth and early twenty-first century: the role of the media (in publicizing and shaping public opinion of the events), of global interconnections (Khomeini's *fatwa*), of grass-roots organizations and networks (in contrast to historic authorities), of relationships between the voluntary sector, the local and national state and transnational norms and institutions (Muslim voluntary organizations, Bradford Town Council, the British government and the European Court) and the importance of arguments about religion and its role in society, among both the religious and the non-believers. Indeed, the cacophony of voices raised in argument approximated to a state of 'hyper-pluralism' (Mayhew 1997) and concerned the public/private nature of religion, social integration and separate collective identities, 'community' leadership, individual and collective rights and freedom of speech.

Again in April and July 2001 Bradford reached the front pages of the national press for reasons of civil disorder. Although the sensibilities of a religious group were no longer the centre of controversy, which appears at least in part to have been provoked by far-right activity, the role of religion in social integration and 'community' leadership was again a focus for discussion. Thus Hashmukh Shah, spokesman for the World Council of Hindus, whose premises were set alight during the July disturbances, blamed the mosques for promoting separatist Muslim identities and militant attitudes: 'They are less religious centres, more like training grounds for the Taliban', he said (in Roy 2001). Lord Ouseley's official report into community relations, *Community Pride not Prejudice,* published shortly after but prepared before the July disturbances, is based on extensive interviews with local people (Ouseley 2001). It reports that Muslim religious leaders are perceived as 'hostile and monocultural' and resented by the white community, and argues that self-segregation along religious and ethnic lines in housing and education is leading to deteriorating community relations. The report adds that such self-separation is exacerbated by government policy which encourages competition among communities for urban renewal funds, a pattern that Baumann also observed in Southall, as we saw in Chapter 3.

While the history and composition of Bradford are, as we shall see, distinctive in a number of respects, this chapter will argue that Bradford provides an illuminating case study of the role of religion in the civil society and public sphere of a Western European city and of the contemporary politics of multiculturalism. Even before 1988 Bradford was seen as 'a microcosm of a larger British society that was struggling to make sense of itself, even as it was undergoing radical change', as the novelist Hanif Kureishi wrote in response to the Honeyford affair in the mid-1980s, a furore sparked by the remarks of a Bradford teacher, and one of a series of controversies in the 1970s and 1980s that forms the background to *The Satanic Verses* controversy, and which we shall consider further below (Kureishi 1986 p. 149, in Lewis 1994 p. 2). But it was *The Satanic Verses* controversy that was to change not only perceptions of Bradford but of community relations in Britain, as Philip Lewis, author of an important full-length study of Bradford's Muslims (1994) explains:

> In 1985 the majority of those concerned with race relations in Britain – whether policy makers, community workers, academics or activists – still thought of the religious identity of the country's ethnic minorities as a somewhat marginal issue with only a limited impact on policy. Even then it was subsumed under the category of multiculturalism. Yet within five years Bradford had become known to the non-Muslim as well as the Muslim world as a city of Islam, an infamous place where an enraged Muslim community had burned a novel. From being culturally and politically invisible, Muslims were suddenly projected as a dangerous fifth column, subversive of western freedoms: a trojan horse in the heart of Europe with a deadly cargo of 'fundamentalist' religiosity. (p. 1)

By way of introduction to this chapter, we shall pick up on two of Lewis's points: the association of Bradford's Muslims with 'fundamentalism' and the lack of awareness of the role of religion in community relations in Britain in the late 1980s.

First, the issue of 'fundamentalism'. As we argued in Chapter 2, even its most systematic users have failed to capture a convincing underlying commonality to the groups they label with this term and this, together with its polemical connotations, led to a rejection of its use as an analytic concept here. However, in this context Lewis is right to observe that the label has been used to describe both British Muslims and groups in the Muslim majority world, and hence to suggest a connection between the two. Therefore, the purpose of this discussion is to provide an initial orientation to the relationship between Bradford's Muslims and the development of political Islamism in the Muslim majority world.

The Iranian revolution of 1979, in spite of Iran's subsequent economic difficulties (Beyer 1994), greatly raised the global profile of Islam as a political force. In the Middle East, the crisis in Arab nationalism precipitated by Arab defeat in the 1967 war with Israel had stimulated the development of Islamist groups in the 1970s. Such groups, sometimes called fundamentalist but here labelled with the more precise and self-recognized label 'Islamist' (*Islami* in Arabic), seek an increased role for Islam in public life, focused especially on the goals of an Islamic state and the implementation of *sharia* (Islamic law). They received an additional boost from the Iranian revolution, since it seemed as though their ideas were being put into practice, in spite of the distinctive Shi'ite form of the Ayatollah's Islam. Through the Middle East and indeed across the Muslim world from Morocco (Dwyer 1991) to Indonesia (Hefner 2000), Islam increasingly became a discourse within which political aspirations came to be articulated, not least because of the denial of alternative forums for discussion and mobilization in many countries. There is also evidence that, in places at least, this increasing social significance of Islam has been accompanied by a revival in practice, as we saw in Chapter 1.

However, viewed from the perspective of the Islamization of public discourse in much of the Muslim majority world, perhaps the most striking feature is the general lack of articulation between Bradford's Muslims and these global developments. This is the case even though the first generation came from Pakistan, which under General Zia in the 1980s underwent a programme of Islamization of law. This is primarily because whereas Islamist movements are predominantly the outgrowth of urban, educated Muslim engagement with modernity, the first generation of most Western European Muslims, including Bradford's, came to Europe from poor rural areas. For example, levels of primary education in Azad Kashmir, from which most of Bradford's Muslims come, were as low as 8 per cent as late as the 1980s (Lewis 1994 p. 77). This contrasts with most of North America's South Asian heritage Muslims, who have come from urban and educated backgrounds. Their rural background means that by the late 1980s most British Muslims had little contact with the new developments in Islamic thinking in the 1970s and 1980s. The impact of the resurgence of Islam in the Muslim world on British Muslims was therefore limited in terms of direct engagement with the thinking of new movements. Thus although close links were maintained with Pakistan, the flows of information concerned predominantly local and regional issues rather than the major issues discussed by Islamists during this period.

Furthermore, even if British Muslims had been part of such debates, much of the discussion would have been of little relevance to their lives as minorities in Western societies. While considerable intellectual effort, as we saw in Chapter 5, went into rethinking aspects of Islamic tradition in relation to modernity, this all tended to presuppose a majority of Muslims in the population and Muslim cultural hegemony. But neither of these is a remote possibility when Muslims constitute perhaps 3 per cent of the population. Hence the main preoccupations of Islamists – creating an Islamic state and implementing *sharia* – were of no direct relevance to British Muslims, except in the latter case to the limited extent that British legal systems permit legal pluralism (Yilmaz 2000). Since the classical traditions of Islamic political thought make the same assumptions, British and other migrants from Muslim majority societies had few historic or contemporary resources to draw on to help them think through their minority situation. Islamist and liberal Islamic rethinking of Islam's relation to human rights and democracy, which began to develop during the 1970s and 1980s (Dwyer 1991; Halliday 1996) was of more relevance, but knowledge of these sources amongst British Muslims in the late 1980s remained very limited.

In the 1990s, a combination of the politicizing effect of *The Satanic Verses* controversy itself and the emergence of a generation of British-born educated urban Muslim youth, led to an increased interest in Islamist ideas. This was mirrored, especially on university campuses, by the growth of small radical Islamist groups including *Hizb-ut-Tahrir* and *al-Muhajiroun*, the latter particularly notorious for its much publicized stance in the aftermath of 11 September 2001. But the influence of such groups was a consequence, not a cause, of *The Satanic Verses* controversy. If, then, Bradford's Muslims at the end of the 1980s are to be called 'fundamentalist' (and some came to own this label in the course of *The Satanic Verses* controversy, for example Akhtar 1989 p. 19), the very different possible connotations of this term should be borne in mind.

Second, awareness of religion as a factor in community relations in the late 1980s. In the Introduction, I have already pointed to the lack of articulation between intellectual discourses on the issues raised by the controversy as a reason for writing this book. In the late 1980s, the study of race and ethnic relations barely considered religion, the study of religion barely considered the interaction between the religious traditions of migrant groups and predominantly post-Christian, secularized culture, while the sociology of the reception of literature had a very marginal place in the study of literature. To some extent, this chapter is my belated attempt to think through the connections between these fields in terms of *The Satanic Verses* controversy. But it also moves on from the events of 1988–91 to the following decade and seeks to develop an understanding of religion in civil society and the public sphere that is of contemporary relevance.

The chapter therefore centres on *The Satanic Verses* controversy, attempting first to understand some of the main themes of the book and then the characteristics of two very different audiences or 'interpreting communities'. These are Bradford's Muslim population, including its history of political activism and the development of empirical civil society, and the book's main 'public', predominantly consumers of sophisticated fiction. It then considers the dissemination of the book to Bradford's Muslims, the course of two events that have been central to the construction of the controversy in the wider British public sphere (the book-burning in Bradford and Ayotollah Khomeini's *fatwa*) and developments in the Muslim public sphere in Bradford as a result of the controversy. The broader development of Muslim public spheres in Britain through the 1990s is then examined, leading to a discussion of some of the legal, ethical and social issues raised by the controversy and its aftermath. In particular, is the lack of legal recourse for Muslims offended by the book a sign of British society's intolerance of diversity or, on the contrary, of tolerance? And how can community pride be achieved without exacerbating community prejudice, and what roles can religion and religious organizations be expected to play in this process?

2. Diversity and Coexistence in *The Satanic Verses*

According to Muslim tradition, a question posed about three pagan goddesses in the Qur'an ('Have you considered al-Lat, al-'Uzza and Manat, the third, the other' 53: 19–20), was once followed by two additional verses: 'These are the exalted birds whose intercession is to be desired'. These words would appear to contradict the central Islamic tenets of the oneness of Allah and the rejection of mediators between Allah and humanity. But a later revelation (17: 73–5) indicates that these verses were a false interpolation inspired by Satan, and hence they were removed from the Qur'anic canon. This incident of the 'Satanic Verses' to which the title of Rushdie's book refers is well attested in early Islamic sources (Akhtar 1989 p. 19). Rushdie uses these verses not only to build a parody of the revelation of the Qur'an and the early Islamic community in two chapters of the book, but also to develop a more general theme across the canvas of the novel. This is the inevitable intermingling of good and bad, and the inability of humans to discern the difference between the two. In this moral universe, he explores the possibilities and dangers of modern multiculturalism:

> 'The modern city,' Otto Cone on his hobbyhorse had lectured his bored family at table, 'is the locus classicus of incompatible realities. Lives that have no business mingling with one another sit side by side upon the omnibus. ... And as long as that's all, they pass in the night, jostling on Tube stations, raising their hats in some hotel corridor, it's not so bad. But if they meet! It's uranium and plutonium, each makes the other decompose, boom.' (Rushdie 1988 p. 314)

In this passage the prognosis for multiculturalism seems bleak. Furthermore, Otto Cone's pessimistic picture would seem justified by the explosion the novel itself precipitated. Yet other voices in the book speak more brightly. The description of Zeeny Vakil's art criticism, in her Bombay context, seems suggestive of a way of living with different cultures beyond communalist strife or homogenizing secular modernity:

> She was an art critic whose book on the confining myth of authenticity – that folkloristic straitjacket which she sought to replace by an ethic of historically validated eclecticism, for was not the entire national culture based on the principle of borrowing whatever clothes seem to fit, Aryan, Mughal, British, take-the-best-and-leave-the-rest? – had created a

predictable stink, especially because of its title. She had called it *The Only Good Indian*. 'Meaning, is a dead,' she told Chamcha when she gave him a copy. (p. 52)

Perhaps this passage also anticipates the opposition to *The Satanic Verses*, another provocatively entitled work. Certainly, there are strong parallels between 'the book' and 'the book within the book'. Both challenge a belief in purity. In *The Satanic Verses* the purity challenged is the possibility of a sacred text revealed without human interpolation, without accommodation to context, while in *The Only Good Indian* the purity challenged is that of aspects of Indian cultural tradition. One is targeted at what the author sees as Islamic fundamentalism, the other at Hindu fundamentalism. Both titles seek to turn an old vice into a new kind of virtue – the colonialist insult and the Orientalist taunt into ironic celebrations of eclecticism.

These excerpts from *The Satanic Verses* give glimpses of Rushdie probing the incongruous juxtapositions of life in multicultural urban settings. While he refers to Bombay, ancient Mecca and, briefly, Teheran, the dominant city in his narrative landscape is 'Ellowen Deeowen', spelt out 'London'. Seen from this perspective, *The Satanic Verses* is not a simple slander on the Prophet of Islam, but a form of diagnosis and even a hint of cure, for the disease of conflict threatening plural, rapidly changing societies. Yet it is a 'disease' which its publication has both tragically and ironically highlighted and exacerbated.

This kind of reading correlates broadly with the critical reception for the book by secularized audiences (to be examined further below) and with Rushdie's expressed intentions. Thus before publication Rushdie commented:

> There are things that seem not to belong together, except that it is part of the metropolitan experience that such things do not belong together and do live side by side – that you can live upstairs from Khomeini. What I've tried to do is set alongside each other in odd, sometimes raw juxtapositions all sorts of different bodies of experience to show what frictions and sparks they make. (In Appignanesi and Maitland 1989 p. 9)

In her review (also pre-publication), Angela Carter too interprets Zeeny Vakil's art criticism as a key to the novel: '*The Satanic Verses*, as if in tribute to Zeeny's ethic, is eclectic as hell' (*The Guardian* 23 September 1988). She describes it as 'an epic into which holes have been punched to let in visions, an epic hung about with ragbag scraps of many different cultures'. These 'holes ... punched to let in visions' identify the genre as magical realism, a style of fiction in which realistic narrative is interspersed with fantastic events, and dreamscapes mingle with political allusion.

Characteristic features of this genre have been outlined by Brennan (1989), using the example of Gabriel García Márquez's *One Hundred Years of Solitude*, which he compares with Rushdie's *Shame* (1984). The comparison also holds for the more recent *The Satanic Verses*. Thus both *The Satanic Verses* and *One Hundred Years of Solitude* feature miraculous defiance of gravity (the gypsies' flying carpet in the former, Gibreel and Saladin's safe fall from the exploding jumbo in the latter), young girls haunted by swarms of butterflies and the frequent appearance of ghosts.[1] While fantasy in many forms can be seen as influencing Rushdie's work, including the pre-Islamic Arabic tradition of storytelling represented in *The Satanic Verses* by the figure of the poet Baal, the debt to Márquez's magical realism goes further. As Brennan (1989 p. 66) comments, 'What Rushdie borrows from Márquez is ... unique in one respect: he theorizes his own use of fantasy and does so by referring to colonialism'. Magical realism, according to Brennan, 'is a genre that serves an ideological role ... as the imaginative expression of freedom' (p. 65). He means political freedom; the idea is that by subverting the realist conventions of modern fiction the hegemony of dominant political ideologies is challenged. Márquez deliberately apes the fantastical style of early white explorers of the continent, ironically adopting a discourse developed to subjugate a continent as a means of challenging present dominant modes of representation; an old insult is transformed into an ironic celebration.

Thus in *The Satanic Verses* in passages in which one of book's main protagonists Gibreel dreams he is the archangel (of the same name) who delivers the Qur'an to Muhammad, the latter is renamed 'Mahound':

> To turn insults into strengths, whigs, tories, Blacks all chose to wear with pride the names they were given in scorn; likewise, our mountain-climbing, prophet-motivated solitary is to be the medieval baby-frightener, the Devil's synonym, Mahound.
> That's him. Mahound the businessman, climbing his hot mountain in the Hijaz. (p. 93).

As Bradney (1993) points out:

> According to the Oxford English Dictionary, Mahound has five meanings, all of them, to one degree or another, derogatory. The term is variously linked [in medieval Christian polemic] with the 'false prophet' Mohammed (imagined also as a god), with a monster, as an alternative name for the Christian devil and so forth. In all its forms the term is one of abuse. (p. 85)

Of course, Rushdie acknowledges this in the text in the passage cited, but claims it as part of a ploy to 'turn insults into strengths'. However, to the reader this may not be apparent, and the 'ironic celebration' may seem remarkably like the old insult. Yet even understanding and accepting this strategy, it is questionable whether Rushdie actually carries it out in *The Satanic Verses*. Rather, to many readers it appeared that he instead developed a new and more sustained insult. Bhikhu Parekh, a secularized Hindu and at the time Professor of Political Philosophy at Hull University and deputy chairman of the Commission for Racial Equality, describes British Muslim reaction to the two chapters about Mahound:

> They did not seem much concerned about its critical discussion of Islam to which most of them had been long accustomed, but felt strongly about its treatment of Muhammad, his disciple and his wives, a sensitive subject for Muslims for centuries. They resented that he had been called an impostor who made up his revelations as he went along, made deals with the Archangel and treated religion as a kind of business. They were deeply offended that he had been called a debauchee who, after his wife's death, had slept with so many women that his beard turned 'half-white' in a year. They resented too that his three revered colleagues were called 'those goons – those f...... clowns', the 'trinity of scum'. ... [They] bitterly complained that *The Satanic Verses* reduced [the Qur'an] to a book about how to

'fart', 'f...' and 'clean one's behind'. They also felt distressed by the brothel scene in which twelve prostitutes increased their earnings by taking the names of and pretending to be, Mahound's wives. (Parekh 1990 p. 61)

It is difficult to see how these passages succeed in turning 'insults into strengths'. Indeed, it is possible to see these unredeemed insults as part of a broader movement in *The Satanic Verses* away from the hopeful engagement in post-colonial struggle that animates his earlier novels like *Midnight's Children* and *Shame*, to nihilistic and cynical acquiescence in Western postmodernism (Brennan 1989). The salient features identified as postmodern here are an abandonment of left-wing struggles, replacing political commitment with heightened aestheticism (most leading intellectual postmodernists have a Marxist background), in which the dominant metaphor is that of the text or work of art, to be shaped and fashioned at will. Ironic juxtaposition becomes an end in itself, mischievous playfulness replaces politics. But as Talal Asad (1990) objects:

> [E]veryday life is not so easily invented, abandoned, reinhabited as this notion of culture, modelled on the postmodern idea of an imaginative work of art, suggests. Nor does everyone in the modern world have an equal power to invent, or resist the imposition of someone else's invention. To say this is not merely to remind ourselves of the enormous inequalities of class, race and gender that still exist. It is also to note that although the strictly privatized role of religion in the modern Western state makes it easy for English believers and non-believers to assimilate it to the category of Literature, most Muslim immigrants in Britain find it difficult to assimilate their practical religious traditions to this category. (p. 251)

Bhikhu Parekh's successive interpretations of *The Satanic Verses*, while not expressed in the language of postmodern/post-colonial, none the less illustrate the differences between political approaches underlying the two. Parekh shifts from a reading oriented by a secularized Western context and emphasizing the aesthetic merits of the text, to one more sensitive to alternative perspectives, and especially to the presumption of power behind postmodernist conceptions of culture. Thus initially Parekh welcomed the book, both for its brilliant use of English and 'because its treatment of religion seemed to advertise the loyalty of a secular Muslim to a secular progressive India' (Asad 1990 p. 245). However, following discussions with Muslim friends he began to revise his opinion, eventually concluding that the book embodies a number of contradictions:

> An immensely daring and persistently probing exploration of the human condition, ... lies ill at ease with timid obeisance to the latest literary and political fashions; profound seriousness lapses suddenly and without warning into pointless playfulness. ... Intensely delicate explorations of human relationships and emotions are overshadowed by an almost childlike urge to shock, hurt and offend. (1989 p. 31)

Parekh's rereading is occasioned by exposure to Muslim sensibilities, yet his understanding of the validity of Muslim offence is not Islamic, but draws instead on liberal understandings of 'fairness'. Even from this perspective, he begins to interpret passages in the book disapprovingly as motivated by 'an almost childlike urge to shock, hurt and offend' (ibid.). His developing views pose sharply the difficulty of reconciling the interest of the literary community in exploring complex issues of identity in a plural society in a playful and innovative way, with that of various Muslim perspectives, offended by the book's insults of the Prophet, his family and friends. We now turn to consider the characteristics of each of these broad audiences in more depth.

3. The Intended Readership: The Public of the Novel

> Most people define themselves by their work, or where they come from, or suchlike; we have lived too far inside our heads. It makes actuality damn hard to handle. ('Mirza Saeed' in Rushdie 1988 p. 490)

This section focuses on the kind of audience Rushdie might expect to read his fiction in the normal course of events, that is, consumers of sophisticated contemporary fiction in English, and the readings of the book which this audience might generate. The 'sophisticated' tag for Rushdie's fiction here refers to the complexity and length of *The Satanic Verses*, which limits the audience. It is an international audience, but one which is likely to be comparatively small in any one country. Sales are not necessarily a reliable guide to readership, as it may be that a high proportion of novels bought are not read.

Of course, anyone in a country where a book is published can buy or read it and hence the contours of this group are difficult to determine. It is easier to identify a 'community' associated with the publishing industry – writers, publishers, critics and so on – but this 'literary establishment' forms only a small part of the audience of a novel. This gives rise to basic methodological problems; as we have noted, purchase or borrowing of a book is no guarantee of actual reading; and interpretation is not easily quantifiable. Perhaps the most salient field of empirical enquiry is market research, which identifies consumer characteristics, sometimes involving quite fine-grained analysis. But such studies focus on correlating consumption with socio-economic characteristics, rather than on the process and meaning of consumption, and are therefore of limited value for us here.

Yet the practice of reading sophisticated fiction, both in terms of the private use of texts and the particular form of 'the novel', is quite historically and culturally specific, and in the context of *The Satanic Verses* controversy, warrants investigation. What, then, can be learned about this audience in the absence of direct studies of it? In the study of religion it is usual to be confronted with a historic text of whose first interpreting community we know little. In this situation, it is usual practice to attempt to imaginatively reconstruct the audience from clues in the text itself, supplemented by archaeological evidence, or evidence from other texts.[2] Something of that method will be used here by asking the following questions: what hints to the identity of its intended audience does *The Satanic Verses* itself and the secondary literature it has generated provide?

The cultural anthropologist Talal Asad (1990 p. 257) suggests that 'The book's stories ... powerfully connect with ... the highly ambivalent emotions generated by an anglicized Indian's gaze at the ruling class of Imperial Britain'. Certainly the central characters of the book, Saladin and Gibreel, are privileged, cosmopolitan, anglicized Indians. Thus Rushdie does not write of a universal experience of migration; rather, when he writes of migration as a metaphor of 'postmodern' life, the life alluded to is that of the high-flying cosmopolitan. We may recall here Inglehart's theory that cultural postmodernity (at least, we have argued, in its 'take-off' phase) requires a high degree of economic security. And yet in many critics' reviews of Rushdie's works universalizing statements abound. With breathtaking disregard for Indian authors (Rushdie was educated at an English public school), *The New York Times*'s reviewer of *Midnight's Children* described the work as 'a continent finding its voice', a comment which the publisher saw fit to repeat on the paperback's cover (Rushdie 1981, cover; Ahmed in Asad 1990, p. 249). Nisha Puri of *The Indian Post*, having confessed that '*The Satanic Verses* is not an easy read', none the less goes on to proclaim: 'Rushdie remains buoyantly accessible to anyone who responds to all that is good and living in the supreme fictions offered by literary genius' (in Appignanesi and Maitland 1989 p. 13).

Clearly, Rushdie is an example of a writer in English from an ethnic minority who has assumed the status of representative by at least some within the literary establishment. This 'critical' material also, like Rushdie, ascribes to literature a moral and hence social function ('all that is good and living'), yet at the same time constructs a clear distinction between literature and politics, so that the latter should not intrude on the former. Yet if literature is to be socially efficacious and to comment on matters of social importance, how can such a wall between literature and politics be sustained? As Asad (1990) argues, *The Satanic Verses*

> is constructed from the start within a field of modern reading-and-writing that extends beyond the activities of literary figures to include the scope of modern politics; the text acquires its representative status by tapping the network of images and power made available in that field and not another. (p. 249)

Within this field are included 'the self-fashioning narratives of militantly atheist readers who remember a repressive religious upbringing' (ibid.). Such memories are in part constructed using the Enlightenment story of secular European civilization's hard-won and relatively recent victory over ecclesiastical authority (Chapter 1) and as we saw in Chapter 5 a whole range of cultural memories is drawn on in the construction of liberal tradition, including the emergence of liberalism from the blight of religious wars. When examining reactions to the burning of *The Satanic Verses* below, we shall consider whether under such perceived attack these memories might sometimes harden into 'secular fundamentalism'.

A prominent theme in such secularist narratives is the functional displacement of religion by the various achievements of modernity – these include, as we have seen, modern 'systems' (Chapter 1) and the nation (Chapter 3), but also 'literature'. This is so not only among literary aesthetes like I. A. Richards and the New Critics in the 1930s; Rushdie's own comments point in this direction. Thus in 1990 he wrote that he possessed 'the same God-shaped hole' as Dr Adam Aziz, the patriarch of

Midnight's Children, and that 'Unable to accept the unarguable absolutes of religion I have filled up that hole with literature' (1990a p. 26). *Is Nothing Sacred?* (1990a) is constructed around an opposition between his love of literature ('I grew up kissing books and bread', p. 2), a love which 'need not be blind' (p. 3) and faith, which, he contends 'must, ultimately, be a leap in the dark' (1990).

The doctrine of salvation through literature reaches its partly self-mocking extreme in Fay Weldon's (1990) notorious defence of Rushdie:

> as a piece of revelatory writing *The Satanic Verses* reads pretty much to me like the works of St. John the Divine at the end of our own Bible ... St Salman the Divine. Too far? Probably. But if into the weevily meal and the brackish water of our awful, awful society, this good yeast is dropped ... all may yet be well and our brave new God of individual conscience may yet arise. (p. 42)

Yet, as Asad points out, it would be a mistake to represent the 'modern field of reading and writing' purely as it represents itself – as a private sphere (and hence in competition with religion), albeit one with public 'significance', from whose consequences it should, however, be protected. Rather, the modern 'private' sphere of writing and reading is made possible – indeed is structured – by the differentiated systems (legal, economic, political, and so on) of modern societies. The 'free speech' enjoyed by novelists is enabled, in Habermas's terms, by the fact that in modern differentiated societies the lifeworld is unburdened of some of its coordinating tasks by functional systems. In contrast, speech that threatens the functioning of systems – or those residual coordination roles still ascribed to the lifeworld – is not free. This can perhaps be seen most clearly by examining what kinds of speech are free – and what kinds cost – in an advanced industrialized democracy like Britain. Once again, the perspective of a British Muslim can help us to 'anthropologize' British norms:

> I do not want to see Salman die, that is immoral and wrong and anyway not what the majority Muslim population here [Bradford] want. I don't even think the book should be banned. But right from the beginning, I have felt that everyone was treating the Muslim protest as if it was completely crazy. This freedom of expression – why do we have pornography and libel laws and a law of blasphemy which applies only to Christianity? How can that be fair? (cited in Alibhai 1989a p. 12)

Speech is (and was in 1988) restricted in the UK in a number of ways: in the interests of private individuals (defamation, for example libel), national security (official secrets legislation), 'racial' minorities (incitement to racial hatred), public morality (restrictions on obscenity, for example pornography) and even Christianity (blasphemy). Informal mechanisms also operate: in 1988 a play called *Perdition*, which portrayed some Jewish communities as complicit in the Holocaust, was pulled during rehearsal stage in London's West End. Furthermore, some legally sanctioned restrictions of free speech may seem a good deal more trivial than the vilification of the central figure of a major religious tradition. For example, in 1993 Elton John was awarded £350,000[3] damages for allegations about his eating habits (*The Guardian* 5 November 1993). So why, Muslims asked, can they not be protected against verbal assaults?

The ways in which societies restrict speech depend on social values and, functionally interpreted, these in turn depend upon the means of social integration. National security is protected because the state is understood to be guarantor of rights and freedoms, and hence the regulator (and integrator) of systems. Restrictions on 'race' hatred are also seen as important for social integration, those on pornography principally now for the protection of minors rather than public propriety. Libel laws originate in the process of the mutual construction of the private sphere and the modern private individual, who is both entitled to speak in the public sphere and bound to observe the 'sphere of privacy' of other private individuals in so doing. In fact, libel is not a protection of privacy *per se*, since anything can be said publicly if it can be proven; rather it protects individuals against false accusation. Yet the impression of cultural bias – in the case of libel protecting individual reputation (of those who can afford it) and in the case of blasphemy and race hate speech protecting only selected forms of collective identity – remains.

Arguments about free speech thus need to be seen to emerge from a field of meaning in which not all speech is, in fact, free and hence to recognize that those less familiar with the conventions of this lifeworld may have difficulties in understanding them. Their puzzlement may in turn expose the limitations of rationalization within this lifeworld. Rushdie shares this lifeworld and hence takes his bearings largely from the expectations of this audience, and through this prism explores in the novel the contradictions of life in a plural society. We now turn to consider the formation of the Muslim public and its reception of *The Satanic Verses*. In doing so we accept, as with the literary public, that we are not referring to mutually exclusive and homogeneous groups, but rather to overlapping and intersecting collections of individuals whose shared history, experiences and assumptions may none the less be reconstructed as ideal-types.

4. Another Interpreting Community: British Muslims

Bradford in the late 1980s had a high density of Muslims among its ethnic minorities: approximately 50,000 compared with 9,000 Hindus and 8,000 Sikhs, in a Metropolitan district of about 450,000 (Lewis 1993 p. 119). Most of these lived (and continue to live, in contrast to the more dispersed settlement patterns amongst other minorities) within a half-dozen or so inner-city wards. In the preceding section we considered how *The Satanic Verses* has been interpreted by some, predominantly literary, critics, moving from sympathetic readings of the work as post-colonial literature to criticisms of it as out of touch with and insensitive to the experience of many migrants, colluding in rather than challenging the dominant discourses of Western societies. Critics who take this latter line contrast Rushdie's relatively privileged background with that of most British Muslims. Thus Asad (1990) writes:

> The remarkable thing about *The Satanic Verses*, considering what's been said about it, is that it isn't about the predicament of most immigrants at all. ... Most Muslims in Britain are proletarian, large numbers of whom have settled in the mill towns of northern England.

... The book's stories do not connect with the political-economic and cultural experiences of this population. (p. 257)

Asad's point is backed up by the available demographic and socio-economic portrait of Britain's, and especially Bradford's, Muslim communities.

(a) Bradford's Muslims in a British Context: Socio-Economic Profile, Prejudice and Honour

The majority of Muslims in Britain are from South Asian backgrounds (c.70–80 per cent, from Nielsen 1992 p. 41), with most of the rest from the Middle East and Africa and probably not more than five thousand white converts (p. 43). The Policy Studies Institute's (PSI) survey *Britain's Ethnic Minorities* (1993) drew on a range of studies conducted during the previous decade to consider the economic and social profile of Britain's minority populations, and is one of the first to pay specific attention to religious factors. Hence it provides a good source of information on British Muslims' economic and social fortunes in 1988–90.

First, geographical distribution. Pakistanis, who predominate in Bradford, are more heavily concentrated in the North of England than other groups, with only 19 per cent living in Greater London, compared with approximately 50 per cent of the other ethnic minority groups comprising the Muslim population. Second, social class. Most immigration from Britain's former colonies, or New Commonwealth immigration, came in the postwar years in response to shortages in the British labour market in manual and low-skilled occupations (with Asian immigration peaking some ten to fifteen years after Caribbean immigration). In the postwar years citizens of these countries could freely enter the UK to live and work and easily obtain full British citizenship; but as the postwar boom declined and immigrant numbers rose, immigration was progressively restricted through the late 1960s and early 1970s. Thus most immigrants joined the bottom rung of Britain's economic ladder. However, the PSI report suggests that in the last twenty years the economic fortunes of these groups have begun to differentiate markedly. Thus 'The essential diversity of the different ethnic groups is perhaps overcoming the common role in which immigrants were cast by British society' (Donaldson 1993 p. 151). So how have the groups which make up the British Muslim population fared? The report concludes:

The findings suggest that the South Asian population contains both the most and least successful of the ethnic minority groups that we have studied. At one extreme we have the African Asian and Indian populations. These groups have higher proportions of well qualified people, have attained comparable (or better) job levels compared to whites and have unemployment levels closest to those found amongst the white population. At the opposite end of the spectrum are the Pakistanis and Bangladeshis. They retain the largest proportion, even among young people, with no formal qualifications of any ethnic groups. They have substantially lower job levels than people of other origins and consistently suffer the highest rates of unemployment. ... Pakistanis and Bangladeshis stand out as the two groups in consistently poorer circumstances than all others. ... These two groups retain high proportions of employees in the semi-skilled and unskilled categories. (pp. 151–4)

It is among the Pakistani and Bangladeshi groups that most of Britain's Muslims are to be found. This pattern is not surprising given the rural background of many first-generation migrants from these countries. The majority of Bradford's first-generation migrants came from Azad Kashmir, an area where as we noted above in the 1980s as few as 8 per cent had completed primary education (Lewis 1994 p. 77). The jet-setting cosmopolitans of *The Satanic Verses* stand a long way from the economic fortunes of these groups. Parekh illustrates the resentment caused by inequalities in social status within the Muslim community by referring to recorded discussions between his colleague and a group of Muslims of mixed educational backgrounds, who had been active in opposition to the book. When asked why they had not involved Muslim intellectuals in 'the struggle' against the book, 'the reaction was immediate and fierce ... "All these scoundrels are useless. They were never ours, they never will be"', was the response of one teacher, while a graduate worker in a textile mill commented: 'They are all stooges of the whites. They talk a lot about struggle, but when have they been beaten up, lost their jobs or suffered a reduction in their salary? They think highly of themselves and hate us. It even seems they are ashamed of us' (Parekh 1991 p. 71). Such conditions and attitudes form the background to this group's response to *The Satanic Verses*. However, the PSI report failed to fully consider one important factor in Pakistani/Bangladeshi Muslim deprivation, and particularly relevant to these groups' reception of *The Satanic Verses*. The PSI report states baldly that: 'Previous research found that racial discrimination was experienced equally by all ethnic minority groups' (Donaldson 1993 p. 155). It continues by asserting that it is 'highly unlikely' that the situation would have changed. The only evidence offered in support of this assumption of stasis is 'the fact that both the most and least successful of the groups in the ethnic minority population *have a similar skin colour*' (p. 166, emphasis added). But is skin colour the only criterion on which people discriminate? Are the clean-shaven Asian professional in a smart Western suit and the *mullah* with traditional dress and full beard discriminated against solely in the same way, on the grounds of colour? Later in the 1990s, the Runnymede Trust's report *British Muslims and Islamophobia* (1997) was to demonstrate prejudice against Muslims on the grounds of perceptions of their culture rather than skin colour. Furthermore, aside from the inherent implausibility that prejudice should suddenly become more discriminating in the mid-1990s, there is considerable evidence of such culture/religion-based prejudice against Muslims from the period of *The Satanic Verses* controversy.

Thus a MORI poll commissioned by the Muslim Iqra trust in 1991 found high levels of specifically anti-Muslim prejudice: 17 per cent said they would not like to have a Muslim family living next door and two-thirds of those who expressed a view expressed a negative perception of Islam. Modood (1990 p. 127) cites a European Commission survey cited in *Today* newspaper (14 March 1990) which found that 'while Muslimophobia had not yet reached French proportions, Asians are the single most disliked minority in this country'. Being the object of such attitudes is likely to trigger a defensive response to perceived criticism.

There is also the matter of *izzat*, or honour, often associated with the *biraderi*, or extended family (Saifullah-Khan 1977; Jacobson 1998; Lewis 1994; Shaw 1988), but which can also be associated with the wider community. Standing up to insult against Mohammed came to be seen as a matter of pride by a community already bruised by the controversies of the 1980s, economic deprivation and racism. Furthermore, it was a community that had already been politicized by a series of local and national controversies running back to the 1960s.

(b) The Politicization of British Muslims: the Example of Bradford

The involvement of Bradford Muslims in campaigning on several local issues (some of which have had national ramifications) in the 1970s and 1980 prepared the community, organized through the Council for Mosques in particular, for a campaigning role. While the next section will look at institutional developments among Bradford's Muslims, this section will consider the substantive issues that helped shape the development of those institutions. Education is a common theme in these 'politicizing' events, central as it is in the reproduction of society.

(i) Bussing. The first of these issues was opposition to the council policy of 'bussing', a policy which lasted from 1964 to 1979 (Halstead 1988 p. 37). This involved taking children from areas with high concentrations of ethnic minorities to predominantly white areas and theoretically, though rarely in practice, vice versa. While Lewis argues that the impact of bussing should not be exaggerated, since only 15 per cent of Asian pupils were ever 'bussed' (1994 p. 71), many Muslim parents objected to this inequality, as well as to the inconvenience caused. For example, Muslim parents had difficulties in attending parents' evenings and other extra-curricular events, because fewer Muslim parents in the inner city had access to cars than suburban parents. There was also the suspicion, well founded in economic terms, that the policy persisted after it had been abandoned elsewhere in the country because it saved money – the rapid growth of the ethnic minority population called for a large building programme in the inner city if all were to be schooled there. Probably the main issue, however, was one of the right of children of minorities to education in their own area and the notion of 'community schooling'. Halstead (1988 p. 39) tells us that 'Councillors Ajeeb and Hameed called the policy racist and considered it an affront to the freedom and dignity of ethnic minority parents'. Parents, teachers and others organized to present a thousand-signature petition to the council in 1979, which together with pressure from the Commission for Racial Equality led to the policy being dropped.

(ii) Halal Meat. Halal ('permitted') meat has been slaughtered in accordance with Islamic law and is the only kind of meat that Muslims are allowed to eat. Although the 1974 Slaughterhouse Act gives local authorities a licence to permit *halal* and *kosher* (Jewish) methods of slaughter, public institutions did not serve any *halal* meat until 1983 (Halstead 1988 pp. 45–6). In Bradford schools, then, Muslim children had to opt for vegetarian meals, and as numbers grew through the 1970s, so pressure from Muslim parents to provide *halal* meat mounted. In 1983 the local education authority piloted a scheme which extended to cover sixty schools within a year; however, opposition followed from an unlikely alliance of animal rights activists and the National Front. Muslims organized in reaction, presenting a petition

with 7,000 signatures to support provision. In March 1984 the council voted by a large majority to continue the service (ibid.).

(iii) Honeyford. The Ray Honeyford affair saw the Muslim community take a leading role in organizing the campaign for the removal of Honeyford, head teacher of Drummond Middle School between 1980 and 1985, a school with 90 per cent Muslim Pakistani children (Lewis 1994 p. 150). Between 1982 and 1984 Honeyford published several articles in the *The Times Educational Supplement* and the right-wing journal *The Salisbury Review*, a publication at that stage committed to the repatriation of ethnic minorities (ibid. p. 151). In these he made offensive remarks about Asian and Afro-Caribbean cultures. He accused Asians of importing 'the hysterical political temperament of the Indian subcontinent' and described Pakistan as 'a country which cannot cope with democracy ... the heroin capital of the world', which, he added, is a 'fact which is now reflected in the drug problems of English cities with Asian populations'. In the same article, Afro-Caribbean homes are portrayed as places 'where educational ambition and the values to support it are conspicuously absent' (Honeyford 1984 p. 31).

Honeyford also provided a New Right justification for monocultural education policies. He argued that in the 'pretty ruthless meritocracy' of the early 1980s Britain children need an education that equips them to compete in terms of mainstream culture. It is therefore a mistake to attempt to 'enhance the self-respect of settler children by teaching the culture of their parents' mother land and a critical view of British imperialism' (in Halstead 1988 p. 57).

A variety of parents, Asian and Muslim groups campaigned for Honeyford's removal, rivalry developing for leadership between the secular and left-wing Asian Youth movement and the Council for Mosques (Samad 1992 p. 513). Bradford Council, while split cross-party over the issue, was at odds with Honeyford over his highly public criticisms of their 'multi-racial' education policies. Support for Honeyford was considerable; the 'Friends of Drummond Middle School' collected some 10,000 signatures in his support and his union, the National Association of Head Teachers, gave him full support throughout (ibid. p. 514). Eventually a controversial settlement was reached whereby Honeyford agreed to early retirement in exchange for a substantial payoff (ibid.).

The extent of support for Honeyford suggests that the affair resulted in, or exposed, considerable ill-feeling toward Bradford's Muslims. As for internal organization, Samad comments that:

> No organization involved in the Honeyford affair emerged as undisputed leader of the Mirpuri community. But it had opened new vistas of agitational politics to the Bradford Council for Mosques and given them credibility in the eyes of the politicized Mirpuri youth. (Ibid.)

In the context of the development of civil society in Bradford, it is notable that this 'agitational' style of politics prevented reasoned discussion of the substantive issues that Honeyford raised, in spite of his inflamatory language. As Lewis (1994 pp. 152–3) comments, 'The headteacher's opinions on three important inter-related issues: racism, free speech and accountability – were never exposed to open debate but merely shouted down'. The result was increased polarization between sections of the white and Muslim populations, creating suspicion on both sides that fanned the flames of *The Satanic Verses* controversy.

(iv) 1988 Education Act. The 1988 Education Act contained controversial provisions relating to religious education and the conduct of assemblies. The Act requires that education be 'mainly' and 'broadly Christian', worship 'mainly or wholly' so; schools wishing to have a lower proportion of Christian assemblies must apply for a special licence renewable every five years, a position which considerably antagonized some Muslims (Akhtar 1993). The provisions for religious education appear to run contrary to the direction of developments during the last thirty years to 'pluralize' religious education in schools. There has been a shift from confessional, religious nurture approaches towards methods which seek to impart an understanding and appreciation of the variety of religious traditions without commitment to any of them.

Muslim views of these approaches vary; more orthodox Muslims are likely to be suspicious of the non-confessional approaches, seeing here the tacit inculcation of secular humanism, in terms ranging from disdain for a 'wishy-washy' approach to the full-blown conspiracy theory of Kalim Siddiqui:

> The western civilization is fundamentally an immoral civilization ... such moral values as survived the Christian experience were systematically eradicated. ... Those parts of our societies that the West has succeeded in disintegrating from the highly integrated Islamic social order all display the same symptoms of corporate selfishness and a shift away from moral behaviour. (In Nielsen 1991 p. 469)

Siddiqui draws attention to the moral implications of 'western civilization', refusing the Western self-image of neutrality. His style may be confrontational, but Siddiqui is not alone in making the latter point; the difficulties with concepts of neutrality in Western political philosophy were discussed in Chapter 5. Some educational theorists have also challenged this perception of neutrality, seeing approaches that attempt to combat prejudice as prejudiced and ethnocentric themselves: 'The comprehensiveness of constituent cultures is subordinated at critical points to the practical judgement of an established educational philosophy which is assumed to be logically prior to all others' (Hulmes 1989 p. 13). In these circumstances, Muslims may prefer a Christian orientation to religious education to secular approaches, the former being seen as closer to an Islamic value system. But the implied normativity of Christianity in the Act also led to resistance, not least in the form of the demand for separate schools.

(v) 'Separate' schools. Until 1998 there were no voluntary-aided Muslim schools, enjoying the same combination of state-funding status and religious foundation as Anglican, Catholic and Jewish schools. There were a number of independent Muslim schools, including the Muslim Girls' High School in Bradford (now Feversham College),[4] which had up to 100 pupils between eleven and eighteen years of age. Repeated applications for voluntary-aided schools with religious foundations outside the Jewish and Christian traditions had consistently been refused by councils

in various parts of the country, though on technicalities rather than issues of principle (Halstead 1988).

In spite of the apparent inequality of this situation, the Muslim community appears to have been divided in its attitude to such schools; for example in 1983 the Bradford Council for Mosques voted 13–8 against a proposal to convert Belle Vue Girls' School into one. The latter is one of the few surviving single sex state schools in the area and has predominantly Muslim pupils. However, numbers of such schools are likely to increase in future, given that support of both major political parties for schools opting out of local education control developed during the 1990s. Then in 1998 the new Labour administration granted voluntary-aided status to two Muslim primary schools, the first non-Jewish or Christian schools to achieve this status (Parker-Jenkins 1999). Their growth raises questions about the role of education in social integration, which will be further discussed below. For now, these five examples each demonstrate the willingness of the Muslim community by the end of the 1980s to contend actively for the maintenance of their sense of community and religious traditions. We consider next the kind of mediating institutions that Bradford's Muslims developed to enable them to mobilize politically, as well as perform other functions of community maintenance and development.

(c) Civil society in Bradford? The growth of Muslim voluntary organizations to 1989

> Writing about South Asians in Bradford in 1972–3 an anthropologist concluded that the community was 'fragmented with no 'grass-root' organizations'. It would not be possible 20 years later to say the same thing. While the mosques represent the largest investment by the Muslim communities to preserve religious, cultural and linguistic distinctiveness, there has also been a proliferation of often complementary and overlapping associations reflecting diverse ... allegiances. Some appeal mainly to elders, others to youth and many straddle both groups. This dense network of voluntary community initiatives – some funded in partnership with local and central government – both support and express a measure of cultural autonomy. (Lewis 1994 p. 67)

In this quotation Lewis provides a concise summary of the dense network of Muslim organizations in Bradford. This section aims to give a sense of the diversity of these organizations, the tensions between them and the function of some of them in representing 'the Muslim community' in its relationship with the local and national state.

Muslim voluntary organizations in Bradford by the late 1980s ranged from the Gujar Khan burial society, which organizes burials in members' home region of Pakistan, through various cultural and regionally based self-help associations, to the numerous mosque organizations that are predominantly related to three streams of Pakistani Islamic tradition. They include bodies part-financed by or self-established to liaise with Bradford Council, the former including various community centres, the latter the Council for Mosques. They also include the networks and initiatives of Bradford's business community, though these were to become much more prominent in the wake of *The Satanic Verses* controversy. As we shall see below, the growth of prominence of the business community's initiatives arguably represents a shift of emphasis from the reproduction and representation of religious traditions (typified by the mosques and Council for Mosques) to the development of open debate between sections of the community (and concern for with community representation) and hence represents the development of what might be termed a Muslim public sphere.

The three main traditions to which Bradford's mosques are affiliated are Barelwi, Deobandi and Jamaati Islami, all with roots in the Indian subcontinent, the former two in nineteenth century colonial India, the latter in the late colonial period (founded 1941) and post-colonial Pakistan. The former has already been linked to special reverence for Muhammad, and the sufi mysticism associated with this group includes belief in the intercessory powers of the Prophet and the ability of holy men to perform miracles including 'walking on water, flying in the air ... [and] raising the dead' (Lewis 1994 p. 88). Good innovation in tradition (*bid'at-i hasana*) is seen as acceptable.

Some commentators on *The Satanic Verses* controversy have pointed out that the strongest protests against the book came predominantly from South Asian heritage Muslims. Thus, with the exception of Iran, the countries most affected by the controversy have been those with substantial populations of South Asian Muslims: India, Pakistan, South Africa and Britain, and within Britain communities most active in the protests were of Pakistani heritage (Samad 1992 p. 510). This is because of the special reverence for Muhammad in these traditions, particularly evident in the case of the *Barelwi* movement, which has been 'accused by its opponents of treating Mohammed like a deity' (Nielsen 1992 p. 133). This further serves to differentiate the anger expressed by British Muslims from the general global development of radical Islamism:

> If Rushdie had successfully attacked fundamentalism, as I believe he intended, many Muslims would have cheered and certainly there would not be the present lines of confrontation. It was not the exploration of religious doubt but the lampooning of the Prophet that provoked the anger. This sensitivity has nothing to do with Qur'anic fundamentalism but with South Asian reverence for Mohammed (deemed by many Muslims, including fundamentalists, to be excessive) and cultural insecurity as experienced in Britain and even more profoundly in India. (Modood 1990 p. 129)

Although they share a strong reverence for Muhammad, the Deobandis seek to reform sufistic traditions and in their seminaries and private schools at Bury and Dewsbury (50 and 10 miles from Bradford) to propagate a puritanical and to some extent rationalized version of Islam, rejecting Barelwi supernaturalism and innovation in the tradition, as well as visually based media and music, since the first are seen as idolatrous, the second as corrupting. Here we see the differential impact of modernization on religious traditions: while miracle-believing Barelwis are open to the use of electronic media, rationalizing Deobandis reject new media.

Instruction at the Deobandi school in Dewsbury illustrates aspects of the difficulties facing traditional Pakistani Islam in British society. In 1989 the morning curriculum for the 300 students consisted largely of studying set texts, with the students learning to translate *hadith* from Arabic into Urdu and reproduce the interpretation of their teacher (Lewis 1994 p. 94). This contrasts with the skills of developing individual judgement needed for reasoned participation in public spheres in Britain. In the afternoon students were taught up to GCSE level in core subjects in the British curriculum; however, no attempt was made to integrate or even relate the morning and afternoon's curricula:

> in the morning they will study *Lessons from Islam*, in Urdu, ... and read about the miracles wrought by the Prophet, including 'splitting the moon', based on sura 54:1 of the Qur'an. This is interpreted literally. In the afternoon they will study general science in English. A possible discordance between these two worlds is neither acknowledged nor addressed. (Lewis 1994 p. 94)

In contrast to the Egyptian case (Starrett 1998), no attempt is made to synthesize Islamic tradition and modern science. The difficulties suggested by this education process are likely to be even greater for *ulema* brought up and educated on the subcontinent within the Barelwi tradition.

While only a small minority of pupils are educated in private or voluntary-aided Muslim schools, perhaps the majority of Muslim children attend supplementary Qur'an schools, held in mosques after state school finishes. English-educated *ulema* remain rare and children (mostly boys – there is limited provision for girls) are often taught in very large (up to 70) mixed age (5–16 years) groups. Most instruction is in Urdu and centres on memorizing the Qur'an and repeating the '*alim*'s intepretation, with discipline administered by a short cane (Lewis 1994 pp. 140–1). As Dr Munir Ahmed of Young Muslims UK commented in 1989, small wonder boys 'at the first opportunity ... rebelled against a religion, which has sometimes literally been beaten into them' (*The Muslim News*, 15 December 1989).

Against this background the appeal and constituency of the third main Islamic group in Britain, which in the late 1980s supported two mosques in Bradford, becomes clear. This is the Jamaati Islami (Society of Islam), formed on the subcontinent by Abul A'la Maududi in 1941, and associated with a number of organizations in Britain. These include the Islamic Foundation (a Leicester-based publishing house and from 1990 tertiary education institution: the Markfield Institute of Higher Education), Young Muslims UK, the UK Islamic Mission and Dawat al-Islam (relating primarily to Bangladeshi Muslims). In Pakistan it has appealed to tertiary-educated urban groups outside the political élite and in Britain to similar groups: for example, in the 1970s and 1980s two of the leaders of the Islamic Foundation were graduates of Leicester University (Lewis 1994 p. 104).

Yet Jamaati Islami has found it difficult to establish a strong following in Bradford (only two mosques in 1994), largely because its Islamist message had little appeal to the rural background first-generation migrants. And while it has had more success in youth work, it has also had problems in Bradford, for different reasons from its failure to establish itself as a major force among the older generation. It seems that young British leaders, while supporting the Islamist critique of traditional Islam, found the uncritical devotion to *pirs* redirected to the person of Maududi and the rhetoric of the Islamic state, of little practical relevance in a UK context (Lewis 1994).

However, through its magazine *Trends* Jamaati Islami's youth wing, Young Muslims UK, shows a willingness to engage with pressing issues facing young Muslims unrivalled by anything the Deobandis have produced: subjects such as masturbation, contraception, divorce, women's rights and religious freedom are addressed in its 'agony aunt' column. Significantly, some of the advice given has begun to depart from the teachings of Maududi and is in line with Islamist thinking elsewhere, for example on the issue of contraception. Its attitude of more open engagement is indicative of a number of initiatives in the 1990s in Bradford and elsewhere that were to signal a new phase in the development of a Muslim public sphere.

The Council for Mosques was founded in 1981 on the initiative of Umar Warraich, a public health inspector unattached to either of the main Barelwi or Deobandi groupings. It aimed to present a united front to advise public bodies in the city, especially on education, to provide a forum for the discussion or at least management of sectarian differences, and a platform from which to appeal for local and national authority funds. Its constitution carefully sought to balance sectarian rivalries and ensured that it consisted mostly of businessmen experienced in dealing with a variety of groups in the city and beyond, rather than *ulema*, but it was not democratic in the sense that members were co-opted rather than voted for by local Muslims. In this sense it resembles the Roundtable groups formed to take forward the transition to democracy in many Eastern European countries (Burgess 1997; below, Chapter 7) and for the same reasons: to ensure broad representation and exclude populist elements that might obstruct the negotiation process.

The Council for Mosques was successful in attracting council funding in the 1980s, establishing a headquarters and broad social programme including centres for the elderly and advice workers, and employing 50 workers, until the rules for receipt of Manpower Services Commission funding changed in 1988. Through shared membership of the Community Relations Council it was able to form strategic alliances with other minority groups and through its connections with Muslim councillors (three in 1981, nine by 1991) it was able to mobilize political support (Lewis 1994 p. 147). The council played a leading role in campaigning for *halal* meat, but its intervention in the Honeyford affair, while effective in removing Honeyford, was, as we have seen, damaging to community relations and open public discussion.

We have now considered something of the contents of *The Satanic Verses*, the assumptions of its primary audience and the composition, history,and organizational development of Bradford's Muslims in the broad British context. We are therefore in a position to consider the critical events of 1988–90 and then the longer-term consequences of the controversy and other developments relevant to British Muslims' role in civil society and the public sphere.

5. Dissemination of *The Satanic Verses* to British Muslims, and the Offending Passages

British Muslims became aware of *The Satanic Verses* controversy through their connections with the Indian subcontinent, rather than through the reviews or publication of the book in Britain; extracts of the offending passages were circulated via Bradford's mosque network (*The Sunday Times* 19 February 1989; in Appignanesi and Maitland 1989 pp. 56–7). This fragmentary form in which the novel was circulated has led to the accusation that British Muslims condemned the book without having taken the trouble to read it (Hulmes 1992 p. 47). This dispute is an interesting one to consider in the context of developing an account of the public sphere(s) in multicultural societies.

First, following the arguments presented in Part I, the differentiated information society is one in which the abundance of information available is so great that it is not practical for any one individual to master it all; in this context, reliance on sources of 'digested' and 'pre-packaged' information becomes essential. It is ironic that the same society that prizes the autonomy of individuals to judge and decide for themselves and through the Internet provides unprecedented access to a diversity of sources from which to do so, also prizes and structurally necessitates specialization, and has multiplied sources of information beyond the individual's capacity to process all of it. Mayhew (1997; Chapter 4 above) recognizes the problem this situation poses for democratic participation and proposes the solution of 'deliberative forums for redemptive communication', where the 'rhetorical tokens of civic leaders' can be redeemed, as a response. Our account of the development of Muslim civil society in Bradford suggests the beginnings of the development of such forums and as we shall describe below, these were to develop further in the 1990s.

But the point to note here is that in accessing information through mediating channels, Bradford's Muslims were not unique: this reliance on mediated information is part of life in the information society. Defenders of the book also often relied on (albeit) different mediating sources, principally the British press. There is also the further argument that if a text is held to be unacceptable by sources of authority deemed reliable by the individual, it is reasonable to decide not to engage with it further (the basis of film certification, for example). However, it is clearly a different matter to argue on such a basis that a work should not be available to others.

It is also important to note that the public sphere to which Bradford's Muslims related was in the late 1980s more oriented to South Asia than to Britain. Hence the whole affair demonstrates the dangers of the fragmentation of the public sphere within a national society and of the cultural isolation of particular communities. Furthermore, it may also be argued that if one wants to challenge social norms of the free circulation of information (albeit constrained in practice, as we shall discuss below), the impetus is on you to research your case. Yet some have sought to justify the outrage of Muslims who had not read the book, by putting it in the context of other important decisions and life-orientations made on the authority of a text without full knowledge of it:

> As for the assertion that one cannot be indignant about a book unless one has read it ..., it is a new qualification about having an opinion: that you cannot form an opinion unless you have experienced the thing yourself. There are millions of believing Christians who *have* read only a few pages of the Bible. There are also Muslims who can read the Qur'an without understanding it. There are also believing Jews who know only a few quotes from the Torah. (Mazrui 1991 p. 28)

Thus traditional lifeworlds, indeed the process of enculturation in all societies, relies on the reception and absorption of knowledge and values without (or at least prior to) what Habermas has called the process of 'discursive deliberation'.

Knowledge is inevitably mediated, not only because of its volume in the modern information society, but also because of the processes of learning and cultural transmission. The important normative lesson, however, would seem not to be a justification of Muslim non-reading of the text, understandable as this may be, but rather the importance of establishing effective communication between different publics in a multicultural society. In this context, let us turn to consider two key events that stand entwined at the centre of media representation, and consequently in public perception, of *The Satanic Verses* controversy. These are the book-burning in Bradford on 16 January 1989 and Ayatollah Khomeini's *fatwa* on 14 February 1989.

A month apart, these events have fused in public perception, symbolized on the envelope of a letter received by Shabbir Akhtar, a leading figure in the Bradford campaign against the book, addressed simply 'The Ayatollah's Bradford Acolyte, Dr Shabbir Akhtar' (Akhtar 1989, p. 50). In particular, public perceptions of the controversy have been almost entirely filtered through the prism of the *fatwa*, with murderous intent read back into the Bradford conflagration. However, there is no evidence that Bradford's book-burners had an inkling of Khomeini's forthcoming judgement (Robinson 1992 p. 39), so that at least the book-burning should be judged independently. Indeed, it will be argued that on close examination each of these incidents appears somewhat differently from their dominant media portrayals.

6. Formative Events of *The Satanic Verses* Controversy

(a) Book-burning

The Bradford book-burning followed five months of peaceful lobbying which had failed to catch the media's attention. Since the book's publication on 26 September 1988, Muslim organizations, first the Islamic Foundation in Leicester, then the Bradford Council for Mosques and the Union of Muslim Organizations (UMO), had been lobbying Viking-Penguin (the publishers) and the government. The first letter from the Bradford Council for Mosques, acting on summaries of the book from Indian-published Urdu newspapers, urged the Prime Minister to follow the example of the Indian government and ban the book. It focused on the distress caused to Muslims and did not threaten or accuse Rushdie of apostasy (Lewis 1994 pp. 156–7). Max Madden, a Bradford MP, suggested that the publishers insert into the book a short explanation of why Muslims found the book offensive and called for a television debate between Rushdie and Muslim critics, which could perhaps have generated public discussion before the situation polarized . The former suggestion appears to have been endorsed by some Muslim leaders: 'At this early stage many Muslim leaders were not asking for the book to be banned but for the insertion of a statement reasserting that it was a piece of fiction' (Samad 1992 p. 514).

However, while Penguin wrote to say that they were 'truly sorry for the distress the book had caused', they insisted that Muslim 'reaction is based on a misreading of the book' and called on the support of 'the critics' to endorse their claim (Ruthven 1990 pp. 102–3). Thus Penguin made a clear judgement as to which interpreting community had made the 'right reading'. Madden's requests were refused. On 11 November, in response to a letter from the UMO's Dr Syed Pasha, the Prime Minister (Margaret Thatcher) stated that 'there are no grounds on which the government would consider banning the book' (*Sunday Times* 19 February 1989, in Appignanesi and Maitland 1989 p. 57). Further approaches to the Home Office by Pasha met with a negative response, while a leading law firm, Kingsley Napley, advised that the blasphemy law applied only to Christianity.

Formal legal and political channels blocked, Muslim activists resorted to non-violent direct action. In an attempt to bring Muslim grievances to public attention, a book-burning was held in Bolton in December 1988, but it was not widely reported in the media (Akhtar 1989 p. 43). Therefore Bradford Council for Mosques deliberately informed the press before the Bradford book-burning (Ruthven 1990 p. 103). However, the publicity that they achieved through this event was not as they had anticipated: 'All the newspapers commented ... *Times, Daily Telegraph, Guardian, Yorkshire Post*. They compared us to Hitler' (Liaqat Hussein of the *Jamiaat Tabligh ul Islami*[5], in Ruthven 1990 p. 99). It is worth pointing out that while in Bradford WH Smith had been forced to withdraw the book due to threats before Khomeini's *fatwa* (Samad 1992 p. 515), the only place in the UK where this was so, no threats had been made to Rushdie or his family (Webster 1989 p. 126). This strongly suggests that anger was directed to the contents of the book, rather than at Rushdie as a person:

Although Muslims were intensely frustrated and angry and although isolated individuals spoke of violence, no Muslims, to my knowledge, threatened Rushdie or his wife's life, or even threw a stone at him or his house, at a time when he was unguarded and vulnerable. (Parekh 1990 p. 62)

While most media attention focused on Muslim outrage, both media presentations of the book-burning and the comments of many non-Muslim commentators also expressed considerable anger. This anger needs to be understood in the context of British, and more widely European, historical memories. In particular, anger was aroused through the association of the book-burning with Khomeini's *fatwa*. Why such a powerful connection? Asad's comments, quoted at the beginning of this chapter (labore p. 157), shed some light on the power of cultural memory in this context.

In the burning of a character in a book with the burning of paper and ink, Asad exposes a liberal sacred space opaque to a crude positivist distinction between metaphor (artifice) and literalism (reality). Broadly liberal reactions to book-burning, especially when the burning is performed by a religious group, need to be understood in the context of cultural memory. These include the still-living memory of the burning of books by the Nazis, the more distant but still-evocative cultural memories of the Inquisition and the emergence of the modern nation-state from the religious strife of post-Reformation Europe. They also include the turbulent history of the West's relations with Islam; of the Crusades, of Turks at the gates of Vienna at the birth of modern Europe, and also of 'Orientalist' representations of Islam which legitimated colonial practices and which continue to form part of influential Western discourses (Said 1978).

Thus liberal responses need to be understood in terms of the history of Europe and the stories that Europeans have told about themselves in response to, and in shaping, this history. Some commentators have gone further, arguing that liberalism, with its connotation of open-minded tolerance, is an inappropriate word to describe popular reaction to the book-burning. For example, D'Costa (1990 p.419) has described media responses to the event as 'secular fundamentalist'. He explains his admittedly provocative use of the term as follows: 'fundamentalism can be said to represent an unquestioned authority given to a particular revelation of the way things are; in this case, a secular metaphysics with its attendant political and social baggage' (ibid.). He admits that there are varieties of secular fundamentalism, but goes on to argue that within this diversity there are certain core characteristics which justify using the term. To make the argument, he analyses a letter printed in *The Independent on Sunday* near the anniversary of the *fatwa* and Rushdie's repudiation of the term in *Is Nothing Sacred?* (D'Costa 1990). D'Costa believes Rushdie's views to be widely shared (p. 419). The text of the letter which he cites runs:

> The events following the publication of Salman Rushdie's *The Satanic Verses* highlight the fundamental obstruction to the further development of society. Belief, that is the dogmatic rejection of reason and the acceptance of ideas on the basis of 'faith' alone, provides man with a box to hide from the realities of life. Belief, be it religious or political, has been the major cause of war, conflict and disunity. ... To build a better society and a better world we must be prepared to question and to reason; belief obstructs the path towards achievement of this ultimate aim. (In D'Costa 1990 pp. 425–6)

Despite its polemic against 'beliefs', D'Costa argues that the letter itself demonstrates the presence of a number of beliefs, in the sense of assertions whose content it is possible to dispute reasonably. First, he points out that the belief that it is possible to have no beliefs is itself a belief. Second, the belief that context-free reason is possible is a view we have contested in Part I following MacIntyre (1985, 1988). Third is the conviction that 'no mode of discourse other than itself can facilitate the conditions where other discourses can survive' (D'Costa 1990 p. 426). This last assertion relates closely one of the main aims of the book, which is to discover whether there is (or could realistically be) a civil society in which a diversity of institutions and worldviews prospers, and which gives rise to a public sphere in which the latter can be freely discussed. We have sought to examine this question both in societies that are culturally dominated by a particular religious tradition (hence Egypt and Poland) and in societies where no single religious tradition has cultural hegemony (hence Britain and Bosnia). We have also set out to establish whether religious organizations can function in civil society in a way that supports public discussion and respect for the basic rights of individuals and communities who may fundamentally disagree.

D'Costa finds a particular answer to these questions to be presumed within the reader's letter: the presumption that only secular discourses can sustain civil society. This view is empirically contestable, because it appears that in some circumstances religious discourses can support normative civil society. But it is also problematic because it implies that religious discourses should be confined to the private sphere, hence undermining some of the diversity in the public sphere that it purports to sustain. D'Costa (1990) finds evidence of a similar position in Rushdie's writings.

First, the claim to be without beliefs:

> [Rushdie] writes 'I have never in my adult life affirmed any belief' (1990a, p. 19), yet he provides us with a manifesto replete with metaphysical, ethical and epistemological beliefs ... Rushdie has found and preaches the truth as he sees it: a godless universe which is self-created and socially constructed, in which all rules, duties and obligations are human made and open to change, in which the individual has Promethean rights to question and write, and a universe in which love is nevertheless worth striving for. (p. 427)

D'Costa is 'certainly not against a person holding such a view', but is concerned that the view is not recognized by its proponents as a 'sacred discourse' (ibid.). This is because without such recognition, disagreements with people holding alternative views of the sacred are likely to be perceived as unprovoked attacks. Second, the claim that only secular discourses can sustain diversity. In the climax of the essay *Is Nothing Sacred?* Rushdie constructs a parable in which literature is represented as a special, set-aside room in the crowded, run-down, dangerous house that represents the world: 'Literature is the one place in any society where, within the secrecy of our own heads, we can hear voices talking about everything in every possible way' (D'Costa 1990 p. 16). The assumptions here are interesting. First, 'literature' is described as a unique and universal location for the exercise of a certain kind of freedom. Second, the private reading of literature is viewed as an activity not just of universal significance (for the exercise of freedom), but also capable of capturing the full range of human meanings in the form of a certain kind of (Cartesian) interior dialogue. Thus the claim is made that everything that can be said can be said through literature and appreciated through its private reading.

From a comparative cultural perspective, these assumptions are highly question-able. Contrast, for example, the meaning of reading in the case of the pedagogical practice of the Deobandi school of Islam, introduced above. More than half the mosques in Bradford are affiliated to this school, and there is substantial continuity between the teaching methods described in the account below of practice at the turn of the century and contemporary methods (Lewis 1994). At one level, the Deobandi movement represents a similar response to modernization to the nineteenth-century reform of Egyptian schooling described in Chapter 1. Thus the Qur'an becomes a source book of moral and practical lessons to be cognitively processed rather than simply memorized and performed, as in a more traditional oral culture (ibid. p. 79).

However, the sphere of learning and doing is not differentiated and both remain public, the process oriented to internalizing conformity rather than to creating an inner private space for reflection. Thus private reading is not encouraged, as Maulana Thanawi's *Bihishti Zewar* ('Heavenly Ornaments', 1906), a book of instruction for women still in use in some Deobandi mosques in Bradford, makes clear. Thanawi's work was intended, as one commentator observes

> for an oral, public world. It was to be read aloud, discussed openly, taught in groups ...[but it] discourage[d] ... the privacy of reading silently, of creating a private world of one's own inner voice by losing oneself – a terrible image, in Thanawi's view – in books like novels. (Metcalf 1990 p. 21; in Lewis 1994 pp. 79–80)

Thus Deobandi pedagogy provides an example of the grafting of literacy onto an established, primarily oral social world, a legacy that persists. The publicity of knowledge in such a world is differently constituted to that in a literacy-based and hence, in part, more highly differentiated society. It is highly questionable whether the private acts of writing and reading – of which novel-writing/reading is only one genre – can reconstruct the forms of knowledge created and shared in such a culture. For if there are elements that are untranslatable between different written languages, how much more so between literacy and orally based cultures (MacIntyre 1988). Indeed, viewed historically, the novel is one mechanism by which oral cultures were 'colonized' by the literacy-based world.

This can be seen by recalling the account of the development of the bourgeois public sphere in Chapter 3. In the late eighteenth and early nineteenth centuries the novel was, in part, constitutive of the creation of this discursive public sphere (Habermas 1989). As European nations colonized other parts of the world, so their literacy-based practices – and the whole panoply of 'disciplinary' practices Foucault describes so vividly – spread with them and impacted in various ways on different strata of the societies they colonized. Cultures of 'secondary orality' – where writing had long been known but practised alongside and in some ways subordinate to oral performance and modes of organizing knowledge – were among the colonized. Thus the practice of reading sophisticated fiction, both in terms of the private use of texts and the particular form of 'the novel', is historically and culturally specific, underlining the case presented in Section 3 above. Yet because of its familiarity to a Western audience and its role in shielding the lifeworld from the incursions of systems, Rushdie's assertion of its universal potentialities for representation and the nurturing of freedom becomes plausible.

In this way, the particular form in which Rushdie presents the argument that only secular discourses can sustain diversity – that is, based on the idea of a literary public sphere – seems to be undermined by the inability of the literary public sphere to represent oral cultures without distortion. As we saw above (Section 3), such claims for the efficacy of a literary public sphere in sustaining diversity in a socially significant way are also damaged by the relative marginality of this sphere in a world dominated by functional systems (economics, politics and so on). At the same time, such an argument itself undermines diversity by denying a public voice to religions. Rushdie has recently developed this argument in the wake of the terrorist attacks of 11 September 2001. In *The Guardian* on 2 November 2001 he argues that Muslims need to accept that Islam should become a private faith in the modern world, drawing a sharp distinction between Islam as a private faith and the political Islam of Islamists. On the basis of this false dichotomy, he proceeds to lump together moderate Islamist groups like the Muslim Brotherhood in Egypt, who condemned the attacks on America and seek Islamization through democratic means, with terrorist organizations like bin Laden's *al-Khajida*.

Such attitudes only make the formation of democratic alliances more difficult. Certainly, there are important questions to ask about Islamist ideas and practices of democracy, as we discuss in Chapter 9. But to attempt to impose a partial reading of the development of church-state relations in Western Europe on the rest of the world robs one of the ability to recognize the diversity of forms of public religion across the world, including in Britain.

In this perspective, it is possible to view the Bradford book-burning as less the calculated action of an organized and dangerous Islamic fifth column, and more as an ill-advised though graphic and non-violent expression of the frustration of a relatively powerless minority. There is certainly no evidence of any direct foreign connection with the demonstrations (Modood 1990 pp. 127–8; Ruthven 1990 pp. 97–8). This brings us to the infamous *fatwa*.

(b) Khomeini's Fatwa

Ironically, whether in ignorance or contempt for the rhythms of the secular season, it was on Valentine's Day 14 February 1989 that Ayatollah Khomeini issued a *fatwa*, or 'learned legal opinion' (Modood 1990 p. 129), which condemned Salman Rushdie, the author of *The Satanic Verses*, to death. The crime for which Rushdie was condemned was not blasphemy, which has no strict equivalent in Islam (Ally 1990 p. 23), but rather *riddah*, literally 'turning back' from the path of Islam, usually translated 'apostasy' (p. 25). According to many contemporary Muslim commentators, including some Islamists, two kinds of *riddah* can be distinguished (ibid.; Tamimi and Mayer in Herbert 2001b). This opinion arises from the Qur'anic testimony. On the one hand, the Qur'an declares that 'There is no compulsion in religion' (2: 256) and indicates punishment in the afterlife rather than the present life for those who turn away from faith (2: 217, 16: 106). On the other hand, a series of severe penalties, including death, is prescribed where apostasy is accompanied by fighting against the Islamic community (5: 36–7). On this basis it is argued that:

> a quiet desertion of personal Islamic duties is not a sufficient reason for inflicting death on a person. Only when the individual's desertion of Islam is used as a political tool for instigating a state disorder, or revolting against the law of Islam, can the individual apostate then be put to death as a just punishment for his act of treason and betrayal of the Muslim community. (Ally 1990 pp. 25–6)

However, it also possible that Khomeini considered Rushdie to be guilty of apostasy in the second sense of 'instigating ... state disorder'. This is because on the two days before the *fatwa* seven people were killed and more than one hundred injured in two separate riots following protests against the book in Islamabad, Pakistan, and Kashmir, India (Appignanesi and Maitland 1989 p. ix). Thus Khomeini may have seen Rushdie's rejection of Islam evidenced in the book and the international means of its dissemination, as deliberately designed to provoke the international Islamic community and so held him and his publishers responsible for these civil disturbances and consequent Muslim deaths. The national day of mourning called in Iran for the victims of the riots on 15 February supports this view. In this light the judgement of what might be termed 'aggravated apostasy' begins to become intelligible.

Khomeini was also playing to the political stage, vying for political leadership of the Muslim world with Saudi Arabia. Thus, ironically, while the *fatwa* led the Western media to perceive a world Muslim conspiracy, one commentator has argued that 'the *fatwa* was the deathblow to the internationalization of the campaign because the ... Organization of Islamic Conference [OIC] refused to endorse Khomeini's diktat' (Samad 1992 p. 511). In fact, the OIC issued a declaration urging the banning the book and a boycotting of its publishers, and from the perspective of the campaign to ban the book dissociation from the *fatwa* was progress, since the *fatwa* was a distraction from that aim.

But the main point here is that Khomeini's *fatwa* lacked legitimacy in international Islamic terms; though not a religious authority, the OIC none the less represents the governments of all Muslim majority countries (Mayer 1995). Furthermore, as a Shi'ite Muslim leader Khomeini had no religious or political authority in the rest of the Muslim world: 90 per cent of the world's Muslims are Sunni, including most of Britain's Muslims. And in Bradford the *fatwa* received only limited and temporary support, principally due to the frustrations of the British campaign. Indeed, a local radio poll conducted in January 1991 by Bradford City Radio, a private radio station catering mainly for ethnic minority communities, suggested that 90 per cent of Muslims were against the *fatwa* (*The Independent* 6 January 1991; in Lewis 1994 p. 170). Indeed anti-Shi'ite feeling was strong in Bradford: the organization for Deobandi *ulama*, to which at least half of Bradford's mosques are affiliated, produced posters in 1989 entitled 'The heretic beliefs of the Shias', while one of their publications anathematized Khomeini's 'perverted assertions and diabolical beliefs' (in Lewis 1994 pp. 96–7).

However, in spite of Deobandi condemnation of Khomeini and the radio poll's evidence that on later reflection most Muslims rejected the *fatwa*, in February 1989 many Muslims felt isolated and stung by the strength of attacks following the book-burning. In this emotional context the *fatwa* 'spoke to the hearts of many Muslims who felt despised, powerless and without recourse in law' (Modood 1990 pp. 129–30). This encouraged British Muslims to raise the stakes, calling for an outright ban on the book and in some cases for reprisals against publisher and author.

7. From Book-burning to Vigil: the Development of Civil Society in Bradford

In this dangerous context, it was the intervention of the leadership of another religious group – of the Anglican Church – that was to prove effective in mediating between Muslim organizations, the council and secular community relations organizations. Philip Lewis, the Anglican bishops' inter-faith adviser, describes the situation:

> In Bradford many of the institutions committed to community building, racial equality and equal opportunities were paralysed and relations sorely strained. The race relations community was split between Muslim outrage and liberal perplexity: the latter appreciated Mr Rushdie's earlier contributions to racial justice and part of his novel could still be construed within this framework. The Labour party, locally, were also split on the relative merits of free speech and advocacy of the concerns of an incensed minority. (Lewis 1993 p. 12)

The bishop's response was to organize meetings with leaders from all Bradford's faith communities and then 'between Muslims, civic leaders, politicians and the police at the highest level. ... at the diocesan retreat centre in the Dales, far from the clamour of the city' (ibid.). This led to a meeting between national Muslim leaders, the bishop and the two archbishops at Lambeth Palace (Lewis 1992, p. 56). These meetings permitted the constructive channelling of the frustration felt by different parties and in particular, by recognizing Muslims' views, perhaps helped the Council for Mosques make its decision to terminate public demonstrations, which 'were in danger of being hijacked by less responsible elements' (1993 p. 12). At a more grass-roots level, the inter-faith dialogue group Concord held a series of public lectures and discussions at which passionate feelings and strong disagreement were voiced. Here a variety of voices were heard and channels of communication that had been built up through the *halal* meat controversy and the Honeyford affair were maintained. This dialogue also led to the publication of public lectures as a collection, further widening the public sphere (Bowen 1992).

The bishop's action here, in facilitating dialogue primarily between male élites, is subject to Yasmin Ali's criticism of British multiculturalist politics that 'subcontinental systems of patronage and obligation fuse with British traditions of representation without democratic mandate', thus excluding women and other less powerful groups (Ali 1992 p. 110). But at least the bishop was able to act at a time when secular institutions were paralysed; indeed, according to the chief executive of the city of Bradford, he was the only one in a position to convene that important meeting in the Dales (Lewis 1992 p. 12).

Partly as a result of this dialogue and in contrast to the Honeyford affair, the Council for Mosques proved able to learn from its mistakes on this occasion. Through its Chair Sher Azam's involvement with the UK Action Committee on Islamic Affairs (UKACIA), formed in October 1988 to campaign against the book and convened by the Saudi diplomat Mughram Al Ghamdi, director of Regent's Park Mosque, the Council began to learn to articulate its argument in terms that began to engage with wider British public culture (Lewis 1994 p. 161). In March 1989 a UKACIA delegation lobbied an Organization of the Islamic Conference (OIC) meeting in Riyadh and succeeded (as we saw in the previous section) in getting a declaration agreed that urged the banning of the book and the boycotting of the publishers (ibid.). In April, when Kalim Siddiqui of the Iranian-backed Muslim Institute called for 'symbolic breaking of the law' (ibid. 1994 p. 162), this was repudiated by UKACIA and Sher Azam managed to contain support for the Iranian position voice in the Council for Mosques.

The Council for Mosques supported UKACIA's response to Home Office Minister John Patten's statement rejecting calls for any change in the law, which argued that special protection for Christians in the blasphemy law undermined Patten's goal of 'mutual respect'. Later in the month they launched a ten-point charter including the idea of making electoral support contingent on support for 'the establishment of a Muslim think-tank to combat ant-Muslim propaganda in the media'. The anniversary of the book-burning in January 1990 was marked by a vigil, symbolising a change in campaigning style, and in April 1990 a national conference with wide participation on the future of Muslims in Britain under the title 'Fair Laws for All' was held.

Thus in 15 months their position had developed from one of symbolic confrontation in an idiom that alienated the British public to the promotion of debate in civil society in the universalist idiom of equality and human rights. This is exactly the strategy Casanova (1994) recommends for religions to find a voice in public life in pluralist democracies, and was taken further by UKACIA in 1993 with the publication of *The Need for Reform: Muslims and the Law in Multifaith Britain*, which sought to articulate a Muslim case for separate schools and extension of racial discrimination legislation to cover religion, an idea adopted by Home Secretary David Blunkett eight years later in the wake of 11 September 2001. Such initiatives can be seen as part of a wider development after *The Satanic Verses* controversy of Muslim organizations oriented to discussing and presenting issues in a manner that articulates with the British public sphere.

For example, in Bradford the 18 months following the book-burning also saw the development of two other initiatives indicative of the future trend of the diversification of Muslim voices in the public sphere. Established in 1989 with investment from Muslim businessmen, Bradford City Radio's chief executive saw its aim as to make public debates within the Muslim community and especially to provide a forum for women to speak publicly. We have already discussed the poll they organized in 1991 on the *fatwa*, and they also hosted a phone-in debate on the Muslim Manifesto, produced by Siddiqui's Muslim Institute and proposing the establishment of a 'Muslim Parliament', with a Muslim councillor and businessmen involved. A total of 60–70 per cent of callers opposed the Manifesto (Lewis 1994 p. 169).

Another organization founded in 1989 was Women Against Fundamentalism (WAF). Launched in London on 6 May 1989, its agenda provides a critical standpoint from which to assess the relationship between empirical and normative civil society in Bradford in the wake of *The Satanic Verses* controversy. The group claims not to be anti-religion, but anti-fundamentalist, seeing the common traits of fundamentalism as 'they claim their version of religion to be the only true one. They use political means to impose it on all members of their religion and feel threatened by pluralist systems of thought' (Saghal and Yuval-Davies 1992 p. 4). Those arguing for increased recognition of religious or cultural identity have criticised multiculturalism as subordinating culture to liberal ideology at crucial points (Hulmes 1989). By contrast, WAF have argued that multiculturalism already goes too far in defining individuals in terms of their cultural background. WAF emphasizes the internal diversity of minority communities and the rights of individuals to shape their own identities. This latter point is especially crucial for women, who, according to WAF, are seen by 'fundamentalist' groups as the main agents in the transmission of tradition and therefore 'women, their roles, and above all their control, are at the heart of all fundamentalism.' (1992 p. 1).

These examples provide a context for the consideration of the relationship between religious organizations and civil society in Bradford during *The Satanic Verses* controversy. The mosques, with the possible exception of those linked to *Jamaati Islami*, provide little experience and no training in the skills of debate and critical evaluation important for participation in the public sphere. Those involved in the mosques acquire those skills elsewhere – in business, networking through the Community Relations Council and in local politics. Women remain largely excluded from mosque life, although for different reasons – more to do with tradition and lack of resources for the *Barelwis*, more ideological for the *Deobandis*.

The Council for Mosques in the period reviewed fits the critique of Baumann (1999; Chapter 3) and WAF of a body created in response to the demands of the British political system, in a tradition that stems back to the colonial period, of communal representation along religious lines. Such a system favours male 'elders' over the voices of women and youth. However, this usually unarticulated practice competes with a secular 'race' relations discourse and institutions which proved unable to respond to *The Satanic Verses* controversy, and in fact required the mediation of the established church. Furthermore, the Council for Mosques proved capable of learning, moderated its tone and began to support and foster the creation of spaces within which a wider range of Muslim voices could be heard and communicate with a wider public. Bradford City Radio and WAF also sought to broaden debate and increase participation, and the same characteristic can be seen in the Young Muslims UK *Trend* magazine.

8. The 1990s and the Broadening of the British Muslim Public Sphere

The decade since *The Satanic Verses* controversy has seen British Muslims achieve important goals. This can be seen by glancing through the pages of *British Muslims Monthly Survey* (BMMS)[6], a digest of references to British Muslims in the Muslim, ethnic minority, national and local press. For example, in March 1997 an article entitled 'Mosques for millennium' (BMMS 5:2, 20 March 1997 p. 1) reported estimates that 100 new mosques were scheduled to be completed by 2000, bringing the national total to over 1000. Alongside this ran comments from national and regional newspapers comparing the rise in mosque attendance with the decline in Christian worship, especially among traditional denominations (as we saw in Chapter 1).

The period has also seen the introduction of state funding for Muslim schools through the granting of voluntary-aided status (as we noted above) and the formation of a national umbrella body for Muslim organizations. This project had often been attempted but never previously achieved, but the Muslim Council, although it remains to be seen how successful it will prove in representing Britian's diverse Muslim population, signifies a considerable advance (BMMS 5:11, 20 December 1997 p. 1). This period also witnessed the serious possibility of legal recognition in anti-discrimination legislation, a possibility made more likely in the wake of 11 September 2001 (BMMS 5:6, 20 June 1997 p. 1). Such developments suggest the increasing maturity, establishment and public recognition of Muslim communities and their contribution to British society, as indeed did Muslim involvement in the millennium celebrations (BMMS 5:1, 20 February 1997 p. 5; 6:7, 20 August 1998, p. 3).

Other signs of development include increased voter participation, membership of professional associations such as The Association of Muslim Lawyers, membership of mainstream political parties, growth in the number of Muslim local councillors (around 150 nationally in 1995) and the national organization of these councillors into a National Forum for Muslim Councillors (Purdam 1996). They also include the development of English-language newspapers (*Q-News, Muslim Times*), satellite television, creating a South Asian public sphere (*Asianet*) and increased publishing activity (*Alkalifah Press*; Lewis 1994.)

Anthropologist Pnina Werbner (1996 p. 68) describes three phases in the development of 'the Islamic politics of identity' in Britain in the 1990s. The first is the increasing visibility of Muslim political activism after *The Satanic Verses* controversy. This, we might add, also involved a diversification of Muslim voices and the growth in public forums for debate. The second is a new development of transnational consciousness resulting not from ties with sending societies, but from areas of the world not strongly represented amongst British Muslims, especially Bosnia. To this we might add Palestine and, controversially in the wake of 11 September 2001, Afghanistan. The third phase is the development of a 'gendered diasporic public sphere in which women's independent collective voice has to be taken seriously by men' (ibid.). In contrast to the male-dominated community activism hitherto, Werbner argues that this gendered and familial space 'is also a space of "fun", that is marked by gaity (sic.), transgressive humour and dance' (p. 58). Werbner illustrates the growth of transnationalism and the gendering of public space using the example of the al-Masoom Foundation Trust in Manchester.

In the early 1990s this women's organization was involved in charitable and campaigning work for Muslim groups in Bosnia, Kashmir and Pakistan. Its members comprised mostly devout Muslim middle-class Pakistani women, motivated by the Islamic notions of *khidmas* and *sadaqa* ('selfless communal work' and 'charitable giving' (Werbner p. 59). Their activities included taking supplies to the Bosnian border for Bosnian refugees, supporting the construction of a children's cancer hospital in Rawalpindi, organizing concerts in Manchester to raise funds for these activities and lobbying MPs to raise the issue of Kashmir in Parliament. Yet at the same time as attracting the attention and approval of members of the political establishment and in spite of their impeccable Islamic credentials, the group had angered sections of the Pakistani male leadership in Manchester: Mrs Khan, the organization's founder, has received death threats. The organization has bypassed the business community, with its traditional male-dominated patronage networks, appealing directly to the local community: one school raised £7,700 through a day of sports activities and fairs. But more than that, it has challenged the dominance of men in the public representation of the Pakistani community.

Werbner sees groups like al-Masoom as drawing on the global development of political Islam (Islamism), which has encouraged the growth of women's organizations and legitimized women's struggles against traditional social norms. It has also legitimized the struggle of youth against elders in terms of a distinction between ' true Islam', reconstructed from early textual sources, and later cultural accretions (*bida*, illicit innovations; Werbner 1996 p. 64). In the context of feminist Islamist interpretation (Mernissi 1988), a figure such as 'Aisha, a wife of the Prophet, comes to serve as a role model for contemporary Islamist women. Muhammad died while 'Aisha was still young and since she never remarried, she conducted the rest of her long life as an independent woman, including leading armies into battle'. One should also add that economic factors, bringing more women into work, as well as education, have been important in transforming gender relations among British Muslims (Shaw 1988; Werbner 1990).

As this account of Islamist hermeneutics implies, skills of critical analysis and autonomy in the interpretation of texts and traditions are developed through it. Islamist movements and thinking have also had some influence in Bosnia and been highly influential in Egypt, as we shall see in Chapters 8 and 9 below. Their modernist attempt to free textual interpretation from traditional straitjackets means that such movements and methods have the potential to (communicatively) rationalize traditional lifeworlds and develop skills that can enable public debate and democratic participation. At the same time, however, their modernist insistence on the univocity of meaning of a text ('true Islam') can foster authoritarianism, as has been the case with their nurturing in predominantly authoritarian political contexts (Egypt, Iran, Tunisia, Nigeria and so on). Furthermore, traditional elements of respect for authority are also blended with this, for example the reverence for Maududi in *Jamaati Islami* discussed above in this chapter, and the participation of the Pakistani branch of this organization in Zia's repressive military government.

The appropriation of Islamist discourse by al-Masoom poses an interesting challenge to the WAF's construction of fundamentalism. Islamists do, on the whole, insist that their version of religion is the only true one. However, the process by which they validate their readings is one that is in principle open to contestation, even if this may be circumscribed in practice. In a British context, the appropriation of Islamist discourse has, alongside other factors, enabled women to challenge 'the control of women's minds and bodies' which WAF see as 'at the heart of all fundamentalist agendas'. In the British context, it would seem that it is less Islamists than traditional religio-cultural configurations that seek to control women's minds and bodies.

Al-Masoom also witnesses to the diversification of the British Muslim public sphere in the 1990s. Such a diversification process is also evident in Bradford, for example in responses to the Gulf War (1991). The strong line taken by the Council in criticizing British government action (and that of other allies and the Saudis) while barely criticizing Saddam Hussein led local politicians to challenge the representative status of the Council. They did so implicitly by presenting alternative perspectives, for example denying Saddam Hussein's interpretation of the conflict as a 'holy war', given the range of Muslim forces on both sides. They also did so explicitly, for example Tory candidate Muhammad Riaz argued that no person or group has ever been given 'a mandate by ... the Muslims of Bradford to act as their representative or spokesman' (in Lewis 1994 p. 168). Further diversification followed. The business community in Bradford took greater responsibility for organizing Eid celebrations through the formation of an Eid Committee (1991), which also sought to foster non-Muslim participation in the celebrations. Fast FM, a radio station set up in 1992 to support those engaged in the annual fast, broadcast a debate amongst *ulama* on the disputed dates for starting and finishing the fast: three different dates were given by different sectarian authorities, causing disruption, confusion and embarrassment (ibid., p. 171).

The 'riot' of 1995 and possibly those of 2001, also witness to the pluralization of the British Muslim public sphere, although to an extension of agitational rather than discursive politics. In the disturbance of 1995, a crowd that had gathered at a police station in a Muslim majority area to protest at the arrest of three youths attacked non-Muslim owned property and business premises, leading to many more arrests (Burlet and Reid 1996). When Council for Mosques leaders addressed the crowd to appeal for calm, they were shouted down with cries of 'police puppets' (ibid. p. 151). Interviews with youths from the area showed that they perceived local community relations mechanisms, including the Council for Mosques, as irrelevant to their needs: 'elders are increasingly out of touch with our reality of unemployment and racism', one young man commented (p. 148).

The youths also blamed local policing tactics: the arrests that triggered the incident were seen as the latest in a pattern of heavy-handed practice, including use of stop and search powers and the construction of a police station described as 'Fortress Lawcroft'. Gender differentiation is also evident in the interviews conducted by Burlet and Reid: one middle-aged woman commented: 'women wouldn't smash up shops, we direct out energy towards peaceful action' (p. 151). Nor did such opinion remain in the private sphere: in response to the riot, a group of Muslim women began a petition aimed at presenting their perspective and facilitating dialogue (ibid.).

Taken together, these developments suggest the pluralization of British Muslim public spheres within different cities, as well as nationally. In many cases they also suggest the rationalization of the Islamic lifeworld of British Muslims, as traditions become open to question and argument and identities become more reflexive as well as more complex. To state this is not to lose sight of Asad's critique of literary critics who see Rushdie's high-flyers as typical of migrant experience. Rioting youths in Bradford do not have the same life-choices as Bollywood film stars (one of Rushdie's protagonists in *The Satanic Verses*), or even Cambridge-educated novelists (Rushdie). But exposure to a combination of state education, the British media, mosque school and links with Pakistan does inevitably confront British Muslims with choices about values and lifestyle and engenders multicultural competences – knowing how to act in different settings, which discourses to deploy when, in Baumann's terms. Such a process has not necessarily or even usually led to the rejection of Islam. Indeed, often the reverse, as Leveau found in France: 'The rigorous intepretation of Islam among intellectual believers appears to be a strategy for coping with French society' (1988 p. 112 in Baumann 1999 p. 103).

Pluralization – the voicing of different Muslim perspectives – has also been accompanied by some signs of convergence, as the development of UKACIA and later the Muslim Council, suggests. One example is the UKACIA document *The Need for Reform: Muslims and the law in multifaith Britain*, presented to the Home Secretary to represent Muslim views on racial equality legislation at the time of the Commission for Racial Equality's (CRE) second review of the 1976 Race Relations Act in 1993, and briefly discussed above. Here, its proposals provide an opportunity for us to revisit some of the substantive issues raised by the chapter. Thus, having demonstrated that at least some aspects of Muslim civil society in Britain are procedurally democratic – in the sense of allowing broad participation, encouraging autonomous reflection and sustaining public debate – we turn to consider whether the specific proposals that have arisen from the Muslim public sphere (especially

increased recognition of collective identity, such as separate schools) are favourable
to the twin concerns of individual freedom and social integration that underlie
normative concepts of civil society.

9. Conclusion: the Politics of Difference and Social Integration

The UKACIA document (1993) suggests some convergence of Muslim opinion on
the direction that campaigning for greater recognition for Muslims should take,
witnessed by the wide range of organizations represented, including the An-Nisa
Society, Muslim Women's Helpline, Muslim Wise, The Muslim Update, Union of
Muslim Organizations. It calls for an end to the dominance of race as the defining
category of difference in British legislation and seeks legislation outlawing racial
vilification, incitement to religious hatred and discrimination on religious grounds
(pp. 17–18). The An-Nisa Society *et al.*'s response to the CRE's review looks at a
wide range of implications of the dominance of racial and ethnic categorization,
pointing to the implications in the areas of fostering and adoption, housing, service
delivery and policy monitoring (pp. 41–50). The sophisticated engagement with
detailed policy issues contrasts with the dualism of the Muslim Institute's
presentation in the Muslim Manifesto; here is a serious engagement with policy
arguments and institutions. Yet the extension of religious identity into more areas of
life is for some groups a cause for great concern, for example WAF, and may even
be seen as more dangerous than the apocalyptic rhetoric of the institute.

The issue of separate religious schools is an important one here. As we have seen,
British Muslims appear to have won the argument with the government, at least
temporarily, and an expansion of the voluntary-aided sector, including religious
schools, is envisaged. However, this is hotly contested in the light of the terrorist
attacks of 11 September 2001. Clearly, a proportion of Muslim parents prefer that
their children be educated in Muslim schools and parental choice is currently a major
factor in the discourse of all major political parties on the issue of schooling. But
there are other considerations, especially the role of education in the reproduction of
society. Do Muslim schools give Muslim pupils confidence and a strong sense of
identity that better equips them to contribute to society, or do they deny the
development of autonomous thinking and action (especially to girls)? Let us
consider these issues further using the arguments of the WAF group and the An-Nisa
Society as presented in the UKACIA document.

While education is not a major issue in the cited UKACIA document, support for
separate Muslim schools is clearly implied in the main statement (1993 pp. 4–6), and
in the supporting evidence the Al-Nisa Society *et al.* write: 'The refusal to grant
Muslim schools, such as Islamia Primary School in Brent, London, voluntary-aided
status is perceived by the vast majority of Muslims as clear evidence of the hostility
and prejudice prevalent in society at large against them' (p. 44). By contrast, WAF's
opposition to religious schools is based on the view that 'All religious schools have
a deeply conformist idea of the role of women. They will deny girls opportunities
which they are just beginning to seize' (Sahgal and Yuval-Davis 1990 p. 2).

But must this be so? Is it necessarily true, or true in practice, that religious schools deny women opportunities? To take one example, the headmistress of Feversham College, Bradford, has justified her school precisely on the grounds that the provision of a supportive Muslim environment gives parents the confidence to allow their daughters to continue in education, and thus to benefit from greater educational opportunities.[7] The small number of girls beginning to progress from Bradford Muslim Girls' School to Bradford and Ilkley Community College to train as teachers in the early 1990s testifies to the fruits of this policy. Thus taking account of religious sensitivities may enable wider participation and individual fulfilment. Separate schools catering for religious needs may be supported along these lines.

However, the opportunities which WAF has in mind may be of a broader nature; it may objected that slightly broadening opportunities from a narrow religiously determined base is an unsatisfactory implementation of equal opportunities – or that education should involve an initiation into pluralism – an empowerment to make individual choices – which is incompatible with the ethos of a religious school. One important question here is whether a religious school can present students with a sufficiently broad and critical perspective to enable them to make their own life-choices.

Also drawing on MacIntyre's work on traditions (above, Chapter 5), Fitzmaurice (1993) proposes that any cultural practice can be characterized in terms of two dimensions of reflectiveness and embeddedness. She argues that all activities can be located on a continuum between the two, but we suggest that keeping the dimensions separate is better, because the two are not necessarily antagonistic on MacIntyre's understanding. For example, educational practices can be characterized in terms of the extent to which they encourage on the one hand critical reflection on and hence autonomy in relation to existing cultural norms and practices, and on the other hand unreflective reproduction of them.

Differences between the WAF and UKACIA positions may be represented in these terms. For the WAF, religious schools will not enable women to develop the autonomy needed to seize the opportunities available, while for UKACIA, without sufficient rootedness in their cultural community and in particular its religious identity, individuals will lose meaning, purpose and even effectiveness, since they will not know who they are, or where they are going. Following Fitzmaurice (1993) in seeing autonomy-tradition/cultural rootedness as representing poles on a continuum neither of which represents a possible or desirable state in their extreme form of loss of identity or petrified tradition, can help us to think around the autonomy-tradition dichotomy posed both by secularist modes of discourse (for example WAF, most pre-1990 political philosophy and race and ethnic studies, some feminist discourse) and the reversed polarity of some forms of conservative Islam (and other religions) which demonize secularism in a similar way. But seeing the two as independent can take us further, towards a self-critical traditionality that does not insist, as Fitzmaurice continues to, that every step towards autonomous thinking is a step away from tradition. One starting-point for the development of such a self-critical traditionality is the recognition that in the case of *The Satanic Verses* controversy, both secularists and Muslims have sacred memories to protect and reasoned arguments to advance.

But before returning to this controversy, the question of the dangers of separate schools to social integration needs further reflection. Differentiated societies may be integrated through systems rather than lifeworlds, but without lifeworld integration they will not be pleasant places to live, as the Bradford riots of 2001 demonstrate. At the time of writing no full analysis of the 2001 rioting has yet been undertaken, but preliminary reports suggest a combination of youth alienation associated with unemployment and racism, the breakdown of respect for parental and other authority, and hostility to non-Muslims fostered by the mosques (Lewis 2001; Roy 2001). Social separation could be implicated in the genesis of all of these factors and Ouseley's report also points to the dangers of a separate social system created initially by housing and solidified on that basis through education, and to some extent reinforced by the reification of community identities in the competition for public funding.

However, on the other hand, attempts at social engineering (for example bussing) have proved ineffective and have been decisively rejected by local people. Furthermore, 'separate' institutions such as schools do not necessarily foster prejudice, depending on their ability, and that of other community institutions, to foster civic pride and achieve participation in local communities in other ways. Thus schools founded on a religious basis – especially where they follow a curriculum that conforms to national standards designed to provide a broad-based education in the skills and knowledge needed to live in today's society, including a measure of personal autonomy and individual thinking – are not necessarily obstacles to wider social integration. Rather, they can in fact aid social integration by developing links with other community groups, through hosting adult education classes, having active parent-teacher associations, encouraging students to engage in voluntary work, and so on. On the other hand, schools on the whole reflect rather than create the communities they draw on, and in divided and impoverished communities they will tend to reflect that background, although in some cases they may be able to transcend it.

In any case, voluntary-aided and private Muslim schools will only educate a small proportion of Bradford's children for the foreseeable future. The issue is more one of separation within the secular (or 'Christian' voluntary-aided) sector partly caused by segregation of housing. Here, the increasing participation of Muslim organizations in the public life of the city can only help matters, as can the active maintenance of a Christian 'presence' in predominantly Muslim areas (Lewis 2001). Yet, clearly, there are parts of the population, especially male youths, who are not being effectively drawn into these public spheres, except sporadically in violent protest or through the confrontational politics of extremist groups like Hizb-ut-Tahrir, which were to be found recruiting in the wake of the 1995 disturbances (Burlet and Reid 1996 p. 152). The state and supplementary school system both have responsibilities here.

These problems should not obscure the progress that has been made in terms of the development of public forums for Muslims to debate (a good thing for both the WAF and UKACIA). Furthermore, the evidence presented here also suggests that Muslim tradition is capable of nurturing organizations which embed respect for basic rights in the Islamic lifeworld, and which support a plural public sphere. True, the development of such organizations in the British context and especially in Bradford has been a struggle, but their growth in the 1990s – ranging from UKACIA (formed to campaign to ban Rushdie's book, but committed to arguing the case within British civil and political society and on the basis of human rights), to Bradford City Radio and Fast FM to al-Masoom in Manchester – suggests that the struggle is bearing fruit. Empirical Muslim civil society is contributing to normative British civil society.

Another question raised in the Introduction was whether the lack of legal recourse to redress religious insult discovered by British Muslims through *The Satanic Verses* controversy is a measure of the tolerance or prejudice of British society. The maintenance of a blasphemy law that protects one religious group but not others is indefensible in a plural society; but its extension would also be inappropriate as well as practically impossible. It would be inappropriate both because it could prove socially divisive and because it is anachronistic, reflecting conditions when the legitimization of the state depended on a dominant religion. It would probably be impractical because of the range of religious beliefs and their sometimes conflicting claims. The persistence of the existing blasphemy law could be described as a kind of institutionalized prejudice in favour of the historically dominant tradition, but its social significance is minimal.

More significant and a more plausible prospect, is the extension of existing race relations legislation to encompass religion, especially the law against incitement to racial hatred. In 2001, the prospect of this in Britain in the wake of 11 September 2001 has provoked unease that satire and other forms of humour would be curtailed. However, as the limited success of prosecutions under the legislation with respect to race suggests, such a law would probably have a limited effect in curtailing free speech. Some of Bradney's (1993) comments on the Rushdie case in the relation to the extension of the blasphemy law would seem also to apply to incitement to hatred:

> Yet, even if the law of blasphemy were extended to encompass Islam, it seems unlikely that any jury would convict a publisher of *The Satanic Verses*. The very opacity of the text, the length and difficulty of the book, general ignorance of Islam and a prevailing orientalist attitude towards the East are all factors that would make such conviction unlikely. (p. 92)

In the case of incitement to hatred, the sheer complexity of the insult makes *The Satanic Verses* ill suited to the purpose in the context of prevailing British ignorance of Islam! Furthermore, the inequity of protecting some religious groups against hate speech because their religious identity happens to coincide with 'racial' identity (for example Jews, Sikhs) while British Muslims lack such protection is apparent. Thus it seems likely that the extension of this legislation would go some way to reassuring British Muslims while curtailing only the crudest expressions of religious prejudice. Some kind of 'artistic purposes' defence, to be discussed below, could further strengthen the protection of free speech.

Simon Lee (1990) argues that the blasphemy law directed public attention in a fruitless and contentious direction, but that the amount of attention focused on it testifies to the power of law, even an archaic and rarely invoked one, to shape public debate (p. 92). He therefore suggests that even a law against incitement to religious hatred on which it is difficult to secure convictions could serve a useful symbolic function and could help shape public debate through more constructive channels: 'A shift in focus of the law [away from blasphemy] might have diminished conflict and dissatisfaction. ... A law against incitement to religious hatred might well have contributed something positive in this direction' (p. 87). Another alternative is some form of group libel offence which serves to introduce the idea of an 'artistic interest' defence. The New South Wales Anti-Discrimination (Racial Vilification) Amendment Act 1989 comes close to this (ibid. p. 90). Moderation in application is promoted by several measures. First, the requirement for prosecutions to gain the consent of the Attorney General; second the Attorney General's power to order an apology; and third, a public interest defence. The last protects from prosecution 'a public act, done reasonably in good faith, for academic, artistic or research purposes in the public interest, including discussion or debate about and expositions of any act or matter' (cited in Lee 1990, p. 90). Here we see a legislative embodiment of the need for an autonomy-promoting society to weigh the educative value of controversial material against any offence caused to minority groups. The inclusion of 'artistic...purposes' here is particularly important and could serve to defend uses of controversial material in comedy and satire. It is not yet clear how the New South Wales legislation is working out in practice, but in principle at least it represents an attempt in law to move toward an engagement with the diversity of values that are at play in a culturally complex society.

In the next chapter we shall consider how Polish Catholicism, like Pakistani and Bangladeshi heritage British Islam long accustomed to cultural dominance, is adapting to the pluralization of Polish society in the post-Communist period and whether empirical civil society is living up to normative expectations generated by the opposition movement in the 1980s.

Notes

1   Rushdie's links with Márquez and Latin American magical realism may be mediated through his experiences of travelling in Latin America, recorded in *The Jaguar's Smile: A Nicaraguan Journey* (1987).
2   This procedure is fundamental to 'redaction criticism', a method which predominates in current New Testament scholarship (Tuckett in Coggins and Houlden 1990 pp. 580–82).
3   Awards for libel may seem unduly high because, almost uniquely in English law, damages are set by the jury and hence are less influenced by precedent than judges in the amounts they award.
4   In *British Muslims Monthly Survey* for March 1996, vol. 4, no. 3, p. 14.
5   An organization affliated to the Barelwi mosques in Bradford, and described by Lewis as 'quietist and revivalist' (1994 p. 36).
6   Produced by Selly Oak Colleges, Birmingham Centre for the Study of Islam and Muslim-Christian Relations, edited by S. Imtiaz, S. and M. Draper.
7   This information was gathered during an interview in 1992.

Chapter 7

After Solidarity

Catholicism, Civil Society and the Public Sphere in Poland

A million pilgrims attended the opening mass of the Great Novena, held in Częstochowa on 26 August 1956. The text of solemn vows [to Mary, renewing King Jan Kazimierz's vow of 1656] was read by Bishop Klepacz. Wyszyński [the Polish Primate] who was still interned in Komańcza, 'stood before the picture of the Madonna at Częstochowa and recited the act of dedication at the same time as Bishop Klepacz at Jasna Gora [the monastery at Częstochowa]'.[1] It was this spectacular ceremony that defined the cultural frame of the conflict between church and state for years to come. (Kubik 1994 p. 111)

In the past, one could have private reservations, but to criticize the Church openly was to stand in favour of the communist regime. After 1989, when the Catholic hierarchy aggressively pursued anti-abortion legislation but did not address the issue of 'shock therapy's' social consequences, political fault lines became visible. (Osa 1997 p. 340)

The Central European experience shows that the ethical view of civil society does not pass the democratic exam. The societies in question reject this view. They even despise those who talk about *ethos* and the rather abstract universal principles of morality without paying attention to the economic conditions of society's functioning. (Skapska 1997 p. 158)

1. Introduction

The Polish Roman Catholic Church (PRCC) is widely recognized as having played an important role in supporting the trade union Solidarity-led opposition to the Communist government which eventually led to the latter's defeat at the ballot box in the elections of 4 June 1989, thus triggering the domino effect that was to see the political transformation of Central and Eastern Europe. Indeed, Poland's transition from Communism was in many ways the classic state versus civil society scenario: Polish intellectuals were among those most responsible for the revival of the normative concept of civil society in the 1980s (Alexander 1998) and the Polish opposition self-consciously adopted a strategy of building a parallel society rather than seeking to reform existing government structures, thus deliberately deepening the state-society dichotomy. As Warsaw Solidarity activist Wictor Kulerski stated in 1982:

This movement should create a situation in which the authorities will control empty stores but not the market; the employment of workers but not their livelihood; the official media, but not the circulation of information; printing plants, but not the publishing movement; the mail and telephones, but not communications; and the school system, but not education. (in Ramet 1995 p. 85)

It is therefore perhaps surprising to find by the early to mid-1990s doubts being expressed about the value both of the normative concept of civil society (Skapska 1997 p. 146) and the social role of the PRCC, by this stage accused of seeking to create a 'para-religious' (Zielinski 1992 p. 3), 'theocratic' (Brzezinski 2000 p. 122) and even 'fundamentalist' state (Załęcki 1999 p. 350).

Furthermore, in spite of wide recognition of the PRCC's significance in the Great Transformation, its exact role remains disputed and, surprisingly, relatively unexplored (Osa 1997 p. 340). More precisely, the articulation between the symbolic and discursive mobilization of the Church and its institutional processes in the late Communist period, that is between the Church's role in the public sphere and the interface between empirical civil society and the state, have not been fully explored together. Therefore, this chapter seeks to elucidate the transformation we have observed in perceptions of normative civil society and the PRCC by examining the development of the Church's role in empirical civil society and church-state relations from the 1950s to 2000. While the main emphasis will be on the later period, an account of Communist times is important in understanding recent transformations, as well as in examining the potentialities and limitations of religion in mobilizing opposition to authoritarian regimes in modern societies. Poland is also an important test case for examining how a culturally hegemonic religious tradition manages the transition to pluralism and for exploring the problematic relationship between the three corners of Baumann's 'multicultural triangle' (religion, nationalism and ethnicity) in a post-Communist society.

2. History

The close relationship between the Catholic religion and Polish nationhood is well known. Central events in Poland's sacred narrative include the common origin of religion and nationhood in Prince Mięszko's baptism and marriage to the daughter of the Prince of Bohemia in 966 and the Black Madonna's miraculous protection of the monastery at Częstochowa and ultimately Polish nationhood from the Swedes in the seventeenth century. The disappearance of the Polish state from the 1780s to 1918 deepened this connection and widened the gulf between state and society. Nazi occupation and Soviet domination reinforced both tendencies. However, historically Poland has been far from monoreligious or monocultural: the current Catholic dominance is rather the result of the impact of twentieth-century totalitarianism. Thus there is early evidence of both Slavic and Greek rites (Davies 1996) and Poland's later empire included Orthodox, Jewish and Protestant (mostly Lutheran) subjects. This diversity persisted until the Second World War, when the Nazis murdered most of the Jewish population – the largest in Europe – and at the outbreak of the cold war Stalin moved Poland's borders 100 km west, thus incorporating most of the Orthodox population into Belarus, then part of the Soviet Union, and displacing most of the German-speaking Lutheran population in the West. Poland in 1948 was thus for the first time approximately 95 per cent Catholic, with, in order of size, minorities of Orthodox, Jews, Lutherans and Muslims. The Jewish population further shrank through postwar pogroms, the last of which was in 1968, leaving a tiny, ageing population of 3,000 as of 1993 (Ramet 1995 p. 440).

Most accounts of the rise of Solidarity trace its development from the increasing organization of workers and intellectuals in the mid-1970s. Worker dissatisfaction stemmed from increasing hardship, with Poland's centralized economy unable to respond effectively to the worldwide recession, intellectuals' dissatisfaction with the Communist authorities' repressive response to expressions of dissent, signalled by the constitutional amendments of 1975 which further restricted civil and political liberties, and manifest in the brutal repression of the riots in the Ursus tractor factory in Radom in 1976. These events led to initiatives such as the creation of KOR, the Workers' Defence Committee, founded by intellectuals, but which began to bring intellectuals and workers together. Deepening economic crisis and government recalcitrance triggered further mobilization of workers and intellectuals, which, morale boosted by the papal visit of 1979, led eventually to emergence of the 'proto' trade union Solidarity in mid-1980. Such accounts 'all draw short arrows of causality from certain economic, social or cultural experiences in the 1970s to 'revolutionary' mass mobilization in 1980–1' (Osa 1997 p. 343).

In such accounts, the Church is recognized as playing a supportive role in the developments of the 1970s, for example in protesting against the constitutional changes of 1975, fostering Catholic intellectual clubs that enabled the development of independent intellectual movements, engaging in dialogue with KOR and making public statements supporting KOR's human rights work. But its role is seen as essentially reactive and supportive rather than leading or constitutive. For example, Sabrina Ramet (1995 p. 184) argues that changes in 'the Church's social presence in the mid-1970s *mirrored* the broader systemic changes occuring at the time', Lawrence Goodwyn (1991 p. 319) that 'the Church was *reactively relevant*. But it was *not a source of causation*'. These accounts exemplify the phenomenon (observed above in Chapter 2) of the effects of the incorporation of assumptions derived from the secularization thesis on mainstream accounts of political change in Eastern Europe. *A priori* assumptions about the role of religion in modernity preclude recognition of the agency of religious groups and institutions, even in Poland where these were most prominent. However, a longer time frame and alternative theoretical perspectives can cast events in a different light, as well as helping to explain the difficulties of the Church in coming to terms with the post-Communist period.

In developing our account we shall give consideration to the role of Polish Catholicism in empirical civil society, from parish and diocese to national and transnational (through the Pope, international philanthropic networks) levels. But first we shall examine the Church's role in the creation of a national oppositional public sphere. Osa (1997) and Kubik (1994) both argue that the Church was determinative in shaping a national public sphere of symbolic confrontation which was crucial to events in the early 1980s and beyond. In contrast to Ramet, who states that under Gomułka (1956–70) 'there was little in the way of organized opposition … and the Church itself still felt very much on the defensive' and therefore neglects this period, we shall argue that to appreciate the development of this public sphere it is important to go back to the 1950s.

3. The Church, Solidarity and Symbolic Politics

As in the other Eastern and Central European societies brought within the Soviet sphere of influence, the immediate postwar period was the toughest, as the new Communist leaderships sought to consolidate their authority. There were widespread arrests of clergy between 1951 and 1953, among them the Polish Primate Cardinal Wyszyński (Ramet 1995 p. 183; Kubik 1994 p. 110). The government also undertook other measures to try to control, or, if not, divide the Church. As in other communist countries, alternative 'patrotic priests' associations' were set up with an aim to divide loyalties, appeal was made directly to the Vatican above the heads of Polish leaders and attempts were made to interfere with church appointments (Ramet 1995 p. 183; Gilarek 1997 p. 114). While still interned (1953–56), Wyszyński developed a strategy to contest the legitimacy of the Communist state not on a directly political ground, but in the symbolic representation of the nation. Thus he developed plans for the 'Great Novena': a decade of celebrations leading to the dual millennium of Polish statehood and conversion to Christianity in 1966, the launch of which was described in the first quotation at the head of this chapter.

The renewal of King Kazimierz's vow by the imprisoned Wyszyński provided a cultural frame within which to interpret the recent Poznań riots (June 1956), the first significant protest against the Communist regime. Taking advantage of party divisions and the presence of foreign journalists in the city for a trade exposition, workers from the Cegielski factory, frustrated at the authorities' refusal to engage with their demands, had marched on the city centre. There they were able, via the journalists' cameras, to appeal over the heads of the government directly to the international public sphere (Osa 1997 p. 350). Three days of street-fighting and many deaths eventually resulted, but not before workers had managed to storm the party building, unjam the apparatus at the state broadcasting station that was blocking BBC transmissions and broaden their demands from 'Bread!' to 'Freedom!' to calls for the release of Wyszyński (ibid.). By recalling the suffering of church and nation in the context of his own imprisonment and in the aftermath of the Poznań riots, Wyszyński created a powerful link with Poland's past through which to interpret its present oppression. The themes of the Great Novena, to which each year from 1957 to 1966 was dedicated, give some indication of the rhetorical weaponry the Church was to deploy against atheistic Communism: 'defence of the life of spirit and flesh', 'holiness of sacramental marriage', 'strength to the family by God', 'justice and social love' and 'the struggle against national vices and the acquisition of Christian virtues' (Kubik 1994 p. 111).

Following the initial vow of dedication, in a journey that was to last 23 years

(Phase 1 1957–66; Phase 2 1966–80), a copy of the icon of the Black Madonna was to tour all parishes in the country, in each parish resting for a night in private households selected by the local priests. This event was to have a substantial impact on both social bonding and religious vitality in Poland:

> These direct encounters with the Black Madonna strengthened social integration on both local and national levels and rejuvenated the religiosity of the Poles; countless incidents of conversion were reported from all over the country; there were massive returns to the sacramental life. (Kubik 1994 p. 112)

But more importantly from a political perspective, the peregrination disseminated and embedded a network of symbols and related discourse which was to 'frame' opposition action in the years to come. Wyszyński's individual contribution to this was considerable; he 'blended Polish legends, folklore and peasant mysticism with the intellectual products of the Polish Romantic poets to create a Mariological vision of the nation and Polish history' (Osa 1997 p. 353). The embedding process of this 'myth' occurred as the touring icon met with opposition from state authorities. A pattern became established whereby the authorities' attempts to disrupt celebrations repeatedly backfired, reinforcing local and national oppositional solidarities.

For example, in Gdańsk in 1960 the authorities refused to allow decoration in the streets along which the procession bearing the icon was to travel to one parish church. In response, the parishioners placed hundreds of candles along the perimeter of the Church boundaries, marking the limit they were allowed to decorate and timed the departure of the icon so that 'the songs of the participants in procession clambered up to the windows of the bureaucrats as they returned from work to their homes' (in Osa 1997 p. 357). Such 'symbolic substitution' to circumvent the state's restrictions was a frequent occurrence. Former journalist Marek Skwarnicki recalls another example:

> It got so absurd that at one point the communist authorities seized the painting to stop its pilgrimage around Poland. It might seem strange that a copy of a religious painting had acquired such a symbolic significance. But those 'clever' Marxists in all their great wisdom were so worried about this image they arrested it and guarded it closely so it wouldn't go on its travels. And what did the Poles do? They simply took candles and lit them and took the candles on pilgrimage instead. It made no difference to them whether they had candles or a painting because to them, the light of the candles represented the light of love from the Virgin Mary. (Interview, in Kozerski and Herbert 2001)

Such examples show the advantage of shifting the ground of conflict from the political plane, where the Church could not hope to compete with the state, to the symbolic plane, where ingenuity counted for more than material strength. This symbolic ground also enabled the Church to appear untainted by petty politics and united, transcending its internal divisions (which we shall later discuss). As Osa (1997) comments on the Gdańsk incident:

> The sumptuous decoration of the Church, the outline, (that is, emphasis) of church boundaries with flickering candles, forceful singing beneath the windows of government offices – all showed the unity of the people and the Church, the protection of Our Lady, Queen of Poland, and the moral purity and force of the participants' symbolic message in contrast to the dirty material politics of the regime. (p. 357)

The effect of the Great Novena and the numerous associated pilgrimages, saints' days, celebrations and dedications between 1956 and 1980, at one level 'purely religious' events with no overt political reference, no alternative programmes or material threat, was none the less to embed a cultural frame within which 'the initial public presentation of Solidarity in the Gdańsk shipyards in August 1980 – with its crosses, flowers, religious pictures, Masses – [was] instantly comprehensible to a mass public' (ibid. p. 352). This 'cultural frame' was to be actively sustained by the Solidarity movement: 'Solidarity's semiology connected the movement to Poland's historical mythology and the touchstones of the Great Novena: the Black Madonna, the suffering Christ, the Christian nation. Elaborate ceremonies and symbolic displays were as essential to Solidarity as the sit-down strike' (p. 362).

The election of a Polish Pope (John Paul II) in 1978, followed by his first visit to Poland in 1979, was to provide particularly important impetus to building national solidarity just before the emergence of the Solidarity movement itself in the summer of 1980. Once again, suffering church and nation were identified in opposition to an oppressive state, this time drawing on the discourse of human rights, an increasing feature of international Catholic rhetoric since its legitimization at the Second Vatican Council (1962–65). In preparation for the papal visit, Wyszyński preached on the myth of St. Stanislaw, bishop of Kraków, who was slain by King Boleslaw the Bold in 1079, and had become symbol of state persecution of the Church:

> The conflict between Boleslaw and Stanislaw revolved around the issues of justice and human rights. It proves that already nine hundred years ago the Church struggled for human rights and already nine hundred years ago there was in Poland a man of the Church who fought for human rights. (In *Tygodnik Powszechny* 21 May 1978; in Kubik 1994 p. 133)

Up to 3 million celebrated the final Mass led by the Pope during his first visit in 1979. Through this generation of national solidarity, the Church provided much of the symbolism and vocabulary for the Solidarity movement that shook the Communist regime in 1980–81 and survived through the years of martial law to negotiate its downfall in 1989.

The symbolic form of mobilization was also arguably to affect the shape of resistance offered by parts of the underground Solidarity movement in the 1980s that were ideologically quite distant from the Church. One such example, which drew to great effect on the absurdist element of the Church's symbolic confrontation to which Skwarnicki (above) refers in commenting on the Communist arrest of a copy of a painting, is the 'Orange Alternative'. This Wrocław-based Dadaist group led by Waldemar Frydrych, aka 'The Major', staged mock 'celebrations' of the Communist system (Ramet 1995 p. 105). On one occasion 'the Major' led 5,000 students dressed in red on a 'march' by the orang-utan enclosure at Wrocław zoo, singing 'Stalinist hymns and wav[ing] red flags' (ibid.). Perhaps drawing on the image of Mary, Queen of Poland, in June 1988, a thousand youths assembled, armed with trumpets and horns and with due cacophany elected General Jaruzelski, the Communist leader, 'King of Poland' (ibid.).

Both the Great Novena, with its combination of solemnity and celebration and the Orange Alternative, with its use of humour to undermine communist pomposity, effectively undermined Communist legitimacy by creating a public space where people's views could be made clear without directly saying anything, because direct criticism of the regime was not tolerated. No public sphere, in the normative sense of a place for unconstrained discussion, was possible. Such mobilization to create an alternative public sphere may be compared with the strategies employed by British Muslims and discussed in the previous chapter, for example the 'gendered and familial Pakistani space of voluntary action (which constitutes) ... a space of ... transgressive humour, music and dance' (Werbner 1996 p. 58), constructed by women's groups like al-Masoom. Here, women cannot participate as equals in the public sphere of male Pakistani 'community leadership', but have created their own spaces in which, among other things, relatively unconstrained discussion is possible. Furthermore, by engaging directly with British public life (by organizing concerts, meeting MPs) they indirectly challenge the male leadership's right to represent the 'community', as well as British stereotypes of Asian women as passive and Islamic religion as inherently repressive of women.

Like the Great Novena and the Orange Alternative, the burning of *The Satanic Verses* was also the symbolic action of a group that perceived itself to be unable to influence the authorities, or even to engage in meaningful discussion with them. However, it illustrates the dangers of symbolic action without effective discursive action, if you misunderstand the cultural codes of your audience. Symbolic action may, in some situations, provoke discussion, but it certainly does not necessarily support or encourage it. This is in part why Habermas's account of the public sphere stresses the primacy of linguistic action, growing as it does out of the Frankfurt school's critique of mass culture. Central to this was the manipulation of mass publics through symbolic media, whether those of Nazi and Stalinist totalitarianism or Western consumerism. Habermas also emphasized the unity of the public sphere, seeing dangers in the fragmentation of public communication. But these examples perhaps allow us to take a more nuanced view.

First, as well as a means of domination or seduction in totalitarian and consumer societies respectively, symbolic communication can also be a powerful means of creating a counter-public for marginalized groups, whether relatively small groups such as Muslim women in Britain, or the whole population in a Communist system where the Party seeks to monopolize public life. Indeed, not only is it a means of communication when discursive channels are blocked, it can communicate in a unique way that cannot be reduced to linguistic form. Thus the Pakistani familial 'space of fun' and the ceremonial space of Polish Catholic liturgy can renew and transform the lifeworld in a way that discussion alone cannot. Second, as Benhabib (1992a; Chapter 3) argues, multiple public spheres enable the empowerment and public participation of marginalized groups; but at the same time this runs the risk of fragmenting public communication and creating a condition of 'hyperpluralism', with many raised voices failing to engage with each other's point of view. This is where the gradual communicative rationalization of each lifeworld context is needed as a counter-trend to diversification.

To return to the Polish case, it may be argued that the weakness of a system of symbolic communication without lifeworld (or strategic) rationalization was exposed when the Communist regime collapsed. There are two components to this, corresponding to the two aspects of rationality delineated by Habermas: strategic and communicative. First, the opposition, led by Solidarity, relied too much on symbolic and 'felt' unity, because that symbolic repertoire, so effective at mobilizing against the Communist system, was ill suited to practical problem-solving, which requires the exercise of strategic rationality. This is Osa's (1997) thesis: during the martial law period (1981–89) symbolic mobilization, mediated through the Church's pastoral networks and Solidarity's underground:

> created a rhetorical framework and developed tactics that were good for the expressive assertion of collective identity and for symbolic confrontations. But the repertoire, conditioned by the constraints on collective action imposed by a repressive regime format, itself became an obstacle for activists faced with the problems of day to day organizing ... Solidarity's symbolic politics deflected instrumentality (interest-based politics) and diffused activism by substituting symbolic for actual victories. ... Ironically, the creation of religiously tinged ideological and solidary frameworks then constrained the movement from transcending the field of symbolic politics. (pp. 363–5)

Second, the development of 'solidary frameworks' based on identification with key symbols and narratives without a parallel development of communicative rationality left Poles ill equiped to deal with 'the Other', with those within society for whom identification with religio-national symbols was in some way problematic: atheists and non-Catholic religious groups. It also left the Church ill equipped to deal with plurality, both within itself and in society, and in particular having so long identified its own interests with the national interest, in disentangling these two when considering constitutional and legal questions.

However, another perspective on the post-Communist difficulties of Solidarity and the Church is presented by Ramet (1995), following the work of Samuel Huntingdon (1968), later to become controversial for his 'Clash of Civilizations' thesis (1993). Ramet argues that during the 1980s Poland was to suffer from Huntingdon's syndrome of 'praetorianism', a condition in which in the absence of adequately developed channels of political communication those groups which happen to have well-organized institutions – such as the military, students, unions and churches – comes to act as a surrogate channel of political communication (Ramet 1995 p. 178). While this can work quite effectively in relatively simple societies, as societies become more differentiated the coordination capacity of such institutions declines (Huntingdon 1968 p. 229). Considered in the perspective of systems theory, the failure of the political subsystem, itself 'artificially' induced by the Communist government's attempt to coordinate all systems through the political one, triggers a 'temporary' de-differentiation process in which a specialist institution once again (in the case of the Church) takes on political functions.

This perspective is not necessarily in conflict with the 'symbolic mobilization theory' developed above. The inherent limitations of symbolic media of coordination can be seen as the means through which the praetorian institution fails. However, as we noted in Part I, there is a danger that such systems-theoretical perspectives reify particular Western European/North American institutional arrangements, as well as downplay the role of conflict in achieving systemic change. In particular, Huntingdon's perspective on Poland points to the limitations of the Church as a channel of political communication, but does nothing to illuminate its role in bringing about conditions through which adequate political institutions could come into being. The assumed superiority of institutional differentiation along Western European/North American lines means that Polish intimations of a 'third way' between church-state separation and fusion (Former PM Mazowiecki, in Brzezinski 2000 p. 122) are ruled out from the start. Furthermore, in doing so it neglects the importance of the lifeworld to political communication.

Therefore, in examining the role of religion in empirical civil society and the public sphere in Poland we must try to guard against such normative presumptions. In particular, we need to keep in mind both of our preliminary hypotheses for explaining the Church and normative civil society's post-Communist failure – praetorianism and inadequate lifeworld rationalization. In this section we have considered the Church's role in symbolic mobilization, the first area that we contended in the Introduction is important to grasping the role of religion in civil society and the public sphere in the Great Transformation in Poland. We now turn to the second area: the relationship between the Church, empirical civil society and the state.

4. The Church, Empirical Civil Society and the State

First, it is important to note that the mythical unity of nation and church was always that – mythical, and that both the Polish Church and society have been heterogeneous throughout the postwar period. For example, within the Church there were tensions between the Church hierarchy, which sought to gain and protect its institutional prerogatives, and more radical elements of the priesthood and laity, who sought to pull the Church towards stronger expressions of opposition to the regime (Gautier 1998 p. 306). Church activity also varied by locality (Bernhard 1993 p. 135). Within the parallel society of the 1980s, there were certainly elements of the underground movement that rejected the Church's role in politics – Fighting Solidarity and Independence, for example (Ramet pp. 189–90). Indeed, there were times when it looked as though the bonds holding together the disparate elements of the Church and the opposition might break. The early 1980s was such a time, when the cautious Cardinal Glemp had succeeded Wyszyński, martial law was at its most repressive, and Solidarity's infant institutions lay shattered. However, we do not need to read an account of this diversity as an exposé of the myth of Solidarity. Rather, following Baumann's (1999, and above, Chapter 5 Section 4) conceptualization of models of culture as discursive we can think of 'culture as process' and 'culture as roots' models of the Church and civil society as useful in different contexts, and therefore as potentially complementary rather than necessarily conflicting. The development of parallel society in Poland has its own rich literature and this short discussion is not intended to reproduce it; rather, it aims briefly to characterize the diversity and development of Poland's civil society and to examine the Church's role in relation to it.

In the Introduction we noted Ramet's characterization of church action in the mid-1970s as 'mirroring' broader developments in society, as one example of a tendency for the Church to be seen as secondary and supportive rather than constitutive of the opposition. The last section argued in response that the Church's role can be seen as more fundamental than this: without the Church's symbolic 'action frame', the predominantly urban and industrially based workers' movements which constituted Solidarity could never have united the country, especially the countryside, and the ecclesiastical development of this frame can be traced back to at least the mid-1950s. Furthermore, as we shall see, it was not only in the arena of symbolic framing that the Church made a seminal contribution to the opposition movement.

However, it is important to note that the Church was able to make these contributions in part because of the position of relative strength it had negotiated for itself by cooperating with the regime. This gave it a stake in preserving the peace to maintain these prerogatives – and hence difficulties arise for interpreting its role as one of straightforward opposition to the government. For example, in 1956 Wyszyński agreed a 19-point accord with the state that guaranteed the Church aspects of the Church's core mission while conceding some regulatory powers of church affairs to the state. Under this agreement, the Church could begin to teach again in public schools and regain a voice in the selection of church personnel, but at the cost of state regulation of many church activities. By the 1970s these prerogatives had grown to include Catholic deputies in the Sejm (Parliament) and finance for the construction of new churches (although, as we shall see below, this remained a contentious issue).

So, from the beginning of the construction of symbolic resistance, the Church hierarchy found itself in a mediating position between the state and opposition forces (which at this early stage lacked institutional form), rather than one of outright opposition. In part, it resolved this dilemma by voicing criticisms of the government on moral grounds and over particular incidents, rather than criticising the system as a whole. In fact, the PRCC never faced quite the dilemmas of cooption that confronted other national churches in Central and Eastern Europe. For example, the 'Church in Socialism' from the 1970s policy confronted the East German church (EKD) with the difficult task of walking a tightrope between cooperation to achieve influence, and collaboration, and has caused long-term damage to its reputation (Burgess 1997). This is partly because of the institutional strength and popularity of the PRCC, in turn related to its historic role in the preservation of national identity, and partly because the Polish communists never succeeded in penetrating society to the extent of their East German counterparts.

Examples of the Church playing a leading role in opposition include criticism of the government-led pogrom in 1968. This was vocally opposed by Wyszyński and the future Pope Karol Wojtyła, as well as by the newly established *Tygodnik Powszechny* Catholic intellectual weekly, whose editor Jerzy Turowicz invited sacked

Jewish journalist Antoni Słonimski on to the staff. *Tygodnik Powszechny* was to provide a significant opposition voice during the following two decades and exemplifies the Church's role in developing a Catholic intelligentsia who were to have significant leadership roles in pre-Solidarity opposition groups in the 1970s and later in Solidarity itself. Thus Catholic intellectuals were part of the discussions in the early 1970s that eventually led to the formation of KOR (Workers' Defence Committee) in 1976, following the suppression of the riots in Radom and Ursus in 1975. As some later commentators reflect on the discussions of the early 1970s 'this process of encounter and rapprochement affected only a small core of dissidents. But most boasted the potential at the time to exert an influence within their respective milieux and have since enjoyed an importance far outweighing their actual numbers' (Luxmoore and Babiuch 1995a p. 75). In addition, the hierarchy gave support to the KOR by praising its human rights work. Catholic opposition was also prominent in reaction to the constitutional amendments of 1975, which strengthened ties with the Soviet Union. Signatories to the *List 59*, which proposed an alternative amendment based on civil rights, included priests and prominent lay church members, among them associates of the Kraków-based Catholic publishing house Znak. Again, the hierarchy also offered support by issuing an official statement asking the government not to react with renewed repression. The case of Znak is also worth noting. In the late 1960s and early 1970s Znak's theological works, inspired by the Second Vatican Council's impetus to political theology, demonstrated the relevance of Catholic moral discourse to contemporary politics. As Norbert Zmijewski argues, 'initially minimalist and apolitical, Znak's Catholicism gave rise to the use of Catholic morality for political purposes, a morality uniting people and nations fighting against unbidden regimes' (in Taras 1995 p. 97). Although Znak's influence was to wane with the rise of the KOR, it provides another example of ecclesiastical precedence in the development of Poland's democratic opposition.

The presence of Catholic voices in this early opposition owed not just to courageous individual action and the hierarchy's attempts at their protection, but, as the presence of Znak associates suggests, to the Church's considerable organizational resources, which the hierarchy's cautious and conciliatory approach had arguably allowed it to develop. Thus by the 1970s there was already a large network of Catholic organizations, in part supported by international Catholic philanthropy. One commentator writes of

> a vast pastoral and educational network (including, at Lublin, the only functioning Catholic University in the then communist world), one that the Church continually expanded for the purposes of training youth, educating religious, nurturing a Catholic lay intelligentsia and, in its thousands of parish halls, defending and promoting workers and human rights. (Della Cava 1997 p. 179)

Catholicism also gave inspiration to other opposition groups before the formation of Solidarity. Thus one of the few active opposition groups that pre-dated Solidarity, and the first to call for an overthrow of Communism and genuine independence, was the Confederation for an Independent Poland (KPN), formed in September 1979.

This drew on traditional Catholic ethics and looked back to the pre-Communist period for historical inspiration. It was committed to legal forms of opposition and during his trial in 1986 its leader Leszek Moczulski maintained that members of his organization had never broken the law, but that the Communist authorities, in failing to implement the Yalta agreement and hold free elections, had done so.

The Church also contributed to the development of civil society during the 1970s by supporting cultural activities. For example, since 1968 the Sacro-Song festival had drawn international participation and a predominantly young audience, while in 1975 the Warsaw Campus Ministry launched its annual week of Christian culture, whose programme included lectures, music, poetry and discussion groups, including prominent writers and artists (Ramet 1995 p. 181). The 1970s also saw a rapid expansion in the Church's building programme, although struggles with the state authorities over construction in some areas, especially the new towns such as Nowa Huta, remained. This is witnessed by the formation of organizations such as the Christian Community of Working People in Nowa Huta in 1979, dedicated to defending illegal chapels (many of these new towns were constructed without churches) and to gain permission to build new ones (Bernhard 1993 p. 139).

However, while these activities demonstrate the importance of the Church in the 1970s in providing organizational, moral and intellectual resources for the development of potential sites of opposition, the emergence of Solidarity and the imposition of martial law were to mark a new phase:

> In contrast to the Solidarity period, when the Church hierarchy attempted to mediate between the union and the party-state, or the 1980s, when the Church provided space and shelter for independent cultural initiatives, Church political involvement in the 1970s was less direct because it posed greater risks. (Ibid. p. 137)

The events of 1980–81 were to change the whole situation radically. As a result of the strikes of the summer of 1980, the Interfactory Strike Committee in Gdańsk was able to negotiate the legal recognition of free trade unions for the first time in the Communist world (including Solidarity, which had first surfaced in July 1980), paving the way for the registration of other autonomous bodies (ibid. p. 193; Ramet 1995 p. 94). In the space of little more than a year, the number of independent organizations of all kinds mushroomed. But on 13 December 1981 the government decided to close the whole experiment down (Ramet 1995 p. 86). Although opposition leaders were aware of Russian troop manoeuvres on the borders and other signs of an imminent clampdown, they had expected it to be initiated through legislation and hence give them to the opportunity to resist through legal channels (p. 88). The proclamation of martial law closed such channels – indeed it closed down or militarized most of the society and economy – leaving the fledgling union movement in disarray.

However, the imposition of martial law failed to close down civil society. On the contrary, Solidarity succeeded in re-forming underground, sometimes from below, beginning at factory level, sometimes from above, as regional bodies that had been established unofficially revived. By mid-1986, 23 of the 38 regional committees had been re-established (Ramet 1995 p. 96). Particularly important for the establishment of an alternative public sphere, the underground press mushroomed: approximately 1,200 different periodicals appeared between 1981 and 1986, with an average circulation of between 500 and 2,000 copies, although *Tygodnik Mazowsze*, widely regarded as Solidarity's official mouthpiece, had a circulation as high as 80,000 weekly in 1985 (*Helsinki Watch* 1986 pp. 44–5). *Robotnik* ('The Worker'), founded in 1977 on KOR initiative, proved important in facilitating communications between workers (Bernhard 1993 pp. 159–70). Although they never succeeded in replacing the state media as the Poles' main source of information, they became a vital source of supplementation and correction and later, as Gorbachov's reforms proceeded in the Soviet Union, of international news (Ramet 1995 p. 111).

Parallel arts, education and public health structures also developed, so that by 1988 'perhaps no part of communal life remained in which parallel society had not penetrated' (ibid. p. 108). But what was the Church's role in these developments? First, there was support at parish level and by priests for striking workers, manifest in the symbolic mobilization we have already discussed; for example at the Lenin shipyard in Gdańsk the gates were opened daily to allow the priest to enter to bring Mass to striking workers. Second, in the period leading up to and following the legalization of Solidarity the Church hierarchy played a significant role in mediating between the developing labour movement and the government. This is the classic 'praetorian' role:

> In early September [1980] Cardinal Wyszyński met for the first time with Solidarity's leader Lech Wałęsa and from Sepember 24 to the end of the year, *a joint commission of the bishops and the government met eighty-one times.* During the spring of 1981 ... Cardinal Wyszyński met with General Wojciech Jaruzelski and, two days later, with Lech Wałęsa. As a result of these meetings, the so-called Warsaw agreement was signed on April 1, 1981. (Strassberg 1988 p. 194, emphasis added)

The intensity of the Church hierarchy's involvement with both the Communist authorities and with Solidarity's leaders – the latter of whom were to form the first post-Communist government within the decade – together with the long frustration of the Communist years, perhaps helps to explain why from 1989 the hierarchy attempted to try to translate 'Christian values' into legislation through government channels without democratic process. However, returning to 1981, a change in leadership style was to occur with the death of Wyszyński on 31 May and the election of Cardinal Glemp. Glemp's leadership coincided with a further deterioration of the relationship between the state and the developing parallel society and saw the imposition of martial law by the end of the year.

Glemp's initial reaction – to plead against the eruption of violence on both sides, 'even if I have to plead on my knees, do not start a fight of Pole against Pole' (in Luxmoore 1987 p. 127) – was consistent with Wyszyński's approach to the strikes the previous summer. But later this even-handedness seemed to critics to amount to an endorsement of the regime, arguing that Solidarity shared the blame for the deterioration of the situation and even stating in early 1984 that 'the Solidarity now in existence has moved away from many of its principles' (in Ramet 1995 p. 188). Such statements earned him the nickname 'Comrade Glemp' and opened up the division between the hierarchy and the lower clergy. Priests such as Jerzy Popiełuszko and Kazimierz Sklarczy were direct in their criticicm of the government, the latter stating that 'Christianity's confrontation with Communism is a war of good against evil, love against hate, truth against lies' (ibid. p. 187). As Casanova (1993 p. 135) has noted, these radical parish priests helped to sustain the socially integrating oppositional power of the initial Solidarity movement through the martial law years: 'By recreating sacramentally, in the Durkheimian sense, the collective effervescence of the original experience of Solidarity, they were helping to [keep] alive the movement as well as its norms and values'. Several bishops were contributing to this 'sacramental maintenance' of solidarity/Solidarity, for example by holding solemn Masses on the fifth anniversary of Solidarity in December 1995. They also made more concrete contributions, Bishop Damian Zimon of Katowice telling a crowd of thousands at Katowice in 1987 that they had a right to 'independent and self-governing trade unions' (Ramet 1995 p. 188).

Indeed, throughout its ranks and the martial law period the Catholic Church was consistent in support of independent trade unions (ibid. p. 191). Even at his most cautious in the early martial law period, and while attributing a share of the blame for the violence to Solidarity, Glemp insisted on unions' right to exist, as when he asked in August 1992 for the recommencement of trade union work 'at least by stages' (p. 187). The Pope's second and third visits in 1983 and 1987 added an international dimension to the Church's support for underground Solidarity. While always supporting Glemp in his statements, the Pope went further in emphasizing the need for self-determination as the context of all dialogue, as well as calling (as Glemp had) for amnesty for political prisoners and the legalization of autonomous trade unions (Walendowski 1983 pp. 5–8).

Between the Pope's second and third visits the outspoken Warsaw priest Jerzy Popiełuszko was murdered by the security forces. In his visit in 1987 the Pope affirmed his support for such radical opposition by praying at Popiełuszko's grave (Ramet 1995 p. 191). In 1988 the Church stepped up it campaign: on 26 August the Polish bishops issued a collective statement that not only specified their support for trade union pluralism but described industrial unrest as a symptom of the diseased socio-political system (ibid. p. 192). In October Catholic intelligentsia clubs nationally issued a nine-point statement calling for parliamentary democracy and the re-legalization of Solidarity, while internationally the Vatican made the latter a precondition for the restoration of diplomatic relations. When the thaw finally came, it is symptomatic that the legalization of Solidarity on 17 May 1989 was followed by the passing of three laws relating to the Church; characteristically, too, the Church had a place at the roundtable talks which were set up to mediate the transition to pluralism and democracy.

These bills gave the Church the right to produce television and radio programmes, guaranteed freedom for the Church press, gave the Church back control over the Catholic charity Caritas and granted powers to establish and run new welfare organizations, including hospitals and old people's homes. It also granted legal recognition to various church institutions, including those of higher education, returned some church property confiscated in the 1950s and gave permission for the Church to establish new schools. In fact in many cases these rights simply enabled the Church to expand activities it was already undertaking. Throughout the 1980s the Church played an important role in the 'bottom-up' development of civil society through its wide-ranging national network: by 1988 it had more than 10,000 churches, 2,500 convents, 400 monasteries and 12 high schools, as well as the Catholic University at Lublin (Ramet 1995 p. 180). At the most basic level, the Church provided space for underground Solidarity to meet. For example, St Brygida's church at Gdańsk was used as the trade union's headquarters while it remained illegal and in the summer of 1984 Solidarity held its first 'summit meeting' since the declaration of martial law in the Jasna Góra monastery at Częstohowa (Ramet 1995 pp. 192, 194).

The Church greatly expanded its role in education, so that by 1987 there were more than 22,000 Catholic places of religious teaching in Poland (Gilarek 1997 p. 128). Although most of these concentrated on 'catechesis' – basic Catholic teaching – many greatly expanded their range of courses across the curriculum, both in practical subjects and for 'consciousness-raising'. For example, at the Institute of Christian Culture in Lubochnia, which offers classes from pre-school to adult education, the latter included lectures on 'Noncommunist resistance in the Second World War' and 'Citizen's Protection under the Law' (ibid. pp. 180–81). The Catholic press and publishing houses also encouraged pluralism, both by the diversity of perspectives they offered and in some cases by their defence of the rights of others. Thus by 1988 there were 32 publishing houses, accounting for 1.2 per cent of the market share. *Tygodnik Powszechny* had published articles by various dissidents, most of them agnostics, during the 1970s and under martial law published poems and columns by jailed Solidarity activists (Ramet 1995 p. 181). We have already noted the importance of Znak in developing the moral discourse of Catholicism for political use (Taras 1995 p. 97).

The Church continued its support of alternative culture, staging Ernest Bryll's banned play *The Circle*, which dealt (aptly enough) with the Apostles' despair between Christ's crucifixion and resurrection in a ruined Warsaw church at Easter 1985, and during a week of Christian culture in 1984 staged a play by known KOR sympathizer Halina Mikołajska (ibid.). The Church also expanded its operations in the welfare sector, with the Rural Pastoral Communities and Pastoral Service to Workers associations established to cater to the needs of rural and urban workers. In this welfare work the Church played an important role as a channel of foreign aid, which became especially important as the economic situation worsened towards the end of the decade. Glemp was particularly concerned for rural workers and had some success in pressurizing the government to give them extra help in this later period. In 1981, following the declaration of martial law, new arrangements were put in place to distribute international aid. American Catholic philanthropic organizations took special responsibility for the North, Austrians for the South and Germans for Central Poland, with the Commission for Charities of the Polish Bishops' Conference playing a leading role in internal coordination (Della Cava 1997 p. 182). Thus:

Between 1981 and 1985, Poland received considerable support for three distinct types of need: food and clothing; agricultural machinery (likely earmarked for members of 'Rural Solidarity', a notably Catholic structure founded on the heels of the workers' initiative); and a variety of financial and material aid to Church social enterprises such as old-age homes, day-care centers, [and] orphanages. (pp. 182–3)

As a result of all these developments, by 1987 the Church's role in empirical civil society was so central that one commentator could accurately claim 'our churches are no longer just churches in the religious sense, they are fully fledged community centers' (Śliwiński 1987 p. 10).

Thus, the Church's contribution to empirical civil society was multi-layered. First, at the level of networks: through its parish, pastoral, educational, intellectual and monastic networks, themselves linked to international philanthropic networks and ecclesiastical authorities (for example the Pope and the Vatican) and its support of the independent arts and journalism, the Church helped develop and sustain an alternative society, as well as at times sheltering and supporting the specifically political underground. Second, at the level of the hierarchy, who, perhaps most clearly under Glemp in the early 1980s, never entirely abandoned the classic ecclesiastical role of government legitimization and at times (especially during periods of political transition in 1980–81 and 1988–89) adopted the 'praetorian' role of an independent 'broker' between the government and political opposition. Third, at the level of symbolic/discursive mobilization, through which the Church provided an alternative public sphere entwining religious and nationalist elements.

The relationship between these levels was sometimes difficult, as illustrated in the popular rather than ecclesiastical 'canonization' of Popiełuszko, only partially redeemed by the Pope's visit to his grave in 1987 (Taras 1995 pp. 99–100). At the same time, the relationship between the levels was closely inter-related: for example, the Pope (hierarchy/transnational network) developed and sustained the symbolic public sphere inherited from Wyszyński (hierarchy), which was in turn re-enacted and developed by local priests such as Popiełuszko (local network). The relationship of this empirical civil society to normative civil society was also complex: the Church undoubtedly fostered pluralism both institutionally and intellectually; at the same time, in mediating between church and opposition it stepped over the boundary between political and civil society central to the normative concept. There are similar tensions in the relationship between the Church-supported empirical public sphere and the normative public sphere: while *Tygodnik Powszechny* provided a forum for public discussion beyond orthodox Catholicism, Wyszyński's synthesis of orthodox and folk Catholicism with nationalist romanticism implicitly identified Polish citizenship with Catholicism and hence restricted participation in the public sphere.

The question to which we now turn is: how would this legacy of thoroughgoing involvement in the development of empirical civil society and the public sphere through the Communist period, yet ambivalent with respect to their normative conceptions, translate into the post-Communist period?

5. Church, Civil Society and the Public Sphere in Post-Communist Poland: Issues, Explanations and Context

There is a positivist attitude that ethics comes from law, that law is, as it were, prior ... that parliament is the root of morality. I do not share this opinion. For me the root of morality is God. This is a great conflict in Poland. ... Is the will of the people primary or are certain ethical principles primary which people are not permitted to change? I as a representative of a Christian party represent the view that the principles of morality are eternal, unchanging and people are not permitted to change them. We have to adjust the law to them. (Stefan Niesolowski, MP, Christian National Union [a political party], January 1993; in Brzezinski 2000 p. 198)

The 20th century was a period of special violence [against] the consciences of people. ... In spite of appearances, the rights of conscience should also be defended today. There is ... more and more intolerance spreading within the mass media under the banner of tolerance in public life. ... attacks on the Church and holding Christian values up to ridicule, noticeable in my fatherland, should arouse anxiety. (Pope John Paul II in Poland in May 1995:in Załęcki 1997 p. 14)

Secular Poles have started to talk of a Khomeinization of Poland at the hands of the Catholic Church and its right wing allies. (Ramet 1995 p. 396)

In the post-Communist period, both in the immediate transition period (1989–93) and since, the Church has become involved in a whole series of complex controversies concerning church-state-civil society relationships. We shall concentrate on two of these. First, the church hierarchy became involved in a protracted and public legal wrangle with the Ombudsman for Citizens' Rights over its close involvement with government over matters of education and abortion policy. Second, elements of grass-roots Catholicism have become associated with the growth of a nationalist Far Right, for example through the sometimes inflammatory rhetoric of Poland's most popular Catholic (but unauthorized by the hierarchy) radio station, Radio Maryja (Załęcki 1997 p. 11). During the same period, public trust in the Church as an institution has plummeted (Borowik 1997 p. 247). Another controversy, though of more significance internationally than for the development of civil society in Poland (although it is in part indicative of anti-semitic attitudes) is the complicated wrangle involving the Church, the government and the international Jewish community over the presence of a Carmelite convent (and later crosses) at the site of the concentration camp at Oswięcim (Auschwitz). A brief discussion of the issues involved is presented below, but for detailed discussions see Wollaston (1994) and Rittner and Roth (1991).

There is not a single 'orthodox' scholarly explanation for response to these developments, but a number of intertwined strands can be discerned. Again, for the purposes of introduction, I shall identify just three and briefly indicate why I think each of them raises significant problems which are important to address, because each prematurely closes off avenues of enquiry and debate that ought to be kept open.

First, following the 'orthodox' secularization thesis some scholars have argued that the Church's popularity was 'artificially inflated' by its role as a cultural defence against Communism, so now this 'pressure' has gone, the popularity of the Church declines. For example, one scholar concludes: 'If the imposed communist system, together with urbanization and industrialization, created the first stage of secularization of Polish society, the last years of transformation to democracy could be treated as a second phase of secularization' (Węcławowicz 1996 p. 112). I have already argued against the 'pressure' model of religious popularity, because it fails to consider the way in which religious discourse and symbols change social reality by entering public space. In the Polish case, it also wrongly equates decline in public trust in the hierarchy with decline in personal belief and religious practice, neither of which is justified by existing data. In particular, we shall consider one study that suggests that personal belief actually *increased* just as trust in the institutional church plummeted (Borowik 1997). More importantly, however, for our concerns in this chapter, the same study also suggests that such high rates of personal belief, in the presence of a culturally dominant religious tradition, are compatible with the basis of normative civil society and the public sphere, namely respect for personal autonomy in matters of moral and religious conviction.

Second, scholars point out that the oppositional role of the Church concealed both its own internal divisions and divisions within the Polish public, which have since re-emerged – hence Osa's statement, quoted in full at the head of the chapter, that in the post-Communist period for the first time 'political fault lines became visible' (1997 p. 340). Part of what was concealed was divergence between lay and hierarchy on much of the Church's teaching, and part the dictatorial attitudes of the church authorities and some of the laity. A problem with this account emerges when these authoritarian attitudes are interpreted as part of a general thesis on post-Communist Central and Eastern Europe. Thus, especially in the light of events in Yugoslavia (to be considered in the next chapter), it is argued that Communism somehow 'kept the lid on' seething ethnic tensions and xenophobic nationalisms.

However, as Ramet (1995) argues, we need to dig deeper than the 'Communist lid' theory if we are to understand the rise of 'uncivil society' in post-Communist Europe:

> I do not subscribe to the common notion that the ethnic hatreds and chauvinisms presently visible in Eastern Europe were there all along, but repressed by communist power, and that as soon as that power collapsed, percolated to the surface. I consider this interpretation facile, simplistic and fallacious. At a minimum, one should always want to know *why* a given ... phenomenon exists and the 'standard' interpretation entirely evades this question by positing ethnic hatred and chauvinism as eternal verities – but not for all humankind, only for Eastern Europe, because we in the West do not need repression to keep our chauvinists in line. So this is a chauvinistic theory about chauvinism. (p. 431)

The 'why' that we shall consider here includes the role of Communism in constructing such chauvinisms – most obvious in Bosnia in the mutual antagonism of Serb and Croat nationalisms developed through a corrupt and competitive federal structure, as we shall see in the next chapter. In Poland we should note that the persecution of Jews in 1968–69 stemmed from government policy. Reasons also include the impact of Communism on social bonds, followed by the sudden arrival of market competition coinciding with the collapse of much industry and welfare provision – conditions hardly conducive to cooperation.

The third point relates to Ramet's criticism of a Western chauvinism that 'we in the West do not need repression to keep our chauvinists in line'. It can be seen when the failure of the hierarchy to come to terms with change – for example, the loss of its 'praetorian' mediating role as other political institutions emerge – is narrated as if there exist 'normal' models of political institutionalization to which Poland should conform. At its extreme, this results in Fukayama's (1992) 'end of history' thesis, whereby with the failure of state socialism all societies supposedly converge on a common liberal democratic capitalist political-economic model. Yet the evidence considered in various places in Part I of this book should give us pause for thought before accepting that there is only one form of political institutionalization that ensures civility. First, Habermas's critique of systems theory shows the lifeworld dependence of modern institutional forms, while our (in part, following Casanova) critique of Habermas shows that a diversity of lifeworld settings (including religious traditions) can function as agents of communicative rationalization. Second, internal critique of the Western tradition of political philosophy has shown that the supposed neutrality of Western forms of political institutionalization are in fact highly problematic (Galston 1991). Third, Baumann's (1999) account of multiculturalism exposes the implicitly religious or 'civil' religious form of Western political institutions (for example in France or America).

These considerations will inform our account of church-state-civil society relations in Poland from 1989. But to understand the controversies involved, an overview of the rapid social change effecting Poland during this period is necessary. After this, primarily using Skapska's (1997) study of local government, we shall consider the impact of these changes and the legacy of Communism for the empirical civil society within which Catholic networks and hierarchies operate. This will equip us to tackle the first set of controversies we shall consider – those concerned with the role of the Church at the level of the state and political society, in the context of debates on procedural and substantive democracy. This relates closely to the problematic assumptions in the democratization literature that we identified – the assumed normativity of Western forms of political institutionalization.

We shall turn then to Borowik's (1997) study of religious and moral belief and its relationship to church authority, because as well as responding to the first, secularization-based, strand of problematic scholarship, this also challenges the third set, because it suggests that a culture in which one religious tradition is dominant is not necessarily hostile to pluralism. This possibility, however, is challenged by the emergence of forms of chauvinism, including the religious, of which we consider two examples: the persecution of Greek Catholic Ukrainians in Przemyśl and a study of anti-semitic attitudes among young Poles and the Church's relation to these. This provides the setting for reviewing the procedural-substantive democracy debate, the arguments developed so far concerning religion's relation to normative civil society and anticipates the fuller discussion of religious chauvinism in the next chapter on Bosnia.

First, then, the political setting. Poland's first postwar free elections occurred on 4 June 1989, with Solidarity winning an overwhelming proportion of those seats that were freely contested. The Communists failed to create a workable coalition and by August were forced to concede the prime ministerial post to the opposition: Wałęsa offered them three candidates. Jaruzelski, still President, chose Taduesz Mazowiecki, former editor of the Catholic monthly *Więź* and editor of Solidarity's weekly *Tygodnik Solidarność* (Ramet 1995 p. 304). The period until the election of Wałęsa as president on 25 November 1990 was one of rapid political and economic change for Poland. Let us first consider political change.

The context for the transition to democracy was created by the abolition of censorship and depoliticization of the police in early 1990. The period proved to be one of fission and formation, as social movements coalesced under the Communist system divided when they reformed as political parties. Thus the Communist Party and structures irreparably weakened, with the party weekly set up to oppose Solidarity, Rzeczwistość, closing and the party (the Polish United Workers' Party) itself eventually dissolving, reconstituting itself as the Social Democracy Party. It immediately split, with the new faction called the Union for Social Democracy. Deprived of state subsidies, both rapidly began propagating the free enterprise they had so long denied: converting the Gdańsk party canteen into a public restaurant and entering the retail, banking and tourism sectors (Ramet 1995 p. 358). Solidarity, until this stage a trade union rather than a political party, was itself to divide as it moved formally into the political arena, with the Centre Alliance formed behind Wałęsa and Democratic Action behind Mazowiecki. The Polish Labour Party, a centre-right, Christian democratic organization emerged, as did the National Party and the Green Party. Indeed, political fragmentation was such that some eighty political parties contested the local elections in May 1990, and in the national election of October 1991 no party polled more than 12 per cent of the vote (ibid. pp. 358 and 387). The fall of Hanna Suchocka's government in May 1993 led to reform, so that no party with less than 5 per cent of the national vote could gain seats, which reduced the parties in Parliament from 29 to 12 (p. 389).

Economically, the government began the process of privatization of state-owned industries and to follow the monetarist policies of Harvard economist Jeffrey Sachs, who advocated abolishing limitations on the currency supply, abolishing price and wage controls and freeing trade. This economic 'shock therapy' was introduced without democratic public deliberation. None the less, it has been continued by subsequent administrations regardless of political persuasion, because it proved successful in curbing inflation and increasing productivity, producing an increase in GDP by 1993 and a trade surplus by 1992 (Ramet 1995 pp. 375–6). But in 1990 industrial sales slumped, unemployment grew rapidly (a problem that has not abated) and farmers complained that they could not afford machinery and fertilizer (p. 359). Furthermore, along with long-term unemployment these policies have also brought a long-term widening of the gap between rich and poor and reductions in health, welfare and social services. Having sketched this broad context, we turn to three case studies to consider the development of civil society and the public sphere and their relation to religion: of civil society in local government, of a national public sphere as reflected in the controversies between the Church and the Ombudsman and of changing religious attitudes to the Church's role in public life. Finally, we shall look at the treatment of religious minorities as a barometer of the development of normative civil society.

6. Parallel Society and Post-Communist Civil Society: Case Studies

(a) Local Government

These changes form the background to Skapska's study of local government in and near Kraków in South-East Poland. A considerable decentralization of government occurred in the early 1990s and Skapska's study investigated how these new powers were being used in practice, interviewing both local politicians and residents in two areas. The first, a city district, had a high profile for Solidarity activity in the 1980s, with the local church playing a leading role in organizing illegal parallel society activities such as the 'flying university' for workers, art exhibitions, charity and self-help groups. From being predominantly an industrial workers' area, it had become infused with small businesses by 1995 (Skapska 1997 p. 152). The second area was more mixed between farmers and workers (ibid.). In both cases Skapska concludes that 'the alternative forms of civil society flourishing before the collapse of Communism proved to be dysfunctional in democratic society' (p. 158).

A major problem, not surprisingly, is that trust in and respect for public officials, institutions and the law are low. Looking for the deeper causes of this, Skapska argues that while social bonds are strong, these are of the 'amoral familism' or 'familial egoism' type discussed in Chapter 2 and therefore do not translate well into orientation to the good of the wider community. Examples include the sale of state property to 'selected bidders' (that is, the families of local officials) and unwillingness to support public spending because they 'do not go outside at night' (street lamps) or 'do not own a car' (public highway) (ibid. p. 155). Such narrow attitudes, looking inwards towards one's family and in opposition to the 'system', was a functional necessity under Communism, but can also easily foster hostility to outsiders.

A further characteristic identified by Skapska is of interest in the light of the importance of the Church's symbolic mobilization to Solidarity. The Communist public sphere, with its orchestrated public demonstrations, may have been false in the sense of forced and lacking articulation with everyday life, but it was also a source of emotional togetherness and common participation in hard work and has become a source of nostalgia for the past. As one of Skapska's respondents states, 'People do not know what to do on May 1. Before, one had to take part in a demonstration, together with the whole factory (or office, or school). Now, it's just a free day' (p. 156). More insidiously, this form of mobilization gave the emotional sense of participation in a wider community, but did not foster a sense of practical responsibility for that community. Again, the lack of an instrumental orientation to the symbolic public sphere, functional for the opposition under Communism because no other form of public opposition was permitted, becomes dysfunctional under post-Communist conditions. As Osa (1997) comments:

> Pastoral mobilization created a rhetorical framework and developed tactics that were good for collective identity and for symbolic confrontations. But the repertoire, conditioned by the constraints of the repressive regime format, itself became an obstacle for activists faced with problems of day-to-day organizing. (p. 363)

It was against this background of economic constraint and struggle to come to terms with a new market system, for which the parallel society of Solidarity and the symbolic mobilization of the Church had ill equipped the Polish people, that the controversy over religious education in schools needs to be understood.

(b) Religious Education, Abortion and the Ombudsman's Challenge to the Church:
Authoritarianism versus Liberalism, or Human Values versus Nihilism?

As we have seen, the Church had already extended its role in education in the 1980s and its rights in this sphere had been extended in May 1989, but there was still no religious education in state schools. The radical changes in the political system during the next year gave the Church the opportunity to press for more, arguably in an effort to enshrine Christian values in the place in which the state had tried to maintain Communist values in the previous system: public education. Stefan Niesolowski of the Christian National Union Party states the argument:

> I demand respect for Christian values in public life because otherwise the state will become possessed by other ideologies. ... Of the other ideologies I have in mind in particular liberal ideology, aiming to build a morally relativist state, a completely secular humanist state ... I fear precisely that. I guard against that. (In Brzezinski 2000 p. 198)

But the Church was to find this vision of a democracy rooted in Christian values contested in the name of a procedural democracy that sought to radically separate church and state, including in the educational field.

In May 1990 the Polish episcopate published its recommendations and in August 1990 the Ministry of Education, following discussions with the Church, issued instructions that authorized the Catholic Church and 'other interested churches' to offer religious instruction in state schools. Appointments were to be made by Church authorities but financed by the state, and parents were required to enrol their children if they wished them to benefit from this instruction. These instructions were to prove controversial in several respects.

First, although provision for non-Catholic confessional education was possible in theory, in practice small numbers have made this very difficult to implement. Second, the instruction was issued without debate in Parliament (the Sejm) or other forms of public debate, but rather on the basis of private discussions between ministers and the PRCC. Other denominations or inter-church bodies, such as the Ecumenical Council, representing other Christian denominations in Poland, were not consulted. Third, the state funding of religious education and the propagation of religion in state schools both arguably violated church-state separation. This accusation was made because the kind of curriculum proposed was not the non-confessional approach to a variety of religious traditions which is usual in Britain,[2] but rather a confessional, specifically Catholic, education.[3] Church-state separation was specified in the constitution of 1952 and the revised version of this was ratified in 1989, as well as in a number of laws including the 1961 Education Act. However, since these were all, in whole or part, passed under the Communist system, their legitimacy was challenged by the Church. None the less the legality of the instruction was challenged by the Ombudsman for Citizens' Rights, first, unsuccessfully, in 1990 and then, following a second instruction, with some success in 1992–93.

It was the battle between supporters of the church hierarchy and the Ombudsman on this second occasion which drew media attention to the issue and it is on this controversy that we shall concentrate, because it raises questions about the role of a 'national religion' in a democratic society.

First, let us consider the role of Ombudsman for Citizens' Rights. This post was first proposed by the Solidarity National Congress in 1981 and introduced by the Communist government in July 1987. It was the first official position designed to protect human rights and independent of government in the Communist world and as such represented a major concession to the democratic opposition. The Ombudsman's powers are limited. S/he cannot compel the state authorities to follow his or her recommendations, but can make recommendations to the Sejm for changes in legislation, petition the Constitutional Tribunal[4] to review state action and initiate proceedings in the courts on behalf of individuals or organizations, up to the Supreme Court if necessary (Brzezinski 2000 p. 79). The first Ombudsman, appointed for a fixed period of four years, was Ewa Letowska (1987–91), the second Taduesz Zielinski (1991–95) (Gilarek 1997 p. 129). Both became controversial figures in Polish public life, largely because they raised uncomfortable questions about the issue of the kind of democracy Poles wanted. In particular, their actions brought out tensions between two models of democracy: one in which the values of the majority or organizations who claim some special relationship with the nation (for example the PRCC) are be enshrined in law, and a second in which the state should attempt to be neutral on questions of value, in a context in which the very idea of neutrality had been undermined by its association with 'scientific' socialism.

Letowska, the first Ombudsman, petitioned the Constitutional Tribunal in response to the Ministry of Education's directive, challenging its legality on the basis of its compatibility with the Religious Education Act of 1961 (which ruled on the secular character of state schools) and with two articles of the 1989 constitution relating to freedom of conscience and the separation of church and state (Article 82 Sections 1 and 2), (Gilarek 1997 p. 129; Brzezinski 2000 p. 178). However, her petition was rejected by the Constitutional Tribunal. The 1961 Act, passed in the Communist period, was considered inconsistent with the directive; but the Tribunal's reaction was to petition the Sejm to pass a new law to replace it – which it did. Second, it was argued that state support for religious education provided by the Church under church appointment did not violate the separation clause, whereas state appointment of teachers of religion (as in Britain) or a state curriculum (as in Britain at a local level) would. Third, it was argued that the requirement for parents to opt their children into this system did not violate freedom of conscience, because it did not force parents to make a public declaration of faith – they could remain silent and children need not receive this education.

It is important to note that during this period and indeed until 1997, Poland's constitution was undergoing reform.[5] In December 1989, as an interim measure, the old 1952 constitution, which had been constructed during the most repressive phase of Communist rule, was ratified with some significant deletions and additions. Gone was all reference to alliance with the Soviet Union and the Party's 'leading role', while a new Article 1 proclaimed that 'Poland is a democratic state ruled by law' (Brzezinski 2000 p. 88). None the less, the legitimacy of the constitution was open to question and this was precisely the response of the Catholic hierarchy when a second instruction on religious education was questioned on constitutional grounds by Letowska's successor, Zielinski, in 1992. Thus the head of the PRCC, Cardinal Glemp, declared:

> I cannot understand ... how anyone could bring the case of religion before the Tribunal – the religion in which the vast majority of Poles believe, which so often helped the nation free itself from oppression throughout its history. In the name of what constitution is religion being taken to court? In the name of that Stalinist constitution with its many amendments? Are we not more in need of an ombudsman capable of telling us that a given action is inconsistent with the will of the nation for in the long run it is that nation and its will which decide what shape the law will take? (24 August 1992, in Pawlik 1995 p. 34)

Zielinski replied in equally forceful terms, expressing his fear that Poland was in danger of becoming a 'para-religious' state:

> As opposed to a theocracy, which is a political system where there is near total rule by the clergy ... , a para-religious state is a political system in which there exists a formal differentiation between church and secular authority and in which the Church has no intention to replace civil governments, but claims pretences in the control of all its doings if these have a moral significance and in moral judgement it is the highest arbiter. In such a state the Church authorities demand that law impose under the threat of penalty the observance of all the rules that the Church demands of its faithful and also that which is a sin in the eyes of the Church also be an offence according to state law. (24 August 1992, in Brzezinski 2000 p. 199).

Shortly before the Constitutional Tribunal announced its decision (April 1993) on the Ombudsman's challenge, pressure from Church officials increased. This led Zielinski to add:

> I am deeply disturbed by the evolution of opinions concerning the relationship between the state and the Catholic Church. The Church is actually interfering with all three spheres of power: legal, executive and court. I am afraid that we are standing at the gateway of a denominational state ... Church officials cannot claim the right to the privilege of putting pressure on the judges of the Constitutional Tribunal, who should announce their verdicts according to their own consciences and legal knowledge. (15 April 1993, in Pawlik 1995 pp. 35–6)

In the event, the Tribunal's decision was mixed, in part favouring the Ombudsman and in part the Church. But for the purposes of understanding the relationship between the Catholic Church and Polish society, the principles involved here are more important than the specifics of the legislation, so we shall concentrate on the former and then consider public reaction to the whole affair.

First, the affair raises questions about the legitimacy of modern legal systems. As we have seen (Chapter 1) modern legal and social theories tend to see law as a kind of autonomous self-regulating sphere, which should operate impartially without political interference. Zielinski's comments are consistent with this opinion. On the other hand, in a democracy law is created through the political process (as Cardinal Glemp argued), so there is always tension when the logic of a legal system contradicts political will. Tension was particularly strong in this case because the political system under which the law was created had come to be seen as illegitimate, although we note that the constitution had been significantly modified by this stage.

Second, the affair raises questions about the role of the Church in relation to the state and political processes. For church officials, certain matters are regarded as so fundamentally good (or bad), so necessary (or detrimental) to the good functioning of society, that their enforcement (or prohibition) by law is justified over any considerations of freedom of choice. In fact in this case the requirement for parents to request RE in order for their children to receive it means that the Church did respect freedom of choice (although this disregards the social pressure there may be in practice). However, there are other cases where this has not been so. For example, abortion, which had been permitted for both 'social and medical' reasons under the Communist system, was greatly restricted in 1993 to circumstances when 'a woman's health is in danger, when the fetus is severely deformed, or when the pregnancy results from incest'. Pressure from Catholic groups was largely responsible (Brzezinski 2000 p. 181), and apparently contrary to public opinion. Thus one 1988 study had found that 59 per cent of Poles held that abortion should also be an option in the case of poverty, a large family, mental illness, or AIDS (Ramet 1995 p. 447). A 1994 study found that 75.7 per cent thought 'everyone should decide for themselves on the issue' (Borowik 1997 p. 250).

In the cases of both RE and abortion the Church did not seek merely to present its case in public debate and leave the outcome up to the democratic process, but rather to influence government policy by negotiating directly with ministers. In the case of RE the process bypassed the Sejm altogether. While the close connections between ministers and church officials make clear how this was socially possible, deeper questions remain: should limits to the public sphere be set and if so how? Are some matters so fundamental to the well-being of society that they should not be up for debate? Are some things too important to leave to the democratic process? In the context of *The Satanic Verses* controversy we saw that democratic societies do place limits on the public sphere, for example in the interests of national security and to protect individual reputation. We also saw in Chapter 3 that theorists of liberalism have conceded that liberalism is not neutral; as Galston (1991 p. 117) states: 'from certain religious standpoints, the stance of liberalism is bound to seem partisan and hostile'. Certainly, this is how media discussion of the issues had begun to look to sections of the Catholic public by the mid-1990s, as the quotation from the Pope at the head of Section 5 shows.

It should also be noted that both sides in this controversy behaved as if some things are so important that they are simply non-negotiable, although very different things in each case. For the Ombudsman, legal and constitutional processes and individual rights enshrined within these, were held to be non-negotiable. Thus certain basic rights of dissenting minorities (for example freedom of conscience) must be respected, even though the majority may disagree. For Catholic officials, rather different rights, such as the foetus's right to life, were non-negotiable. One may, however, argue that the two approaches are fundamentally different because for the Ombudsman laws and even the constitution can be changed through the political process, whereas the Church appeals to a sacred principle, beyond the political process. In response it may be argued that any form of liberal democracy rests on some non-negotiable basic rights.

There are important arguments here about the extent to which a religious ethos ought to be embodied in a constitution and whether it can be so embodied without compromising the rights and freedoms of others and hence form the basis of normative civil society. The Church also made other attempts to infuse a Christian ethos into the structure of the state during the 1990s. In December 1992 the Broadcasting Law was amended to require all broadcasting to 'respect the religious feelings of the audience and in particular the Christian system of values' (in Brzezinski 2000 p. 198). In 1994 the powers of the National Broadcasting Council to regulate this were amended because prior censorship is unconstitutional, but broadcasters could still find themselves subject to retrospective action. A 'Concordat' – an agreement between the Polish government and the Vatican – was agreed in 1993, although its ratification was suspended following a change of government. Practically, it caused concern because of the implications of the powers it granted the Church over the regulation of cemeteries, but in principle the idea of an international agreement with a religious authority seemed to violate church-state separation.

Elements of the Church have also been active at the level of political society. 'Fatherland', the Catholic voters' alliance founded with the support of Archbishop Gocłowski of Gdańsk, sought to lobby voters to support Catholic candidates who supported 'traditional values' (Ramet 1995 p. 396). Such views were endorsed by deputy Prime Minister Henryk Goryszewski, who addressed voters in the 1993 general election with the words: 'It is a Catholic's duty to elect another Catholic. We, in our overwhelming majority, want a Catholic Poland, such that will not sell the Lord for material goods' (in Brzezinski 2000 p. 197).

However, it appears that Goryszewski had misjudged the Polish public, and the 1993 elections saw the post-Communist parties victorious for the first time. The Church, in the sense of the Church hierarchy and those seeking to monopolize politically on a Catholic basis, also appeared to have fallen out of favour with public opinion by 1993. Thus from a highest-ever rating of 87.8 per cent in May 1989, approval of the functioning of the Catholic Church slumped to 41 per cent by January 1993, at the height of the Ombudsman controversy concerning both abortion and RE. On the Ombudsman controversy in particular, a slightly later survey (May 1993) showed that 87 per cent of respondents knew something of his work, half of these had heard of the motion to dismiss him, and 80 per cent disagreed with it. It is important, though, to be clear on just what this popular rejection of Catholic policy in the early 1990s implies. As a first stage in doing that we shall examine Borowik's (1997) study of Polish beliefs and in the conclusion return to the relationship between religious values and democracy.

(c) Piety, Politics and the Public Sphere: a Reappraisal

Reduction in support for Catholic political parties and the hierarchy's policy in 1993 does not appear to have dented Polish piety. Thus in a study conducted on over 1,000 respondents in November 1994 Borowik found that personal belief in items such as the resurrection of the body, Hell and angels – usually the first to drop on the 'orthodox model' – actually increased by large (30 per cent, 23 per cent and 19 per cent respectively) and statistically significant amounts between 1990 and 1994 (1997 p. 249). She also found no decline in ritual performance, although cautions that since this was based on self-report, this may be due to the 'precedence' effect, whereby self-perception of behaviour lags behind actual change (p. 254).

Borowik also examined relationships between trust, religious belief, moral belief and views of the proper role of the Church in public life. She reports increases in the belief that 'everyone should decide for themselves' as against 'everyone should be obedient to the Church' on issues ranging from politics (93 per cent : 3.4 per cent) through contraception (81.7 per cent : 15.4 per cent) to abortion (75.7 per cent : 20.3 per cent) and fasting (55.2 per cent : 42.5 per cent) (ibid. p. 250). These data suggest that most Poles view issues outside the purely ritual as properly a matter of individual conscience.

Yet this does not mean that they disagree with the Church's teaching – only that such agreement should not be enforced. For example, nearly 50 per cent unconditionally condemn adultery, but only 30 per cent believe that this should be out of obedience to the Church. In morality, as in religious belief, the view that these should be self-chosen rather than accepted on the basis of received authority does not translate into a decline in belief. Although too much should not be read into a single study, the implication in terms of secularization theory is that choice does not appear to undermine belief. In terms of communicative action theory, it implies that rationalization of the lifeworld does not necessarily entail a decline in belief in either moral absolutes or religious dogma. The implications of this for thinking about the role of religion in civil society and the public sphere are considerable. It suggests that normative versions of these – based on communicative rationalization of the lifeworld and respect for basic human rights – can function in a cultural context with a dominant and thriving religious tradition. What it appears to require – in contrast to the hierarchy's efforts to enshrine Catholic values in the sphere of the state, but in line with Casanova's (1994) thinking – is the self-restriction of the Church to civil society – a separation of religion from coercion. We shall return to this point in the conclusion.

Borowik also measured perceptions of the influence and authority of the Church on society compared with other public institutions, and opinions as to the appropriateness of this influence. Astonishingly, she found that the Church's influence was rated highest of all – above that of the mass media (which came second), big business, the government, Parliament and the national bank (1997 p. 242). In this context, she found that large numbers thought that the Church had too much influence and authority (14.7 per cent 'decidedly too much' and 29.7 per cent 'too much'), as against 42.5 per cent who thought the influence and authority of the Church was 'about right' (p. 244). This would seem to suggest that, contrary to other indicators of trust in the Church, nearly 50 per cent of the population thought that the Church had about the right amount or too little influence. Furthermore, those who thought the Church had too much influence did so in a context in which the Church was perceived as the most influential institution of all. This is hardly a resounding rejection of the Church having a public role in the state or political society, let alone in the public sphere of civil society.

However, if Borowik's evidence suggests the psychological compatibility of strong religious convictions and support of personal autonomy and hence individual difference, some aspects of post-Communist social life do not.

(d) Religious and Ethnic Minorities: a Barometer of Civil Society

This brings us to our final major issue to consider in assessing the PRCC's role in post-Communist Poland: the treatment of minorities. As we noted earlier, the combination of the Holocaust and postwar pogroms means that the Jewish population in Poland is very small, so that most people have no first-hand contact with Jewish people or Jewish culture. As a result, images of Jews are based on cultural stereotypes, which are predominantly negative:

> In a large part of Polish society, the word 'Jew' (like the word 'Gypsy') is used to label an enemy ... . For example, anti-Jewish graffiti in recent years often referred to the 'Jewish-Communist system' (*zydo-komuna*) of the Democratic Left Alliance. Or the word is used to insult an enemy such as the members of an opposing football club. (Ambrosewicz-Jacobs and Mirski 1999 p. 394)

Such negative stereotypes of Jews have been part of popular culture in Europe for hundreds of years, but whereas in many parts of Western Europe such attitudes have been challenged since the Second World War, so that they are no longer an acceptable part of public discourse, in CEE, in spite of its official rhetoric, the Communist system seems to have been largely ineffective in tackling prejudice. Furthermore, Ambrosewicz-Jacobs shows that such attitudes are being reproduced among teenagers who have grown up under the post-Communist system. Her survey was conducted in June 1996 among 173 fourteen year olds in six schools in different areas of Kraków, in southern Poland.

Ninety per cent of the sample did not know any Jew and had never met one, yet 42.9 per cent agreed with the statement that 'Polish culture needs to be protected from Jewish influence', 61.5 per cent did not find anti-Jewish graffiti 'disturbing or shameful' and 22.4 per cent even found it 'amusing' (Ambrosewicz-Jacobs 1999 pp. 392–7). Some 37.8 per cent would 'probably not vote for a Jewish political candidate' (p. 394). On the specific point of 'majority identity' versus 'citizenship rights', highlighted by the Ombudsman controversy, 42.9 per cent agreed with the proposition that 'a Jew cannot be a true Pole' and 46.4 per cent agreed that 'the Jews have Israel, so Poland should be for Christians'. However, on a positive note, (if rather inconsistently) most students thought it was not good to have a negative opinion about Jews and agreed with the proposition that Jews are the same as everyone else. Furthermore, 65.5 per cent said that schools were not teaching enough about the Jewish people and 64.6 per cent that 'the whole question of Poland and the Jews is important to them', indicating at least a willingness to learn (p. 392).

Negative attitudes persist in spite of official Catholic teaching on anti-Semitism (there was a special letter from the episcopate to be read in all parishes in 1991 condemning anti-Semitism) and the leading role of the Catholic intelligentsia in attempting to combat it (including publications and exhibitions promoting knowledge about Jewish culture; ibid. p. 395). The government has also taken action, creating a Presidential Commission on Anti-Semitism. In view of the controversy concerning RE, it is also interesting to note that students perceived their RE teachers (that is, priests, under the arrangements described above) to have unusually positive opinions about Jews (22.6 per cent very positive, 40.5 per cent positive, 17.3 per cent slightly positive), compared with the 2.4 per cent very positive and 18.6 per cent positive attributed by the students to the adult population as a whole (ibid). However, the curriculum in RE and history contains little information about Jews, Jewish history or Judaism (Kapralska 1995). Ambrosewicz-Jacobs (1999) further argues that the opinions of RE teachers have considerable influence on students. Therefore, if the church authorities made more effort to ensure that Catholic teaching since the Second Vatican Council was actually taught in schools, it seems likely that this could have a strong positive effect, alongside curriculum developments in history and Literature that reflect the contribution of Jews to Poland's history and culture.

The one issue concerning attitudes to religious and ethnic minorities in Poland that has reached public attention in the West has been the controversy concerning the Catholic Carmel that operated at Oświęcim ('Auschwitz' in German) from 1984–93. For example, Clifford Longley wrote in *The Times* in May 1989:

> A small group of Carmelite nuns in Poland have somehow managed to put at risk all the precious goodwill built up since the war between the Jewish community and Christianity. The problem is not what they are doing – they are praying – but where they are doing it. They have opened a convent in the grounds of Auschwitz concentration camp (Longley 1989, quoted in Wollaston 1994 p. 19).

However, while the Carmelites present at the site may have been a 'small group' they were there, at least initially, with the approval of the Catholic hierarchy both in Poland and internationally, and with the support of many Polish people, as survey evidence indicates (Sułek 1998 p. 64). Indeed, this support remained visible several years after the nuns had moved, when crosses began appearing outside the perimeter fence of the camp, sparking further controversy in 1988–9 (ibid.). However, the problem is not simply one of Polish anti-Semitism, nor even insensitivity to the centrality of Auschwitz to Jewish (and international) memorialization of the Holocaust. Rather, a key factor is the different (and incompatible) way in which Jewish and Christian (especially Catholic) religious traditions view and commemorate sites associated with death, and especially mass death. As Wollaston comments:

> To a Catholic audience ... [i]t is traditional to build convents or shrines on sites where blood has been shed in order to pray for reconciliation. ... However, such an understanding is totally alien, indeed is fundamentally inappropriate, when seen from a Jewish

perspective. A place of massacre (or *tel olam*) should be left untouched; it should never become a place of institutionalized prayer (1994 pp. 26–7).

As another commentator explains, these different practices refer to different theologies:

> Jews do pray in cemeteries, both on the day of burial and on the anniversaries of the death of loved ones. But the prayer texts for those occasions do not refer directly to death. ... Instead they focus first and foremost on the sanctification of God. ... [C]lassical Jewry today accepts the notion of the resurrection of the faithful individual. But this point of belief is emphasized far less than it is in Catholic theology. And one does not find in Judaism any sense of temporary purgation akin to the Catholic view of purgatory. Hence there exists no sense of responsibility on the part of the living community of faith to assist those who have gone before them in finally attaining heaven (Pawlikowski 1991 p. 68).

Historical factors including recent Polish independence, Communist memorialization of the Second World War and the Holocaust, and indeed traditional anti-Semitism, are also important in shaping the attitudes of many Polish Catholics towards the 'right' to Catholic memorialization at Oświęcim. Jewish (and perhaps especially Jewish American) perceptions of Poles are in turn sometimes shaped by a perception of Polish complicity in the Holocaust, and more generally by a view of contemporary Poland seen through the lens of the events of the Second World War (Rittner and Roth 1991). But much as these factors have fanned the flames, the core of the dispute was a different understanding of sacred space. Hence the resolution of the dispute at an official level in 1989 by the Catholic agreement to relocate the Carmel outside the camp, although this move did not in fact occur until 1993. The agreement also changed and 'softened' the function of the Carmel to become a centre of information and education as well as prayer.

Since 1989 Polish Catholic attitudes have shifted somewhat, so that a significant Minority now recognise the complexity of the situation, and even the validity of Jewish claims to control memorialization at Auschwitz. Thus a survey in 1998 found that while 58 per cent still believed that 'every nation has a right to put their religious symbols in Oświęcim, 32 per cent believed that 'there should not be any religious symbols there', a belief coinciding with (though not necessarily caused by) Jewish wishes (Sułek 1998 p. 68).

In conclusion, the case of the Carmel and crosses at Oświęcim would seem to have several implications for our understanding of the relationship between the PRCC and civil society. First, it again illustrates differences between official Catholic teaching and popular attitudes. Second, it further demonstrates the limitations of religiously based symbolic mobilization in a plural society, since Catholic and Jewish positions on memorialization cannot be reconciled, exposing the limits of Catholicism to represent the nation, or rather narrowing the scope of national identity affirmed through the tradition. Third, it witnesses to the ongoing importance of symbolic mobilization in identity formation in post-Communist societies, something we shall consider further in Chapter 7 in relation to Bosnia, and the significance of which we shall now consider in relation to other minorities in Poland.

If the knowledge about Judaism conveyed in the state education system is limited, that of other religious and ethnic minorities is even more so (Kapralska 1995). There is evidence of negative attitudes towards non-Catholic new religious movements (NRMs) such as Jehovah's Witnesses, ISKCON and the Unification Church in surveys, the media and among Church officials (Urban 1999). There is also increasingly restrictive legal regulation of NRMs in line with developments both elsewhere in post-Communist Europe and in Western Europe, as Poland moves further away from an American-style religious free market (albeit one in which the Catholic Church is dominant) to a European-style state-regulated religious market, under the influence of the Council of Europe and European Community (Doktor 1999).

Hann (1997) describes the situation facing Greek Catholic minorities (who are also ethnically Ukrainian) in South-Eastern Poland, drawing on anthropological fieldwork conducted in and around the town of Przemyśl. Greek Catholics practice the Greek rite of the Eastern Orthodox liturgy, but are in communion with the Roman Catholic Church[6] (Keleher 1992). Several factors are relevant to escalating tensions between ethnic Poles and ethnic Ukrainians. First, new movements of goods and people, as Eastern Europe's borders have become more porous. In particular, prejudice against Ukrainians has been exacerbated by the flood of traders from nearby Ukraine anxious to sell their goods in comparatively well-off Poland and by ethnic Ukrainians (displaced by Stalin in 1948) returning with money from Poland's relatively rich western border with Germany, seeking to reclaim and buy property. Second, a back-lash was provoked by the central government's efforts to promote local Ukrainian identity (and strengthen political ties with the Ukraine) by holding the biannual festival of Ukrainian culture in Przemyśl. The festival went ahead despite obstruction from the local council, but was marred by an arson attack on the Ukrainian Club and anti-Ukrainian graffiti (Hann 1997 p. 41). Third, tensions have been increased by controversy over the Orthodox-style cupola (onion-shaped tower) of the local Carmelite convent, which had been a Greek Catholic cathedral until it was confiscated and handed over to the Carmelites (a Roman Catholic religious order) by the Communists in 1946. Local Polish nationalists led a successful campaign to replace the cupola with a 'Western-style' tower, and cost the protesting conservation officer (an ethnic Pole) his job in the process.

Hann's conclusion is that in South-East Poland the breaking down of national frontiers and the arrival of a democratic political system have not liberalized culture, but rather 'unleash[ed] forces that exaggerate and strengthen national and confessional barriers' (ibid. p. 29).

7. Conclusion

Hann's view of the growth of 'uncivil society' in South-East Poland powerfully connects with our next case study, Bosnia. But before we turn to consider this, we need to reflect on the role of religion in civil society and the public sphere in Poland. Clearly, Poland in the postwar period, and especially from the 1970s, developed a parallel society that grew out of and significantly drew on the Church as the only partly autonomous national institution permitted in Communist society. In particular, the Church created 'action-frameworks' later mobilized by Solidarity. But while symbolic mobilization was an essential mode of resistance under Communism, its lack of instrumental orientation led to problems when faced with the practical challenges of post-Communist reconstruction.

Furthermore, the necessarily covert development of parallel society and the lack of legal institutionalization of civil society, together with other features of the Communist system, bred habits and ways of relating to authority which have also subsequently proved dysfunctional. The hierarchy's efforts to institutionalize 'religious values' at the heart of the state can also be read as a symptom of a dysfunctional post-Communist syndrome. But, alternatively, they can also be read as religion standing up for 'human values' against the institutionalization of a juridical liberalism that would allow the rampant colonization of lifeworld by the dominant systems of the modern world. The truth is probably somewhere between the two. Either way, the apparent buoyancy of Polish religiosity and autonomous but religiously grounded ethical sensibility, despite disillusionment with the hierarchy, suggest at least the potential for the emergence of a robust Catholic liberalism to avoid the future polarization of society into religio-nationalist and secularist factions.

Notes

1   Micewski (1984 p. 158), in Kubik (1994 p. 111).
2   Although this is complicated by the requirement for a 'mainly Christian' act of daily worship in the 1988 Education Act.
3   Indeed, more generally in Eastern Europe, the concept of non-confessional religious education (RE) is treated with great suspicion after years of Communist propaganda about religion, so that the introduction of RE in schools is seen primarily in terms of allowing religious professionals or other representatives into schools to teach children about their particular tradition. However, in higher education, groups such as the Institute for the Study of Religion at Jagiellonian University, Kraków, Poland, pioneered a non-confessional, non-Marxist approach under Communism and in contemporary Bosnia there is interest in developing a non-confessional multi-faith curriculum in schools.
4   Another concession to democratic pressure was made in 1982, though initially extremely limited in its powers (Brzezinski 2000 p. 77).
5   Subsequent progress towards a fully reformed constitution was slow, largely as a result of the political fragmentation of Solidarity into a range of splinter post-Solidarity political parties. In 1992 a 'Small Constitution' was agreed as an interim measure, but it was not until 1997 that a full new Constitution was ratified (Brzezinski 2000 p. 93, 123).
6   The re-emergence of Greek Catholic communities which had been suppressed under Communism has caused tensions in Catholic-Orthodox relations, especially in the Ukraine and Russia.

Chapter 8

After Genocide

Religion and Civil Society in Bosnia

Muslims, Serbs and Croats lived in peace for most of the five hundred years they cohabited in Bosnia-Hercegovina. The intercommunal violence which accompanied the Second World War was an important deviation from this pattern, but ... The Serbian Insurrectionary War of 1991–5[1] was different in that, with the exception of the defenders of Sarajevo, each of the respective sides tended to recruit almost exclusively from the nationality it claimed to represent. (Ramet 1999 p. 202)

Today there is not a single politician in power establishments from any of the 'national bodies', at any level of government, who does not declare himself a hard-line believer in one of the three religions that practically act as if they were state religions, each one of them in 'its own space'. (Lovrenović 2000 p. 77)

'Civil society' has become perhaps the buzzword for progressive politics and the rearticulation of nationalist space in Bosnia and is the most common signifier for nonnationalist perspectives and programs. ... experience in the former Yugoslavia demonstrates that 'civil society' is not inherently progressive: in Croatia and Slovenia it has hosted varying degrees of nationalist sentiment and has been the modus operandi of a 'new globalized middle class' more concerned with the political assumptions and parameters of their international funders than the requirements of local communities. (Campbell 1998 p. 236)

1. Introduction

In the last chapter, in the context of the growth of religio-nationalist tensions in post-Communist Poland, we argued against the view that such developments can be explained satisfactorily in terms of the idea that communist repression 'kept the lid' on seething ethnic tensions. Rather, such tensions need to be understood in terms of the impact of modernity on Central and Eastern Europe, including the indirect and direct consequences of Communism. This process can be seen particularly clearly in the case of Yugoslavia. Hence, as the first quotation indicates, the war in Yugoslavia needs to be understood as a distinctive modern development rather than 'ancient animosities', contrary to the stereotype propagated both by warring parties and much media coverage.

However, as the second and third quotations indicate, if one is looking for confirmation of a positive relationship between religion and normative civil society,

229

Bosnia might seem the worst possible place to search. In the 1990s religion regained social significance in the worst possible way from the normative perspective of civil society: as the former federal republic disintegrated, forms of nationalism often mobilized around religious symbols and discourse emerged as a divisive social force. Indeed, between 1992 and 1995 Bosnia became the site of the worst military conflict in Europe since the Second World War, as the shell-scarred apartments of Sarajevo, the bombed-out farmhouses of the countryside, the dynamited mosques and damaged churches and the hundreds of thousands of displaced people bear continuing testimony. Moreover, as the second quotation indicates, religious nationalism is now built into the postwar structures. Thus people from different communities face the formidable task of building social trust in a context where religion has re-emerged as a highly divisive factor in public life.

Bosnia has the added significance of being a kind of European and international 'laboratory'; for it is here that European and other international bodies, backed by a significant military presence, aim not only to restore and maintain public order, but also, more ambitiously, to build a viable 'civil society' as a basis for a lasting, pluralist, democracy. However, as the third quotation suggests, the international community's supposedly 'ethical' policy of 'civil society building' as a strategy for democratization has been criticized for reinforcing nationalist interests, stressing societal cleavages by supporting a local élite divorced from grass-roots concerns, and failing to increase grass-roots participation in civic and political processes (Chandler 1998; Campbell 1998).

Yet, precisely because of this dual process of instrumentalization and because the policies of the 'international community', major political parties, local state actors and official religious institutions have repeatedly failed to sustain multicultural spaces within Bosnia, it is particularly important to ask whether other actors in the non-governmental sphere, including those identified as religious or specializing in mediation between religions, can and do contribute to the creation of such spaces. Can such groups help build alliances in Celia Cockburn's sense of 'a creative structuring of a relational space between collectivities marked by problematic differences' (1998 p. 211)?

'Bosnia' is currently partitioned between the Muslim-Croat (Muslim majority) Federation of Bosnia-Hercegovina and the Serb majority Serbian Republic (Republika Srpska, RS). When these two entities are taken together, Muslims form the largest minority, a unique position in Europe (Muslims 44 per cent, Serbs 31 per cent, Croats 17 per cent; Malcolm 1996 p. 223).[2] Historically, Bosnia stands at the crossroads of two major world religions (Islam and Christianity) and of Eastern and Western Christianity (Eastern Orthodoxy and Roman Catholicism). In contrast with Poland in the previous chapter, in Yugoslavia religious groups played a relatively minor role in the transition from Communism, although Serbian mobilization of Orthodox identity as a source of nationalism and in reaction Croatian mobilization of Catholic identity, both developed through the 1980s. However, during the wars (1991–95) religious mobilization on all sides (including Muslim) has played a significant role in the polarization of society, accompanied by some evidence of religious revival; religious participation among Catholic Croats was already high and this has increased among Muslims and Serb Orthodox too (Ramet 1999 p. 80; Poulton 1997 p. 239). In the postwar period some religious groups and inter-religious organizations are attempting to play a constructive role in the reintegration of society, as we shall see.

However, the Communist period did furnish Bosnia with some similarities to Poland. Here, too, the period immediately after the Second World War (1945–c.1953) saw the most severe repression of religious groups by a Communist regime seeking to establish its authority over society. Religious organizations were banned, religious leaders imprisoned, religious presses and educational establishments at all levels closed, as the state sought to monopolize public space and the transmission of culture. Tito's postwar attack on religious organizations also followed severe repression under the Nazis, especially of the Serb Orthodox Church.

This had long-term consequences for the ability of religious organizations to effectively transmit and renew their traditions, and especially for Orthodoxy in the development of defensive, inward-looking attitudes and susceptibility to the lure of a nationalism which gave favoured status to the Church. In some ways Islam suffered doubly under Communism, because as well as being a religion it was also associated in Marxist-Leninist ideology with 'Oriental backwardness' (Malcolm 1996). However, Muslim identity (as opposed to Islamic teaching or institutions) later became useful to Tito in his bid to lead the non-aligned world. Furthermore, Bosnia's isolation by Western sanctions in the war of 1992–5 led Bosnians to look to the Muslim world for moral and material support and to reconsider their relation to the worldwide Muslim community. Some postwar aid has also favoured Islamization, with continued support from Muslim countries, especially from the Gulf States. However, such aid is viewed with some suspicion, as a long history of minority status, the influence of Sufism and the experience of European modernity have made Bosnian Islam very different from that of the Gulf. Thus Islamization is in tension with more dominant forces, for example towards closer European integration.

As in the chapter on Poland, we are concerned here with what the Bosnian story has to tell us about the relationship between religion and civil society. To this end it is important to understand something of Bosnia's history, not because 'ancient religious rivalries' caused the war, but because this history has been used to misrepresent the conflict, not just by warring participants but also by Western politicians and the media.[3] So we must turn to consider some of the historical factors that shaped the peoples of the former Yugoslavia, something of the role of religion in the social life of local communities, and the reasons for the disintegration of Communist Yugoslavia. In particular, we shall need to examine how this affected multi-ethnic, multi-religious Bosnia, the wars that followed and resulted in the massive displacement of people divided on religious/ethnic lines and the postwar reconstruction process in a religiously/ethnically partitioned state.

2. Bosnia to 1989

(a) The Ottoman Empire to the Second World War

The contemporary religious mix of Bosnia stems from the Ottoman influence in (later occupation of) the Balkans, beginning in the fourteenth century. During this period the recently formed Serb kingdom was defeated by the Ottoman Turks, for example at the battle of Kosovo (28 June 1389), an event which led eventually to Serb veneration of the Kosovo area as a site of historic martyrdom. This was later to become a crucial symbolic element in the construction of Serb nationalism in the nineteenth century and again at the end of the twentieth under Milosevič. As regards Bosnia, some of the population, at the time a mixture of Catholics and Serbian Orthodox, with a small Jewish minority,[4] converted to Islam. This appears to have been a gradual, unforced, process; although benefits would accrue from converting to the religion of an occupying power, there is no evidence of forced conversions.

Islam has a tradition of providing for recognized religions to live under Islamic rule which stems from the time of the Prophet – and in particular the Constitution of Medina drawn up when Muhammad became the ruler of Medina makes provision for Jewish and Christian minorities (Bulac 1998). The particular version of this used by the Ottomans was called the *millet* system. In comparison with the position of non-Christian (mostly Jewish) minorities in medieval Europe, this was a tolerant system. Non-Muslims had to pay a poll tax which supported the Ottoman military, were (mostly) unable to take part in the military and were subject to other limitations on their participation in public life, although a small number were promoted to high office. They were forbidden from proselytising – that is trying to convert Muslims – and had to apply for special permission to build new churches and monasteries. Their political representation was through religious leaders – producing a tradition of a close association between religion, politics and ethnicity in the area.

However, while the Ottoman system was less restrictive – and there was less persecution of minority religions – than those in medieval Christendom, it was basically a system of collective subordination of minorities on a religious basis and as such incompatible with the individualist and egalitarian political traditions which sprang up in Europe from the seventeenth century. Today these traditions are represented in the constitutions and legal systems of democratic nations and in international treaties such as the United Nations' Universal Declaration on Human Rights (UDHR). Here we can note the legacy of the *millet* system for the relationship between religion and politics in Bosnia, which was to reinforce their association, at the same time as deterritorializing political authority – the *millets* did not have a territorial basis. We can also note that while the *millet* system is collective in orientation, this did not mean that individuals were without certain rights. This set of institutional arrangements is also important for understanding the Egyptian case in Chapter 9 below. However, while we have stressed the collectivist orientation of Ottoman arrangements, it should be remembered that modern political traditions are not entirely individualist in orientation either. Rather, two traditions of collective identity came to be extremely important in modernity: nationalism and Communism, and both were to have a strong influence on Yugoslavia.

Ottoman influence in the area declined through the nineteenth century, with Serbia gaining independence in 1829 and the Habsburg Austro-Hungarian Empire taking over the administration of Bosnia-Hercegovina in 1878, with full annexation following in 1908. The Austro-Hungarian policy was to make only gradual changes to the social system – under which many Catholics and Orthodox remained serfs working Muslim lands – but to try to develop the economy as much as possible (Malcolm 1996 p. 140–41). While the failure to redistribute land caused some resentment among Christian serfs and peasants, economic prosperity in both agriculture and manufacturing, together with government support for schools organized according to religious affiliation (primary education became compulsory in 1909) and even-handed treatment of religious communities (ibid. p. 145), seems to have led to good inter-faith relationships. An English visitor in 1897 commented of Christian attitudes: 'It is strange that they should bear so little hatred to their former oppressors' (in ibid. p. 149). Continuing practice established under the Ottomans, the Orthodox patriarch and the Pope gave the emperor the right to appoint bishops. In a departure from Ottoman practice and on the suggestion of Bosnian Muslims themselves, Islamic leadership independent of Istanbul was established in 1882, with the establishment of a *Reis-ul-ulema* ('head of the religious community') appointed by the emperor, leading a council of four advisers (p. 145).

However, there was also a growth of nationalist consciousness, particularly among Serbs (Orthodox) and Catholics (Croats) in the area (pp. 149–52). Serbia and Montenegro's success in driving the Turks out of Kosovo in the First Balkan War (1912–13) heightened anti-Habsburg feeling in Bosnia, especially among Serbs and Croats, but also among some Muslims, since for the first time (from 1907) groups such as Mlada Bosna (Young Bosnia) organized on a pan-Slav basis including Muslims and seeking a common South Slav state. Tension between Austria and Serbia grew; the Austrian army organized troop manoeuvres in Bosnia as a show of strength, with the heir to the Habsburg throne due to inspect troops in Sarajevo on 28 June 1914, the anniversary of the battle of Kosovo. A month after that fateful day and the assassination of Archduke Franz Ferdinand by a Bosnian Serb, Austria declared war on Serbia, thus precipitating the cataclysm of the First World War.

After the war, a Serb-dominated Kingdom of Serbs, Croats and Slovenes was established (1921). This also included all the territories which were later to become the Federal Republic of Yugoslavia (1945–91), that is, Bosnia-Hercegovina, Montenegro, Kosovo and Vojvodina, as well as Serbia, Croatia and Slovenia. The Kingdom survived until the Nazi invasion in 1941, changing its name to the Kingdom of Yugoslavia in 1929. Some historians have pointed out the very different positions with which the Serbs and the Croats, Bosnians and Slovenians entered the Kingdom: the former as victors, the latter as part of the conquered empire. Under King Alexander (reigned 1921–34) Serbs monopolized most high government and military positions (Ramet 1999 p. 102), resentment of which contributed to the emergence of the Croatian fascist movement (the Ustashe) in 1929. The rise of fascism in Italy and Germany and the economic depression of the 1930s also contributed to increasing polarization. The Serbian dominance in politics was paralleled by the Serbian Orthodox Church's privileged position, receiving generous subsidies from the monarchy and successfully opposing the signing of a concordat with the Vatican (an agreement, as we saw in Chapter 5 with post-Communist Poland), between the government and the papacy) and laws which would have given Catholics the right to proselytize.

(b) The Second World War

After defeat by the Nazis in April 1941, a German-supported Croatian nationalist (NDH) Ustashe state was established, encompassing all of prewar Croatia and Bosnia-Hercegovina. It was divided between Italian and German zones of occupation, with the Italians occupying a roughly 100 km wide strip inland from the coast, the Germans the territory further inland. Serbia was occupied and partitioned by the Germans, with some Serb territory to the East handed to Bulgaria and Italian controlled Albania, and in the North Slovenia was partitioned between Italy and Hungary. Throughout the former Yugoslavia the Orthodox Church suffered greatly in a period that became known as 'The Great Catastrophe', but in Ustashe (NDH) Croatia the persecution was particularly intense:

> In April 1941, there had been 577 Serbian Orthodox clergymen in the territory of the NDH. By the end of 1941, all of them had been removed from the scene: 3 were in prison, 5 had died of natural causes, 217 had been killed by the *Ustaše*, 334 had been deported to Serbia and 18 had fled to Serbia earlier. (Ramet 1999 p. 104)

In Yugoslavia as a whole by the end of the war perhaps 20 per cent of Serbian Orthodox clergy had been killed and 50 per cent of their churches seriously damaged.

The role of the Catholic Church in the war is complex. Although the Communist regime later tried to portray the Catholic Church as simply supporting Ustashe rule, many Catholic priests fought alongside or supported the partisans, while relatively few supported the fascists (Ramet 1999 p. 81). Archbishop Stepinac in Zagreb, for example, privately sought the release of Orthodox believers from prison, wrote to the Ministry of the Interior to object to laws discriminating against Catholics of Jewish descent and publicly preached against 'racism, genocide and Ustashe policies' (p. 82). However, while the Catholic Church was somewhat equivocal in its attitude to fascism, interwar experiences of Catholics in the Soviet Union led the Vatican to unequivocal condemnation of Communism. As a Croatian Catholic newspaper had put it in 1937, 'Communism is in its very essence evil. Therefore, the person who values Christian culture will not cooperate with [Communists] in a single thing' (in Ramet 1999 p. 82).

Bosnian Muslims found themselves caught between hostile Ustashe and hostile Cetnik (Serb) resistance. Although most Muslims were more sympathetic to Zagreb than Belgrade before the war, given the dominance of Serbs in the Kingdom, the abuses of the Nazi-sponsored regimes soon led to Muslim opposition. In the summer and autumn of 1941 Muslim clergy issued a series of protests against the mistreatment of Jews and Serbs, which make interesting reading in the light of the recent ascription of 'ancient ethnic hatreds' to the area. These resolutions complained of the forced conversion (that is, to Catholicism) of Orthodox Serbs (in Mostar), of the theft and looting of Jewish and Serbian property (in Banja Luka) and of violence against Jews and Serbs (in Sarajevo) (Malcolm 1996 p. 186). Yet for the most part violence by Serbs against Muslim villagers in rural areas prevented them from joining the Cetnik resistance, attached to the Serbian-dominated government in exile in which they were not represented. However, as the Communist-led Partisan resistance under Tito (the Communists had been a very small movement before the war) grew and separated from the Cetniks, Muslims began to join. As Communist policy developed (although it remained vague), the prospect for Bosnian autonomy within a federal structure seemed a better long-term prospect than absorption into, or partition between, Croatia and Serbia.

However, some Muslims, especially the religious leadership, were reluctant to support atheistic Communism and disinclined to accept Tito's propaganda pamphlets which portrayed Stalinist Russia as a 'wonderland of tolerance and Islamic religious freedom' (Malcolm 1996 p. 187). Under increasing pressure of indiscriminate attacks on civilians by both Cetniks (majority Serb) and the Ustashe (majority Croatian), some appealed directly to the Germans for a separate Bosnian state, putting forward proposals that included the expansion of the Muslim Volunteer Legion under direct German control. The Germans knew that the Ustashe would not accept Bosnian autonomy, but on Himmler's suggestion a Muslim SS division was created, following precedents in occupied France, Belgium, Holland and Denmark (ibid. p. 189). In the spring and summer of 1944 this took part in indiscriminate reprisals against Serbs in Northern and Western Bosnia (p. 191). Thus atrocities were committed by all ethnic groups in the war; but this does not mean that all groups were equally affected or responsible. We have noted the appalling toll on the Serbian Orthodox Church; while the Muslim religious establishment were not effected in this way, Muslims none the less suffered a greater loss of life (8.5 per cent of the population) than the Serbs (7.5 per cent), or any group except Jews and Gypsies (Malcolm 1996 p. 192). As Malcolm concludes:

> Muslims had fought on all sides – Ustaša, German, Cetnik, Partisan – and had been killed by all sides. Many had been killed in Croatian and German death camps, including Jsenovac, Buchenwald, Dachau and Auschwitz. They had not started this war and had fought above all to defend themselves. But the killing was not yet over. (Ibid.)

(c) Religion in Communist Yugoslavia (1945–89)

Partisan forces took Sarajevo on 6 April 1945 and had consolidated control of Bosnia by the end of the month. There was hope for national reconciliation, but Tito, still a close follower of Stalin at this time, imposed Communist power on Yugoslavia ruthlessly and at high cost: an estimated 250,000 were killed as a result of his consolidation of power in 1945–6. In the late 1940s and early 1950s all sources of possible opposition – and that meant any autonomous organizations – were ruthlessly suppressed, mirroring the pattern elsewhere in the postwar Communist world. Among these were religious organizations. Between 1945 and 1953 religious schools were closed, religious education in state schools was replaced with classes in atheism, religious professionals were harassed, arrested and in some cases killed, the formation of independent associations on a religious or ethnic basis was banned and much property of religious organizations was confiscated. In tandem with this attack on the influence of religious organizations in society, the Communist authorities also sought to coopt religious groups, for example by encouraging priests' associations independent of the Catholic and Orthodox hierarchies.

As we have seen, the Vatican position on Communism up to this time had been uncompromising. Combine this with the fact that the Ustashe regime had been supported mostly by Croats, who were mainly Catholics, and it is unsurprising to find that the Communists were particularly harsh in their treatment of Catholicism. Archbishop Stepinac was imprisoned in 1945, officially for collaboration with the Ustashe, but as the chief prosecutor Jakov Blazevic later (1985) admitted, 'That trial of Stepinac was forced on us. If Stepinac had only been more flexible, there would have been no need of a trial' (in Ramet 1999 p. 87). 'Flexibility' would have involved severing ties with Rome, giving up his calls for freedom of speech (Catholic periodicals were cut from around 100 prewar to three in 1953 under the Communists). After conviction, Stepinac was offered the choice of freedom in exile, but chose to remain in Yugoslavia in prison. He was released but confined to his home village in 1951, where he died in 1960.

Like the Catholic Church, the Orthodox Church was deprived of property, the means to educate its laity and reduced to one official newspaper with a small circulation until 1958. There were also attacks on its unity and the patriarchate lost jurisdiction over its dioceses in Czechoslovakia (1945–8), America-Canada (1963), Romania (1969) and, on Yugoslav soil, with Macedonia (1967). On the other hand, the Church could also be useful to the regime by giving the lie to the accusation that it was anti-Serb and by enabling links with other Communist countries with prominent Orthodox Churches (Ramet 1999 p. 105).

Islam suffered the double disadvantage of being a perceived by the Communist regime as a threat because of its social dimensions and as 'backward and Asiatic' in Marxist-Leninist ideology (Malcolm 1996 p. 195). It likewise suffered the destruction of its presses and educational institutions, except for a single 'carefully supervised' *medresa* (theological training college) for the training of *imams*. Dervish orders and other cultural associations were banned; just one official Islamic association was permitted. The *vakuf* – charitable foundations stemming back to the sixteenth century – were liquidated.

After May 1953 (Ramet 1999 p. 106) a new Law of Religious Communities was passed, which eased the situation somewhat. Islam in particular benefited from Tito's new self-styled role as leader of the non-aligned world (after a trip to Egypt and India in 1955; Stalin had expelled Yugoslavia from the Cominform in 1948), with Islam being a common connection between many non-aligned countries. However, as we shall see below with the issue of Muslim 'nationality', this was more a question of appearance than substance, measuring the latter in terms of knowledge of and adherence to the Islamic tradition. As Malcolm (1996 p. 197) comments on the new breed of Muslim diplomats in the 1960s, 'That these were Communist Party members who had largely abandoned their religion seemed not to matter, so long as they had names such as Mehmed, Ahmed and Mustafa'.

However, as Muslims were allowed greater contact with the wider world, so opportunities for nominal Muslims to become more knowledgeable about and influenced by Islamic tradition increased: growing numbers studied abroad at Arab universities in the 1970s, and in 1977 Saudi money financed the establishment of a Faculty of Islamic Theology at Sarajevo University (ibid. p. 201). This increased awareness of Islamic tradition can also be seen as an unintended (indeed ironic) effect of secular Muslims within the Communist Party struggling for greater recognition of Muslim 'nationality'. They reasoned that Bosnia's poor economic condition compared with other Yugoslav republics owed much to Bosnian political under-representation in the federal administration and this in turn to the lack of membership of a distinctive national group through which to lobby.[5]

The changing Communist conceptualization of the relationship between Muslim identity and nationality provides a fascinating case study in identity politics. The first postwar Party Congress declared: 'Bosnia cannot be divided between Serbia and Croatia, not only because Serbs and Croats are found throughout the territory, but also because the territory is inhabited by Muslims *who have not yet decided on their national identity*' (in Malcolm 1996 p. 197, emphasis added). The underlying logic seems to be that to belong to a modern state, even a multinational one, you need a nationality: religious identity on its own will not suffice. There had never been a Muslim nation in Bosnia: as we have seen, Bosnian Muslims were Slavs who had converted to Islam during the Ottoman occupation and had never constituted a majority or even the largest minority (until the late 1960s) in the area. However, since Tito's ideology of 'brotherhood and unity' called for federal unity on the basis of national identity, from 1948 Muslims came under pressure to choose between a Serb and Croat national identity, but repeatedly refused to do so. Eventually in 1968 the Bosnian branch of the Communist Party (under internal pressure from secularized Muslims seeking to increase Bosnia's influence in the federation) recognized Muslim 'nationhood' (Malcolm 1996 p. 199).

Thus far, the Communist legacy to religious identity was greatly to weaken religious institutions while tying religious identity more closely to secularized forms of national identity. However, in spite of the increased awareness of national identity as economic failure exposed political fault-lines through the 1970s and 1980s, in urban areas social integration between the communities was relatively high, one sign of which was the 30 per cent rate of intermarriage found in urban areas by the late 1980s (Malcolm 1996 p. 222).

The early 1970s saw the increasing decentralization of Yugoslavia, at least in theory, with the introduction of the cumbersome 1974 Constitution. It was based on a rotating presidency – 'political musical chairs' (Glenny 1999 p. 623) – in which senior positions changed hands annually between the republics, to prevent any one republic gaining too much power. It was created partly in reaction to the 'Croatian Spring' of 1971 – a protest in part at the predominance of Serbians in top jobs in the federation, but also, like the Prague Spring of 1968, a movement of broader democratic activity including the growth of independent publications in response to an easing of censorship by the Croatian Communist Party. This liberalization was ended by Tito in the winter of 1971–2, as were similar developments in Serbia in 1972. Following the tensions in Serb-Croat relations during these events, Tito sought to curb rising nationalism by playing Serbia off against Croatia – which was to prove a dangerous long-term strategy.

Thus the early 1970s saw two developments which were to prove crucial in the eventual disintegration of Yugoslavia: first, the re-emergence of tensions between Serbia and Croatia for the first time since the Second World War; and second, the creation of a federal system which, while in practice still controlled by Tito and his close advisers, was potentially cumbersome, ineffective and unstable. A third change which was important to developments in Bosnia was demographic: the shift of Serbs away from the area due to the republic's economic backwardness, world recession and the prospect of better fortunes in more prosperous Serbia. This created insecurities in the Serbs who remained, who were no longer the largest minority (Malcolm 1996 p. 202).

The death of Tito on 4 May 1980 left a federation that was politically divided, dominated by corrupt Communist Party systems and economically weak. As Malcolm comments:

> History suggests that federations of different national entities can work successfully only if they are based on a genuinely democratic political system; but this was not the case in Communist Yugoslavia. … It is easy to persuade one nation that it is being oppressed by another, when the whole political system in which both nations are locked is undemocratic and intrinsically oppressive (p. 203)

However, in spite of the evident weaknesses of the system, it was the actions of particular groups and key individuals which led the system to fall apart in the way that it did.

Thus during the 1980s, the federal structures lurched from crisis to crisis, unable to agree on constitutional reform, which would require unanimity. But it was tensions building over Kosovo during this period that were eventually to lead to Yugoslavia's implosion.

Before continuing with the political-historical narrative, it is worth giving brief consideration to the impact of these developments on Bosnian social life. Bringa's (1995) study *Being Muslim the Bosnian Way* shows that while in urban areas religious identification under the impact of Communist secularization policies was becoming a declining factor in social life, in rural areas it remained significant, but primarily in a socially integrative way. Bringa argues that recognition and sharing of religious differences, especially through traditional festivities, was an important dynamic in social life which rarely became a source of tension or hostility. However, as we have seen, political developments, together with Serbia's monopoly of Serbian State television from the mid-1980s, also watched by many Bosnian Serbs, was to lead to a rapid deterioration in these relationships.

One particular feature of the 1974 Constitution was the autonomy it granted to two provinces of Serbia: Kosovo, of which the majority were ethnically Albanian (and nominally Muslim), and Vojvodina. In 1981 calls for Kosovo to become a fully independent republic increased and this triggered a nationalist backlash in Serbia, as so many of the holy sites associated with its sense of nationhood to be found there. The Serbian Orthodox Church played a major role in increasing Serb fears of a 'genocide' directed against Serbs by ethnic Albanians. In September 1986 matters came to a head with the publication in a Belgrade newspaper of 'the Memorandum', a document which became a manifesto for Serbian nationalism and was written by an anonymous team of academics at the Serbian Academy of Sciences (SANU) (Glenny 1999 p. 625). It claimed that Serbs in Kosovo faced extinction at the hands of aggressive Albanians, drawing a comparison between their plight and that of Serbs in wartime (Ustashe) Croatia.

The Memorandum was unequivocally condemned by all Communist leaders, with one exception, who restricted his criticism to an audience of secret police leaders – a context where it could reassure Communist leaders without reaching public attention. This was Slobodan Milosevič, former banker and newly elected President of the Serbian Communist Party (May 1986). Seizing his opportunity, Milosevič consolidated his grip on power in Serbia with remarkable speed. In 1987 he dismissed officials opposed to his policy of reasserting Serbian control over the autonomous provinces within Serbia and between 1987 and 1989 he sought, with partial success, to recentralize the federal system under Serbian domination. During the same period he rehabilitated and sought to coopt the Serbian Orthodox Church, so that it would promote a revived Serbian nationalism (Ramet 1999 p. 25). As Ramet comments, these policies 'Destroyed what remained of any consensus in the system and by late 1989, for all practical purposes, Yugoslavia had already ceased to exist' (pp. 25–6). With the functional disappearance of Yugoslavia came the demise of Yugoslav Communism. Two factors in particular set the scene for a show-down between the republics at the Fourteenth Extraordinary Congress of the Yugoslav Communist Party in January 1990: first, the Slovenian Communist Party's decision to allow multi-party elections in the republic in the spring of 1990, a precedent soon followed by other republics; and second, Ivica Racan, an advocate of decentralization, the free market and multi-party politics was elected to the leadership of the Communist Party of Croatia in December 1989.

At the Congress Serbian delegates refused successive Slovenian demands to end political trials and the use of torture and for the reform of the Communist Party into an association of independent political parties. As a result, Slovenian and Croatian delegates walked out of the Congress and with the Bosnian and Macedonian delegates refusing to continue in their absence, the Congress was dissolved (Ramet 1999 p. 54). Elections in April 1990 brought anti-Communist democratic alliances to power in Slovenia and Croatia; in Serbia, Milosevič founded the Serbian Socialist Party in July and swept to presidential power with 64 per cent of the vote, aided by a massive unsecured loan to the Serbian republic of $1.2 billion from the National Bank of Yugoslavia which effectively ended the federal government's plans for economic reform (ibid.). Thus Communism in Yugoslavia also ended in 1989–90, but for very different reasons and under very different circumstances from its demise in Poland.

What of Bosnia as Yugoslavia fell apart through the 1980s? In response to events in Croatia and Slovenia, Bosnia also held multi-party elections in November 1990. As a result of these, a fragile coalition of Muslim, Serb and Croat nationalists defeated the Communists, with the Muslim majority SDA (Party of Democratic Action) uneasily allied with the Bosnian Serb majority SDS (Serb Democratic Party), whose Croatian counterpart was already agitating for Serbian autonomy in the Krajina region of Croatia (Malcolm 1996 p. 218). As a multi-ethnic republic[6] in a federation falling apart along ethnic fault-lines, Bosnia faced a particularly difficult situation. The victory of ethnically based parties in the elections of November 1990 suggests that Bosnia had already began to fragment along ethnic lines, although it should also be noted that these parties made common cause sufficient to form a coalition in opposition to the former Communists, even if this was to prove unstable (Ramet 1999 p. 54). This instability is hardly surprising in view of the escalation of hostilities between republics along ethnic fault-lines and the frequent use of religious symbols and discourse during the 1980s. The pressure of Serbian nationalist propaganda was particularly intense. Serbian commemorations for the 600th anniversary of the battle of Kosovo on 28 June 1989 illustrate the extent to which Serbian Orthodoxy became entwined in this process of nationalist mobilization by the end of the 1980s:

> On 28 June several hundred thousand Serbs assembled at the battlefield site of Gazimestan, outside the Kosovar capital, Pristina, to celebrate the six-hundreth anniversary of the Battle of Kosovo. For many weeks a ferment of national feeling had been created inside Serbia; the bones of Prince Lazar, who died at the battle, had been taken on a tour of the country, becoming an object of pilgrimage wherever they were. In the courtyard of the monastery at Gracanica (south of Pristina), while people queued to pay their devotions to the Prince's bones inside, stalls sold icon-style posters of Jesus Christ, Prince Lazar and Slobodan Milosevic side by side. At the ceremony on the battlefield Milosevic was accompanied by black robed metropolitans of the Orthodox Church, singers in traditional Serbian folk costumes and members of the security police in their traditional dress of dark suits and sunglasses. 'After six centuries', Milosevic told the crowds, 'we are again engaged in battles and quarrels. They are not armed battles, but this cannot be excluded yet.' The crowd roared its approval. (Malcolm 1996 p. 213)

They would not have long to wait.

3. From the End of Communism to the End of the War in Bosnia (1989–95)

As we have seen, Communism in Yugoslavia ended not on a wave of popular protest as in the case of Poland, but largely in reaction to Serbian attempts to dominate the Yugoslav federation. True, through the 1980s and especially in Slovenia and Croatia, there had been a growth of political parties and agitation for democratization, parallel to developments elsewhere in Communist Central Europe. But such developments came later and were on a much smaller scale in Bosnia-Hercegovina. Furthermore, as tensions between Serbia and Croatia grew, Bosnian Serbs and

Croats were drawn into conflict. From September 1990 Bosnian Serbs began forming illegal local militias, with secret support and training from Serbia (Ramet 1999 p. 202). Driving these developments was an escalating propaganda war:

> The propaganda of extremist organizations … swamped the public arena with instrumentalized historical memories. In Serbia, most of these symbols, myths and martyrdoms recalled the Second World War, quite the most violent period in Yugoslav history. The identification of 'Croat' and 'Ustase' was too often taken for granted in them. The Croats … also began rehabilitating the Ustase state. … If ordinary Serbs believed that the Ustase were about to return, or if Croats in Croatia could be convinced that their neighbours were preparing for a Cetnik onslaught, then it would be much easier to mobilize them for war, according to the principle 'Kill before you are killed'. (Glenny 1999 p. 629)

As we saw at the end of the previous section, religion, and especially the Serbian Orthodox Church, played a significant part in the propagation of these 'instrumentalized historical memories', as illustrated there in the commemoration of the Battle of Kosovo. However, while in the case of confrontation between Serbia and Croatia it was sufficient to recall the Ustashe regime to mobilize Serb fears of Croatian hostility, no similar Muslim threat from recent historical memory could plausibly be recalled. Instead, Serb and Croat propaganda drew on three, somewhat contradictory and implausible associations: with contemporary Islamic militancy; with Ottoman occupation (both of which drew on broader Western orientalist caricature); and, in the Serb case, on nineteenth-century nationalist mythologies which identified Slavic Muslims as Christ-killers and Serbia with the slain Christ (Malcolm 1996; Sells 1996).

The genesis and course of the war is complex and controversial and the detail is not central to our concerns here, so only a basic analysis will be given of how Yugoslavia moved from disintegration into conflict, first between Serbia and Croatia (1991–92) and then within Bosnia (1992–95). While Communism ended, and most cooperation between republics had ended in 1990, no republic had yet declared its independence from the federation. However, by 1991 Milosevič's actions were driving Slovenia and Croatia towards declaring independence, leaving Bosnia vulnerable. In particular, by revoking the autonomous status of the provinces of Kosovo and Vojvodina and putting pressure on Montenegro, Milosevič had managed to get the votes of four of the eight republics under his control. Furthermore, by entering a trade war with Slovenia and beginning an insurrection among Croatian Serbs in the Croatian area of the Krajina he provoked Slovenia and Croatia to exit from the Federation.

Thus on 25 June Slovenia and Croatia simultaneously declared independence, following near-unanimous referenda (Malcolm 1996 p. 225). Encouraged by recent EC and American pledges to the territorial integrity of Yugoslavia, Milosevič sent tanks to the Slovenian border, but during the previous week the Slovene military had called up it reserves and reinforced the border posts. The federal army backed down and Milosevič let Slovenia go, with its small population of ethnic Serbs. In Croatia the policy of agitating local Serb insurrection (through propaganda and supply arms), response to which could then be used as pretext for 'federal' intervention, was employed, which had escalated to full-scale war by September. This war was to last until the UN brokered a peace and agreed to send 10,000 troops to Croatia in January 1992.

This peace, however, was not to help Bosnia: on the contrary, it laid the foundations for a possible division between Serbia and Croatia, whose two leaders had met secretly in March 1991 to discuss the division of Bosnia between them (Glenny 1999 p. 633). In Bosnia, too, Milosevič employed similar insurrectionary tactics and in September 1991 the federal army moved in to 'protect' four self-declared 'Serbian autonomous regions' in Bosnia-Hercegovina. Positions in Bosnia (for example at Banja Luka) had already been used as a base for attacking Croatia from August, and during the autumn of 1991 communications centres across the republic were taken over by federal forces and heavy artillery positions were constructed around major towns (Malcolm 1996 pp. 228–30). In order to appear to comply with the terms of the peace, from January 1992 Milosevič replaced Serbian military commanders in Bosnia with Bosnian Serbs, who would thus be Bosnian citizens were Bosnia to declare its independence, but whose sympathies had clearly been shown to lie with Milosevič's goal of a Greater Serbia.

Thus, by 1992 the situation had become intolerable for Bosnia's beleaguered government. Military responses seemed hopeless, with the highly armed Bosnian Serb militias and the federal army holding key positions. Matters were made worse when Izetbegovic allowed the federal army to begin confiscating the weapons of local defence units, perhaps in the hope that local Serbian militias would also be disarmed (there is evidence of this on a small scale) and perhaps with the hope of gaining the international support for this refusal to escalate the conflict. As a result, when Bosnian Serbs attacked Sarajevo a few months later, only the local criminals had weapons left to defend the city (Sells 1996 p. 117). The best option, then, seemed to be to go for independence, in the hope that international recognition would bring international protection. A referendum was held on 29 February and 1 March. In spite of the SDS's (Serbian Nationalist Party) boycott – including road blocks to prevent the entry of ballot boxes into territory it controlled – 63.4 per cent of the electorate voted, including many urban Serbs, with 99.4 per cent answering 'yes' to the question: 'Are you in favour of a sovereign and independent Bosnia-Hercegovina, a state of equal citizens and nations of Muslims, Serbs and Croats and others who live it it?' (Malcolm 1996 p. 231; Ramet 1999 p. 205). When the results were announced on 2 March Serbian paramilitary forces set up barricades and sniper positions near the Parliament building in Sarajevo. Only the protests of thousands of Sarajevans on the streets appears to have arrested the *coup*. A month later (5 April), after a desperate flurry of internationally mediated diplomacy and escalating Serb paramilitary activity, such protests no longer proved effective, as Serb paramilitaries opened fire on a crowd of 50,000 and 100,000 Bosnian protestors of all national groups (Malcolm 1996 p. 235).

On the following day, 6 April, the EC recognized Bosnia's independence. But instead of triggering international support for the fledgling democracy, the only action that followed came from Milosevič, who escalated military action on the pretext of restoring order between local factions. In fact, he used a combination of federal army forces and Bosnian Serb paramilitaries and tactics of intimidation, rape and murder against an undefended civilian population, to take control of more than 60 per cent of Bosnian territory in the space of six weeks (ibid. p. 238). Differences between the Bosnian Serb leadership and Milosevič did emerge in the spring of 1993, but, in spite of official Serbian propaganda and Western credulity,[7] contemporary eye-witness and subsequent evidence clearly show that Serb and Bosnian Serb fought side by side for the first year of the conflict (ibid.; Ramet 1999 pp. 206–7).

However, constructing the conflict as a civil war rather than a continuation of the campaign for a Greater Serbia (and, later, a Greater Croatia), the international community was slow to impose sanctions on Serbia, yet, under the terms of the UN arms embargo imposed on the whole of the former Yugoslavia on 25 September 1991, refused to allow arms into Bosnia to help Muslim forces mount some resistance against the Serb onslaught.[8] Thus the international community helped to ensure the falsity of its own description of the Bosnian conflict as a 'civil war':

> What occurred from April through September has been labelled a war and even a civil war. A war, however, is a conflict between armed adversaries. The Serb army took towns and villages that lacked significant military defences. Where there was any Bosnian defence at all, Serb militants used heavy artillery to shell the defenders into submission. Once the town or village was taken, the killings of civilians would begin.
>
> This was not a war but organized destruction of a largely civilian population. With weapons and weapons factories under their control and with the arms embargo in place and stubbornly maintained for years, Serb militants were able to carry out their campaigns with impunity. (Sells 1996 p. 117)

For reasons of space, we shall not go into the details of Bosnian resistance and the ensuing events of the conflict. The basic points to note, however, are these. First, the international community refused to lift the arms embargo, in spite of overwhelming Serb military superiority.[9] Second, all proposed peace solutions, such as the Vance-Owen plan and later the Dayton agreement reneged on an established principle of international law which refused to legitimize aggressive territorial gains (Ramet 1999 p. 209). Third, while the war involved atrocities on all sides, the Serb case is distinctive in that there is evidence of systematic genocide and rape authorized from the highest levels. Fourth, it was not until 5 February 1994, when the carnage caused by Serb shelling of the main outdoor market in Sarajevo reached Western television screens that large scale and effective international intervention ensued. Pictures of Serb death camps, which had been available since the summer of 1992, had failed to produce:[10] large-scale any effective response.

Fifth, although Milosevič and Karadzič had repeatedly prevaricated, misled the international community and reneged on agreements, it was the change of military fortunes resulting from the Western change of policy that eventually led to a 'successful' return to the negotiating table, leading to the peace agreement signed in Dayton, Ohio, on 21 November 1995, that forms the basis for the present arrangements (2001) in Bosnia-Hercegovina.

4. The Dayton Peace Accord

> The new Bosnia-Hercegovina was hailed as a triumph of the West's commitment to a
> multi-ethnic state but in reality confirmed its total partition. ... Dayton brought the
> fighting to an end, in itself a considerable achievement. But as a model for reconciliation
> and for rebuilding a shattered society, it was and remains severely limited. (Glenny 1999
> pp. 647, 651)

The Dayton agreement was thrashed out between Izetbegovic, Tudjman and
Milosevič with American mediation in the first three weeks of November 1995. But
the mediators brought a formula of territorial division to the table which had first
been proposed by international negotiators in the spring of 1994, a period when Serb
forces were in a very much stronger position than in the autumn of 1995. Thus
questions have been asked as to why, given the much-weakened position of Serb
forces, the international community did not bring pressure to bear for a solution
which not only made a territorial settlement that more closely reflected the size of
the respective populations and prewar conditions, but also sought to ensure its future
unity and multi-ethnicity (Malcolm 1996, Glenny 1999, Ramet 1999). For the
Dayton agreement divided the former republic 51 : 49 between a Muslim-Croat
federation and Serb administered territory (Republika Srpska, RS), with each entity
having predominantly separate institutions (for example police, military, media,
parliament, education). There is also a combined Parliament, council of ministers
and three-person presidency; but (beyond practical matters, such as air-traffic
control) its powers are restricted to foreign and monetary policy, and its procedures
such that the veto of any one ethnic constituency can render them inoperative.

The agreement embeds the European Convention on Human Rights in the
constitution, bars indicted war criminals from holding public office (which led to the
departure from office of Karadzič and later Mladic, although neither has, to date,
been arrested), guarantees freedom of movement and the return of refugees to their
prewar homes and also set up elections for the Federation and RS respectively in
September and November 1996. A NATO-led force of 60,000 (Implementation
Force, IFOR) was put in place for one year to police the agreement, then reduced to
35,000 (Stabilization Force, SFOR). The September 1996 elections were
overwhelmingly won by the main nationalist parties of each of the three main
national groups, while the November elections saw a sharp rise in the vote for the
Serbian Radical Party – linked to the fascistic party of the same name in Serbia. The
Organization for Security and Cooperation in Europe (OSCE) oversaw these
elections, which were deemed acceptably fair, although there were some
irregularities, including the unusual result of rather more votes cast (2.6 m) than the
voters in the electorate (2.3 m) (Ramet 1999 pp. 283–4). Intermittent 'ethnic
cleansing' continued through 1996 (c.90,000 people were removed from their homes
between January and August) and freedom of movement was compromised by
Bosnian Serbs charging illegal tolls in German marks (ibid. p. 278).

However, since 1998, in spite of some incidents, stability has improved. The
larger problem is one of whether reintegration of the two entities is a practical
proposition under the present arrangements. The RS has concluded a security treaty

and joint citizenship arrangements with Serbia, and the Serbian Radical Party leader won the RS's presidential seat in September 1998, a result confirmed two years later. At the time of writing (late 2000) it is too early the assess the impact on RS politics of the fall from power of Milosevič in the autumn of 2000 and his subsequent arrest and deportation to face the International War Crimes Tribunal in the Hague. Although some progress has been made in the return of refugees, especially in 2000, this remains a major problem. In particular, in a context of extreme housing shortages and because Bosnian Serbs tend to feel more confident about reclaiming their property in the Federation than vice versa, the return policy has had the unfortunate consequence of Muslim refugees who had been resettled in accommodation abandoned by Serbs being evicted and the Serb owners returning only to refurbish the accommodation and sell it on the open market, returning themselves to live in RS. It has also proved impossible (at least until April 2000) to rebuild mosques in RS, an issue we shall examine further below. Furthermore, polarization between RS and the Federation has arguably been increased by the fact that to punish RS for lack of compliance with Dayton, international aid has mainly been directed to the Federation. Unemployment and dependence on international aid remain high.

One argument is that the polarization of Bosnia into Serb and non-Serb entities could have been tackled more effectively in the long run had the international community opted for the kind of measures adopted in Germany and Japan after the Second World War, when the education systems of those countries were completely overhauled. Other measures – given legal precedents in other European countries – would have been the banning of hate speech, which might have helped to control the media that had played such a large role in generating antagonisms. Such measures have not been taken – although, somewhat more crudely, NATO did take control of RS television transmitters in September 1997, which had continued to 'churn out hate propaganda' (Ramet 1999 p. 281). Thus a criticism that has been levelled is that the agreement has favoured procedural democracy (elections) over 'liberal substance' (ensuring that all parties represented are committed to respecting the rights of others) (p. 278). The UN has, however, put in place a 'democratization' programme, consisting of '"top-down" international regulation of elections, institutional development and economic management, accompanied by "bottom-up" assiatance to develop a democratic political culture through civil society building' (Chandler 1998 p. 78). Chandler's assessment of these strategies, as put into practice by the OSCE, is that the insistence of the international community on parties showing a prior commitment to constitutional democracy before benefiting from international support has limited civil society building efforts to the production of middle-class talking shops. This view – that the international community is too controlling of the development of civil society – thus appears to be the opposite of Ramet's opinion that the international community should have extended further its control to education and the regulation of public speech. We shall return to these contentious issues when we consider the role of religion in the reconstruction process. But first, we turn to consider the equally contentious issue of the role of religion in the war.

5. Religion and the War

The violence in Bosnia was a religious genocide in several senses: the people destroyed were chosen on the basis of their religious identity; those carrying out the killings acted [in the Serb case] with the blessing and support of Christian church leaders; the violence [again, in the Serb case] was grounded in a religious mythology that characterized the targeted people as a sacred act; and the perpetrators of the violence were protected by a policy designed by the policy makers of a Western world that is culturally dominated by Christianity. (Sells 1996 p. 144)

It is not my belief that the Serbian Insurrectionary War was about religion. When Serbs blew up mosques and Catholic Churches and when Croats destroyed mosques and other religious buildings, they were not, in fact, doing so to spread their own faiths, but rather to destroy the architectural artefacts that established other people's history in the area and that helped members of other nationalities remember their past and hold on to their cultural identity. In other words, attacks on religious objects served strictly political purposes; politics was primary, not religion. (Ramet 1999 p. 79)

As these quotations demonstrate, opinion on the role of religion in the war differs. Thus, while Michael Sells argues that the war was 'religiously motivated and religiously justified' (1996 p. 89), Sabrina Ramet believes that the war was not about religion (1999 p. 79). What is not disputed, however, is that religious symbols and discourse were mobilized by all parties in the conflict and especially by Serbs and Muslims. The dispute is rather as to the significance of this mobilization. What is also not disputed is the polarizing effect that the war had on the religious communities in a previously highly integrated society, one sign of which is the 30 per cent rate of intermarriage found in urban areas by the late 1980s (Malcolm 1996 p. 222).

(a) Serbian Orthodoxy

We shall look first at the Serbian Orthodox Church. We have already considered an example of the relationship between Milosevič and the leadership of the Serb Orthodox Church in the commemoration of the Battle of Kosovo in 1989. Sells (1996 pp. 38–52) explains further how one Serbian reading of the passion narrative came to identify Serbia's suffering at the hands of the Ottoman Turks with Christ's suffering in his passion, in fact at the hands of Roman authorities, but blamed on the Jews in medieval Christianity. As Christ was betrayed by Judas Iscariot, so the Serb prince Lazar was betrayed by Vuk Brankovic, a figure who later comes to be identified with Slavs who converted to Islam under Ottoman rule. Nineteenth-century Serbian nationalist literature further identified such Slav converts as 'Turks' – by changing religion, they were also held to have changed race (Sells 1996 p. 45). The Orthodox church responded to these nationalist developments by beginning to celebrate the feast of St Lazar. In 1892 this was combined with the feast day of Vid, a pre-Christian Slavic god, and appeared for the first time as an official holiday in the Church's calendar as 'Prophet Amos and Prince Lazar (Vid's Day)' (ibid. p. 44).

Again, in the 1980s the Serbian Church, which had suffered so badly in the Second World War and under the Communists, responded to a rising nationalism.

The main Serbian theologians of the twentieth-century had prepared it to take such a role, having 'developed their theological concepts on the basis of the idea that Serbian Orthodoxy forms the heart of the Serbian national identity and that from a historical perspective the Serbia nation is under constant threat' (van Dartel 1992 p. 281). Milosevič had also sought to win the Church's favour. Before the 600th anniversary of the Battle of Kosovo (June 1989), he had allowed the Church to build and reconstruct churches in previously forbidden areas and he later allowed the Church newspaper *Pravoslavje* to be sold at public news stands, and replaced the teaching of Marxism in schools with RE along Orthodox lines (December 1989–January 1990; Ramet 1999 pp. 112–3). At the anniversary celebrations, the hierarchy indicated its support for Milosevič's policy of revoking the autonomy of Kosovo and Vojvodina, describing acceptance of their autonomy as 'only a temporary solution' (ibid. p. 36). Furthermore, in the early 1980s, the Church had played a leading role in creating scare stories about an Albanian campaign of 'genocide' against ethnic Serbs.

However, the Orthodox Church should not be regarded as simply the creature of Milosevič. On 14 June 1992, at the height of the insurrection in Bosnia, the same Patriarch Pavel who had stood alongside Milosevič at the anniversary celebrations three years before, led 10,000 people in a march and prayers for peace in Belgrade in protest against the Milosevič regime. Again, in the autumn of 2000, Pavel voiced criticism of the Milosevič regime, shortly before the latter's fall from power. The position of the institutional Serbian Orthodox Church is thus perhaps best characterized as a defensively ethnocentric national Church, shaped by a history of suffering and more recent international isolation. The Church supported Milosevic's plans in so far as these furthered the security of Serbia and Serb control over sacred sites (especially Kosovo) and it also contributed to propagating nationalist mythologies, even though it did not originate these.

The role of the Serbian Orthodox religion more generally in the war – as opposed to that of the institutional Church – is difficult to assess. The relationship between the 'folk culture' shared by Karadzič and his Bosnian Serb troops and institutional Serb Orthodoxy is complex. Certainly, Christian symbolism is blended with its mixture of folk-songs, music and romantic attachment to the countryside, away from the 'impure' mixing of the towns (Sells 1996 p. 50). Furthermore, the Church's own identification with the Serbian nation reinforced such connections. On the other hand, before the war the active membership of the Church was probably less than 10 per cent and probably lowest among young men, religious instruction in schools was not permitted under the Communist system, and 'in the Orthodox church, religious education, at least of a systematic kind, was hardly known' (van Dartel 1992 p. 278). So the chances of such soldiers playing an active part in church life or being educated in church teachings are slim.

Thus much depends on what one means by 'religion' – if one means this in a rather Western sense of a consciously chosen belief system that informs actions in a reflective way, Serbian Orthodoxy had not been very effective in transmitting itself in this way and hence its impact in this sense could not have been great. If, on the other hand, one means sets of symbols, rituals and stories that may float free of authorizing institutions, but continue to exert influence via other media (for example TV, folk-songs, word of mouth), then Serbian Orthodoxy appears to have been rather more influential in informing Serbian insurrectionary ideology.

So differences between analysts such as Ramet and Sells may perhaps be explained by differences in their understanding of religion. Ramet seems to understand religion in the former, reflective-systemic sense, so that for a war to be religiously motivated and justified, as Sells claims, some substantial argument derived from the tradition must be shown to be involved. Thus Ramet asks: 'Though one can easily cite Serbian bishops who justified the war, is the endorsement of even several bishops tantamount to *religious* justification as such?' (1999 p. 79). Furthermore, in the quotation that opened this section she also implies an understanding of a division between politics and religion and of their essentially different nature. Yet, where religious identity is considered by participants in the situation to be part of political identity, the utility of such a distinction becomes questionable. Religion is not necessarily defined by a wish to convert others, but also, sometimes, by a need or desire to mark boundaries, to say what is self and what is other. This is not to say that religion is nothing but politics or boundary-marking, but rather that to understand religion as essentially something apart from politics is to foreclose on important possibilities for understanding its action.

Working with a different understanding of religion, Sells argues that the widespread use of Christian symbols and discourse by Serb soldiers and leaders, together with insults against the Catholic and Islamic religions, shows that Serbs were 'performing the passion' of the Slavic Christ. They were transforming nineteenth-century folktales based around the 'Kosovo passion' into 'the daily rituals for ethnoreligious purification' (Sells 1996 p. 51). He gives many examples of this, including the following four. The first is a 1990 political cartoon depicting a Roman Catholic priest and a Muslim *imam* fighting over a Serb baby (p. 64). The second is the declaration of the Serb 'warlord' Arkan, friend of Karadzič and Milosevič, on the occasion of his wedding: 'we are fighting for our faith, the Serbian Orthodox church' (p. 82). Third, when the city of Foca was cleared of its Muslim population and all architectural traces of their presence removed, it was renamed *Srbinje* ('Serb place') and the renaming celebrated by visits from high church officials (p. 80). Finally, Metropolitan Nicolaj, the highest-ranking church official in Bosnia, stood between Mladic and Karadzič at the 1993 Easter service and described the Bosnian Serbs under these leaders as 'following the hard road of Christ' (p. 82).

Such examples should be put into perspective by pointing out that not all Serbs shared such views. In the case of the Bosnian Serbs, the Serb Civic Council formed in Bosnian government areas to articulate the views of Serbs in favour of a multi-religious society points out that less than half of the Bosnian Serb population lives in RS in the postwar period; 150,000 choose to live in Federation areas and half a million have fled abroad including to Serbia (Sells 1996 pp. 78–9). It should also be remembered that Serbs were not alone in committing atrocities – all sides were guilty, as subsequent war crimes trials have shown (Ramet 1999 p. 286). However, the fact that individuals on all sides committed atrocities does not imply equal collective responsibility. The evidence shows that first Croats and later Muslims, copied Serb tactics of ethnic cleansing (Sells 1996 pp. 20–1). Furthermore, although of course it makes no difference to those individuals affected, Serb atrocities were committed on a far larger scale and as part of an orchestrated and systematic campaign to carve out swathes of Serb-only territory.

Nor do the examples cited by Sells prove that religion 'caused the war'. Many other factors, as we have seen, were also involved – the ambitions of Milosević, the unstable federal structure, economic decline, Serb domination of the federal army and so on. Indeed, expressions of religious motivation played relatively little part in the build-up to the conflict, except in the case of the Serb Orthodox Church's concern over Kosovo:

> In fact, the war was ignited by rising tempers of ethnic hatreds and did not at first have the character of a 'religious' war, but as time passed, the war took on ever more religious characteristics. Imams and Christian clergy followed their troops into battle, blessing them and praying for their success in battle. (Ramet 1999 p. 254)

However, in the case of Muslims, as we shall see, religion was mobilized only in reaction to other events. In the case of Serbs, Serbian Orthodoxy is seen as a core constituent of Serbian national identity both by many perpetrators of violence in Bosnia and by the Church itself, and the symbols and discourse of the Church were used by both parties to legitimate Serb actions in Bosnia. But it should also be remembered that the Church did not instigate the policy of ethnic cleansing, nor was it the most powerful propaganda tool of the Milosević and Karadzić regimes: rather the state-controlled media – TV, radio and newspapers – were. As one writer with a long acquaintance with Bosnia concludes:

> Having travelled widely in Bosnia over fifteen years and having stayed in Muslim, Serb and Croat villages, I cannot believe that the country was forever seething with ethnic hatreds. But having watched Radio Television Belgrade in the period 1991–2, I can see why simple Bosnian Serbs came to believe they were under threat, from Ustashe hordes, fundamentalist jihads or whatever. As the independent Belgrade journalist Milos Vasic put it to an American audience, it was as if all television in the USA had been taken over by the Ku Klux Klan. (Malcolm 1996 p. 252).

(b) Islam

Like the Serbian Church until it began to lobby the government over Kosovo in the early 1980s, up to 1990 Islamic institutions in Bosnia tended to be politically quietist. However, under attack for what was most distinctive about their identity, that is their religion, many Muslims reacted with a positive affirmation of their tradition. Such an affirmation needs to be put in context: a 1985 survey had suggested that only 17 per cent of Bosnians were religious believers (Malcolm 1996 p. 222). Other work, for example Sorabji's (1989) anthropological study of a Sarajevo suburb suggests rather higher levels of religious identification and participation among Muslims. Furthermore, in contrast to Orthodoxy (and like the Catholic Church), the Muslim community had put considerable efforts into religious education, so that by 1980 across Yugoslavia some 120,000 children were receiving

Islamic instruction at primary level (Ramet 1999 p. 120). Thus, in spite of rather low levels of active participation, it is likely that many Muslims had some basis in their tradition to which to turn in the new situation, both of a formal kind and received via broader cultural transmission. There was, however, little tradition of Islamic political activism on which to draw: 'in spite of [its] formidable institutional base, the Islamic leadership adopted a much lower profile then either the Roman Catholic Church or the Serbian Orthodox Church' (ibid.).

As early as the 1960s some thinkers, such as the future President Izetbegovic, had thought through the issues that would come to characterize 'political Islam' from the 1970s. Thus concern with the nature of Islamic society and Islamic government forms the subject of his work the *Islamic Declaration*, written in the late 1960s, a time of considerable rethinking across the Muslim world. In this work, addressed to the Islamic world in general, Izetbegovic argues that Islamic government is only appropriate for societies in which a majority of people are sincere and practising Muslims, without which 'The Islamic order is reduced to mere power ... and can turn into tyranny' (in Malcolm 1996 p. 220). Thus he anticipated some of the problems associated with Islamic regimes that emerged in the 1970s and 1980s (Iran, Sudan), as well as ruling out the possibility of such a regime in Bosnia, where nominal Muslims formed a minority and practising Muslims a small proportion of those. Izetbegovic also points towards a positive synthesis of Islam and Western culture, a theme developed much further in a later work written in the early 1980s, *Islam Between East and West*:

> From its first foundations, Islam undertook, without prejudice, the study and collection of the sum of knowledge bequeathed it by earlier civilizations. We do not see why Islam today should take a different approach to the achievements of the Euro-American civilization with which it has such broad contact. (ibid. p. 221)

However, none of this prevented him being labelled 'fundamentalist' by Serbs and nationalists, nor the former describing Bosnia as in the grip of a 'fundamentalist-Ustashe' coalition at various times during the conflict. In this new context in which their religious identity was under direct attack, Bosnian Muslims reacted in two ways, strengthening their religious identity, for example in the green banners and crescents of Izetbegovic's SDA (the main Muslim political party), but also stressing that they 'stood for the preservation of Bosnia's unique character as a multinational, multi-religious republic' (Malcolm 1996 p. 218–9). There were strong tensions between these two elements, which persisted throughout the war and indeed to the present.

Certainly, Islamic identity was increasingly mobilized in the war effort, aided in part by the flood of less cosmopolitan rural refugees into urban areas with the tide of Serb ethnic cleansing (Glenny 1999 p. 644). From late 1993 new exclusively Muslim brigades were established, for example the 7th Brigade in Zenica:

> The new recruits were men who had been 'cleansed' from their homes and understandably they did not pay lip-service to the concept of a multinational or multi-ethnic Bosnia. For the first time a strident Mulsim nationalism appeared on the scene, rivalling that of the Serbs and Croats. The brigade's officers sported Islamic insignia and beards and adopted

anti-Western positions. Their wives and daughters increasingly adopted Islamic dress and head covering. Shops selling alcohol were attacked and pigs were slaughtered and their carcasses destroyed. (Poulton 1997 p. 233)

Such developments were paralleled in the official public sphere in 1994: the *reis-ul-ulema* (Islamic religious leader) criticized mixed marriages, and journalists committed to multiculturalism were removed from state television (ibid.). However, such religious exclusivism did not go uncontested and SDA policy has remained officially multiculturalist in principle and in practice: Serbs stayed in the coalition government throughout the war. One example from 1996 of the ongoing struggle between religious exclusivism and other tendencies (in this case a secular multiculturalism) concerned the issue of the appropriate form of commemoration for Muslim war dead. When Izetbegovic used Islamic terminology and symbols as official Bosnian forms, the father of a slain soldier objected in an open letter published in the nationalist newspaper *Ljilian*:

> Why do you use the religious term *shehid* [Arabic word for martyr] for my son and other soldiers who have died? My son is not one and I do not allow you to call him so. Why do you say a *fatiha* [Arabic word for prayer for the dead] for those who have been killed? When it comes to my son, remain silent. It is better not to say anything than to speak a language which neither he nor I understand. (Osman Tica, reported in *BosNews* (Digest 112), 27 March 1996, in Campbell 1998 p. 113)

So Islam too was instrumentalized during the conflict, that is, used to mobilize a sense of national identity deployed in opposition to other religious nationalisms and implicitly exclusive both of other religious identities and of non-religious identities. Controversy about this public identification of 'Bosnian-ness' with Islam continued to prove controversial during the 1996 elections, as when Izetbegovic addressed an election rally which featured Islamic religious music and verses from the Qur'an (Ramet 1999 p. 283). Furthermore, during the war this identification of Bosnian identity with Islam was rejected by some religious Muslims close to Izetbegovic, who subsequently broke away from the SDA. One example is the academic Rusmir Mahmutcehajic, who is influenced by the Sufi tradition of Islam influential in Bosnia's history and strongly critical of the ethnic division of Bosnia enshrined at Dayton. In response, he has formed 'Bosnia Forum', an organization for academics from all groups in Bosnia aimed at working towards a deeper form of reconciliation premised on the idea of multi-ethic, multi-religious Bosnia.

None the less, whether because of the multi-religious and cosmopolitan constituency of Sarajevo or for some other reason, in Sarajevo at least Muslim nationalism never spilled over into violence directed against religious property, in contrast to Croatian and Serbian nationalism (Ramet 1999 p. 255). Furthermore, incidents of this kind outside Sarajevo in Bosnian government-controlled areas were less frequent and severe than elsewhere, although not entirely absent: as late as March 1997 explosives destroyed the Catholic parish church in Humac, a Muslim-Croat area.

These attacks on religious property need to be seen in the context of what Bosnian Muslims describe as 'the war against culture', of which a key example is the shelling of the historic National Library in Sarajevo, which destroyed many historic rare books and manuscripts. Indeed, the Bosnian government has decided to leave several major public buildings unrepaired as monuments to this war, including the Parliament building. However, by far the most common form of destruction was that of places of worship. Religious buildings provided the most prominent witness to the long-term settlement of a 'cleansed' community, one that Serbs in particular were keen to eradicate entirely – hence, as we have seen, the destruction of all 211 mosques in Banja Luka, including two of historic importance from the late sixteenth century. By August 1994, Serb forces had destroyed 650 mosques across Bosnia-Herzegovia (Ramet 1999 p. 255). This has subsequently become one of the most controversial areas of reconstruction, with the international community unable to persuade the local authorities in Banja Luka to grant permission to re-build. In refusing the initial request to rebuild the Ferhadija mosque of 1579 the then Mayor of Banja Luka rebutted Carlos Westendorp, the international community's highest representative in Bosnia, with these words: 'The international community has got to stop insulting the Serbs and asking them to rebuild the monuments from the darkest days of slavery' (in Ramet 1999 p. 285). Indeed, by March 2000 not a single mosque in the Serb Republic had been rebuilt and an attempt to lay a foundation stone on the site of the historic Ferhadija mosque in the spring of 2002 was again thwarted by local pressure. In the meantime, many new mosques can be seen springing up in the suburbs of Sarajevo. Thus the practical partition of Bosnia is being constructed at the level of religious buildings too. But this also needs to be seen in the context of attempts at religious reconciliation, which we shall consider in the next section. First, though, what of the role of the Catholic Church?

(c) The Catholic Church

Although nominally Serbian Orthodox members outnumbered Catholics in Yugoslavia, the Catholic Church had the largest active membership of any religious group (Ramet 1999 p. 80). It was also the most politically active during the Communist period, beginning with Cardinal Stepinac's criticism in the immediate postwar period, which resulted in his imprisonment and internal exile until his death in 1960. Comparison of the leading newspapers of the three major religious traditions illustrates the differences in their political stances. Throughout the Communist period, *Glas koncila* (Catholic) openly and often took issue with the Communist press, publishing interviews and articles on 'state atheism, Christian-Marxist dialogue, proposals to change laws governing religious life in Yugoslavia and other social issues' (ibid. p. 121). In contrast, *Pravoslavje* (Orthodox) did not become active until 1981, after which it became 'ever more strident in its defence of Serbian interests in Kosovo and its advocacy of Serbian Orthodox nationalism generally' (ibid.). *Preporod* (Muslim) rarely touched on social issues, focusing instead on mosque-building, reports of religious festivals and information about basic Islamic teaching (ibid.).

State oppression decreased after 1970, but several areas of conflict between the Catholic Church and the state remained. Issues on which the Church continued to challenge the state included: school teaching of atheism, the exclusion of believers from the Communist Party, and in general their treatment as second-class citizens; denial of access to broadcasting for religious groups; and human rights, including wrongful imprisonment and denial of access to religious services for prisoners and military personnel (ibid. pp. 91–3).

Although Croat leaders such as Tudjman tried to harness Catholicism to the nationalist cause, in contrast to the Serb Orthodox case they received no support from the Church leadership or Catholic teaching. Perhaps as a result, when Croat soldiers committed atrocities against Muslims and Serbs, it was to Ustashe and not to Catholic symbolism that they appealed. Catholic leaders in Croatia and Slovenia had supported multi-party elections, but warned priests not to take sides in party politics (ibid. p. 94). Subsequently, under Catholic pressure, Catholic religious instruction was introduced as a compulsory subject in Croatian schools (ibid.). From the beginning of the conflict, Pope John Paul II called for peace and for nationalist passions to be set aside. Later in the conflict (September 1994) he visited Croatia and tried to visit Serbia and Bosnia, but was refused in the first case by Patriarch Pavel and Milosevič, in the second by UN officials concerned for his safety. Addressing an audience of one million in Croatia on 11 September 1994, he spoke against 'the risk of idolizing a nation, race [or] a party and justifying in their name hatred, discrimination and violence', continuing by calling on Croatian Catholics to 'become apostles of a new concord between peoples' (in ibid. p. 258).

Earlier, in 1993, when the Croat-Muslim alliance had fallen apart, the president of the Council of Islamic Elders for Croatia and Slovenia had praised the Catholic Church's role in non-partisan relief work across the former Yugoslavia:

> I am convinced that with this war the Catholic Church has gained lasting [esteem], which we Muslims will know how to foster and develop. That quality is actually the biggest guarantee that it will be possible to resolve the Croatian-Muslim dispute considerably more easily than it appears at this present moment. (In ibid.)

In this context, let us turn to consider the role of religion in the postwar reconstruction period.

6. Religion and the NGO Sector in Post-Dayton Bosnia

> Catholic, Orthodox and Muslim clergy carry out appropriate religious rituals at almost every economic, military, edicational or civic event, jubilee or celebration and the media conscientiously record and transmit them. …
>
> Here today, a politican proved to be corrupt would bear the consequences much more easily than one who dared, even in a civilized way, publicly to demonstrate his indifference to religion. (Lovrenović 2000 p. 77)

As this quotation suggests and as we have seen, religion became highly politicized and instrumentalized through the conflict in Bosnia. In neighbouring Croatia, in a poll conducted in September 1994, the most respected person was found to be the Catholic leader Franjo Cardinal Kuharić, ahead of Tudjman. When asked whom they hated, 68.4 per cent named Serbian Orthodox leader Pavle, although 96 per cent named Milosevič (in Ramet 1999 p. 256). However, while the quotation suggests that a public show of adherence to religion is universally required, not all public shows are equally welcome; in particular, young women who have chosen to adopt Muslim *hijab* may be criticized, insulted or discriminated against by other Muslims. For example, a woman respondent who runs a secular NGO told of critical comments on her attire from her boss, and even in the canteen at Sarajevo University it was evident that her dress aroused suspicion.[11] The pages of *Dani*, a Bosnian magazine, also witness to the controversy caused by the small numbers of young women who have adopted Islamic dress.

Interviews conducted in March 2000 demonstrate a range of understandings among Bosnians of the role of religion, both in the war and in the reconstruction process. Among Bosnian Muslims, these views were quite polarized. For some, especially with continuing Communist sympathies, religion could not be the cause of or solution to anything, but rather had been manipulated by politicians. One interesting feature of this response was how the increased religious observance of some was understood to be purely a political act of conformity to impress those now in power; even though, for most women for example, increased observance has meant mostly praying at home, unseen.

Those who had increased their observance in this way tended simply to say that the war had made them think about the meaning of life more and that they had found answers in their religion. Several respondents said they were pleased that a foreigner was showing an interest in something that they felt was positive that had come out of the war, rather than in the negative consequences. These remain devastating. Apart from the physical destruction, injury and displacement, there is the psychological damage, especially that caused by rape. Among Muslims alone, it is estimated that between 20,000 and 50,000 women were raped by Bosnian Serb soldiers 'in a systematic campaign of humiliation and psychological terror' (Ramet 1999 p. 239). There is little support available for these victims of rape, but as we shall see further below, organizations like Medica in Zenica have been attempting to address their needs since December 1992 (Cockburn 1998 p. 174).

Other conditions in Bosnia remain very difficult. Corruption is widespread and unemployment is massive: between 1991 and 1999 the workforce has dropped by some 300,000 (Ombudsman Institution 2000 p. 29). As the Ombudsman Institution's report for 1999 states:

> Nepotism, corruption and other … illegal ways of making [a] fortune … take place. [The] authorities do not respond properly to these irregularities. On the contrary, it is usual practice that state officials [at] all levels are at the same time members of one or more steering boards of public enterprises.
> All this [has] widened [the] gap between the rich, various carpetbaggers and [the] majority of the population which lives in extreme poverty, many of them under any acceptable level of human dignity. … Publicly presented official data states: 70 per cent of

citizens are in need of some kind of social aid, 200 000 households live in poverty, 145 000 receive some kind of social aid. (p. 28)

Media independence remains compromised by reliance on political and international sources of funding, insecurity, fragmentation of professional journalists' organizations and high levels of taxation (pp. 45–6). Cases of reported intimidation of journalists remain frequent (p. 47). The development of a normative public sphere under such circumstances remains difficult, to say the least.

We have already mentioned problems associated with the policy of return. Under this policy, Muslims who had fled Serb majority areas, where many of them and their families were raped and murdered, face the prospect of being evicted from their present accommodation if the Serb owners choose to return. Their choice is then to return to the place where they experienced these atrocities, or to live in some kind of temporary accommodation, for example in military barracks. At present, however, any alternative to this policy of return is seen by the international community as condoning ethnic cleansing.

Responses by members of the international community to issues of religion were rather different to those of local Bosnians. One way of categorizing them is to make a distinction between the major international institutions, for example lawyers working for the European Union and representatives of the Federal Ombudsman (set up to monitor human rights) and smaller organizations. The last include Helsinki Citizens' Assemblies (set up to provide local forums for citizens' participation), small scale groups oriented to reconciliation (such as the Yanta Communications Centre in Banja Luka) and inter-faith groups. We shall discuss the work of some small groups in detail below. Bosnians work at both levels in such internationally supported organizations, but are more strongly represented in the latter.

All groups agreed that religion had become too politicized or 'instrumentalized', in the words of one respondent, as a result of the war. However, they diverged sharply on the appropriate response to this. For the large-scale and secular organizations the unanimous response seemed to be to ignore religion and proceed on a universalist or 'religion-blind' basis. Among larger-scale international organizations there was a sense that religion is too difficult to handle and also that smaller-scale peace initiatives, while well intentioned, were of little practical value. Some smaller secular initiatives, such as a conflict resolution project (the Yanta Communications Centre) in Banja Luka, also held that it was better to focus on what unites people – the practical challenges of reconstruction – rather than on religion, which could be a potential source of division.

In a context in which religious memories have become so instrumentalized and official religious institutions so identified with nationalist political parties and the state, the relationship of religious affiliation, belief, symbols, discourse and organizations to the NGO sector is bound to be problematic. An illuminating way into the discussion of the role of religion in this sector is provided by Celia Cockburn's (1998) study of the Medica organization in Zenica, part of a comparative study of women's organizations in conflict situations in Bosnia, Croatia, Northern Ireland and Israel. Cockburn brings out the complex and ambiguous role of religious identity in the life of women who run and use the centre, and can help us gain some insight into the 'lifeworld' in which Bosnian religion and civil society come into being.

During the war Zenica became a major centre for Muslim refugees, victims of ethnic cleansing in what came to be Serb- and Croat-controlled areas. Although some distance behind the front line, the town well illustrates the dynamics of ethnic cleansing. The 1992 population was about 120,000, roughly a third of which was Serb and Croat in similar numbers. Within months, all but 3,000 Serbs and 3,000 Croats had fled and 70,000 Muslims had flooded into the town (Cockburn 1998 p. 192). The centre began in early 1993 to combine medical and psycho-social therapy for women traumatized by the war, especially the experience of rape (ibid. p. 175). At this stage there was no government provision for rape victims and even to discuss the issue was very difficult, partly due to the stigma attached to victims, in spite of the widespread use of rape as a weapon of war, especially by Serb forces (ibid.).

Nearly all the refugees were Muslim, but the staff had three Bosnian Serbs, three Bosnian Croats and a Slovenian. However, as Cockburn emphasizes, 'these distinctions felt new and distasteful to them. They simplified belonging beyond anything they recognised' (p. 192). For example, one Catholic Slovenian woman had not realized her partner was 'Croatian' until they registered their marriage, in spite of seven years of living together. Cockburn states that 'religion was perhaps more meaningful' as a source of identificiation, although she also notes the low rate of observance among those interviewed: only two out of 18 claimed to be practising (ibid.). She comments:

> Because the Yugoslav state had discouraged religion and disadvantaged those who practised it, the present generation of women in Medica mainly had parents who had been non-religious, members of the officially atheist Communist Party. But they often mentioned grandmothers who had been religious, whose beliefs and practices they had been intrigued by and had respected. Probably most women in Medica in principle welcomed the re-enfranchisement of religions in the region. But for these women personally, being 'Muslim' was 'only' a matter of family and community culture. They were anxious that religion 'know its place', not a matter for the state or party politics but one of individual spirituality. (p. 193)

In terms of the debate developing through this book about the social location of religion, it might be argued that 'family' and 'community' already exceeds the scope of 'individual spirituality'. But the key point is that private and community spheres rather than state or political society are seen as the legitimate sites of religious identification and activity, although this evidence suggests practice is more a matter of 'belonging without believing' than 'believing without belonging'.

Through the story of Rada, ethnically a Bosnian Serb but an atheist who had always identified as 'Yugoslav, nationally undeclared', Cockburn also shows how the absence in public celebratory space created by the disappearance of Yugoslav civil religion came to be filled with rediscovered religion:

> All around her in Zenica, neighbours and friends who were unresponsive to the interpellation of the new nationalisms were nevertheless tending to fill the gap left by a vanished

Yugoslavia with revived religious identities. Catholics were discovering Christian culture, celebrating Christmas and Easter. Muslims were showing renewed enthusiasm for the fast of Ramadan and festivals such as Bajram [the Turkish for *Eid ul Adha*, the 'feast of the sacrifice' at the end of Ramadan]. 'They take their children to the mosque. Why don't I take mine to the Orthodox church? I feel guilty about the empty space I'm bringing my children up in' she said. 'In the old days, in Yugoslavia, we used to celebrate unifying socialist holidays: New Year was the biggest. And May Day. Now I miss the cultural celebrations and I try to make a cake, light a candle. But somehow it's only improvization.' (p. 218)

However, even the religious festivities of one tradition can sometimes become a source of bonding across confessional barriers at a social level. For example in 1995 the workers at the project decided to celebrate Christmas – they had previously only celebrated Bajram. As part of the celebrations, each of the 'Christians' there was given a present. Cockburn presents the views of two women, the first described as a practising Muslim, narrating and reflecting on this event:

Of course we would invite the refugees too. We weren't sure if they could accept the idea of celebrating a Christian holiday. Most of them at that time had just been expelled from Srebrenica. But they did come and we celebrated together and it was very very positive. …

I think it was a sign Medica grew up, that we really understood what we've been fighting for. (p. 199)

Sharing in Christmas celebrations in a context where society had been pulled apart along religiously demarcated lines, where many women had felt betrayed by Christian friends and neighbours and had been abused and displaced by soldiers bearing Christian symbols, served as a powerful sign of the refusal of nationalist logics. By de-instrumentalizing an identity that has become so profoundly instrumentalized, a simple celebration and the giving of gifts across religious boundaries becomes a subversive act. It also helped to re-create in a new setting the multi-confessional social life that had existed in Bosnian villages before the war (Bringa 1995 p. 198). We shall see this largely unselfconscious reconciling act become a conscious strategy for NGOs seeking deliberately to build relationships across religious boundaries.

Medica also illustrates the capacity of women's organizations to build relationships across 'entity' barriers (that is, the border between the Muslim-Croat Federation and Republika Srpska). This in turn will indicate some of the weaknesses of the international community's civil society building initiatives, a context that also shapes the work of religious and religion-oriented NGOs. Cockburn (1998) explains the Medica initiative:

In May 1996 a group from Medica (facilitated and accompanied by feminists from Zagreb [Croatia] and Belgrade [Serbia]) went north into the 'Bosnian Serb Entity' (the Republika Srpska) for an exploratory meeting with Duga, a women's group in Banja Luka. Duga was known to be non-nationalist, even though not feminist and Medica believed they might be suitable partners in re-establishing common ground, despite the total non-cooperation of the authorities of the Entity with the reminder of the Bosnian state. (p. 197)

Contact was established and relationships across entity and 'ethnic' boundaries have developed, often facilitated by the international network of women's organizations (Helms 1999; Cockburn 1998). They have, for example, given women the opportunity to rebuild relationships with families from which they had been separated by war, now living in the other entity (Cockburn 1998 pp. 220–21). The fact that Medica's cooperation here was with Duga, a non- or not explicitly feminist group working mostly with Serb women, exposes a problem with the international community's civil-society-building-policies. This is because such women's groups do not share the discourses of civil society, multi-ethnicity, secularism and feminism that most sponsors require before they will fund groups:

> International agencies such as USAID, the European Union, OSCE and their implementing partners (vitrually the only sources of funding for local initiatives) fund and support organizations whose proposals demonstrate a commitment to multi-ethnic and cross-entity cooperation, to the establishment of secular, democratic structures and to respect for the human rights and members of all ethnic/religious groups in Bosnia. And in some cases, donors also look for commitment to feminist goals, as defined by the donor agencies. (Helms 1999 p. 4)

While this approach sounds fine in theory, as an ethical sponsoring policy it fails in practice because it does not engage with the lifeworld in which local groups are constructed. The result is a well-funded sector of civil society with shallow roots in local communities and a less overtly politically correct sector deprived of funds. Two recent studies have examined both sides of this problem (Helms 1999, Chandler 1998).

David Chandler (1998) examines the OSCE's civil-society-building strategy in the context of the UN's dual approach to 'peace-building': '"top-down" international regulation of elections, institutional development and economic management, accompanied by "bottom-up" assistance to develop a democratic political culture through civil society building' (p. 78). The idea is to support any initiative that seeks to build multi-ethnic or cross-entity cooperation, in the hope that such organizations will generate political voices critical of the dominant nationalist parties. As Chandler indicates, these groups have begun to voice such opposition, for example two NGOs in Banja Luka who in 1997 raised the politically sensitive issue of the return of refugees (p. 85). However, participation in many internationally sponsored NGOs remains confined to a small group of people, as Adrien Marti, the OSCE's Coordinator for Political Party Development explains: 'The Citizen's Alternative Parliament, the Shadow Government and the coalition for return are basically the same 20 people when you scratch the surface. There is no depth to this' (in Chandler 1998 p. 87). Chandler's interviews with OSCE officials suggest that most NGO activists are middle-class urban intellectuals – those already conversant with the discourse of the international community – who have little influence beyond their circle. Moreover, the problem with funding such groups is that it may actually reduce their articulation with the broader society:

> The unintended consequence of creating civil society NGOs which are reliant on external support has been that they are never forced to build their own base of popular support or

to take on the arguments or political programmes of the nationalists. ... the reliance on external funders can tend to fragment society rather than create a pluralistic exchange of political opinions. (p. 89)

The other side of the effects of the international community's policies is shown by Helms's study of Muslim women's groups. Given the radically divisive nature of the war, in terms of both gender and religious identity, organization by gender and religious heritage is often the most effective, indeed, the only way to support many women, to begin to rebuild their trust and confidence. However, 'the emphasis which these women's NGOs place on affirming Bošnjak and Muslim identity means that Western funding agencies do not see them as encouraging multi-ethnicity in Bosnia – indeed they are often referred to as nationalist – and therefore do not fund them' (Helms 1999 p. 5). Such groups, whether they have an explicit religious basis or purpose or not, provide vital support to women who are often isolated; as a result of war deaths and emigration, a disproportionate number of the adult population of Bosnia is now female, more among refugees.

Such groups are more likely to articulate their desire for tolerance in terms of their desire for 'a society in which Muslims are free to lead an Islamic life and one with strong morality and family values' (ibid. p. 6). They are likely to be critical of feminist discourse, because, as elsewhere in post-Communist Europe (Ramet 1999 pp. 259–62), it is associated with a discredited and imposed Communist ideology and with an image of 'man-hating, anti-family militant Western women' (Helms 1999 p. 7). Yet as their confidence builds, such groups have begun to reach out to other women's groups and – through contact with groups like Medica – to rethink their relationship with feminism. Thus, in spite of a lack of international support:

[S]ome women's groups ... have begun to combine their affirmation of Bošnjak-hood (*Bošnjaštvo*) with efforts to network with women's NGOs in Serb and Croat areas. And, despite their continued relative isolation from western-sponsored initiatives, these same groups have begun to discuss ideas of women's rights and even feminism without first rejecting them out of hand, weighing these ideas to see which aspects might be applied to Bosnian society. (p. 8)

Ironically, while the international community has been discriminating in its funding of civil society, it has been largely indiscriminate in its funding of political society (Campbell 1998). Thus 'free speech' was the criterion for America's 'more than US$5 million in aid' to fund political parties in the run-up to the 1996 elections, regardless of their support for a multi-ethnic Bosnia. In the same campaign the OSCE even gave a quarter of a million US$ to the Serb Unity Party led by the 'warlord' Raznatović, alias 'Arkan', named by the United States as a war criminal (ibid. p. 223). At first, this inconsistency seems perversely contradictory – requiring a higher standard of democratic discourse from grass-roots organizations than from political parties. But it is the result of the fact that the nationalist parties retain the trust of the majority of the electorate – a fact underscored by the results of the 2000 election (Strauss 2000) – and that the OSCE does not want to appear partisan in its sponsorship of political society. Therefore, the only way the international community feels that it can break the stranglehold of the nationalist parties is by encouraging alternative voices in civil society; yet it does so in such a way that may in fact be contributing of the fragmentation of civil society.

It is in this complicated context, with respect both to religious identity and the conditions of civil society, that religiously based and religion-oriented NGOs must operate. We shall consider three examples of such organizations, drawing on interviews conducted by the author in Sarajevo and Banja Luka in March 2000. The first, *Oci u Oci Interreligijska Sluzba* (Face-to-Face Inter-faith Service), based in Sarajevo, is led by the Franciscan (Catholic) Ivo Markovic and aims to promote dialogue among religious leaders, but it is also involved in more grass-roots work, including supporting local NGOs. Thus they have succeeded in setting up inter-faith seminars between trainees at the main Muslim, Orthodox and Catholic training colleges which it is hoped will affect the attitudes of a new generation of religious leaders.

They have established an inter-faith choir, Pontanima, which sings religious music from the different religious traditions of Bosnia. It has toured internationally and released a CD and is seen as a contribution to changing the perception of relationships between religions, both within Bosnia and internationally. It has also transformed relationships within the group, helping to form friendships across confessional boundaries; in this sense it is seen as a contribution to the 'de-instrumentalization' of religion in Bosnia. As an example of supporting another NGO, they helped a small organization called 'Protector', which collects testimony from people helped by someone from another religious group during the war, to publish a book of such stories. They also supported the publication of a 'religious glossary' (1999) explaining key concepts and practices from each of the four historic religions of Bosnia – Orthodox, Muslim, Catholic and Jewish. In its preface it includes a 'statement of shared moral commitment' from 1997 made by the leaders of each of these traditions and which 'Face-to-Face' had helped to mediate. The statement laments the 'visibly slow and inefficient implementation of the Dayton Accords as they pertain to civil society' and goes on to condemn:

- Acts of hatred based on ethnicity or religious differences. We express our especial concern at the burning of houses, the desecration of religious buildings and the destruction of graveyards;
- The obstruction of the free right to return;
- Acts of revenge;
- The abuse of the media with the aim of spreading hatred. (p. 7)

While the religious establishments, especially in the Serb and Muslim cases, remain closely associated with the nationalist parties, such statements witness to the gradual differentiation of religion from the political sphere.

The second organization, Ibrahim/Abraham, was founded in Sarajevo in March 1998 by Cristof Ziemar, an East German Lutheran who had been involved in the mobilization of the Churches in the peace movement there in the 1980s. Their office is in a back street on one of the precipitously steep hillsides overlooking Sarajevo. Ziemar sought the cooperation of local Christians, Jews and Muslims in Sarajevo, with a view to establishing dialogue to promote understanding of their respective faiths. For the first year the project focused on establishing a core group who met weekly to study and discuss aspects of each tradition and to celebrate one another's major festivals. In the second year they attempted a couple of activities that were to prove controversial. One was to lead a mixed-faith group to clean up the Orthodox cemetery in Sarajevo, which had fallen into a state of disrepair. While participants felt that the action was worthwhile, relatives and colleagues were less convinced. Another venture involved taking a mixed group to Germany, including to a Christian meeting, which had made the four Muslims in the group feel uneasy because of being so heavily outnumbered. Some mutual understanding seems to have been achieved by drawing a parallel between the Muslim situation on this trip and the situation of Christians in Sarajevo – both heavily outnumbered.

In spite of these difficulties, the group has held together and has even grown – with approximately fifty members and a regular monthly meeting. Possibly as a result of the German experience they have also established a series of multi-faith 'seminars' in three locations within the republic with a dominant majority population (a common situation, as a result of ethnic cleansing), different in each case. In all cases, 'the religious community which is in the position of [the] majority is not so open for dialogue'. People from each religious community in the three locations were brought together by a local coordinator. The first seminar in each series involved sharing perceptions of the current situation and its problems in a structured setting, the second involved participants form outside presenting their perspectives. A final seminar planned to bring together all three groups in Sarajevo.

The experience of Ibrahim illustrates some of the problems and possibilities of inter-faith work in Bosnia. Ziemar spoke of the incredulity of other NGOs at Ibrahim's activities: 'mostly people said, "oh, please, if you want to do something for ... living together in this country ... go far away from the religious communities and from religion". 'However, the result of the seminars and the development of the membership had changed the minds of some, turning them from incredulity to curiosity to approval: 'Then they said it is very good ... it is normal for our country and such things'. But trust hangs by slender threads, as the cemetery and Germany trip illustrate; there have also been problems with leadership. But the possibility of building relationships at this level is an important one given the future that Ziemar predicts, given his experience of the dramatic loss of confidence in the East German of the early 1990s:

> It's difficult for the religious communities, because in the Tito era they were a little suppressed. ... Then after this there came new opportunities and in the war they [have] more influence and power. ... And now they will lose this power and so, then they must find a way in civil society. ... [A]ll the religious communities have in this time of power dangerous dreams, dreams about Orthodox state or Islamic state or such things, [but] they must change these dreams that religion can determine the whole culture of a society and this is the way now, to find a way without big influence and power, but to bring to society the religious point of view.

The final organization that we shall consider has a religious foundation, but like many such NGOs its activities are focused on reconstruction and development work.

International Orthodox Christian Charities (IOCC) was founded in Baltimore, Maryland in 1992 as the official humanitarian organization of the Orthodox Christians in the United States and Canada. It began relief work at the invitation of the local Serbian Orthodox Church in 1992, when it began needs-based donations of food and hygiene parcels to people regardless of religious or ethnic affiliation. After the signing of the Dayton agreement, along with many other international NGOs, it established a centre in Banja Luka, where I interviewed its director, Mark Onahain, a Syrian Orthodox Christian.

Since 1995 IOCC have been involved in food distribution, working closely with the Muslim charity Mehemed and helping returning refugees to find housing and a livelihood, for example by providing seed and agricultural equipment. They have also been involved in supporting local NGO activity, for example by organizing an NGO fair in Banja Luka and holding news conferences to disseminate information to the local media, 'because the public here don't know much about what an NGO is'. They have been active in initiatives trying to overcome some of the problems of refugee return. These include refugee exchanges, whereby for example a group of Serb refugees from the Federation occupying former Muslim homes in RS would return to the Federation to homes vacated by Muslim refugees returning to RS and so on. They have also been working closely with NGOs in other areas and countries in an attempt to coordinate these efforts, for example with the Serb Democratic Forum, which is active in Croatia.

Links with the local Orthodox Churches in the former Yugoslavia have varied: in RS their non-partisan approach has sometimes caused problems where local churches have expected to benefit from their help as a matter of priority. They have worked closely with the Circle of Serbian sisters, a charity run by Orthodox nuns, and in Serbia close cooperation with the Orthodox Church has been vital to their operations: '[we] wouldn't be able to import any goods from abroad for distribution if we didn't have permission from the local church'. The IOCC illustrates the importance of international philanthropy sponsored by religious organizations in Bosnia. By practical cooperation with other religious and non-religiously based NGOs and by their practical non-partisan support they can indirectly help to break down prejudices.

7. Conclusion

What does Bosnia tell us about the relationship between religion, civil society and the public sphere? First, there are some factors common to post-Communist societies and thus similar to the Polish case we considered in Chapter 7. The distrust of official authority, the necessary reliance on an illegal economy and on family networks all make the establishment of an open, legally protected civil society difficult, and the fear and suspicion of other religious and ethnic groups created by the war have greatly exacerbated these factors. In Chapter 2 and then expanded in Chapter 5, we identified religion as involved in the transition from Communism in CEE in four ways. These were: by providing space for opposition groups to meet; by providing symbols and discourse which contributed to the formation of social solidarity; by providing spatial and historical connections which transcended those of the Communist regimes; and by their contribution to intellectual discourse. It may be argued that each of these dimensions was also present in the war in Bosnia, though in different forms, and hence provides a useful way to summarize our findings in this chapter.

Rather than providing a space in which opposition movements could organize, churches and mosques became the battlegrounds for cultural warfare. But they also became, certainly in the case of mosques, spaces for organization of resistance and community support. Rather than forging social solidarity across society, religious mobilization in multi-faith Bosnia tended to reinforce social divisions. Yet the networks formed within religious communities may in the postwar situation enable the reconstruction of community relations across ethnic divisions, for example in the case of religion-based women's NGOs establishing connections with Serb and Croat NGOs (Helms 1999).

As in Poland, religious organizations and discourse provided connections with the world beyond the conflict. This is perhaps especially true for Muslims, who in the face of the arms embargo looked to other Muslim nations for support in a largely unprecedented way. This has led to a strange mixture in postwar Bosnia, with the influence of radical Islamist groups from the Middle East jostling uneasily alongside Ottoman-originating Bosnian Islam institutionalized under Communism and attempting to re-present itself for closer European integration. This tension is manifest in disputes over Islamic dress and the continued presence of foreign *mujahaddin* in certain villages. Again, the consequences for civil society are complex. Divisions between religio-ethnic groups are reinforced by such external identifications, but at the same time such developments pluralize Bosnian Muslim identity, contributing to the development of diversity in civil society.

Religious discourse has also contributed to intellectual responses to the fall of Communism, the war and postwar reconstruction, again, both negatively and positively. Intellectuals in the Serbian Academy and Serbian theologians who provided a religious justification for the cult of Serbian martyrdom deepened religio-ethnic cleavages, while on the positive side intellectuals have also sought to legitimize a multicultural Bosnia by drawing on Ottoman traditions of toleration (Izetbegovic 1984; and Mahmutcehajic 2000).

These four dimensions of religious functioning in societies undergoing transformation in the post-Communist period can help us to compare the role of religion in otherwise quite different societies. In the cases of Bosnia and Poland, each demonstrates the functionalization of religion in modern social systems, but also suggests different problems and limitations on potential development. For all religious groups in Bosnia, the war has served to heighten religious identity, but in a problematic association with nationalism that presents an enormous challenge to the religious communities in the reconstruction process. The extensive role of the religious organizations in the NGO sector, in practical reconstruction as well as inter-faith mediation, suggests an alternative form of functionalization arising in part from the de-instrumentalization of religion. Here religion becomes a space of shared celebration and cooperation, as well as the non-partisan role of religious philanthropy. The possibility for groups organized on the basis of religious identity to reach out to other symmetrically constructed groups provides another source of hope and a way of rebuilding on the heritage of a multi-faith Bosnia (Bringa 1995). At the same time it demonstrates the shortcomings of international policies which, as in Habermas, underestimate the role of religious groups that can contribute to the communicative rationalizion of the lifeworld. We shall see further challenges to such underestimation in the next chapter on Egypt.

Notes

1 Ramet refers to the Serbian-Croatian war (1991–2) and the war in Bosnia (1992–5) in which Bosnian Serbs were supported by the FRY (Federal Republic of Yugoslavia – that is, Serbia) as 'The Serbian Insurrectionary War'. This is because she regards both as the result of Serbian expansionism, rather than seeing the war in Bosnia as a separate, civil war. As we shall see, there is considerable evidence to support this interpretation.

2 In Albania, Muslims form a simple majority (Clayer 1997). The population figures given here are from the 1991 census; considerable displacements (and losses) have subsequently occurred.

3 One example of 'Balkanist' stereotyping – attributing essential animosities to people living in the Balkans – comes from US Secretary of State Lawrence Eagleburger, who asserted shortly after Dutch UN 'peace-keepers' stood by and watched Bosnian Serbs take UN-designated 'safe area' Srebrenica that 'They have been killing each other with certain amount of glee in that part of the world for some time now' (in Sells 1996 p. 124).

4 The Bosnian Orthodox Church appears to have all but disappeared by this stage (Malcolm 1995).

5 Muslims had good reason to believe that their lack of status as a nation was indeed a cause of Bosnia's economic stagnation in Yugoslavia's politically dominated economy: Bosnia's average national income dropped from 20 per cent below the Yugoslav average in 1947 to 38 per cent below in 1967.

6 The figures are 43.8 per cent Muslim, 31.5 per cent Serb, 17.3 per cent Croat, 7 per cent 'Yugoslav' in 1991 (Ramet 1999 p. 118).

7 For example, at the end of May 1992 Britain and France were still arguing against imposing sanctions on Serbia, saying that they wanted to give Milosevič 'a further opportunity to halt the violence in Bosnia' (in Malcolm 1996 p. 242).

8 Milosevič had welcomed the arms embargo which had been negotiated by Lord Carrington and imposed by the UN on the whole of Yugoslavia, because this meant that Serbia could continue to supply federal and Bosnian Serb positions in Bosnia while Bosnian Muslims had a very small munitions industry.

9 It is estimated that in Sept. 1992 Bosnian government forces had 2 armoured personnel carriers (ACPs), 2 tanks and no aircraft; Serb forces in Bosnia had 200 APCs, 300 tanks and 40 aircraft (malcom 1996 p. 243).

10 On 6th August 1992 Western television first showed pictures of the Omarska and Trnopolje camps, near Banja Luka (Sells 1996 p. 11).

11 Some information in this section comes from interviews and information gathered in Sarajevo, Zenica and Banja Luka in March 2000. My thanks to the British Academy for funding to undertake this research trip and to Emina Hadzhalilovic for translating for me.

Chapter 9

After Nasser

The Islamization of Civil Society and the Public Sphere in Egypt

1. Introduction: Civil Society in Cross-Cultural Perspective

Our insurance system is American and Islamic at the same time ... It's American because we have instituted a payment system for those who suffer from terminal illnesses, such as cancer. It is Islamic because we never cut off the payments, no matter what happens. We keep paying until the patients are either cured or dead. (The scheme's unnamed architect, in Abdo 2000 p. 18)

As long as I am president, religion and state will remain separate. (Hosni Mubarak, interview in *Der Spiegel*, April 1994; in ibid. p. 78)

To take power, no. We are ready to share power. (Essam El-Eryan, Muslim Brother, personal interview,[1] March 2001)

Our first quotation above illustrates the impossibility of keeping cultures and systems compartmentalized in a globalized environment. It also illustrates the role of religion as a moral-practical challenge to the dominant logics of global systems. In this case Islamic morality is used to challenge the economic imperative to offer insurance products at the lowest premium in a competitive health insurance market (the American model), with the side-effect or 'residual problem' that liability is limited. It also illustrates the social and cultural construction of markets, for if a product is socially or culturally unacceptable then it won't sell, no matter how 'efficient' it is; although, of course, society and culture themselves also change in response to systemic influences.

This example suggests that while global systems and ideas are operational in Egypt, care must be taken in discerning the terms of their appropriation. Thus, in moving from Europe to the Middle East and to a Muslim majority society, we are taking our concepts of civil society and the public sphere into new territory and need to proceed with care. With regard to Islam, it was argued in Chapter 3 (against Gellner) that while Islam and Christianity clearly have important differences, there is nothing intrinsic to Islam that renders it necessarily resistant to secularization, incompatible with civil society or otherwise immune to the effects of modernization. Furthermore, with regard to using the concept of civil society in non-Western cultural contexts, we have argued that this can be justified in theory on the grounds of the global penetration of systems and interpenetration of cultures, and the existing use of the concept in non-Western contexts. It may then be justified in practice if used with sensitivity to the different cultural forms that might perform the core tasks of normative civil society (that is, building trust, diversity, openness to diversity and public expression of diversity). Here we shall proceed on this basis.

Our differentiation of empirical and normative civil society means that civil society can be decoupled from the Western liberal project and used as a tool of comparative analysis. Although, like all concepts, it frames the world in a particular way, such framing can be justified, again by arguments like those developed in the previous paragraph. However, it was also argued in Chapter 5 that civil society can legitimately be used as a tool of normative engagement. As Galston (1991) argues, liberalism has reason to engage in cross-cultural argument once it moves from a purely juridical self-conception to offer 'an account of [the] goods and virtues that enable it to oppose the extremes of unfettered individual choice and unchecked state coercion' (pp. 258–9). Given the extent of state coercion in Egypt, this is an argument that needs to be made there (Amnesty International 2001). Binder's argument in *Islamic Liberalism* is of particular relevance here. He contends both that liberalism's principles logically require it to engage in a Middle Eastern context; and that the 'social and intellectual pre-requisites [for political liberalism] already exist in some parts of the Islamic Middle East, including Egypt, (1988 p. 2). There have been substantial developments in Egypt's civil society since Binder wrote, and part of our task in this chapter will be to assess whether they have been in a direction that favours or undermines political liberalism.

Part of the concern expressed by Western scholars about using the term 'civil society' to describe developments in Egypt is that whereas 'civil society … in its liberal conception … is not merely a sphere outside government but rather one endowed with a legally mandated autonomy, involving legal rights and protections backed by the law-state', such legal protection is largely absent in Egypt (Wickham 1997 p. 507). As we have seen in the case of Poland, the necessarily illegal character of parallel society in an authoritarian state distorts its development, building culture and habits that do not adapt well to a democratic environment. There is also evidence in Egypt, though in a different form, of the praetorian syndrome. We have already seen in Chapter 1 that the role of Islam in Egyptian state education gives lie to Mubarak's claim above to sustain a religion/state division, but it is not only at a discursive level that the state seeks to coopt religion.

Through the 1990s the Mubarak regime seized control of thousands of private mosques, requiring preachers to conform to government standards. It also transferred powers of censorship to al-Azhar, mirroring developments in broadcasting regulations in post-Communist Poland (Abdo 2000 p. 66). As in post-Communist Bosnia, Islam in Egypt has become highly instrumentalized, but unlike Bosnia there is no sign of demobilization. However, there are signs that in spite of a repressive state some Islamic movements are developing an Islamic identity as a source of political mobilization in an inclusive direction: the election of Muslim Brothers to the leadership of professional associations (for example the pharmacists), while drawing a substantial proportion of the Coptic Christian vote, is one sign of this, (ibid. p. 100). El-Eryan's proposal for power-sharing (the third quotation at the start of the chapter) is another. Indeed, as the next section will argue, such changes would seem to signal a new stage in the development of Islamic movements in Egypt.

2. Islamic Movements in Egypt: a Changing Picture

We begin by considering the comments of three scholars who have recently conducted extensive fieldwork in Egypt:

[i] Nearly everything I had read before coming to Egypt in 1993 described the Islamic revival as a movement reserved for the poor. The common explanation in press accounts and academic circles for Egypt's return to its Islamic identity had become a cliché: After experimenting with socialism, Arab nationalism and capitalism under successive leaders … a vast majority of Egyptians were left poverty stricken and embittered towards the West. The failures of Western-oriented ideologies and economic development, went the argument, fueled a rejectionist movement – hence, the nostalgic search for Islamic 'roots'.

But as I watched the men dressed in imitation Pierre Cardin sweaters and fine starched cotton suits sprawled out along the green mats in the street, that theory rang false. …

In place of the militant threat, a new type of Islamic revival, untested in the casbah of Algiers, the mountains of Afghanistan and the back alleys of Tehran, has quietly taken shape and poses a far more significant challenge to Western interests in the Middle East. Egypt's 'Popular Islam', a grass-roots movement emerging from the streets, aims to transform the social structure of Islam from the bottom up, creating an Islamic order. (Abdo 2000 p. 3)

[ii] One might dispute the claim that the community the Islamists are creating within the [professional] associations is democratic, at least in the liberal sense of the term. The model which inspires them might be better described as a political community in which the ruler and the ruled are united by faith and adherence to Islamic law. The key point is that intermediary associations registered, and in some cases initiated by the state have become the sites of political innovation, perhaps the equivalent of the parallel polis [city] which emerged under Communism in Central and Eastern Europe to contest official norms and practices well before the collapse of authoritarian rule.

The rise of the Islamic Trend[2] in several of Egypt's professional associations is part of a broader process of evolutionary change. By penetrating official intermediary institutions and creating new ones, the Muslim Brothers and affiliated groups have initiated a gradual appropriation of … public space from the bottom up. While the violent acts of armed Islamists have commanded greater media attention, it is the incremental, legal activities of Islamists which have had the greatest impact in reshaping public life. (Wickham 1997 pp. 130–31).

[iii] If we are to make sense of these developments within the institutional context of Egyptian society, we cannot dismiss religious concerns as benighted survivals of earlier social stages, or merely 'inflammations' symptomatic of social pathology and political strife. Instead, we must see them as perennial questions which persist in an active manner, adapting and reproducing themselves within and between generations through increasingly complex interactions with institutions and communications media whose own advent was supposed to reduce rather than increase the influence of religious ideas in society. (Starrett 1998 p. 91)

These three quotations from recent accounts of the growth of the Islamic movements in Egypt reflect a growing consensus – at least among scholars who have conducted fieldwork in Egypt since the mid-1980s – that such movements are developing in new and unanticipated ways.[3] Indeed, their penetration of society is such that it is questionable whether it is appropriate to call them 'movements' at all, as if they were somehow divorced from the 'mainstream' of society. Rather, as Starrett argues, 'the Trend has moved beyond the level of a movement to become one of the most important contexts in which everyday life is lived' (p. 192). Furthermore, as Abdo's quotation clearly states, they have evolved in a manner unanticipated by standard Western models of Islamic revival movements. In particular, mainstream Islamic movements in Egypt have rejected the violent revolutionary path that would seek to replace the government from the 'top down' and have opted for transformation from the 'bottom up'.

Starrett spells out the methodological implications of Abdo's rejection of the standard psycho-social reductionist model, a model which 'explains' revivalism in terms of a psychological need (for consolation, certainty and the like) that in turn reflects economic disappointment and social dislocation. Rather, the new turn of events calls for closer scrutiny of the processes of cultural reproduction and adaptation that enables religious tradition to perform these new roles, as we argued in Chapters 1 and 2. The standard model also postulates that energies that 'should' be channelled politically find such channels blocked and so are diverted into religious channels 'inappropriate' to contain and direct them, by those insufficiently 'modern' and educated to know better. The popularity of such movements among the wealthy of Zamalek – the upmarket part of Cairo where Abdo observed the praying designer sweaters – calls for a reconsideration of the assumptions underlying this standard account.

Relevant to these normative considerations is Wickham's query about the democratic credentials of Islamic groups in the running of professional associations, which she relates to the model of Islamic governance that inspires them – the idea of an Islamic state. For alongside the Islamic parallel society of hospitals, schools, training centres, newspapers, banks, saving schemes, businesses and fashion there is also a growing industry of state-licensed but, arguably, society-driven, religious censorship. The well-publicized case of Abu Zaid, Assistant Professor in Islamic and Arabic studies at Cairo University until 1995, illustrates this point and will be considered below.

However, first it is crucial to consider another element often missing from psychological accounts of socio-political religious revivalism: the political context. Therefore the next sections summarize Egypt's history of post-Independence politics.

3. The Political Context of Islamization in Egypt

Like other countries in the Middle East, the postwar, post-Independence (1952) period of Egyptian history saw a secular, Arab nationalist government with socialist leanings. Nasser emphasized pan-Arab unity, and a United Arab Republic (UAR) with Syria and Yemen was formed, although Syria pulled out in 1961. One of the groups that supported Nasser in the struggle for Independence was the Muslim Brotherhood. Founded by Hasan al-Banna in 1928, this group was the first in the modern period to see the Islamic tradition as the source of a holistic vision of a modern Islamic social and political order. However, having helped Nasser consolidate his power, they were brutally suppressed (Roussillon 1998), leading many to flee into exile, while others were imprisoned or executed. Groups today that reject the legitimacy of the modern state often trace their roots to the prison writing of Sayyid Qutb, one of the Brothers executed by Nasser after an attempt on his life was made in 1965.

During the cold war, Nasser played a leading role in the Non-Aligned Movement, seeking to create a third force in world politics independent of both the Soviet Union and America. However, he became increasingly dependent on foreign aid, first from America and then from the Soviet Union. Indeed, by the mid-1960s it was clear that the Egyptian economy under Nasser was in serious trouble. At the same time, political tensions in the region were increasing: Arab nations bordering Israel had never accepted its legitimacy since its formation in 1948 and tensions were mounting on the Syrian-Israeli border. Arguably seeking a distraction from domestic troubles, Nasser asked the United Nations force to leave the Sinai and closed the straits of Tiran, Israel's only outlet into the Red Sea. Soon after, Jordan and Iraq signed a defence pact with the UAR. In response, on 5 June 1967 Israel attacked, with devastating results: 'in just six days [they] destroyed the Egyptian air force, captured the Sinai and closed the Suez canal, as well as taking the Golan Heights from Syria and the West Bank from Jordan' (Wayne and Simonis 1994 p. 23).

This was a severe psychological blow to Arabs across the region and precipitated a crisis in Arab nationalism. However, this was perceived by some as an opportunity to rethink the role of the Arab world in the international order, although the Islamist response to this crisis was to remain muted until the death of Nasser in 1970. Fortunes then changed, as Anwar al-Sadat (in power 1970–81) initially actively promoted an Islamic movement, although the Muslim Brotherhood remained illegal (Roussillon 1998 p. 370). This was because although Sadat wished to use religion to support the state, he had no wish for it to foster an independent political opposition. Sadat set up Islamic youth camps at universities and supported Islamist students in their takeover of students' unions in 1976, in an attempt to counterbalance the perceived threat of left-wing groups. He also opened debate on the issue of the Islamization of legislation, introducing the law on apostasy – which was to be invoked against the writer Abu-Zaid – in 1977.

However, Sadat's conciliatory approach to Israel and especially his signature of the Camp David Peace Accords (1979), led him to lose popularity with the Islamic movement and indeed made Egypt a pariah in the Arab world (Roussillon 1998 p. 364). Sadat's attempts to pacify the Islamic movement he had promoted – including promoting *sharia* from *one* to *the principal* source of legislation (1980) failed. On 5 September 1981, in response to a sense that he was losing control, Sadat set about arresting representatives of just about every source of possible opposition – Islamists, Communists, intellectuals, left- and right-wing, civilians and mullahs – on

the charge of plotting to overthrow him. Before the end of the month he was dead –
assassinated by army officers who were also members of al-Jihad, a radical Islamist
organization.

However, in spite of some Islamization measures under Sadat, it was only under
Mubarak (1981–) that an Islamist agenda has become part of the political
mainstream (Roussillon 1998). Mubarak's policy has been to try to accommodate
moderate Islamists – defined by their opposition to violent means of achieving the
Islamization of society and their willingness to partake in the political process – and
to violently suppress Islamic extremists – those who advocate violent means of
achieving change. One means of incorporating the former has been to permit the
Muslim Brotherhood to participate in politics while technically remaining illegal –
by forming informal alliances with legitimate political parties.

Thus the Muslim Brotherhood formed alliances with the Wafd in 1984 and the
Labour Party in 1987. Indeed, they staged a virtual takeover of the Labour Party, thus
gaining access to its newspaper and enabling the election of several leaders of the
still-illegal organization. The other aspect of the policy was to try to clamp down
hard on militants, a policy that intensified during the 1990s. However, the ability of
the security forces to discriminate between moderate and militant Islamists has
proved questionable, to say the least (Boyle and Sheen 1997 pp. 26–7; Starrett 1998
191–219). Furthermore, from the mid-1990s the government realized that it was
losing ground to moderate Islamists and also tried to clamp down on the Muslim
Brotherhood's presence in the professional associations (Gerges 1999) (which we
shall examine further below), attacking their headquarters and arresting leading
members, including independent MPs, thus preventing their participation in
elections in the autumn of 1995.

On 22 January 1995 Essam el-Eryan was one of those arrested. A student activist
in the 1970s, a lawyer and a doctor, el-Eryan had long been a thorn in the side of the
regime, critical of the government and able to back his counter-claim 'Islam is the
solution' (the slogan of the Muslim Brotherhood) with the proven effectiveness of his
work in student and then professional associations (Abdo 2000 pp. 71–6). At the time
of his arrest he was deputy secretary general of the Medical Association and in 1992
had demonstrated to a world audience the effectiveness of the Association in
responding to the needs of victims of the earthquake in Sayyeda Zeinab, when he
appeared regularly on BBC broadcasts. In contrast, government services had proved
slow and inefficient in their response, a public relations disaster the government was
unable to tolerate. So: 'Troops marched into Sayyeda Zeinab and razed the tents
constructed by the doctors of the Muslim Brotherhood' (ibid. p. 97). The 'crimes' for
which Eryan was convicted were: organizing a group, holding gatherings and
disseminating leaflets critical of the government. The holding of meetings without
government permission is forbidden in Egypt (Singerman 1995). What Eryan was
doing was organizing a pressure group or political party; but the Muslim Brotherhood
is forbidden registration as such. The potential for government forces to abuse their
power is exacerbated by the continuation of the Emergency Law. This was brought
into effect in the aftermath of Sadat's assassination. It 'allows for certain press
restrictions, the banning of public political gatherings and the detention without

charge of people suspected of certain categories of crime, including subversion and political violence' (Starrett 1998 p. 191). The Human rights abuses by the military and police, particularly severe in 1993, continued through the 1990s, as did large numbers of deaths, of both civilians and military (Middle East Watch 1992; Amnesty International 1992, Egyptian Organization for Human Rights 1997), detention without trial and extraction of 'confessions' by torture (Amnesty International 2001).

Such developments indicate the central role of the authoritarian state in all aspects of Egyptian life. However, what is not widely realized because of the state's interest in portraying itself to supportive Western governments as secular, is its role in the Islamization of political discourse. In Chapter 1 we have already seen how the state education system has played a role in this, but while central to the process this is not the only way in which this happens. The Egyptian state's policy on religion in public life is confusing and probably confused, and this is reflected in the very different perceptions of different groups in Egyptian society on the matter. Thus, as we shall see below, among feminist and other secularist activists the state is perceived as Islamist it is seen as secularist by Islamists. What seems to be happening is that in spite of its foreign policy image, the state has always looked to establishment Islam for legitimacy. Dependence on this has increased as its legitimacy has been undermined for other reasons (economic and political, as we have seen). As Islamist opposition has grown, to placate moderate Islamists the state began further Islamization of law, thus further legitimizing Islamic discourse. As the power of moderate Islamists has grown, these too are now seen as a threat, but Islam has become so embedded in public discourse that the state cannot legitimate itself in any other medium, so it is increasingly forced to confront Islamists on their own ground. We shall now consider this process in more detail.

4. The Role of the State in the Growth of Public Islam

> [W]hen newspapers in the U.S. claim that radical Islamic movements are threatening to topple 'Egypt's secular government', they are not only engaging in a complex strategy of distancing (the secular West versus the religious East; the (necessarily) secular allied government versus the (fanatically) religious internal threat. They are also ... constructing an astounding fiction: that Egypt's government is a secular one. Although this fiction is useful for the purposes of political convenience and Western self-definition, it makes understanding the current political tensions in Egypt impossible. (Starrett 1998 p. 16)

Through all the social systems that it can influence, the Egyptian government seeks to promote its particular version of Islam as a public religion. Such systems are both domestic and international in scope. Domestically, they include education, the law, state television and newspapers (as well as censorship of private media) and the unique institution of al-Azhar mosque/university. Internationally, they include tourist information and international diplomacy. In this section we shall look in more detail at some connections between the state and official versions of Islam. This will show that the social and political mobilization of Islamic discourse by Islamist groups has developed in response to the intervention of the Egyptian state in the field of culture.[4]

We have already seen that under Sadat laws on apostasy were introduced and *sharia* became the principal source of Egyptian law. Furthermore, this process of Islamization of law has continued under Mubarak, exemplified in the introduction of the *hisbah* ('public decency') law, centralized under the state prosecutor. However, it should be noted that while the state is responsible for this Islamization of Egyptian law, such changes reflect competition between the state and Islamists to prove their Islamic credentials, as well as the influence of Islamist lawyers through the Egyptian Bar Council (Wickham 1997 p. 120). This combination of the state entering into competition to 'out Islam the Islamists', together with Islamist influence through state and non-state channels, is repeated in other social systems and is a key feature of the process of the progressive Islamization of Egyptian society.

Television is a crucial communication medium in Egypt, with one survey showing that 73 per cent of Egyptians rely on it for news, as well as entertainment (Gerges 1999 p. 173 n. 6). Hence it has become an important means for the state to transmit its version of public Islam, especially as it has a monopoly over broadcasting:

> Internally, the Mubarak regime retreated from secular politics and culture by Islamicising sociopolitical space. The official discourse is becoming more Islamic, with the government emphasising the virtues of religion. Nowhere is this more evident than in the domains of education and communication, particularly in television, a critical medium for shaping public opinion. (Ibid. 1999 p. 173)

Mubarak is not the first Egyptian leader to use television to promote an official version of Islam: Sadat also did so. An example from Sadat's era (1970–81) is Mustafa Mahmud's *Science and Faith* series, whose title corresponded exactly with Sadat's political slogan. Second, the state's monopoly of the airwaves does not mean that Islamists have no influence here. As Abu-Lughod argues (1997 p. 280), both the content of programmes generally and the volume of specifically religious broadcasting, are probably both affected. This provides another example of how the dialectic between the state and Islamists is leading to the progressive Islamization of Egyptian society.

Al-Azhar provides a third example of a public institution with a complex relationship to the state. Karam (1997 p. 158) describes the institution of al-Azhar in Cairo and the office of the Grand Mufti, or Sheikh, resident there, as uniquely incorporating the functions of 'mosque, university, state legitimization, interpretative authority and centre of Islamic propaganda all in one'. Centrally situated in Cairo, it is an important focus of religious life, a centre for theological education throughout the Sunni world, as well as a 'secular' university providing education in all disciplines, including science, medicine and humanities. It also runs various other educational institutions across the country.

The Sheikh of al-Azhar is appointed by the state and issues *fatwas* (religious opinions) that historically have tended to support state policies, often commenting on actions beyond Egypt's borders in other Arab countries such as Jordan, Palestine, Lebanon and Syria. The Sheikh's *fatwa* in support of Sadat's (1979) peace initiative with Israel, which, as we have seen, led to Egypt's diplomatic isolation in the Arab world and was deeply unpopular with most of the Egyptian population, showed the extent to which the ancient university had become a government mouthpiece. We shall consider further below two works by scholars associated with al-Azhar (al-Raziq's *Islam and the Basis of Government* and al-'Ashmawi's *Political Islam*), both of which delegitimate the role of Islam in political society and hence oppose opposition Islamist groups. Yet the relationship remains a complex one; under Gad al-Haq, Grand Sheikh from 1982 to 1996, groups such as the Scholars' Front and the Islamic Research Academy based in al-Azhar became a powerful source of criticism of the government and al-Haq's *fatwa*s were frequently in conflict with government policy (Abdo 2000 pp. 56–67). By the time of the appointment of the more acquiescent Mohamed Sayyed Tantawi in 1996 these groups had grown in confidence and are proving difficult to rein in. In 1994 the state also extended al-Azhar's powers over the cultural sphere through censorship:

> In July 1993 Gad al-Haq asked the General Assenbly of the Board of Fatwa and legislation, the state body in charge of safeguarding civil society, to clearly define al-Azhar's role in censoring film, music and video-cassettes and to clarify the responsibility for such matters between the institution and the state. …
>
> The General Assembly's response, issued in February 1994, was a victory for al-Azhar and a blow to Egypt's secular intellectuals. The Assembly ruled that the Islamic Research Academy must protect public order and morality in general, extending its authority beyond the traditional confines of religious issues. But the Assembly went further, declaring that al-Azhar's opinions were binding and could not be overturned by the Ministry of Culture. (p. 67)

This may seem a strange decision in view of the Research Academy's record of criticizing the government. But it seems to have been motivated by an attempt to divide Islamists and to hide behind al-Azhar's decisions when coming under fire from other Islamists, as well as to recapture religious credibility by association with al-Azhar's influence both in Egypt and throughout the Sunni world. However, by legitimizing Islamic discourse in this way in an information age when it has proved incapable of controlling the flow of information, authority is vested more in products than in institutions, and the public education system has equipped the population to interpret sacred texts for themselves, the government seems to be digging a deeper and deeper hole for itself:

> Each new attempt to correct mistaken ideas by furthering the penetration of Islamic discourse in public space creates an intensification of the conflict between parties seeking to control the discourse. In becoming hegemonic, Islam … is forced by necessity not only to provoke limited counter-languages, but to become itself the language in which cultural and political battles are fought by the vast majority of interested parties. (p. 219)

In inadvertent concert with action in the educational sphere (Chapter 1), the state's mobilization of Islam in the legal, media and cultural spheres has coincidentally led to the emergence of social and political Islamism, the former threatening the state's competence-based claim to legitimacy, the latter both its competence- and concept-based claims, as we shall see below. It has done so by making available a functionalized Islamic discourse and creating a largely literate mass public which has become a ready audience for the ideas of Islamist authors when political and economic conditions are ripe.

This sketch of the current Egyptian context has, it is hoped, served to suggest something of the historical and political situation in which Islam has re-emerged as a major factor in the public life of Egypt. We now need to look in more depth at different aspects of this phenomenon. As we have already seen, Islamization is not restricted to the political sphere, but also affects much of social and cultural life. Indeed, as Guenena (1997 p. 135) comments, 'While "Political Islam" may have captured the limelight, it is "Social Islam" that has impacted more significantly on the lives of people'. Furthermore, the basis of its support is vastly wider than that of the more militant political groups. Next, therefore, we shall briefly consider a range of such Islamic NGOs, including Islamic banks, savings schemes and companies, but concentrating on Islamic private voluntary organizations (PVOs). As Ayubi (1991) argues, there is no coherent Islamic ideology underlying all these enterprises, but rather the sharing of a broad Islamic ethos often with strong local roots, in reaction and contrast to the stultifying bureaucratization which characterizes much government provision. We therefore begin our more detailed look at the Islamization of Egyptian society by examining this phenomenon of social Islam.

5. Faces of Social Islam in Egypt

(a) Health and Social Welfare

First we consider the health and social welfare sector. Egypt's rapidly growing population,[5] together with economic problems and an inflexible and bureaucratic state delivery service, has left large and growing gaps in the provision of these services. Sadat's policy of economic liberalization (*infatah* – 'open door') and initially encouraging attitudes towards Islamic groups provided the conditions for development of Islamic and Coptic charitable organizations to fill some of these gaps. The professional associations are also an important channel of welfare, but we shall consider those separately below.

Sullivan (1994) has described the extent and nature of Islamic and Coptic enterprises, profit-making and charitable, particularly in the health and welfare sector. Let us consider some examples. The first is the Community Association of Esbet Zein, a settlement that has grown out of a squatter camp developed around a factory in the early 1960s on the southern edge of Cairo. The settlement lacked public schools and sewerage until the mid-1980s (Sullivan 1994 p. 68). Rural-urban migration and population growth, as well as inefficient bureaucracy and corruption, has left public sources struggling to provide adequate services in such areas (Ayubi 1991 p. 196). Community leaders approached the Ministry of Social Affairs (MOSA) in the late 1970s with plans to build a permanent mosque. They were told that public funding was not available for mosque-building,[6] but that help could be given for community development if they formed a Community Development Association (CDA), which they did. The result was a two-storey mosque building, with facilities for worship on the ground floor and for community development on the first. By 1986 the latter included vocational training (sewing), daycare/nursery school (MOSA provides the teacher, the CDA pays a third of her salary), medical care (a doctor rents a room and charges low fees), remedial tutoring, septic tank cleaning and a food cooperative, which in 1986 had 1,300 members. In 1983 the CDA raised 80 per cent of its budget through *zakat*[7] and other donations from the community.

This centre provides an example of community initiative working with some government support to extend the scope of traditional Islamic societies (such as Qur'an memorization, religious publication and burial of the dead – Ayubi 1991 p. 167) into new areas of social service provision. Such facilities, usually based around a mosque building, are found in middle-class suburbs, poor urban areas and villages across Egypt. Typically, they provide a range of services including basic medical care at a fraction of the cost elsewhere,[8] child daycare, remedial education, religious instruction and vocational training – often sewing for women, carpentry and mechanics for men. Equipment kept at the centre provides a community resource for domestic maintenance. The state has been the traditional provider of employment for graduates, but has been increasingly unable to provide work for them, so one aim has been to provide skills to enable them to become self-employed. Such developments have given local mosques a new importance as a centre of community life, renewing and extending their traditional functions. They have also enabled religious leaders to extend their leadership roles in local communities.

The Young Men's Muslim Association (YMMA), a national association with branches throughout Egypt, provides a range of educational and vocational facilities and gives us an example of a PVO on a different scale, although performing many similar functions to the Community Association of Esbet Zein. For example, the branch in Tanta, Egypt's third largest city and situated in the Nile Delta, has over 1,000 members aged 18+ (Sullivan 1994 pp. 73–6). It provides free training in sewing and carpentry for unemployed college graduates and charges a nominal £E10 for English language and computer training courses. It also has a 900-strong elementary school employing 26 teachers, and a daycare centre. Other services include recreational activities – films, trips (to Alexandria and the Mediterranean coast) and sports. One comment on the content of films gives some sense of the cultural mix in contemporary Egypt: '[Elsewhere] the kids watch a lot of American and Japanese films, especially karate movies. We give them religious and other films, like Indian movies' (ibid. p. 73). YMMA in Tanta also runs a clinic. Each year the association receives 1–5 volunteers from MOSA – mostly women who have to do a year's public service after graduating from high school, instead of the male requirement for military service. As well as the fees charged, it also receives donations from abroad, particularly the US.

An interesting feature of Sullivan's study is the popularity and high esteem in which Islamic social and medical services are apparently held in Egypt. He comments that public perception is that 'a patient receives better care from PVO hospitals. Moreover many patients come to an Islamic hospital because it is Islamic' (1994 p. 79). As most of the doctors who work for them also work in state and sometimes other private facilities, this is at first sight rather puzzling. Sullivan offers two concrete examples: first, a maid who visits an Islamic hospital for family planning, when she could get the service free from a state hospital, explaining 'it is Islamic and therefore better'; second, a woman whose husband had been severely injured in a car accident insisted on having him moved from a state hospital to an Islamic hospital, where he died. Yet she attributed blame for his death not to the extent of his injuries or the care received at the Islamic hospital, but to the poor care initially received at the state hospital. Sullivan argues that regardless of the facts of a particular case, such attitudes spring from the perception that Islamic services combine the supposed efficiency of the private sector (but not its profit orientation) with the supposed care for the poor of the public sector (but not its inefficiency).

As we shall see, Islamic banks and businesses have also benefited from this perception that 'Islamic enterprises' work for the public good and are efficient. However, in these cases such a reputation is less well justified.

(b) Islamic Companies and Financial Institutions

Sadat's policy of *infitah*, 'economic openness', led to an increase in entrepeneurial activity during the 1970s, also stimulated by the sudden increase in oil wealth among the neighbouring Gulf states – many Egyptian entrepeneurs made their initial fortune in the Gulf. Some of these include members of the Muslim Brothers, who went into exile under Nasser. One former Brother, 'Uthman Ahmad, an engineer whose company played an important role in the construction of the Aswan dam, played a key role in persuading Sadat to allow exiled Brothers (and their fortunes) back into the country to 'participate in the *infitah* carnival' (Ayubi 1991 p. 189). One example of a returnee was the millionaire 'Abd al-'Azim Abu Luqma, who bought the former Swiss Groppi tea halls and 'Islamicized' them by forbidding the sale of alcoholic drinks. From the late 1970s increasing numbers of entrepreneurs began to call their businesses 'Islamic', with the 'Islamic' character associated with 'no-interest' transactions, holding prayers at work and other signs of piety. Such businesses vary in size from the al-Sharif Plastic Company (estimated capital value £E450m) to sole-proprieter enterprises such as Islamic grocery stores, which emphasize their careful scrutiny of food and drinks to ensure their *halal* content.

'Islamic' financial institutions are another sector of broadly 'social' Islam, ranging from the large banks which emerged in the 1970s to soak up surplus 'petrodollars' to Islamic investment companies (IICs) whose activities were largely unregulated by the government until 1988. The rationale for distinctive 'Islamic' financial institutions derives from the 'perceived Islamic prohibition on *riba* (usury)' (Ayubi 1991 p. 178). Although there are juridic disputes over what precisely this entails – whether, for example, it applies only to interest rates on credit used for consumption, or also to returns on productive investments (p. 179). However, the majority position is that it refers to any predetermined return on capital. This means that various ways of encouraging people to invest in an inflationary context (driven largely by the international economic system) have had to be sought, especially profit-sharing schemes.

The principle of keeping a close connection between the client and his or her money is important in Islamic jurisprudence (*fiqh*) and hence an initial concentration in the early phase of the Islamic banking movement on cooperative and mutual banking and on financing small-scale enterprises, as with the Mit Ghamr bank established in the rural Nile delta area in 1963, later nationalized to become the Nasser Social Bank in 1971. Although this followed West German models, it could claim some continuity with local traditions of mutual savings arrangements. This formed the blueprint for the oil boom Islamic banks of the 1970s, whose popularity has even led ordinary banks to open special 'Islamic departments'. However, cooperative and mutual arrangements have gradually become ever more marginal and increasingly replaced by more conventional banking practices, with increasingly ingenious attempts to preserve the 'no interest' status. Thus Ayubi concludes: 'whereas Islamic banks appeared initially to favour financing small artisans and entrepreneurs in order to emphasise the role of work and diligence, they have ended up financing the already well to do' (p. 184).

In contrast, Islamic money utilization companies, otherwise known as IICs, have been more influential for the majority of Egyptians: in 1988, more than 100 such companies had over 400,000 depositors and total funds of US$4.3 billion (Sullivan 1994 p. 63). These claimed to operate on the same non-interest profit-sharing basis and to offer up to 20 per cent profit annually. Until 1988 they operated outside the government's financial legislation, but concern over their activities, particularly the extent of overseas investment and the possibility of fraud, led to a new law (June 1988; Law 143), which required them to open their books to official inspection. As a result of refusal to cooperate with the authorities, the assets of the largest group, al-Rayan, were seized in November 1988. It turned out that, among other illegal practices, the 'pyramid-scam' (no joke intended!) was in operation, whereby deposits of new customers were being used to pay the dividends of existing ones (Ayubi 1991 p. 190). In January 1992 the assets of the third largest IIC were also seized. As a result of corruption in these large enterprises hundreds of thousands of investors have lost out and, more importantly for the IIC movement, have lost confidence in the sector, in spite of increased government legislation to protect investors (Sullivan 1994 p. 64).

There is little that is distinctively Islamic about either Islamic banks or IICs. Profit-sharing schemes have in practice turned out to differ little from conventional banking methods. Indeed, some Islamic banks have even invested in foreign banks which pay interest, justifying this on the grounds that such interest is administratively set rather then dependent on market fluctuations (Ayubi 1991 p. 184). Thus, in some ways, the 'Islamization' of the business and financial sector has amounted to little more than a re-branding of existing or adopted business and financial practices. Yet the very fact that the 'Islamic brand' continues to sell, in spite of disasters like the IIC scandal, tells us something about the public influence of Islam in Egypt. Islamic discourse and symbols have become a valued medium of communication, at the very least. And this in itself stands in need of explanation.

In contrast, medical and welfare services can be seen as a more organic outgrowth from the existing philanthropic activities of Islamic associations and indeed as making a substantial contribution to the social system. Here are the conclusions of two researchers:

> Islam may not be the solution to Egypt's socioeconomic conundrum, but it is certainly an important part of a larger solution. Certain aspects of Islam can help provide solutions to basic problems such as lack of education, health care, literacy and day care. (Sullivan 1994 p. 97)
>
> There is little doubt that the Islamic societies are increasingly providing an alternative social and organisational network to that sponsored by the state. They fill in gaps created by the state from some of its previous areas of activity and build closer and more intimate links with the people at a grass roots level, thus constraining the penetration of the state into society and eroding a great deal of the State's 'achievement-based' claim to legitimacy. (Ayubi 1991 p. 198)

Ayubi's final point here – the implicit challenge to the state by taking over functions previously performed by it and hence undermining its legitimacy – is taken further by some commentators. They see Islamic associations 'as the means by which the Islamists control and direct the masses' (Zubaida 1992 pp. 9–10; quotation from Guenena 1997 p. 139). Ayubi also points to the fact that some Islamic companies provide funds for mosques whose preachers are critical of the regime (1991 p. 197), and indeed that some extremist organizations raise funds through businesses enterprises (for example the Takfir group's sale of vegetables through kiosks, p. 192). However, he argues that it is predominantly conservative and traditional elements of the rising entrepreneurial class seeking religious credibility by supporting elements of the Islamic movement, rather than that radical Islamists are using Islamic companies as a front for their activities, who have benefited from the growth of Islamic companies (p. 193). Similarly:

> Islamic social services involve people who belong to very different social classes, who may speak the same religious vocabulary, but who speak different political languages. The 'culture' of the users of these services may bring them together at some level and many of them may share feelings towards the state that would range between hostility and frustration. Only in times of acute crisis, however, might they really act collectively (and most probably only tentatively), to use their growing 'alternative' networks. (p. 199)

None the less, the success of Islamic PVOs in meeting social needs contributes to the credibility and popularity of Islamist discourses in Egypt, serving to legitimate Islamists' claim that Islam can provide answers to all people's needs. As with political Islam, the rise of such groups coincided with the low point of secular nationalism after the Arab defeat in the 1967 war against Israel. Their steady growth and penetration of society through networks of mutual support and obligation provides a crucial and often neglected context for understanding the rise of political Islam. As we saw in Chapter 5, liberal Muslims argue that the sacred texts of Islam provide no justification for the concept of an Islamic state. But such arguments do not count for much if Islamic PVOs provide support and care that appear to demonstrate in practice the Muslim Brotherhood claim that 'Islam is the solution'.

In conclusion, these two subsections have presented Islamic health and social services as developing from traditional Islamic charitable organizations in response to the shortcomings of the welfare state. This is a kind of reversal of the situation in twentieth-century Britain, where, until the last couple of decades at least, the state increasingly took over many education, health and welfare services from religious organizations. Islamic PVOs are 'Islamic' in the sense that they have (often literally) grown out of mosques, which have retained and extended their traditional worship and teaching functions. They also witness to and promote the credibility of 'Islam' as able to deliver where the state cannot, thus legitimising the Islamist slogan 'Islam is the solution'. In contrast, the Islamic companies and financial organizations that have grown up during the same period (from the 1970s on), have not generally grown out of traditional Muslim organizations. But they also trade on, and either enhance or diminish, the credibility of the 'Islamic brand' as 'able to deliver the goods'.

However, as we indicated in Section 2, there is another side to 'civil' Islamization: the extension of illiberal interpretations of *sharia* into the legal sector. We now to turn to consider one well-publicized example of this.

(c) Abu Zaid, the Islamization of Law and Implications for the Public Sphere

Until 1995 Abu Zaid was Assistant Professor in Islamic and Arabic studies at Cairo University. His work applies a social scientific mode of analysis to literary texts, including, controversially, the Qur'an. The implications of his particular Marxist-inspired method seem to leave little room for traditional conceptions of divine inspiration: 'The cognitive horizons of a historical group are determined by the nature of its social and economic structures and that both the base and superstructure interact in an intricate dialectic' (in Najjar 2000 p. 196). Abu Zaid further claims to have reached 'an objective understanding of the religious texts' and apparently subscribes to the view that only secularism can protect a diversity of opinion: 'Secularism ... is the true safeguard of civil society, without which it would not exist' (p. 185). While events lend some support to the latter view in the Egyptian case, it should also be noted that neither historical materialism nor claims to 'objective understanding' would seem to leave much theoretical space for alternative opinions either. But as well as espousing these methodologies, Abu Zaid had been particularly critical of the ways in which many contemporary Islamic groups read Islam's sacred sources, which he describes as 'the contemporary religious discourse' and attacked in his 1992 book *Critique of Islamic Discourse* (p. 184; Abdo 2000 p. 163).

In 1992 Abu Zaid applied for promotion to full professorial rank, but was turned down by the University authorities on the advice of two of the three university professors called upon to assess his work (Najjar 2000 pp. 178–81). One of these also called for the withdrawal from public circulation of Abu Zaid's work on al-Shafi'i, a central figure in the history of Islamic jurisprudence (p. 181). We shall return to the substantive issues in this case later in the chapter, but for now concentrate on the development of 'external' events and in particular on the intertwining of relationships between professional competence, religious confession, institutional autonomy, the public sphere, the judiciary and the state. Again, we shall describe many of the institutions and parties involved in more detail below. But the purpose here is to signal two problems in the use of civil society as an analytic concept in the Egyptian context; first, the extensive interpenetration of state, religious institutions and academic authorities; and second, the pervasive (though not universal) expectation of deference to key religious norms, especially the authority of the Qur'an and the Sunni jurisprudential tradition.

The University's announcement of its decision was followed by an outcry from 'liberal-secularists' and a vociferous exchange among secularists, Islamic associations and the scholars of al-Azhar (the Islamic University). This escalated into a battle between corresponding interests in the media. Eventually, an alliance of scholars from al-Azhar and Cairo University initiated legal proceedings against Abu Zaid, accusing him of *riddah* (apostasy), initially heard before the Personal Status and Domestic Relations Department of the Giza Court of First Instance on 10 June 1993 (Najjar 2000 p. 189). Apostasy is an offence under Egyptian law, whose principal source since 1980 has been *sharia* (Islamic law). Conviction could lead to enforced separation from his wife, since a non-believer is not allowed to be married to a Muslim woman under *sharia*.[9] In January 1995 the Giza Court rejected the lawsuit on the grounds that the plaintiffs had no interest in the case (that is, the relationship between Abu Zaid and his wife) recognizable by law. But it was overturned by the Cairo Appeals Court, which ruled that the principle of *hisbah* is applicable in matters of personal status (p. 191).

This principle allows for prosecution on the grounds of something like 'public morality'. Although its status as part of *sharia* is contested because it does not appear in early sources, it has a long history in Egyptian law until its status became uncertain with the abolition of religious courts in 1952 (p. 192; Abdo 2000 p. 171). The Cairo Court ruled that this could apply in a civil case, even if the case was brought by a party not directly involved. Subsequent legal changes (1996) have restricted the ability to bring *hisbah* cases to the public prosecutor. But such changes came too late to save Abu Zaid, whose appeal was refused by the Cairo Supreme Court of Appeal on 5 August 1996 (Najjar 2000 p. 194). As a result of these events and the threats on his life from extremist elements in the Islamic movement, Abu Zaid has moved, with his wife, to the Netherlands (Tibi 1998 p. x).

Thus we have seen two faces of the present process of Islamization in Egypt, a process which might be defined as 'the increasing influence of Islamic symbols and discourse on the social systems of a society'. One face is represented by the proliferation of Islam-inspired organizations that are contributing to the development of a parallel society and led by a new generation of Islamists who seek to promote Islamization non-violently from the bottom up, a movement which embraces many if not all sections of Egyptian society. Although some question its democratic credentials (Wickham 1997), for many close observers this parallel society is rightly to be identified with civil society and it is the government that is the main obstacle to its development: 'Civil society exists in Egypt, but it is severely restricted and ever under siege by a government concerned first and foremost with its own survival' (Sullivan and Abed-Kotob 1999 p. 135). Another face is represented by the hounding and exile of Abu Zaid, suggesting the development of a public sphere, at least in part through pressure from this alternative society, in which speech is restricted, academic competence is tied to confession and certain scholarly methods are ruled out of bounds. Perhaps more shocking, the privacy of the domestic sphere can be invaded by the guardians of public morality. From this perspective, Islamization appears as a 'slap in the face of civil society'.[10]

It is, however, worth reflecting on the Abu Zaid case in the light of the normative debates about the ideal form of Islamic governance discussed in Chapter 5. It should be remembered that hermeneutical devices like *ijtihad* allow for flexibility in the interpretation of Islamic law. The debate about freedom of religion held by the Human Rights League of Tunisia when seeking to develop their human rights charter is especially relevant. This debate included all members of the organization – from secularists to Islamists (Dwyer 1991). And as we saw, it produced agreement on the personal right to *ijtihad* which, it may be argued, would have protected Abu Zaid.

However, while it may not be possible to reconcile the differences of the parties in this controversy, from an analytic point of view the challenge is to understand the articulation between these two facets and perceptions of Islamization. Before drawing conclusions on this, we need to look at two phenomena which shed light on the extent to which the Islamist movement acts democratically when it holds power and on a crucial issue in the evaluation of the depth of the democratizing processes – the role of women. Both of these phenomena witness to the alternative forms of political participation developed when formal channels are denied by an authoritarian regime, forms which show significant cultural variation.

6. Alternative Avenues of Political Participation

(a) The Professional Associations or Syndicates

In the absence of a strong independent trade union movement and forbidden to form their own political parties, the professional associations have provided a platform on which the Muslim Brotherhood has been able to mobilize politically. These 'syndicates' were originally established by the government as an alternative to independent trade unions, but, as in the case of Polish political parties established by the Communist government, under certain conditions (the turmoil of 1980–81 in Poland's case), such bodies can take on an independent life. Their free elections provide a rare opportunity for democracy in a context where government-run elections are widely reported to be rigged (Kassem 1999).

Between 1984 and 1992 the Brotherhood had gained control of the Egyptian Bar Association, the Engineers' Association and the Medical Association. Initially, while they were able to gain power in these élite professional bodies, Islamists were less successful in the associations of less prestigious professions. In an Egyptian context, these include the associations of teachers, agronomists and vets, 'sectors characterised by low wages, poor working conditions and low social status' (Wickham 1997 p. 128). It may be noted that this greater influence in the élite professions contradicts the stereotype that Islamists recruit mostly from the less well off or most excluded sections of society. However, by 1997 Islamists had also won control of the agronomists, and pharmacists' unions, the latter a particularly notable victory as approximately 30 per cent of pharmacists are Coptic Christians (Abdo 2000 p. 100).

As the pharmacists' vote suggests, the Brotherhood owes its success not so much to the opportunity to provide expression of Islamic political identity but to their promises to deliver services to members and then to their track record of delivering them. As one Muslim but non-Islamist member comments:

> I didn't want the syndicate to become a front for the Muslim brothers. But after a while you see that they help any member, whether he is a Coptic or Muslim. Before the Islamists came, there was no-one to meet you at the syndicate. If you had a problem with the tax authority, there was no-one. Once the Islamists came, there were people in the syndicate headquarters waiting to help at all times of the day. My feeling now is that their performance has been excellent. (in ibid. p. 101)

A Coptic Christian supports this view: 'We can trust the Islamists to work for us, no matter what problems we face. This isn't a syndicate for Muslims. It's a syndicate for pharmacists' (ibid.). Turnout in elections to the boards of professional associations has tended to be low (between 5 per cent and 30 per cent), which has led to accusations that Islamists 'undemocratically' gain office by mobilizing a small section of the electorate. However, these figures compare favourably with national election turnouts in Egypt, where voter apathy has resulted from a parliament that 'serves as an instrument of state policy rather than a constraint upon it' (Wickham 1997 p. 121). Furthermore, Islamists point out that since their involvement began participation has greatly increased, for example from 9 per cent to 30 per cent between 1982 and 1992 in the Medical Association. Underlining their democratic credentials, Islamists decided not to contest 20 of the 25 seats on the Medical Association Board in 1992, to allow for other voices: they won the other 20 (p. 126).

Islamists have particularly targeted younger members, building on their high profile in most universities and on the frustrations of graduates qualified beyond the level of work that the public-sector-dominated economy is able to offer them – hence 'accountants waiting tables … lawyers … working the fields' (p. 122). Even those lucky enough to secure an appropriate job find public sector salaries inadequate to meet their expenses. Hence the Islamist leadership of professional associations have 'initiated projects in the areas of housing, health care and insurance' (p. 123). They have come up with creative solutions to practical problems such as providing shared cars for lawyers with meetings all over Cairo but too poor to afford them and providing loans to help people set up home and get married – huge expenses in Egypt for all but the wealthiest (Abdo 2000 p. 92).

Beyond the interests of their professional groups, Islamists have sought to build on traditions in these professions of a sense of social responsibility and of acting as advocates for 'the Egyptian people' (*al-sha'b*) (Wickham 1997 p. 129). They have taken a stand on democracy and human rights and in some cases sought to build alliances with secularist opponents (p. 130). Concretely, after the 1992 earthquake volunteers from the Medical Association arrived on the scene first in many of the worst-affected areas (p. 130). These events prompted the Minister of the Interior to ask, 'what is this becoming, a state within a state?' To this, a representative of the Engineers' Association responded in the negative; rather, he claims, 'we are creating islands of democracy in a sea of dictatorship' (ibid.). The government's initial response of sending in troops, as we saw above, lent legitimacy to his claims: its subsequent actions were to underline them further.

Frustrated at the Islamists' success, the government passed the notorious 'Law 100' in February 1993, which required a 50 per cent voter turnout or the government would nominate the syndicate board itself. It also restricted the distribution of funds to non-members, to prevent a repeat of the earthquake relief scenario. As we have seen, the requirement for a 50 per cent voter turnout has had little impact: the Islamists' success with the pharmacists and agronomists was achieved under these rules. The government then took more direct action, taking first the engineering syndicate, then the lawyers' syndicate under *hirasa*, official state custodianship (Abdo 2000 pp. 102–5). As Abdo concludes:

> The use of the *hirasa* laws has given Mubarak and his allies some respite from the Islamist onslaught in the syndicates, but only after doing enormous damage to what remained of the legal and political credibility of the government. Court rulings invalidating all or parts of the *hirasa* decisions have been routinely ignored, depriving union members of elected representation and access to union funds. ...
>
> Despite these setbacks, the syndicate movement under the new Islamists has touched Egyptian society in a way few could have imagined when Abu al-Ela Mady, Esam al-Eryan and their comrades launched their extraordinary venture. In a society bereft of democracy they proved free elections and free debate were in fact possible. In a nation crying out for moral guidance, they successfully married a vision of social justice, rooted in the Koran, with the demands and stresses of modern life. ...
>
> The new leadership raised standards of living for union members, eased pervasive corruption and cronyism and filled in for an incompetent state that could no longer address the concerns of the middle classes. The syndicates also demonstrated a remarkable degree of democracy, in contrast to the Mubarak regime. (p. 105)

In this way, the practical manifestation of moderate political Islam complements social Islam by challenging the competence-based legitimacy claims of the state. In practical terms, the professional associations must be judged one of the most successful parts of the Islamization process. From the perspective of normative civil society they clearly satisfy the criteria of building trust within the unions and belief in the possibility of change. They also promote diversity in terms of the institutional plurality of Egyptian society and have proven respectful of equal rights for the Coptic minority within the orbit of a trades union oriented to reaching out into society to improve the lot of its members. In this last respect they have begun to heal some of the wounds inflicted on Coptic-Muslim relations by extremist Islamists. But questions remain about the fourth criterion, the public expression of diversity, in the sense of the free expression of ideas, including those offensive to religion.

In the light of the debates on ideal Islamic social and political arrangements in Chapter 5, it is worth asking what kind of Islamic state the reformers of the Muslim Brotherhood who have led the professional associations envisage, given theirs is perhaps the most credible claim to provide the democratic alternative to the government. Adbo (2000), who corresponded with Eryan during his imprisonment and has interviewed many of these leaders, comments:

> The final configuration of the state was not central to the thinking of Egypt's new Islamists. Nor, as critics of the modern Islamist movement maintain, does it require any return to an imagined order of medieval Arabia. The existing parliamentary democracy in Egypt, however imperfect under Mubarak and his predecessors, could be made to coexist comfortably with Islamic principles. The goal was the creation of an 'Islamic order', not a theocratic 'religious state'. (p. 75)

As we saw in Chapter 5, part of the problem for such reforming Islamists is that the concept of an Islamic state is not clearly spelled out in Islam's textual sources, and the concept formulated by earlier Islamists is problematic. Their handling of power, however, appears to give some grounds for optimism.

To 'join up' our thinking, though, it is also important to reflect back on the Abu Zaid case. What was the response of reformist Muslim Brothers – pro-democracy and pro-pluralism (in the sense of equal rights for Copts) – to this case? Dr Muhammad Imara, a prolific Islamist writer, argues that freedom of thought and pluralism are 'fundamental Islamic values' and therefore that, although he strongly disagrees with Abu Zaid's views, the case is intellectual and not legal and should therefore 'be challenged and debated by argument', not settled in court (in Najjar 2000 p. 194). Such a position has also been voiced by Azzam Tamini, an Islamist scholar resident in Britain (in Herbert 2001b).

However, in a personal interview, Mohammed Abd al-Qaddus, a convert to the Brotherhood from a secular liberal upper-class background, was somewhat evasive on the point: 'if this was Islam, why had it never happened before?' was his reply. 'But surely, it was an attempt to make the law more "Islamic" that had led to this prosecution?' I asked; but that was as far as he was prepared to be drawn. Restricting free speech runs very much against the grain for Al-Qaddus, who is proud of the fact that he shared his house with his secular father and seems to see this as model for Egypt: 'There wasn't really a lot of difference between me and my father. Even though we had opposing political views and religious beliefs we respected each other – which is why we could live in the same house.' His awkwardness on the Abu Zaid case perhaps reflects his unease at a polarization within society that seems to have followed the Abu Zaid affair, shifting mainstream Islamist opinion. As Abdo (2000 p.171) comments; 'At first, cases involving writers such as Abu Zeid [*sic*] were brought only by Islamists on the periphery of the movement. ... But over time, the opinions of figures on the margins came to coincide with those of the mainstream Islamic movement.' Abdo concludes that 'the Islamic world's general consensus about freedom of expression ... is that such liberties are not absolute. Freedom of expression cannot be applied to the most sacred figures and precepts in Islam' (p. 183). In conclusion, it seems that more liberal opinion within the Islamist movement in Egypt is uncomfortable with the Islamist legal pursuit of Abu Zaid, and a minority will say that the case should have been pursued through the courts. Others imply that the case results from the less-than-liberal political situation, but are unwilling to challenge directly what appears to be considerable grass-roots opposition to Abu Zaid. On these grounds, the Islamist movement as a site of empirical civil society must at present not match the fourth 'encouragement of expression of public diversity' feature of normative civil society. The apparent change within the Islamist movement on this issue, however, suggests that the current climate does not reflect the unchanging nature of Islam, but rather current political conditions, which are not conducive to the development of liberal culture (Dalacoura 1998).

In this context, we turn to consider an issue of great importance both within Egypt and to the Western world – the role of women as Islamist discourse becomes more influential in Egyptian society.

(b) Women's Organizations and Women Organizing

The evidence here is drawn from two studies. The first by Azza Karam, *Women, Islamisms and the State: Contemporary Feminisms in Egypt* (1998), examines the discourses of women activists from across the spectrum of opinion on the relationships between women, religion and society. As Karam acknowledges, women active in this way are mostly upper and middle class, although through the dissemination of their writings the Islamists reach a wider audience (ibid. p. 234). Therefore, to broaden the social backgrounds considered, the second work used is an observation of family networks among the *sha'b* (people, popular sector) in central Cairo. This is Diane Singerman's *Avenues of Participation: Family, Politics and Networks in Urban Quarters of Cairo* (1995).

In Egypt the word 'feminism' is widely associated with the West and colonialism and is therefore not a label 'owned' by most women activists, except for secularists. None the less, Karam uses it to describe those women whom she sees engaged in activities that would be identified as feminist in a Western context. She defines feminism as:

> An individual or collective awareness that women have been and continue to be oppressed in diverse ways and for diverse reasons and attempts towards liberation from this oppression involving a more equitable society with improved relations between men and women (ibid. p. 5)

Feminist activists are therefore those involved in seeking to propagate discourses that challenge women's current position on the grounds that women as a group are currently oppressed, however this oppression is perceived, in contrast to those engaged in charity work. She distinguishes three main groups: secularist, Muslim and Islamist.

The former 'unanimously perceive Islam as enemy No. 1 and the state as already Islamist to all intents and purposes' (pp. 234–5). They think the state should enforce the privatization of religion. As Karam comments:

> In their manner of rejecting any discourses of emancipation within religious frameworks, secular feminists are effectively risking both estrangement from, as well as exclusion of, many contemporary Egyptian women activists. In that respect, secular feminists maintain

a politics of Othering – where 'the Other' is the one who thinks differently vis-à-vis religion. (p. 235)

In contrast, Muslim feminists acknowledge the cultural and social importance of Islam and therefore seek to articulate an Islamic feminist counter-discourse against what they see as the hegemonic patriarchal Islamic discourse. In helping to sustain this, they see the state as a 'guilty bystander and sometimes knowing accomplice' (p. 236). Karam sees this group as particularly significant for promoting the feminist cause because it is best placed to bridge the divide between secularists and Islamists and because its discourse is in principle inclusive of both. In MacIntyre's terms, as we have loosely reinterpreted them, they stand at the confluence of traditions and hence can play a key role in resolving the epistemological crisis with which globalizing modernity confronts both.

Islamist feminists see the state in a diametrically opposed role to the secularists; for them, 'the state oppresses all in society – men as well as women – precisely because of the lack of true Islamic laws, as a result of succumbing to Western ideology' (p. 235). They are also inclined to engage in the 'politics of Othering', in the form of 'Islamists versus the rest' and especially the state and secularists. Brief summaries of the three Islamist women on which Karam centres her account give some flavour of the themes and personalities of Islamist women activists. It is on these that we shall focus, both because of the widespread influence of Islamist discourse and because there is most likely to be dissonance between their position and that of normative civil society.

Each individual argues that women are particularly oppressed because they are forced into economic and social roles that conflict with their 'natural' orientation to the domestic sphere, for example:

> For a few limited pennies we have sold our motherhood and then we ask about the role of women in society. What kind of society is this where the home that forms the seed of society has been ruined by tearing women between the home and workplace? (Al-Ghazali 1985 p. 4, in Karam 1998 p. 210)

Such assertions come against the background of increasing participation of women in the workforce, which in the context of increased male unemployment has meant that women are the sole breadwinners in some 30 per cent of households (ibid. p. 163). Pressures from the IMF (International Monetary Fund) and the World Bank for the public sector to become more competitive have led to short-term contracts, hiring of underage women workers and reduction in social benefits for employees (ibid.). Thus not only is women's employment seen as threatening male roles, but many women's experience of work has been that it is unsupportive of their domestic roles.

Al-Ghazali represents an older generation of Islamist woman activist. Born in 1917, she founded the Muslim Women's Association in 1936, as a parallel women's organization to the Muslim Brotherhood. She joined the latter in a personal capacity, but refused the offer of institutional merger, insisting on a separate women's organization. In her personal life she has arguably acted as a strong independent woman, travelling internationally to lecture, imprisoned under Nasser, bearing no children, divorcing her first husband because he interfered with her Islamist mission and stipulating that the second should not do so as a condition of marriage. Yet her remarks until the mid-1980s relentlessly stressed the role of woman as home-maker, wife and mother, although since then she has introduced an element of 'choice' in her rhetoric, perhaps in response to developments stemming from younger generations of Islamist feminists.

Safinaz Qazim (born *c*.1939), a disciple of al-Ghazali, sees the world sharply polarized between Islam and the West: her view that modernization is not a neutral process but a Western plot to subdue Islam is well expressed in the quotation from her writing given at the beginning of Chapter 1. What is interesting, however, given this, is the appeal she makes to concepts such as freedom and citizenship, the latter of which at least presumes a basis in human rights, in opposition to the state's treatment of its subjects as 'hostages or captives' (Karam 1998 p. 217). Yet at the same time she rejects civil institutions such as human rights organizations. She sees the oppression of women as being due to the pre-Islamic legacy in Egyptian society (*jahiliyya*), Western influence and failure to properly follow Islam. She argues that a woman can play an active role in Muslim society and advocates an 'equal but different' position on gender relations.

Heba Ra'uf (born *c*.1965) is a Western-educated mother of two, agony aunt for *Al-Sha'b* (The People, a Labour Party/Muslim Brothers weekly) and teaching assistant in political science at Cairo University. She represents a younger generation of Islamist feminists. Her Master's dissertation argues from Islamic sources that qualified women can legitimately occupy the highest public functions, with the implication that this includes the judiciary and government, still very much male preserves in Egypt and a controversial issue within the Muslim Brotherhood. The basis of her argument about contemporary society would seem to be an attempt to reverse conventional polarities of value between public and private life. She argues that the family is the fundamental source of resistance to an oppressive state ('No state can ever forbid people to have families') and the basic unit from which successful society building begins: 'Islam considers the family as the starting point for any real Islamic society' (Karam 1998 p. 226). Hence her views can be regarded as a radical challenge to Western theories of civil society, which tend to exclude the family as contradicting the ideal of the autonomous individual.

Ra'uf affirms al-Ghazali's emphasis on the domestic sphere, but argues against the former's earlier work that women do not need to be exclusively confined to it, rather that it provides the basis from which public work can proceed:

Women who stay at home ... bringing up children, are participating in ... society; practising ... socialisation, giving their children ... positive values. Then these women can go and perform other public and equally important roles. No one has 24 hours to devote to only one sphere. (Karam 1998 p. 227)

Such views make interesting reading in the light of Singerman's study. Singerman argues that conventional political studies focused on participation in recognized institutions, unions, parties and protest groups neglect the political significance of informal networks and institutions, especially in authoritarian states like Egypt where the former activities are severely circumscribed (1995 p. 3). The people in the poorer neighbourhoods of Cairo that Singerman studied in the mid to late 1980s had few of the former affiliations, although charitable Christian and Muslim PVOs were active there, under increasing government surveillance (ibid. pp. 252–3). However, based on the fundamental economic unit of the extended family, 'they organize networks within the community that work to satisfy their basic economic, social and political needs and desires' (p. 45). It is notable that although 90 per cent of Cairo's families live in nuclear family households, kinship networks remain strong and highly functional, contrary to the expectations of the societalization component of the secularization thesis.

While there is gender separation in certain public contexts among the *Sha'b* – for example men predominate in local cafés and restaurants and in some local crafts and trades – this is not the case in many sectors of employment (for example schools, stores, some factories). Furthermore, it does not reflect the balance of power observed by Singerman in domestic contexts, in which women often exercised power over men, but which is inaccessible to most male researchers (pp. 31–2). Shedding light on official employment rates, Singerman states from a sample of 350 people some 172 men and 120 women were economically active, according to UN criteria (p. 33). Sixty per cent were active in some way in the informal economy (black market) and for 28 per cent this was their primary economic activity (p. 31).

Pointing to such evidence, she reflects back on the problem of male researchers (in part, because of access) accepting the views of Egyptian men on authority within the household, whereas at a macro-political level they would not accept the claims of omnipotence by governments (p. 47). The resulting 'distorted picture of the patriarchal family supports orientalist views of Middle Eastern women as "subjected, oppressed and invisible"'. In fact, she argues, 'Intrahousehold politics is far more competitive and confrontational than is generally believed' (ibid.).

Clearly, in practice most Egyptian women do not have '24 hours to devote to only one sphere', not as a result of ideological commitment but economic necessity. Political discourses – Islamist or otherwise – articulate with this reality or risk irrelevance. Furthermore, while it is indeed a response to economic necessity, the economic and social activism of Muslim women in the popular sector builds on a tradition of female participation in these spheres, long unrecognized by predominantly male researchers. Alongside this, pressure for women to move into more overtly public and political roles comes from middle- and upper-class secular and Muslim feminists, apparently increasingly supplemented by younger voices among Islamist feminists, the most significant voice for reaching the popular sector.

Singerman's study also has implications for conceptualizing civil society as the channel through which messages arising in the lifeworld are translated into the public sphere. As she writes:

> In the ideology and practice of liberal politics, individual self-interest is mediated by institutions that serve the collective good. Individual spirit, ambition and independence are valued and honoured in the political culture of Western liberalism. In other societies, where the cult of the individual is less pronounced and individual rights are not protected by

enforced legal codes, the political system and political culture reflect alternative norms and preferences. In the Middle East the family, rather than the individual, continues to be the more relevant unit of society. However, negative connotations surround the family in analyses of Middle Eastern politics and society as patrimonial politics, nepotism and corruption are blamed on the familial ethos, without any regard for the structure of national and international politics and political economy in the region. (p. 45)

Singerman therefore calls for a reassessment of the relationship between informal and formal politics in constituting civil society and the public sphere in this region and challenges dominant Western models of these concepts that rest on patriarchal and ethnocentric assumptions.

7. Conclusion

This chapter has sought to counter dominant anti-Islamist views in Western journalism and political science with the more sympathetic and engaged perspective of field studies of these groups. The problem with the anti-Islamist literature is its lack of recognition of the diversity of contemporary Islamic movements in Egypt, of engagement with the lifeworlds that generate them and of any kind of critical reflection on the normative conventions (or lack of them) of public spheres in Western societies (Tibi 1998; Al-Najjar 1977). The problem with more sympathetic and engaged perspectives – although I contend it is a lesser one – is the reluctance to move beyond the exposition of the institutions and lifeworld that make Islamization plausible and possible, to tackle to normative issues posed in an intersecting, globalizing world. Understanding is of course the basis for negotiation and there is some legitimacy in scholarly defence of their primarily descriptive and expository role. Yet arguably the expository task is unfinished if the reader is left understanding something of how the Islamist might arrive at his or her worldview – indeed even that such a view is not necessarily antithetical to democracy – but without an understanding of how such a perspective articulates with the reader's own, beyond problematizing it.

In the wake of 11 September 2001, this articulation is particularly important. It is clear that cultural isolationism is not an option in a structurally globalized world. In particular, the Egyptian case shows that a privatized Islam is not an option for the foreseeable future. It is therefore crucial to develop a critical and discriminating understanding of the diverse forms of public Islam and not to continue unquestioningly to prop up, as Western governments have tended to, unrepresentative and isolated political élites. There are forms of political Islam, as Egypt shows, that not only espouse democratic rhetoric but back this up with democratic practice within the highly circumscribed civil society in which authoritarian governments allow them to operate. This is not to say that there are not aspects of this developing Islamic civil society that differ from – indeed are shocking, from the perspective of – Western norms, as the Abu Zaid case demonstrates. But just as an evaluation of women's role in society should not stop at a reflex response to the veil, neither should the advances towards democratization within Islamic civil society be dismissed because of such cases, which arise in any case partly as a result of state intervention

Notes

1   Conducted while working as academic consultant producing an educational video for the Open University with the BBC (Video 1 AD317 *Religion Today: Tradition, Modernity and Change*). My thanks to Romany Helmy for arranging the interviews and to Lionel Mill at the BBC and Katerina Dalacoura at the LSE.
2   In this context, an alternative term for the Muslim Brotherhood. However, Starrett (1998) defines the term more broadly: 'The Islamic Trend, as I have labeled the range of cultural and social phenomena that include specifically political movements, is extremely complex. It ranges from the Islamization of the publishing industry and the increase in enrollment in Islamic studies programs, to the odious violence of terrorist organizations and the sophisticated legal maneuvering of Islamist lawyers within the court system. From the network of private businesses that are funded by and contribute to Islamic political and charitable activities to the quotidian spats and arguments that reveal just "how close religion is to the surface"' (p. 191).
3   Other examples include Sullivan and Abed-Kotob (1999), Karam (1998), Singerman (1995), Ghadbian (1997).
4   Islamization in Iran and Syria have also been linked to this process (Moaddel 1996).
5   The annual growth rate of 2.3 per cent in the 1990s is down from 2.8 per cent in the 1980s, but is still one of the highest in the world. Half the population is under 18 years of age and the number of Egyptians is estimated to have increased fivefold between 1900 and 2000 (Wayne and Simonis 1994 p. 29).
6   According to Ayubi (1991 pp. 196–7) the Ministry of Awqaf (Religious Affairs) has been committed to providing an official preacher for all mosques since the 1940s. However, it has been unable to keep up with demand and by 1981 there were more than 40,000 *ahli* (private) mosques, compared with only 6,000 official ones.
7   'Alms' – this is one of the five 'pillars' of Islam, or duties owed to God. Notionally set at $2\frac{1}{2}$ per cent of production per annum, arrangements for the collection and distribution of *zakat* varies widely across the Muslim world.
8   Ayubi (1991 p. 198) says 'Islamic clinics' charge about 10 per cent of the fee elsewhere, between £1 and £2; Sullivan (1994 pp. 69, 73) cites fees of between £E1.50 and £E5.
9   This is disputed; for example the relatively conservative European Sharia Council is deliberating over whether to permit women who convert to Islam to remain married to non-Muslim husbands and is likely to rule in favour of the 'greater good' of preserving the family (interview with Azzam Tamimi, June 2001).
10 Secretary General of the Egyptian Organization for Human Rights, *New York Times*, 6 August 1996.

Conclusion

In Part I we reconsidered the relationship between religion and modernization, and especially the ideals and social spaces delineated by the concepts of civil society and the public sphere. In Part II we have tested out our theories and developed our concepts in relation to the recent articulation between religion, civil society and the public sphere in four very different societies. While it is clear that there is no uniform relationship between these spheres across societies, certain patterns have none the less emerged. Religion has shown a surprising capacity (from the perspective of the Enlightenment critique of religion and secularization theory) to adapt to changing social conditions. Three forms of such adaptation are particularly prominent.

First, religions have adapted by functionalizing within the dominant instrumental systems of modernity, especially health and social welfare and in the private voluntary sector, from Britain to Egypt. Second, religious symbols and discourse, often disembedded from historically dominant institutions, have become influential media of communication, whether on Indian television, in Egyptian fashion, Polish newspapers or on Serbian militia helmets. This symbolic and discursive power can be used for good or ill, but there is no doubt that in many parts of the world religion retains a cultural resonance which means that it can mobilize and be mobilized effectively within new media. Third, religion can become a powerful social agent in the critique of dominant social forces, whether Communism in Poland or the military state in Egypt or Turkey. This critical power is also evident in less oppressive social conditions, for example in American debates on ethical issues or in support of peace and environment movements in Europe.

While each is unique, the four case studies can also be taken as illustrative of the relationship between religion and civil society in several broad types of society, categorized by their history of church-state relations, modernization and of the liberal tradition within them. Thus Britain represents a Western European type of society in which both structural modernization and the liberal tradition developed internally, and where (except in the case of Northern Ireland) religion did not become a central source of antagonistic communal identities. While we have also shown that there are substantial differences among Western European societies with respect to their national civic cultures and the role of religion within them, these societies are none the less distinct from North and Latin American societies predominantly settled by people of Western European (and African) descent. This is because the church-state relation was either deliberately severed from the start (US) or greatly weakened (Brazil), with the result that secular critiques of religion found less purchase – but so too, in the Latin American case, did the liberal tradition. In Western European societies, then, religious belonging and practice are generally lower than elsewhere, but where there is a tradition of a strong voluntary sector independent of the state (Britain) or of state-organized communal representation (the

Netherlands) religion may exercise an influence in civil society disproportionate to the number of its regular worshippers. Even in contexts where there is a strong tradition of excluding religion from public life (for example France), religious identity may become a channel of political mobilization, and is especially likely to come into conflict with the state-sponsored national civic tradition.

Both Polish and Bosnian case studies provide examples of the role of religion in civil society where during the Communist period modernization was centrally organized, and the state attempted to eliminate any autonomous civil society and to exclude both religious and liberal traditions from public life. However, in practice in the Polish case the authorities were unable to entirely suppress the Church, which largely because of the predominance of Catholicism became a focus of opposition to state domination and an umbrella for the formation of civil society, including, but not only, liberal elements. The Polish case is unusual with respect to church-state relations, for Poland lacked a state during the crucial period of modernization from the late eighteenth century to after the First World War. The multiconfessional nature of Yugoslavia (and indeed Bosnia) made it difficult for religion to play this unifying role. Hence in spite of fairly consistent but limited opposition by the Catholic Church and limited intellectual-led opposition among Muslims beginning in the 1970s, religion did not become a key factor in the mobilization of civil society against the state. Only with the weakening of the Federation following the death of Tito in the 1980s did religion become a significant source of identity mobilization, and then predominantly in support of militant rather than civic forms of nationalism, with the partial exception of Izetbegovic's SDA.

In both cases the Communist legacy for civil society has been a culture of low public trust and predominantly conservative religious institutions developed in defence of national and ethnic identities. The Polish case, however, raises questions about the adequacy of a proceduralist liberalism to handle cultural complexity, while the Bosnian case offers the hope of some religious and inter-faith organizations oriented to building relationships across communal boundaries.

While the British and Bosnian cases illustrate the relationship between Islam and civil society for Muslim minorities (or a regionally marginal and recent majority in the latter case), Egypt is a historic Muslim majority and Arab society, and one in which modernization has been mediated predominantly through Ottoman and then indigenous élites, under colonial influence from the mid-nineteenth to mid-twentieth centuries. Egypt thus has long experience of modernization and exposure to liberal traditions among an indigenous élite, although for most people these developments have been perceived as having come from outside rather than having developed within Egyptian society. Yet in spite of this we have reviewed evidence which has shown that the discourses of democracy, human rights, women's empowerment and, more recently, civil society have become important if contested discourses in Egypt. The authoritarian character of the state remains a major obstacle to further development of civil society in many Middle Eastern societies. Islamic discourse is also certainly a factor in this development, one that is complex to evaluate. Islamic and Islamist groups have a strong track record in health and social services, and where they have been able to exercise limited political power have shown themselves both effective and democratic. At the same time, the rhetoric of the implementation of *sharia* and increasing restrictions on the public sphere through a combination of Islamist lawyers and the government-appointed judiciary raises doubts about the liberal character of this influence. However, while it may not be true, as Halliday claims, that 'you can get Islam to say anything you like' (in Herbert 2001c), the development of democratic practice and rhetoric alongside Islamist rhetoric, as well as broader debate on the nature and development of Islamic tradition, suggests that Islamic forms of civil society both exist and can be further developed. Part of the force of Islamist rhetoric and its attraction in Egypt and elsewhere is its critique of what are seen to be Western-dominated global, political and cultural systems.

This is one example of religion's critical force in the contemporary world, and we have considered a variety of theoretical frameworks within which this critical force can be understood. These include: as an agent of moral/practical lifeworld rationalization (Habermas/Casanova); at the interstices of modern systems (Wilson); addressing the residual problems of world systems (Beyer); and as witness to teleological traditions of enquiry in the fragmented world of modern moral discourse (MacIntyre). Such frameworks can help us to see how religion articulates with other factors in shaping the contemporary world, especially through the sphere of empirical civil society. However, we have not only seen evidence of religion's role as mobilizing discourse and social capital, but also of its capacity to become harnessed to forces of destruction (Bosnia), to block democratic participation (post-Communist Poland), to restrict (or try to restrict) communication in the public sphere (Egypt and Britain), and of its limitations when active predominantly as a symbolic medium of social integration to adapt to a plural civil society (post-Communist Poland).

In examining the role of religion in civil society we have also critically developed the idea of civil society itself and the normative basis for it, and the related concept of human rights. We have argued that application of the concept of civil society can be justified cross-culturally both theoretically and empirically, but within MacIntyre's metatheory of traditions, which requires that in cross-cultural communication concepts must be validated from within a developing tradition of enquiry rather than imposed from outside. In this context we also advanced an argument for the cross-cultural validity of human rights. This appealed to the now global experience of modernization, and brings us back to the quotation from the anthropologist Clifford Geertz with which we started the book. It is hoped that we have shown that in this world in which 'nobody is going to leave anyone else alone and isn't ever again going to' religion is neither the terminally declining nor necessarily destructive force the Enlightenment critique of religion supposes it to be. Public religion is here to stay, and it is hoped that in such a context this book has suggested ways to help us to 'imagine principled lives [we] can practically lead [together]'.

Bibliography

Abdo, G. (2000) *No God But God: Egypt and the Triumph of Islam* (Oxford: Oxford University Press).

Abercrombie, N. *et al.* (1994) *The Penguin Dictionary of Sociology* (3rd edition, London: Penguin).

Abu-Lughod, L. (1997) 'Dramatic Reversals: political Islam and Egyptian television', in J. Beinin and J. Stork (eds) *Political Islam: Essays from Middle East Report* (London: I.B. Travis) pp. 209–52.

Ahmad, M. (1991) 'Islamic Fundamentalism in South Asia', in M. Marty and R. Scott Appleby *Fundamentalisms Observed* (Chicago: Chicago University Press).

Ahmed, A. (1992) *Postmodernism and Islam* (London: Routledge).

Ahsan, M. and Kidawi, A. (eds) (1991) *Sacrilege versus Civility: Muslim Perspectives on The Satanic Verses Affair* (Leicester: The Islamic Foundation).

Akhtar, S. (1989) *Be Careful With Muhammad* (London: Bellew).

Akhtar, S. (1993) *The Muslim Parents' Handbook* (London: Ta-Ha).

Al-Azmeh, A. (1993) *Islams and Modernities* (London: Verso).

Alexander, J. (ed.) (1998) *Real Civil Societies: Dilemmas of Institionalization* (London: Routledge).

Ali, Y. (1992) 'Muslim Women and the Politics of Ethnicity in Northern England', in Saghal Gita and Yuval-Davis Nira, *Refusing Holy Orders: Women and Fundamentalism in Britain* (London: Virago).

Alibhai, Y. (1989a) Satanic Betrayals, *New Statesman and Society*, 2 February p.12.

Alibhai, Y. (1989b) Beyond Fundamentalism and Liberalism *New Statesman and Society*, 3 March pp. 34–5.

Ally, M. (1990) 'Second Introductory Paper' in Commission for Racial Equality *Law, Blasphemy and the Multi-Faith Society* (London: Commission for Racial Equality) pp. 21–9.

Al-Najjar, H. *Islam and Politics: an Inquiry into the Origins of Political Theory and the Political System of Islam* [in Arabic] (Cairo: Daral-Sha'b, 1977).

Ambrosewicz-Jacobs, J. and Mitski, A. (1999) 'The Influence of Religious Instructors on the Attitude of the Youth of Kraków Towards Jews', in I. Borowik (ed.) *Church-state Relations in Catholic Eastern Europe* (Kraków: Nomos) pp. 388–402.

Amnesty International (1992) *Egypt: Security Police Detentions Undermine the Rule of Law* (AI Index, MDE 12.01.92).

Amnesty International (1994) *Tunisia: Rhetoric Vesus Reality: The Failure of a Human Rights Bureaucracy* (London: Amnesty International) January.

Amnesty International (1997) *Tunisia: A Widening Circle of Repression* (London: Amnesty International) June.

Amnesty International (2001) *Egypt: Rough Planet* (London: Amnesty International).

An-Na'im, A.A. (1992) 'Cultural Foundations for International Protection of Human Rights' in A.A. An-Na'im (ed.) *Human Rights in Cross-Cultural Perspectives* (Philadelphia: University of Pennsylvania Press) pp. 19–43.

An-Na'im, A.A. (1998) '*Shari'a* and Basic Human Rights Concerns', in C. Curzmann (ed.) *Liberal Islam: A Sourcebook* (Oxford: OUP) pp. 222–38.

Anaya, J. (1995) 'The Capacity of International Law to Advance Ethics or Nationality Rights Claims', in W. Kymlicka (ed.) *The Rights of Minority Cultures* (Oxford: OUP) pp. 321–330.

Antov, N. and Nash, J. (1999) 'Islamic Civil Society in Turkey', unpublished paper presented at Islam and Human Rights in Post-Communist Europe conference organized by Columbia University, Sofia, 15–16 March.

Appignanesi, L. and Maitland, S. (1989) *The Rushdie File* (London: Fourth Estate).

Archer, M. (1979) *The Social Origins of Educational Systems* (London: Sage).

Arendt, H. (1972) *Crises of the Republic* (New York: Harcourt, Brace Jovanovich).

Arkhoun, M. (1994) *Rethinking Islam: Common Questions, Uncommon Answers* (tr. and ed. R. Lee) (Oxford: Westview).

Asad, T. (1990) 'Ethnography, Literature and Politics: Some Readings and Uses of Salman Rushdie's "The Satanic Verses"', *Cultural Anthropology*, **5**, 230–69.

Asad, T. (1993) *Genealogies of Religion: Disciplines and Reasons of Power in Christianity and Islam* (Baltimore and London: Johns Hopkins University Press).

Asad, T. (1999) 'Religion, Nation-State and Secularism', in P. van der Veer and H. Lehmann (eds) *Nation and Religion: Perspectives on Europe and Asia* (Princeton, NJ: Princeton University Press).

Ashcroft, B., Griffiths, G. and Tiffin, H. (1989) *The Empire Writes Back: Theory and Practice in Post-Colonial Literatures* (London: Routledge).

Ayubi, N. (1991) *Political Islam* (London: Routledge).

Ayubi, N. (1995) *Over-stating the Arab State: Politics and Society in the Middle East* (London: IB Tauris).

Barber, B. (1998) *A Place For Us: How to Make Society Civil and Democracy Strong* (New York: Hillard Wang).

Baron, M., Petit, P. and Slote, M. (1997) *Three Methods of Ethics* (Oxford: Blackwell).

Bauman, Z. (1987) *Legislators and Interpreters* (Cambridge: Polity).

Bauman, Z. (1989) *Modernity and the Holocaust* (Oxford: Blackwell).

Bauman, Z. (1993) *Postmodern Ethics* (Oxford: Blackwell).

Baumann, G. (1996) *Contesting Culture: Discourse of Identity in Multicultural London* (Cambridge: CUP).

Baumann, G. (1999) *The Multicultural Riddle: Rethinking National, Ethnic and Religious Identities* (London: Routledge).

Bayrou, F. (1994) 'Directive aux Chefs d'Etablissement', *Le Figaro*, 21 September p. 3; and paraphrased in Baumann (1999), pp. 49–51.

Beckerlegge, G. (ed.) (2001) *From Sacred Text to Internet* (Aldershot: Ashgate).

Beckford, J. (1989) *Religion in Advanced Industrial Society* (London: Unwin Hyman).

Beckman, B. (1997) 'Explaining Democratization: Notes on the Concept of Civil Society' in E. Özdalga and S. Persson (eds) *Civil Society and Democracy in the Muslim World* (Istanbul: Swedish Research Institute) pp. 1–7.

Bellah, R. *et al*. (1985) *Habits of the Heart: Individualism and Commitment in American Life* (Los Angeles: University of California Press).

Benhabib, S. (1992a) 'Models of Public Space: Hannah Arendt, the Liberal Tradition and Jörgen Habermas', in C. Calhoun (ed.) *Habermas and the Public Sphere* (Cambridge, MA: MIT Press).

Benhabib, S. (1992b) 'The Generalized and Concrete Other', in E. Frazer *et al*. (eds) *Ethics: A Feminist Reader* (Oxford: Blackwell) pp. 267–300.

Berger, P. and Luckmann, T. (1967) 'Aspects sociologiques du pluralisme', *Archives de Sociologie des Religions*, **23**.

Bernhard, M. (1993) *The Origins of Democratization in Poland*, (New York: Columbia University Press).

Beyer, P. (1992) 'The Global Environment as a Religious Issue: a Sociological Analysis', *Religion*, pp. 1–19.

Beyer, P. (1994) *Religion and Globalization* (London: Sage).

Binder, L. (1988) *Islamic Liberalism: A Critique of Development Ideologies* (Chicago: University of Chicago Press).

Boone, K. (1989) *The Bible Tells Them So: the Discourse of Protestant Fundamentalism* (London: SCM).

Borowik, I. (1997) 'Institutional and Private Religion in Poland 1990–1994', in I. Borowik and G. Babiński (eds) *New Religious Phenomena in Central and Eastern Europe* (Kraków: Nomos), pp. 235–55.

Borowik, I. and Babiński, G. (eds) (1997) *New Religious Phenomena in Central and Eastern Europe* (Kraków: Nomos).

Borowik, I. and Jablonski, P. (1995) *The Future of Religion. East and West* (Kraków: Nomos).

Bowen, D. (ed.) (1992) *The Satanic Verses: Bradford Responds* (Bradford: Bradford and Ilkley Community College).

Bowman, M. (1992) *Phenomenology, Fieldwork and Folk Religion* (Cardiff: BASR occasional papers no. 6).

Bowman, M. (1999) 'Healing in the Spiritual Marketplace: Consumers, Courses and Credentialism', *Social Compass*, **46**(2), 181–9.

Boyle, K. and Sheen, J. (1997) *Freedom of Religion: A World Survey* (London: Routledge).

Bradney, A. (1993) *Religion, Rights and Law* (London: Leicester University Press).

Brennan, T. (1989) *Salman Rushdie and the Third World* (Basingstoke: Macmillan).

Bringa, T. (1995) *Being Muslim the Bosnian Way: identity and community in a central Bosnian village* (Princeton NJ, Chichester: Princeton University Press).

Brown, C. (1992) 'A Revisionist Approach to Religious Change', in S. Bruce and R. Wallis (eds) *Religion and Modernization: Sociologists and Historians Debate the Secularization Thesis* (Oxford: Clarendon Press), pp. 31–58.

Brown, C. (2001) *The Death of Christian Britain* (London: Routledge).

Browning, S. and Fiorenza, F. (eds) (1991) *Habermas, Modernity and Public Theology* (New York: Crossroad).

Bruce, S. (1996) *Religion in the Modern World* (Oxford: OUP).

Bruce, S. (1998) *Conservative Protestant Politics* (Oxford: OUP).

Bruce, S. (1999) *Choice and Religion: A Critique of Rational Choice Theory* (Oxford: OUP).

Bruce, S. and Wallis, R. (1992) 'Secularization: the Orthodox Model', in S. Bruce and R. Wallis (eds) *Religion and Modernization: Sociologists and Historians Debate the Secularization Thesis* (Oxford: Clarendon Press) pp. 8–30.

Brzezinski, M. (2000) *The Struggle for Constitutionalism in Poland* (Basingstoke: Macmillan).

Bulac, A. (1998) 'The Medina Document', in C. Curzmann (ed.) *Liberal Islam: A Sourcebook* (New York: OUP), pp. 169–78.

Burgess, J. (1997) *The East German Church and the End of Communism* (Oxford: OUP).

Burlet, S. and Reid, H. (1996) 'Riots, Representation and Responsibilities: the Role of Young Men in Pakistani Heritage Muslim Communities', in W. Shadid and P. van Koningsveld *Political Participation and Identities of Muslims in Non-Muslim States* (Kampen: Kok Pharas), pp. 144–59.

Calhoun, C. (ed.) (1993) *Habermas and the Public Sphere* (Cambridge, MA: MIT Press).

Campbell, D. (1998) *National Deconstruction: Violence, Identity and Justice in Bosnia* (Minneapolis: Minnesota University Press).

Canovan, M. (1992) *Hannah Arendt: A Reinterpretation of her Political Thought* (Cambridge: CUP).

Cantrell, B. and Kemp, U. (1993) 'The Role of the Protestant Churches in Eastern Germany: Some Personal Experiences and Reflections', *Religion, State and Society*, **21** 2–3, 277–88.

Cantrell, B. and Kemp, U. (1995) ''East Germany Revisited', *Religion, State and Society*, **23**, (3), 279–89.

Caplow, T., Bahr, H. and Chadwick, B. (1983) *All Faithful People: Change and continuity in Middleton's religion* (Minneapolis: University of Minnesota Press).

Casanova, J. (1993) 'Church, State, Nation and Civil Society in Spain and Poland', in S Arjomand (ed.) *The Political Dimensions of Religion* (Albany, NY: State University Press of New York).

Casanova, J. (1994) *Public Religions in the Modern World* (Chicago: Chicago University Press).

Casanova, J. (1996) 'Global Catholicism and the Politics of Civil Society', *Sociological Inquiry*, **66**(3), 356–73.

Castells, M. (1996) *The Information Age: Economy, Society and Culture. Vol. 1: The Rise of the Network Society* (Oxford: Blackwell).

Castells, M. (1997a) *The Information Age: Economy, Society, Culture. Vol. 2: The Power of Identity, III: End of Millennium* (Oxford: Blackwell).

Castells, M. (1997b) *The Information Age: Economy, Society, Culture. Vol. 3: End of Millennium* (Oxford: Blackwell).

Chadwick, H. (1967) *The Early Church* (London: Pelican).

Chandler, D. (1998) 'Democratization in Bosnia: the Limits of Civil Society Building Strategies', *Democratization*, **5**(4) 78–102.

Chaplin, J. (1993) 'How Much Cultural and Religious Pluralism can Liberalism Tolerate?', in J. Horton (ed.) *Liberalism, Multiculturalism and Toleration* (London: Macmillan).

Chaves, M. (1994) 'Secularization as Declining Religious Authority' *Social Forces*, **72**(3), 749–74.

Clayer, N. (1997) 'Islam, State and Society in Post-Communist Albania', in H. Poulton and S. Taji-Farouki (eds), *Muslim Identity and the Balkan State* (London: Hurst) pp. 115–38.

Cockburn, C. (1998) *The Space Between Us: Negotiating Gender and National Identities in Conflict* (London: Zed).

Coggins, R.J. and Houlden, J.L. (1990) *A Dictionary of Biblical Interpretation* (London: SCM).

Cohen, J. and Arato, A. (1992) A *Civil Society and Political Theory* (Cambridge MA. and London: MIT Press).

Conway, J. (1990) 'How to Serve God in a Post-Marxist Land? East German Protestantism's Contribution to a Peaceful Revolution', *Journal of Religious History*, **16**(2), 126–39.

Cordell, K. (1995) 'The Church: Coming to Terms with Change', in E. Kolinsky asst. by S.Wilsdorf (eds) *Between Hope and Fear: Everyday Life in Post-Unification East Germany, A Case Study of Leipzig* (Keele, Staffs: University Press), pp. 123–34.

Coupland, D. (1991) *Generation X: Tales for an Accelerated Culture* (New York: St. Martin's Press).

Court, J. (1990) 'Revelation of John', in R. Coggins and J. Houlden (eds) *A Dictionary of Biblical Interpretation* (London: SCM) pp. 593–5.

Csepeli, G. (1991) 'Competing Patterns of National Identity in Post-Communist Hungary', *Media, Culture and Society*, **13**(328).

Curzmann, C. (ed.) (1998) *Liberal Islam: A Sourcebook* (Oxford: OUP).

Dalacoura, K. (1998) *Islam, Liberalism and Human Rights* (London: I.B. Tauris).

Dalrymple, W. (1999) *The Age of Kuli: Indian Travels and Encounters* (London: Flamingo).

Davie, G. (1993) Review of P. Michel (1991) *Politics and Religion in Eastern Europe* (Cambridge: Polity) in *Religion, State and Society*, **21**(2), 237–9.

Davie, G. (2000) *Religion in Modern Europe* (Oxford: OUP).

Davies, N. (1996) *Europe: A History* (Oxford: OUP).

Davis, G. (ed.) (1996) *Religion and Justice in the War Over Bosnia* (London: Routledge).

D'Costa, G. (1990) 'Secular Discourse and the Clash of Faiths: 'The Satanic Verses' in British Society', *New Blackfriars*, **71**, (842), 418–32.

De Gruchy, J. (1995) *Christianity and Democracy* (Cambridge: CUP).

Deacon, T. (1997) *The Symbolizing Species: The Co-Evolution of Language and the Brain* (New York: W.W. Norton).

Decker, P. and Ester, P. (1996) 'Depillarization, Deconfessionalization and Deinstitutionalization: Empirical Trends in Dutch Society 1958–1992', *Review of Religious Research*, **37**, 325–41.

Deflem, M. (ed.) (1996) *Habermas, Modernity and Law* (London: Sage).

Della Cava, R. (1997) 'Religious Resource Networks: Roman Catholic Philanthropy in Central and East Europe', in S. Hoeber Rudolph and J. Piscatori (eds) *Transnational Religions and Fading States* (Boulder, Colorado: Westview), pp. 173–211.

Devereux, G. and Loeb, E. (1943) 'Antagonistic Enculturation' *American Sociological Review*, **8**(2), 133–47.

Doktor, T. (1999) 'State, Church and New Religions in Poland', in I. Borowik, *Church-State Relations in Central and Eastern Europe* (Kraków: Nomos), pp. 178–188.

Donaldson, T. (ed.) (1993) *Britain's Ethnic Minorities* (London: Policy Studies Institute).

Dorrien, G. (1990) *Reconstructing the Common Good: Theology and Social Order* (Maryknoll, New York: Orbis).

Douglass, C. and Friedmann, J. (1998) *Cities for Citizens: planning and the rise of civil society in a global age* (Chichester: Wiley).

Dryzeck, J. (1990) *Discursive Democracy* (Cambridge: CUP).

Dryzeck, J. (1995) 'Critical Theory as a Research Programme', in S. White (ed.) *The Cambridge Companion to Habermas* (Cambridge: CUP), pp. 97–119.

Duffy, D. *et al.* (1993) ''Patriotic Perspectives in Contemporary Poland: Conflict or Consensus?' *The Polish Review*, **38**(3), pp. 259–98.

Durkheim, E. (1984 [1893]) *The Division of Labour in Society* (London: Macmillan).

Dwyer, K. (1991) *Arab Voices: the Human Rights Debate in the Middle East* (London: Routledge).

Egyptian Organization for Human Rights [EOHR] (1997) *Torture Inside Police Stations Must Be Stopped* (Cairo: EOHR).

Ekiert, G. (1996) *The State Against Society: Political Crises and their Aftermath in East Central Europe* (Princeton, NJ: Princeton University Press).

Eminov, A. (1997) *Turkish and Other Muslim Minorities of Bulgaria* (London: Hurst).

Enayat, H. (1982) *Modern Islamic Political Thought* (Austin, TX: Texas University Press).

Esack, F. (1991) 'Contemporary Religious Thought in South Africa and the Emergence of Qu'ranic Hermeneutical Notions', *Islam and Christian Relations*, 2 December, pp. 206–26.

Esposito, J. (1992) *The Islamic Threat: Myth or Reality?* (Oxford: OUP).

Esposito, J. (1994) *Islam: The Straight Path* (2nd edition, Oxford: OUP).

Evans, M. (1997) *Religious Liberty and International Law* (Cambridge: CUP).

Everett, W. (1997) *Religion, Federalism and the Struggle for Public Life* (Oxford: OUP).

Faksh, M. (1997) *The Future of Islam in the Middle East* (Westport, CT: Praeger).

Falk, R. (1992) 'Cultural Foundations for International Human Rights Protection', in A.A. An-Na'im (ed.) *Human Rights in Cross-Cultural Perspectives* (Philadelphia: University of Pennsylvania Press), pp. 44–64.

Farnsley, A. (2000) 'Congregations as the focal point of American religious life', paper presented to the BSA Sociology of Religion Study Group annual conference, Exeter, March.

Fein, H. (1990) 'Genocide: A Sociological Perspective', *Current Sociology*, **38**, 1–126.

Feirabend, J. and Rath, J. (1996) 'Making a Place for Islam in Politics', in W. Shahid and P. van Koningsveld (eds) *Muslims in the Margin: Political Responses to the Presence of Islam in Western Europe* (Kampen, the Netherlands: Kok Pharos) pp. 243–58.

Fergusson, D. (1998) *Community, Liberalism and Christian Ethics* (Cambridge: CUP).

Finke, R. and Stark, R. (1992) *The Churching of America* (New Brunswick, NJ: Rutgers University Press.

Fischer, H. (1991) 'The Catholic Church: a Look Back in Anger', *Religion in Communist Lands*, **19**(3–4), 211–17.

Fitzmaurice, D. (1993) 'Liberal Neutrality, Traditional Minorities and Education', in Horton (ed.), *Liberalism, Multiculturalism and Toleration* (London: Longman).

Flores, A. (1997) 'Secularism, Integralism and Political Islam: the Egyptian Debate', in J. Stork and J. Benin (eds) *Political Islam: Essays from Middle East Report* (London: I.B. Tauris).

Flory, R. and Miller, D. (eds) (2000) *GenX Religion* (London: Routledge).

Foucault, M. (1979) *The History of Sexuality, volume 1: An Introduction* (Harmondsworth: Penguin).

Foucault, M. (1980) *Power/Knowledge: Selected Interviews and Other Writings 1972–1977*, tr. R. Hurley (Harmondsworth: Penguin).

Foucault, M. (1988) *Politics, Philosophy, Culture: Interviews and Other Writings 1977–1984*, tr. A. Sheridan *et al.* (London: Routledge).

Foucault M. (1991 [1977]) *Discipline and Punish: the Birth of the Prison* tr. A. Sheridan (Harmondsworth: Penguin).

Foucault, M. (1992 [1970]) *The Order of Things* (London: Routledge).

Fraser, N. (1992) 'Rethinking the Public Sphere: A Contribution to the Critique of Actually Existing Democracy', in C. Calhoun (ed.) *Habermas and the Public Sphere* (Cambridge, MA and London: MIT Press), pp. 109–42.

Frazer, J. Hornsby, J. and Lovisand, S. (eds) (1992) *Ethics: A Feminist Reader* (Oxford: Blackwell).

Frykenburg, R. (1997) 'The Emergence of "Modern Hinduism"', in G. Sontheimer and H. Kulke (eds) *Hinduism Reconsidered* (Delhi: Manohar).

Fukuyama, F. (1992) *The End of History and the Last Man* (New York: Free Press).

Fuller, S. (1997) *Science* (Buckingham: Open University Press).

Galston, W. A. (1991) *Liberal Purposes: Goods, Virtues and Diversity in the Liberal State* (Cambridge: CUP).

Galtung, J. (1995) *Human Rights in Another Key* (Cambridge: Polity).

Gautier, M. (1998) 'Church Élites and the Restoration of Civil Society in the Communist Societies of Central Europe', *Journal of Church and State*, **40**(2) 289–317.

Geertz, C. (1966) 'Religion as Cultural System', in M. Bouton (ed.) *Anthropological Approaches to the Study of Religion* (New York: Praeger), pp. 1–46.

Geertz, C. (1983) *Local Knowledge* (New York: Basic Books).

Gellner, E. (1981) *Muslim Society* (Cambridge: CUP).

Gellner, E. (1994) *The Conditions of Liberty: Civil Society and its Rivals* (London: Penguin).

Gerges, F. (1999) *America and Political Islam: Clash of Cultures or Clash of Interests?* (Cambridge: CUP).

Ghadbian, (1997) *Democratization and the Islamist Challenge in the Arab World* (Boulder, CO: Westview Press).

al-Ghazali, Z. (1985) *Dawr Al-Mar'a Fi Bina Al-Mujtama* (The Role of Woman in the Building of Society) unpublished paper presented at the Conference of Muslim Women, Lahore, November 1985 (in Arabic).

Giddens, A. (1987) *The Nation State and Violence* (Berkeley: University of California Press).

Gifford, P. (1998) *African Christianity: its Public Role* (London: Hurst).

Gilarek, K. (1997) 'Coping with the Challenges of Modernity. The Church of England in Great Britain and the Catholic Church in Poland', unpublished MA Thesis, University of Exeter/Jagiellonian University, Kraków.

Gilarek, K. (1999) 'Coping with the Challenges of Modernity. The Church of England in Great Britain and the Catholic Church in Poland', in I.Borowik (ed.) *Church-State Relations in Central and Eastern Europe* (Kraków: Nomos) pp. 189–203.

Gill, R. (1992) *Moral Communities* (Exeter: University of Exeter Press).

Gill, R. (1998) *Churchgoing and Christian Ethics* (Cambridge: CUP).

Gill, R., Hadaway, C. and Marler, P. (1998) 'Is Religious Belief Declining in Britain?', *Journal for the Scientific Study of Religion*, **37**(3).

Gilligan, C. (1982) *In a Different Voice: Psychological Theory and Women's Development* (Cambridge, MA: Harvard University Press).

Glenny, M. (1999) *The Balkans 1804–1999: Nationalism, War and the Great Powers* (London: Granta).

Goddard, H. (1999) 'Islam and Democracy', paper presented to Politics and Religion Specialist Group of the Political Studies Association annual conference, Lincoln Theological Institute, Sheffield, 24 February.

Goldberg, E. (1991) 'Smashing Idols and the State: The Protestant Ethic and Egyptian Sunni Radicalism', *Comparative Studies in Society and History*, **33**, 3–35.

Goldschmitt, A. (1988) *Modern Egypt: the Formation of a Nation-State* (Boulder, CO: Westview Press).

Goodwyn, L. (1991) *Breaking the Barrier: the Rise of Solidarity in Poland* (Oxford: Oxford University Press).

Gowricharn, R. and Mungra, B. (1996) 'The Politics of Integration in the Netherlands', in W. Shahid and P. van Koningsveld (eds) *Muslims in the Margin: Political Response to the Presence of Islam in Western Europe* (Kampen: Kok Pharos) (1996), pp. 114–29.

Grabowska, M. (1993) 'The Political Activation of Social Groups', in R. Staar (ed.) *Transition to Democracy in Poland* (New York: St. Martin's Press), pp. 41–55.

Gray, J. (1986) *Liberalism* (Buckingham: Open University Press).

Gray, J. (1995) *Enlightenment's Wake* (London: Routledge).

Greeley, A. (1989) *Religious Change in America* (Cambridge, MA: Harvard University Press).

Greeley, A. (1999) 'The Tilted Playing Field: Accounting for Religious Tastes. A More General Model for the Sociology of Religion', *Journal of Contemporary Religion*, **14**(2), 189–202.

Guenena, N. (1997) 'Islamic Activism in Egypt 1974–1996', in A. Jerichow and J. Baek Simonsen (1997), pp. 128–43.

Habermas, J. (1976) *Legitimation Crisis*, tr. T. McCarthy (London: Heinemann).

Habermas, J. (1986) *Autonomy and Solidarity: Interviews with Jörgen Habermas* (ed. P. Dews, London: Verso).

Habermas, J. (1987) *Theory of Communicative Action. Vol. 2: Lifeworld and System: A Critique of Functionalist Reason* (Cambridge: Polity/Blackwell).

Habermas, J. (1989 [1962]) *The Structural Transformation of the Public Sphere* (Cambridge: Polity).

Habermas, J. (1990) *Moral Consciousness and Communicative Action* (Cambridge MA: MIT Press).

Habermas, J. (1991) 'Transcendence from Within, Transcendence in this World', in S. Browning and F. Fiorenza (eds), *Habermas, Modernity and Public Theology* (New York: Crossroad) pp. 226–50.

Habermas, J. (1992) *Postmetaphysical Thinking* (Cambridge: Polity).

Habermas, J. (1993) 'Further Reflections on the Public Sphere', in Calhoun pp. 421–61.

Habermas, J. (1994a) 'Struggles for Recognition in the Democratic Constitutional State', in C. Taylor with A. Gutmann *Multiculturalism* (Princeton: Princeton University Press), pp. 107–48; p. 113.

Habermas, J. (1994b) *The Past as Future,* tr. M. Pensky (Cambridge: Polity).

Habermas, J. (1996) *Between Facts and Norms* (Cambridge: Polity).

Habermas, J. (1997) 'Israel or Athens, or to Whom Does *Anamnestic* Reason Belong?' in D. Batstone *et al.* (eds) *Liberation Theologies, Postmodernity and the Americas* (London: Routledge), pp. 243–52.

Hadden, J. (1987) 'Toward desacralizing secularization theory' *Social Forces* **65**(3) 587–611.

Hall, J. (1998) 'Genealogies of Civility', in R. Hefner *Democratic Civility: The History and Cross-Cultural Possibility of a Modern Political Ideal* (London and New Brunswick, NJ: Transaction).

Halliday, F. (1996) *Islam and the Myth of Confrontation: Religion and Politics in the Middle East.*

Halstead, J. (1988) *Education and Cultural Diversity* (London: Falmer).

Hann, C. (ed.) (1996) *Civil Society: Challenging Western Models* (London: Routledge).

Hann, C. (1997) 'The Nation-State, Religion and Uncivil Society: Two Perspectives from the Periphery', *Human Diversity,* **126**(2), 27–43.

Hanson, S. (1997) 'The Secularization Thesis: Talking at Cross Purposes', *Journal of Contemporary Religion,* **12**(2), 159–79.

Havel, V. (1987) *Living in Truth: 22 essays published on the occasion of the award of the Erasmus prize to Vacláv* Havel, edited by J. Vladislav (London: Faber).

Hawley, C. (2000) ' "Sharia swimsuit" gives cover at beach', the *Independent,* 2 September p. 14.

Hearn, J. (2000) 'The "Uses and Abuses" of Civil Society in Africa', paper presented to the Review of African Political Economy Conference, University of Leeds, April.

Heelas, P. (1996) *The New Age Movement: the Celebration of Self and the Sacralization of Modernity* (Oxford: Blackwell).

Hefner, R. (2000) *Civil Islam: Muslims and Democratization in Indonesia* (Princeton, NJ: Princeton University Press).

Heins, C. (1994) *The Wall Falls: an oral history of the reunification of the Two Germanies* (London: Gray Seal).

Helms, E. (1999) 'Muslim Women's NGOs Between Discourse of Secular Civil Society and Religion-based National Identity in Boönjak-Majority Areas of Bosnia-Hercegovina', unpublished paper presented to Islam and Human Rights in Post-Communist Europe conference, Sofia, March 15–16.

Helsinki Watch (1986) Reinventing Civil Society: Poland's Quiet Revolution (New York: Helsinki Watch).

Herbert, D. (1993a) 'Shabbir Akhtar on Muslims, Christians and British Society', *Islam and Christian-Muslim Relations,* **4**(1), 100–17.

Herbert, D. (1999) 'Christianity, Democratization and Secularization in Central and Eastern Europe', *Religion, State and Society,* **27**(3–4), 277–94.

Herbert, D. (2000) 'Virtue Ethics, Justice and Religion in Multicultural Societies', in K. Flanagan and P. Jupp (eds), *Virtue Ethics and Sociology: Issues of Religion and Modernity* (London: Palgrave).

Herbert, D. (ed.) (2001a) *Religion and Social Transformations* (Aldershot: Ashgate).

Herbert, D. (ed.) (2001b) 'Islam and Human Rights', Audiocassette 1 of Open University course *AD317 Religion Today: Tradition: Modernity and Change* (Milton Keynes: Open University).

Herbert, D. (ed.) (2001c) 'Rethinking Religion and Modernity', Audiocassette 4 of Open University course *AD317 Religion Today: Tradition: Modernity and Change* (Milton Keynes: Open University).

Herbert, D. (2001d) 'Representing Islam: The Islamization of Egypt 1970–2000', in G Beckerlegge (ed.) (2001) *From Sacred Text to Internet* (Aldershot: Ashgate).

Hervieu-Léger, D. (1997) 'Faces of Catholic Transnationalism: In and Beyond France', tr. R Gleason, in S. Rudolph and J. Piscatori *Transnational Religion and Fading States* (Boulder, CO: Westview).

Hervieu-Léger, D. (2000) *Religion as a Chain of Memory* (Cambridge: Polity).

Hiro, D. (1988) *Islamic Fundamentalism* (London: Paladin Grafton).

Holub, R. (1991) *Jörgen Habermas: Critic in the Public Sphere* (London: Routledge).

Honeyford, R. (1984) 'Educational Race – an alternative view', *The Salisbury Review* 6 pp.30–2.

Horton, J. and Mendus, S. (eds) (1994) *After MacIntyre: Critical Perspectives on the Work of Alasdair MacIntyre* (Cambridge: Polity).

Horton, J. (ed.) (1993) *Liberalism, Multiculturalism and Toleration* (London: Macmillan).

Hudick, A. (1999) *NGOs and Civil Society: Democracy by Proxy?* (Cambridge: Polity).

Hulmes, E. (1989) *Education and Cultural Diversity* (London: Longman).

Huntingdon, S. (1968) *Political Order in Changing Societies* (New Haven, CT: Yale University Press).

Huntingdon, S. (1993) 'The Clash of Civilizations?' *Foreign Affairs,* **72**(2), 22–43.

Iannaccone, L. (1996) 'Looking backward: Estimating long-run attendance trends across eighteen countries', paper presented at the annual meeting of the Society for the Scientific Study of Religion.

Ibrahim, S. (1996) *The Copts of Egypt* (London: Minority Rights Group International).

Ibrahim, S. (1997a) 'From Taliban to Erbakan: The Case of Islam, Civil Society and Democracy', in E. Özdalga and S. Persson (eds) *Civil Society and Democracy in the Muslim World* (Istanbul: Swedish Research Institute), pp. 33–44.

Ibrahim, S. (1997b) 'The Troubled Triangle: Populism, Islam and Civil Society in the Arab World', in A. Jerichow and J.B. Simonsen (1997)13–29.

Inglehart, R. (1997) *Modernization and Postmodernization: Cultural, Economic and Political Change in 43 Societies* (Princeton, NJ: Princeton University Press).

Inglehart, R., Basanez, M and Moreno, A. (1998) *Human Values and Beliefs: a Cross-Cultural Sourcebook* (Ann Arbor: University of Michigan Press).

Iqra Trust, (1990) *Research on Public Attitudes to Islam* (London: Iqra Trust).

Irwin, Z. (1984) 'The Islamic Revival and the Muslims of Bosnia-Hercegovina', *Eastern European Quarterly*, **17**, 437–58.

Izetbegovic, A. (1984) *Islam Between East and West* (2nd edn. Indianapolis: American Trust).

Jacobson, J. (1998) *Islam in Transition: Religion and Identity Among Pakistani Youth* (London: Routledge).

Janis, M. (1997) 'Russia and the "Legality" of Strasbourg Law', *European Journal of International Law*, **1**, 93–9.

Jerichow, A. and Simonsen, J.B. (eds) (1997) *Islam in a Changing World: Europe and the Middle East* (London: Curzon).

Jones, T. (ed.) (1993) *Britain's Ethnic Minorities* (London: Policy Studies Institute).

Jurecyznska, E. (1993) 'Changing Cultural Patterns in Polish Society', in J. Coenen-Huther and B. Synak (eds) *From Totalitarianism to Democracy?* (Nova Science) pp. 67–84.

Kamali, M.H. (1991) *Principles of Islamic Jurisprudence* (Cambridge: Islamic Texts Society).

Kapralska, K. (1995) 'Jewish Topics in the History Curriculum of Polish Schools', unpublished report for Tempos programme *Ethnic Identity in Europe After Aushwitz:the case of Polish-Jewish Relations (post 1989).*

Karam, A. (1997) 'Islamist Parties in the Arab World: Ambiguities, Contradictions and Perseverance' *Democratization*, **4**(4), 157–74.

Karam, A. (1998) *Women, Islamisms and the State*: *Contemporary Feminisms in Egypt* (London: Macmillan).

Kassem, M. (1999) *In the Guise of Democracy: Governance in Contemporary Egypt* (Reading: Ithaca).

Keane, J. (1998) *Civil Society* (Cambridge: Polity).

Kee, A. (1990) *Marx and the Failure of Liberation Theology* (London: SCM).

Keleher, S. (1992) 'Church in the Middle: Greek Catholics in Central and Eastern Europe', *Religion, State and Society*, **20**(3 and 4), 289–302.

Koepping, K.-P. 'Empowerment through embodiment in liturgy and ideology: an apocalyptic religious movement in modern Japan', paper presented to the BSA Sociology of Religion Study Group annual conference, Exeter, March.

Kotva, J. (1994) 'Christian Virtue Ethics and the "Sectarian Tempatation"' *Heythrop Journal*, **35**(1), 35–52.

Kozerski, A. and Herbert, D. (2001) *Church, State and Society in Poland*, a video produced by the BBC (Milton Keynes: Open University).

Krusche, G. (1994) 'The Church Between Accommodation and Refusal: the Significance of the Lutheran Doctrine of the "Two Kingdoms" for the Churches of the GDR', *Religion, State and* Society, **22**(3), 324–32.

Kubik, K.(1994) *The Power of Symbols Against the Symbols of Power: The Rise of Solidarity and the Fall of State Socialism in Poland* (Philadelphia: Pennsylvania State University).

Kubik, K. (1995) Review of R. Zuzowski *Political Dissent and Opposition in Poland. The Workers' Defence Committee 'KOR'* (Westport, CT: Praeger, 1994), in *Polish Review*, **40**(3), 357–60.

Kuhn, T. (1970 [1962]) *The Structure of Scientific Revolutions* (Chicago: Chicago University Press).

Küng, H. (1991) *Global Responsibility* (tr. John Bowden, London: SCM).

Kureishi, H. (1986) '*Bradford'*, *Granta.*

Kymlicka, W. (1991) *Liberalism, Community and Culture* (Oxford:OUP).

Kymlicka,W. (1995) *Multicultural Citizenship* (Oxford: OUP).

Kymlicka, W. (ed.) (1995) *The Rights of Minority Cultures* (Oxford: OUP).

Lambert, Y. (1994) 'Un paysage religieux en profonde évolution', in H. Riffault (ed.) *Les Valeurs des français* (Paris: PUF).

Lanham, H. and Forsythe D. (1994) 'Human Rights in the New Europe: A Balance Sheet', in D. Forsythe (ed.) *Human Rights in the New Europe: problems and progress* (Lincoln, NE: University of Nebraska Press), pp. 214–57.

Lapidus, I. (1992) 'The Golden Age: The Political Concepts of Islam', *Annals of the American Academy*, **524**, 13–25.

Lash, S. (1990) *Sociology of Postmodernism* (London: Routledge).

Lawrence, B. (1989) 'Defenders of God: The Fundamentalist Revolt Against the Modern Age' (San Francisco: Harper and Row).

Lehmann, D. (1996) *Struggle for the Spirit: religious tradition and popular culture in Brazil and Latin America* (Cambridge: Polity)

Leveau, R. (1988) 'The Islamic Presence in France', in T. Gerholm and Y. Lithman *The New Islamic Presence in Western Europe* (London: Mansell) pp. 107–22.

Leveau, R. (1991) 'Islam in France: New Perspectives', in W. Shahid and P. van Konigsveld (eds.) *The Integration of Islam and Hinduism in Western Europe* (Kampen: Kok Pharos) pp. 122–33.

Levine, D. (1999) 'Progressive Catholicism, Liberation Theology, and the Challenge of Democracy in Latin America', unpublished paper presented to the Politics and Religion Specialist Group of the Political Studies Association, Sheffield, 24 February.

Lewis, P. (Paul) (1997) 'Democratization in Eastern Europe', in D. Potter *et al.* (eds) *Democratization* (Cambridge: Polity) pp. 399–420.

Lewis, P. (Philip) (1992) 'From book-burning to vigil: Bradford Muslims a year on', in D. Bowen (ed.) *The Satanic Verses: Bradford Responds* (Bradford: Bradford and Ilkley Community College) pp. 54–8.

Lewis, P. (1993a) 'Beyond Babel: An Anglican Perspective in Bradford' (The Eighth Lambeth Interfaith Lecture), *Islam and Christian-Muslim Relations*, 4(1) 118–38.

Lewis, P. (1994a) *Islamic Britain* (London: I.B. Tauris).

Lewis, P. (2001) 'Bradford – more than a race war', *The Tablet*, 21 July, pp. 1040–2.

Lipschutz, R. (1992) 'Reconstructing World Politics: the Emergence of Global Civil Society', *Millennium: Journal of International Studies*, 21(3) 389–420.

Liu, Z. and Wang, S. (1988) 'From "Mass Society" to "Civil Society"', *Xinhua wenzhai* [New China Digest], 11, 119.

Longley, C. (1989) 'Shadow over Auschwitz', *The Times*, 20 May.

Lovrenović, I. (2000) 'Five Fragments about Implosion', in F. Duve and N. Popović (eds) tr. G. McMaster *In Defence of the Future: Searching the Minefield* (Vienna: Folio/OSCE) pp. 77–92.

Lovin, R.W. and Reynolds, F.E. (1992) 'Ethical Naturalism and Indigenous Cultures', *Journal of Religious Ethics*, 267–78.

Luckmann, T. 'Social Reconstruction of Transcendence', in *Secularization and Religion: the Persisting Tension* (Acts of the XIXth International Conference for the Sociology of Religion, Tübingen, 1987, 25–29 August) pp. 23–31.

Luhmann, N. (1982) *The Differentiation of Societies* (New York: Columbia University Press).

Lukes, S. (1986) *Power* (Oxford: Blackwell).

Lukes, S. (1991) *Modern Conflict and Politics* (Oxford: Clarendon).

Luxmoore, J. (1987) 'The Polish Church under Martial Law', *Religion in Communist Lands*, 25(2), 124–66.

Luxmoore, J. (1995) 'Eastern Europe 1994: a Review of Religious Life in Bulgaria, Romania, Hungary, Slovakia, the Czech Republic and Poland', *Religion, State and Society*, 23(2), 213–18.

Luxmoore, J. (1996) 'Eastern Europe 1995: a Review of Religious Life in Bulgaria, Romania, Hungary, Slovakia, the Czech Republic and Poland', *Religion, State and Society*, 24(4), 357–65.

Luxmoore, J. (1997) 'Eastern Europe 1996: a Review of Religious Life in Bulgaria, Romania, Hungary, Slovakia, the Czech Republic and Poland', *Religion, State and Society*, 25(1), 89–101.

Luxmoore, J. and Babiuch, J. (1995a) 'In Search of Faith: the Metaphysical Dialogue Between Poland's Opposition Intellectuals in the 1970s', *Religion, State and Society*, 23(1), 75–95.

Luxmoore, J. and Babiuch, J. (1995b) 'In Search of Faith, Part 2: Charter 77 and the Return to Spiritual Values in the Czech Republic', *Religion, State and Society*, **23**(1), 291-304.

Lyon, R. (2000) *Jesus in Disneyland* (London: Routledge).

Lyotard, J-F. (1986) *The Postmodern Condition: A Report on Knowledge* (Manchester: Manchester University Press).

Lyotard, J-F. (1988) *The Differend: Phrases in Dispute* (tr. G. Van Den Abbeele, Manchester: Manchester University Press).

MacIntyre, A. (1967a) *A Short History of Ethics* (London: Routledge).

MacIntyre, A. (1967b) *Secularization and Moral Change* (Oxford: OUP).

MacIntyre, A. (1971) 'Rationality and the Explanation of Action', in A. MacIntyre *Against the Self-Images of the Age: Essays on Ideology and Philosophy* (London: Duckworth) pp. 244–59.

MacIntyre A (1973) 'The Essential Contestability of Some Social Science Concepts', *Ethics*, **84**(4), 1–9.

MacIntyre, A. (1977) 'Epistemological Crises, Dramatic Narrative and the Philosophy of Science', *The Monist*, **60**, 453–72.

MacIntyre, A. (1982) 'Public Virtue: a review of *Explaining America: The Federalist* by Gary Willis and *James McCosh and the Scottish Intellectual Tradition* by David Hoeveler', *London Review of Books*, 18 February–3 March.

MacIntyre, A. (1983) 'Moral Rationality, Tradition and Aristotle: a Reply to Onora O'Neill, Raimond Gaita and Stephen R.L. Clark', *Inquiry*, **26**, pp. 447–66.

MacIntyre, A. (1985) (second edition) *After Virtue* (London: Duckworth).

MacIntyre, A. (1987) 'The Idea of an Educated Public', in G. Haydon (ed.) *Education and Values* (London: Institute of Education).

MacIntyre, A. (1988) *Whose Justice? Which Rationality* (London: Duckworth).

MacIntyre, A. (1991) *Three Rival Versions of Moral Enquiry* (London: Duckworth).

MacIntyre, A. (1994) 'A Partial Response to My Critics', in J. Horton and S. Mendus *After MacIntyre* (Cambridge: Polity) pp. 283–304.

MacIntyre, A. and Emmet, D. (eds) (1970) *Sociological Theory and Philosphical Analysis* (London: Macmillan).

Macleod, A. (1991) *Accommodating Protest: working women, the new veiling, and change in Cairo* (New York: Columbia University Press).

Mahmutćehajić, R. (1998) 'The Downhill Path *and* Defence, Not Surrender', in C. Curzmann *Liberal Islam: A Source Book* (New York: OUP).

Mahmutćehajić, R. (2000) 'From the Tropic of the Millennium', in F. Duve and N. Popović *In Defence of the Future: Searching in the Minefield* (Vienna: Folio Verlag) pp. 15–49.

Maitland, S. (1990) 'Blasphemy and Creativity', in D. Cohn-Sherbok (ed.) '*The Satanic Verses' Controversy in Interfaith Perspective* (Lampeter: Edwin Mellen Press).

Makdisi, J. (1985) 'Legal Logic and Equity in Islamic Law', *American Journal of Comparative Law*, **32**, pp. 63–92.

Malcolm, N. (1996) *Bosnia: A Short History* (2nd edition Basingstoke: Macmillan)

Marshalls, J. (1998) 'French Row Over Race Poll', *Times Higher Education Supplement*, 27 November, p. 56.

Mardin, S. (1995) 'Civil Society and Islam', in J. Hall (ed.) *Civil Society: Theory, History, Comparison* (Cambridge: Polity).

Martin, D. (1996a) *Forbidden Revolutions: Pentecostalism in Latin America, Catholicism in Eastern Europe* (London: SPCK).

Martin, D. (1996b) 'Religion, Secularization and Postmodernity: Lessons form the Latin American Case', in P. Repstadt *Religion and Modernity: models of co-existence* (Oslo: Scandinavian University Press) pp. 35–43.

Marty, M. and Appleby, R. (eds) (1991) *Fundamentalisms Observed* (Chicago and London: Chicago University Press).

May, T. (1996) *Situating Social Theory* (Buckingham: Open University Press).

Mayer, A. (1994) 'Universal Versus Islamic Human Rights: Clash of Cultures or a Clash with a Construct?', *Michigan Journal of International Law*, **15**, pp. 307–402.

Mayer, A. (1995) *Islam and Human Rights: Tradition and Politics* (London: Pinter).

Mayhew, L. (1997) *The New Public: Professional communication and the means of social influence* (Cambridge: CUP).

Mazrui, A. (1991) 'Satanic verses or a satanic novel? Moral dilemmas of the Rushdie Affair', *Third World Quarterly*, April, 116–39.

McLuhan, H.M. (1975) 'The Medium is the Message', in A. Wells (ed.) *Mass Media and Society* (Paolo Alto, CA: Mayfield).

McMylor, P. (1994) *Alasdair MacIntyre: Critic of Modernity* (London: Routledge).

Mellor, P. and Shilling, C. (1995) *Re-forming the Body: Religion, Community and Modernity* (London: Sage).

Melucci, A. (1985) 'The symbolic challenge of contemporary movements', *Social Research*, **52**(4), 789–816.

Mendelson, O. and Vicziany, M. (1998) *The Untouchables: Subordination, Poverty and the State in Modern India* (Cambridge: CUP).

Mernissi, F. (1988) *Women and Islam* (Oxford: Blackwell).

Mernissi, F. (1993) *Islam and Democracy* (London: Virago).

Mestrovic, S. (1993) 'Explaining War in the Land of Medjugorje', in S. Mestrovic with S. Letica and M. Goreta (eds) *Explaining War in the Land of Medjugorje* (Austin TX: Texas A&M University Press) pp. 108–30.

Mestrovic, S. (1994) *The Balkanization of the West* (London: Routledge).

Metcalf, B. (1990) *Perfecting Women: Maulana Ashraf 'Ali Thanawi's Bihishti Zewar* (Berkeley: University of California Press).

Metz, H. (ed.) (1991) *Egypt: A Country Study* (5th edn, Washington DC: Federal Research Division, Library of Congress).

Meyer, J. (1980) 'The world polity and the authority of the nation-state', in A. Bergeson (ed.) *Studies of the World System* (New York: Academic Press) pp. 109–37.

Michel, P. (1991) *Politics and Religion in Eastern Europe* (Cambridge: Polity).

Michel, P. (1992) 'Religious Renewal or Political Deficiency: Religion and Democracy in Central Europe', *Religion, State and Society*, **20**(3–4), 339–44.

Middle East Watch (1992) *Behind Closed Doors: Torture and Detention in Egypt* (New York: Human Rights Watch).

Midgely, M. (1989) *Wisdom, Information and Wonder* (London: Routledge).

Milbank, J. (1987) 'An Essay Against Secular Order', *Journal of Religious Ethics*, December, 199–224.

Milbank, J. (1990) *Theology and Social Theory: Beyond Secular Reason* (Oxford: Blackwell).

Mitchell, T. (1988) *Colonising Egypt* (Cambridge: CUP).

Moaddel, M. (1996) 'The Social Bases and Discursive Context of the Rise of Islamic Fundamentalism: the cases of Iran and Syria, *Sociological Inquiry*, **66**(3), 330–55.

Modood, T. (1990) 'Muslims, Race and Equality in Britain: Some Post-Rushdie Affair Reflections', *Third Text*, **11**, 127–34.

Modood, T. (1997) *Ethnic Minorities in Britain: Diversity and Disadvantage* (London: Policy Studies Institute).

Mucha, J. (1993) 'Cultural Minorities and Majority Rule', in J. Coenen-Huther and B. Synak (eds) *From Totalitarianism to Democracy?* (Nova Science) pp. 85–94.

Musial, S. (1989) 'Sprawa Karmelu w Oswiecimiu', 1–3 in *Niedziela Tygodnik Katolicki*, 32, 27–9.

Mutlu, K. (1996) 'Examining religious beliefs among university students in Ankara', *British Journal of Sociology*, **47**, 353–9.

Nagle, R. (1997) *Claiming the Virgin: The Broken Promise of Liberation Theology* (London: Routledge).

Najjar, F. (2000) 'Islamic Fundamentalism and the Intellectuals: The Case of Nasr Hamid Abu Zayd', *British Journal of Middle Eastern Studies*, **27**(2), 177–200.

Neuhaus, R. (1984) *The Naked Public Square: Religion and Democracy in American Grand Rapids* (Michigan: Eeordmans).

Nicholas, R. (1990) *The Catholic Church and the French Nation* (London: Routledge).

Nielsen, J. (1991) 'A Muslim Agenda for Britain: Some Reflections', *New Community*, 17(3), 467–75.

Nielsen, J. (1992) *Muslims in Western Europe* (Edinburgh: Edinburgh University Press).

Olson, D. (1998) 'Religious Pluralism in Contemporary US Countries', *American Sociological Review*, **63**, 757–61.

Osa, M. (1997) 'Creating Solidarity: The Relgious Foundations of the Polish Social Movement', *East European Politics and Societies*, **11**(2), 339–65.

Ousley, H. (2001) *Community Pride Not Prejudice: making diversity work in Bradford* (Bradford: Bradford Race Review).

Outhwaite, W. (1994) *Habermas: A Critical Introduction* (Cambridge: Polity).

Özdalga, E. (1997) 'Civil Society and Its Enemies: Reflections on a Debate in the Light of Recent Developments within the Islamic Student Movement in Turkey', in E. Özdalga and S. Persson (eds) *Civil Society and Democracy in the Muslim World* (Istanbul: Swedish Research Institute) pp. 73–84.

Parekh, B. (1990) 'The Rushdie Affair and The British Press: Some Salutory Lessons', in *Law, Blasphemy and the Multi-Faith Society*, Report of a Seminar, Discussion Paper 2: Free Speech (London: Commission for Racial Equality/Inter Faith Network) pp. 59–78.

Parker-Jenkins, M. (1999) 'Equality Before the Law: An Exploration of the Pursuit of Government Funding by Muslim Schools in Britain', *Brigham Young University Education and Law Journal*, Winter, 119–37.

Pawlikowski, J. (1991) 'The Auschwitz Convent Controversy: Mutual Misperceptions', in C. Rittner and J. Roth (eds) *Memory Offended: the Auschwitz Convent Controversy* (New York: Praeger) pp. 63–73.

Pawlik, W. (1995) 'The Church and its Critics: The Spell of the Polish Ombudsman', *Polish Sociological Review*, **109**(1), 31–45.

Perdue, W. (1995) *The Paradox of Change: the Rise and Fall of Solidarity in the New Poland* (Westport, Connecticut: Praeger).

Piscatori, J. (1993) 'Islamic Fundamentalism in the Wake of the Six Day War: Religious Self-Assertion in Political Conflict', in L.J. Siberstein (ed.) *Jewish Fundamentalism in Comparative Perspective* (New York: New York University Press).

Pollack, D. (1995) 'Post Wende Citizens' Movements', in E. Kolinsky asst. by S. Wilsdorf (eds) *Between Hope and Fear: Everyday Life in Post-Unification East Germany, A Case Study of Leipzig* (Keele: Keele University Press) pp. 101–22.

Poole, R. (1991) *Morality and Modernity* (London: Routledge).

Potter, D., Goldblatt, D., Kiloh, M. and Lewis, P. (eds) (1997) *Democratization* (Cambridge: Polity).

Poulton, H. (1997) 'After Dayton', in H. Poulton and S. Taji-Faruuki (eds) *Muslim Identity and the Balkan State* (London: Hurst) pp. 232–42.

Przeworski, A. 'Economic reforms, public opinion and political institutions: Poland in the Eastern European perspective', in L. Pereirer *et al.*, (eds) *Economic Reforms in New Democracies: A Social Democratic Approach* (Cambridge) pp. 132–98.

Purdom, K. (1996) 'Settler Political Participation: Local Councillors', in W. Shadid and P. van Koningsveld *Political Participation and Identities of Muslims in Non-Muslim States* (Kampen, the Netherlands: Kok Pharos) pp. 129–43.

Qazim, S. (1986) 'An Al-Sijn wa Al-Hurriyya (On Prison and Freedom)' (Cairo: Al-Zahra' li Al-ʹElam Al-Arabi) in Arabic.

Rahman, A. (1984) *Shari'ah: The Islamic Law* (London: Ta-Ha).

Rajagopal, A. (2001) *Politics After Television: Hindu Nationalism and the Reshaping of the Public in India* (Cambridge: CUP).

Ramet, S. (1991) 'Protestantism in East Germany 1949–1989: A Summing Up', *Religion in Communist Lands*, **19**(3–4) 161–95.

Ramet, S. (1995) *Social Currents in Eastern Europe: Causes and Consequences of the Great Transformation* (London: Duke UP).

Ramet, S. (1999) *Balkan Babel: The Disintegration of Yugoslavia from the Death of Tito to the War for Kosovo* (3rd edn, Boulder, CO: Westview).

Ramet, S. (2000) 'Religion and politics in Germany since 1945: The Evangelical and Catholic Churches', *Journal of Church and State*, **42**(1), 115–45.

Rao, U. (2000) 'Social empowerment through prophetic embodiment: belief in divine guidance in an urban Indian environment', paper presented to the BSA Sociology of Religion Study Group annual conference, Exeter, March.

Rasch, W. (2000) *Niklas Luhmann's Modernity: The Paradoxes of Differentiation* (Stanford, CA: Stanford University Press).

Rawls, J. (1973) *A Theory of Justice* (Oxford: OUP).

Rawls, J. (1985) 'Justice as Fairness: Political not Metaphysical', *Philosophy and Public Affairs*, **14**(3), 223–51.

Rawls, J. (1988) 'The Priority of Right and Ideas of the Good', *Philosophy and Public Affairs*, **17**(4), 251–76.

Rawls, J. (1993) *Political Liberalism* (New York: Columbia University Press).

Raz, J. (1986) *The Morality of Freedom* (Oxford: Clarendon).

Rémond, R. (1997) 'The Christian Churches in Europe 1918–1996', *Religion, State and Society*, **25**(1), 11–16.

Reynolds, V. and Tanner, R. (1995) *The Social Ecology of Religion* (Oxford: OUP).

Rippin, A. (1993) *Muslims: their Religious Beliefs and Practices. Volume 2: The Contemporary Period* (London: Routledge).

Rittner, C. and Roth, J. (1991) *Memory Offended: the Auschwitz Convent Controversy* (New York: Praeger).

Robertson, R. (1990) 'Mapping the Global Condition: Globalization as the Central Concept', *Theory, Culture and Society*, 7(2–3), 15–30.

Robinson, N. (1992) 'Reflections on the Rushdie Affair – 18 April 1989', in B.D. Bowen (ed.) *The Satanic Verses: Bradford Responds* (Bradford: Bradford and Ilkley Community College) pp. 33–44.

Roof, W. (1996) 'God is in the Details: Reflections on Religion's Public Presence in the United States in the Mid 1990s', *Sociology of Religion*, **57**.

Rorty, R. (1979) *Philosophy and the Mirror of Nature* (Princeton NJ: Princeton University Press).

Rorty, R. (1982) *Consequences of Pragmatism* (Minneapolis MN: University of Minnesota Press).

Rossouw, G. (1992) 'From a Just to a Good Society: the Role of Christianity in the Transformation of Former Eastern-Bloc Countries', *Religion, State and Society*, **20**(3–4), 321–9.

Roussillon, A. (1998) 'Republican Egypt Interpreted: revolution and beyond', in M. Daly (ed.) *Cambridge History of Egypt vol. 2 Modern Egypt from 1517 to the end of the Twentieth Century* (Cambridge: CUP).

Roy, A. (2001) 'Muslim parents and mosques are to blame, says Hindu leader', *Daily Telegraph*, 9th July.

Runnymede Trust (1997) *British Muslims and Islamphobia* (London: Runnymede Trust).

Rushdie, S. (1981) *Midnight's Children* (London: Cape).

Rushdie, S. (1988) *The Satanic Verses* (London: Viking Penguin).

Rushdie, S. (1990a) *In Good Faith* (London: Granta).

Rushdie, S. (1990b) *Is Nothing Sacred?* (London: Granta).

Ruthven, M. (1990) *A Satanic Affair* (London: Chatto and Windus).

Ruthven, M. (1991) *Islam in the World* (2nd edn. London: Penguin).

Sacks, J. (1990) 'The Persistence of Faith: The 1990 Reith Lectures', *The Listener*, 15 November 1990–3 January 1991.

Sacks, J. (2001) 'In a world run by MTV, nobody has time to think', *The Daily Telegraph*, 6 September.

Sahgal, G. and Yuval-Davis, N. (1990) 'Editorial', *Women Against Fundamentalism*, **2**(1), 1–2.

Sahgal, G. and Yuval-Davis, N. (eds) (1992) *Refusing Holy Orders: Women and Fundamentalism in Britain* (London: Virago).

Said, E. (1978) *Orientalism* (London: Penguin).

Saifullah Khan, V. (1977) 'The Pakistanis: Mirpuri Villagers at Home in Bradford', in J. Watson (ed.) *Between Two Cultures* (Oxford Blackwell) pp. 57–89.

Samad, Y. (1992) 'Book Burning and Race Relations: Political mobilisation of Bradford Muslims', *New Community*, **18**(4), 507–19.

al-Sayyid, M. (1993) 'A Civil Society in Egypt?', *Middle East Journal*, **47**(2), 228–42.

Schank, R. (1990) *Tell Me a Story* (New York: Charles Scribner).

Schiffauer, W. (1988) 'Migration and Religiousness', in T. Gerholm and Y. Lithman (eds) *The New Islamic Presence in Western Europe* (London: Mansell) pp. 146–58.

Schmitt, C. (1985 [1923]) *The Crisis of Parliamentary Democracy* (Cambridge, MA: MIT Press).

Schönherr (1991) 'Church and State in the GDR', *Religion in Communist Lands*, **19**(3–4), 197–210.

Schwartlander, J. and Bielefeldt, H. (1994) *Christians and Muslims Facing the Challenge of Human Rights* (Bonn: Deutsche Kommission Justitia et Pax).

Seligman, A. (1992) *The Idea of Civil Society* (Chichester: Princeton University Press).

Seligman, A. (1997) *The Problem of Trust* (Chichester: Princeton University Press).

Seligman, A. (1998a) 'Civil Society: Between Jerusalem and Los Angeles', paper presented to the IJPR, London, 7 September.

Seligman, A. (1998b) 'Theorising Trust and Confidence', keynote paper presented to NCVO Annual Research Conference, Loughborough, 9 September.

Sells, M. (1996) 'Religion, History and Genocide in Bosnia-Herzegovina', in G. Davis (ed.) *Religion and Justice in the War Over Bosnia* (London: Routledge) pp. 23–44.

Sells, M. (1996) *The Bridge Betrayed: Religion and Genocide in Bosnia* (Berkeley and Los Angeles: University of California Press).

Sennett, R. (1994 [1974]) *The Fall of Public Man* (New York: W.W. Norton)

Shadid, W. and van Koningsveld, P. (eds) (1996) *Muslims in the Margin: Political Response to the Presence of Islam in Western Europe* (Kampen, the Netherlands: Kok Pharos).

Shanks, A. (1995) *Civil Society, Civil Religion* (Oxford: Blackwell).

Sharabi, H. (1966) *Nationalism and Revolution in the Arab World* (Princeton, NJ: Princeton UP).

Shaw, A. (1988) *A Pakistani Community in Britain* (Oxford: Blackwell).

Shilling, C. and Mellor, P. (1995) *The Body and Society* (London: Sage).

Singerman, D. (1995) *Avenues of Participation: Family, Politics and Networks in Urban Quarters of Cairo* (Princeton, NJ and Chichester: Princeton University Press).

Skapska, G. (1997) 'Learning to be a Citizen: Cognitive and Ethical Aspects of Post-Communist Society Transformation', in R. Fine (ed.) *Civil Society: Democratic Perspectives* (London: Cass) pp. 145–60.

Skinner, Q. (1978) *The Foundations of Modern Political Thought* vols 1 and 2 (Cambridge: CUP).

Śliwiński, K. (1987) *Christian Science Monitor*, 8 June, p. 10.

Smith, C. (1998) *American Evangelicalism: Embattled and Thriving* (Chicago: University of Chicago Press).

Sorabji, C. (1989) 'Muslim Identity and Islamic Faith in Socialist Sarajevo', unpublished PhD thesis, University of Cambridge.

Soysal, Y. (1994) *Post-national Citizenship* (Yale University Press).

Spülbeck, S. (1996) 'Anti-semitism and fear of the public sphere in a post-totalitarian society: East Germany', in C. Hann (ed.) *Civil Society: Challenging Western Models* (London: Routledge).

Stark, R. (1999) 'Secularization R.I.P.', *Sociology of Religion*, **60**(3), 249–73.

Stark, R. and Iannoccone, L. (1994) 'A Supply-Side Interpretation of the Secularization of Europe', *Journal for the Scientific Study of Religion*, **33**(2), 30–52.

Starrett, G. (1998) *Putting Islam to Work: Education, Politics and Religious Transformation in Egypt* (Berkeley, Los Angeles and London: University of California Press).

Statszewki, M. (1994) *State-Church Relations in East Central Europe: Legal and Institutional Issues* (Warsaw).

Stout, J. (1988) *Ethics After Babel* (Cambridge, MA: James Clarke and Co.).

Strand, D. (1990) 'Protest in Beijing: Civil Society and Public Sphere in China', *Problems of Communism, **34**, May–June.

Strassberg, B. (1988) 'Polish Catholicism in Transition', in T. Gannon (ed.) *World Catholicism in Transition* (New York: Macmillan) pp. 184–202.

Straus, J. (2000) 'Nationalist hatred divides Bosnian voters', *Daily Telegraph*, 11 November.

Stepan, A. and Linz, J. (1996) *Problems of Democratic Transition and Consolidation: Southern Europe, South America and Post-Communist Europe* (Baltimore and London: Johns Hopkins University Press).

Suggate, A. (1992) 'Personal Responsibility: Hayek and Havel in a Christian Perspective', *Religion, State and Society*, **20**(3–4), 303–19.

Sułek, A. (1998) 'Wokół Oświęcimia: Spór o kryże na tle wyobrażeń Polaków osobie I Żydach' ['What do Poles think about the controversies which have arisen around crosses at Auschwitz?'] *Więź* no. 481 November pp. 61–70.

Sullivan, D. (1994) *Private Voluntary Organizations in Egypt* (Gainesville: University of Florida Press).

Sullivan, D. and Abed-Kotob, S. (1999) *Islam in contemporary Egypt: civil society vs. the state* (Boulder, CO: Lynne Rienner).

Sunier, T. (1995) 'Muslims in Nederland, Nederlandse Moslims: Sociale Integratie in thesfeer van der Islam', in G. Engbersen and R. Gabriels (eds) *Sferen van Integratie Naar een Gedifferencieered Allochtsnonbeleid* (The Netherlands: Boom).

Sutcliffe, S. (1997) 'Seekers, Networks and the "New Age"', *Scottish Journal of Religious Studies*, **15**(2), 97–116.

Swatos, W. and Christiano, K. (1999) 'Secularization Theory: the Course of a Concept', *Sociology of Religion*, **60**(3), 209–28.

Talbi, M. (1998) 'Religious Liberty', in C. Curzmann (ed.) *Liberal Islam: A Sourcebook* (Oxford: OUP).

Tamney, J. (1979) 'Established religiosity in modern society: Islam in Indonesia', *Sociological Analysis*, **40**, 125–35.

Taras, R. (1995) *Consolidating Democracy in Poland* (Westview).

Taylor, C. with Guttmann, A. (ed.) (1994) *Multiculturalism and 'the politics of recognition'* (Princeton, Chichester: Princeton University Press).

Tester, K. (1992) *Civil Society* (London: Routledge).

Therborn, G. (1997) 'Beyond Civil Society: Democratic Experiences and their relevance to the "Middle East"', in E,.Özdalga and S. Persson (eds.) *Civil Society and Democracy in the Muslim World* (Istanbul: Swedish Research Institute) pp. 45–54.

Thumala, A. (2000) 'The applicability of the concept of secularization out of Western Europe: the case of Latin America', unpublished MA thesis, University of Warwick.

Tibi, B. (1998) *The Challenge of Fundamentalism: Political Islam and the New World Disorder* (Berkeley: University of California Press).

Tischner, J. 'Christianity in the Post-Communist Vacuum', *Religion, State and Society*, **20**(3–4), 331–7.

Touraine, A. (1985) 'An introduction to the study of social movements', *Social Research*, **52**(4), 749–87.

Tschannen, O. (1991) 'The Secularization Paradigm: a Systematization', *Journal for the Scientific Study of Religion*, **30**(4), 395–415.

Turner, M. (1996) *The Literary Mind* (New York: OUP).

Turner, S. (1990) 'Whose Tradition About Tradition?', *Theory, Culture and Society*, **7**, 175–85.

United Kingdom Action Committee on Islamic Affairs (UKACIA) (1993) *Need for Reform: Muslims and the Law in Multi-Faith Britain* (London: UKACIA).

Urbun, K. (1999) 'Issues Related to the Process of Legislation Concerning New Religious Associations in Poland (1977–1997)', in I. Borowik *Church-State Relations in Central and Eastern Europe* (Krakow: Nomos) pp. 165–77.

van Dartel, G. (1992) 'The Nations and Churches in Yugoslavia', *Religion, State and Society*, **20**(2–3), 275–88.

van der Veer, P. (1999) 'The Moral State: Religion, Nation and Empire in Victorian Britain and British India', in P. van der Veer and H. Lehmann (eds) *Nation and Religion: Perspectives on Europe and Asia* (New Jersey: Princeton) pp. 15–43.

van der Veer, P. *et al.* (1997) 'Transnationalism: a Three-Level Comparative Approach. Transfamilism, Politicio-Religious Transnationalism and Cross-Diasporic Dynamics among Turks and Moroccans in the Netherlands', project application submitted to NOW, the Hague (Amsterdam, The Netherlands: Research Centre Religion and Society).

van Meerbeck, A. (1995) 'The Importance of a Religious Service at birth: the Persistent Demand for Baptism in Flanders, *Social Compass*, **42**, 47–58.

Walendowski, T. (1983) 'The Pope in Poland', *Poland Watch*, **3** (Spring/Summer), 5–8.

Wallerstein, I. (1979) *The Capitalist World Economy* (Cambridge: CUP).

Walters, P. 'Who Are the Poor? Theology of Liberation in Eastern Europe Under Communism', *Religion, State and Society*, **21**(1), 53–70.

Wayne, S. and Simonis, D. (1994) *Egypt and Sudan: a travel survival kit* (London: Lonely Planet).

Weber, P. (1996) 'Public Spaces and Political Voices: Gender, Feminism and Spects of British Muslim Participation in the Public Sphere', in W. Shadid and P. van Koningsveld *Political Participation and Identities of Muslims in Non-Muslim States* (Kampen: Kok Pharos) pp. 53–70.

Webster, J. (1989) *A Brief History of Blasphemy* (Southwold, Suffolk: Orwell).

Węcławowicz, G. (1996) *Contemporary Poland: Space and Society* (London: University College).

Weeramantry, C. (1988) *Islamic Jurisprudence: an International Perspective* (Basingstoke and London: Macmillan).

Werber, P. (1990) *The Migration Process: Capital, GPIs and offerings among British Muslims* (New York: Berg).

White, G. (1994) 'Civil Society, Democratization and Development (I): Clearing the Analytical Ground', *Democratization*, **1**(3), 378.

White, J. (1996) 'Civic culture and Islam in Turkey', in C. Hann (ed.) *Civil Society: Challenging Western Models* (London: Routledge).

White, S. (1988) *The Recent Work of Jürgen Habermas* (Cambridge: CUP).

Wickham, C. (1997) 'Islamic Mobilization and Political Change: the Islamist Trend in Egypt's Political Associations', in J. Stork and J. Benin (eds) *Political Islam: Essays from Middle East Report* (London: I B Tauris) pp. 120–35.

Wihtol de Wendel, Catherine (1996) 'Muslims in France', in W. Shahid and P. van Koningsveld (eds) *Muslims in the Margin: Political Responses to the Presence of Islam in Western Europe* (Kampen: Kok Pharos) pp. 52–65.

Williams, R. (1981) *The Sociology of Culture* (New York: Schocken Books).

Williams, Z. (2001) 'Faith Hope and Chastity', *The Guardian Weekend*, 20 October, pp. 62–72.

Wilson, B. (1966) *Religion in Secular Society: A Sociological Comment* (London: C.A. Watts).

Wilson, B. (1975) 'The debate over "secularization": Religion, society and faith', *Encounter*, **45** (October), 77–84.

Wilson, B. (1982) *Religion in Sociological Perspective* (Oxford: OUP).

Wilson. B. (1992) 'Reflections on a Many Sided Controversy', in S. Bruce and R. Wallis (eds) *Religion and Modernization: Sociologists and Historians Debate the Secularization Thesis* (Oxford: Clarendon Press) pp. 195–210.

Wilson, B. (1994) *The Changing Functions of Religion: Toleration and Cohesion in a Secularized Society* (Maidenhead, Berks: The Institute of Oriental Philosophy European Centre).

Wilson, J. and Janoski, T. (1995) 'The Contribution of Religion to Volunteer Work', *Sociology of Religion*, **56**(2).

Witte, J. and van der Vyver, J. (eds) (1996) *Religious Human Rights in Global Perspective* (The Hague and London: M. Nijhoff).

Wollaston, I. (1994) 'Sharing Sacred Space? The Carmelite Controversy and the Politics of Commemoration', *Patterns of Prejudice*, **28**(3–4) 19–27.

Wollenberger, V. 'The Role of the Lutheran Church in the Democratic Movement in the GDR' *Religion in Communist Lands*, **19**(3–4), 207–10.

Yilmaz, I. (2000) 'Muslim Law in Britain: Reflections in the Socio-legal Sphere and Differential Legal Treatment', *Journal of Muslim Minority Affairs*, **20**(2), 353–60.

Zatęcki, P. (1997) 'The Biggest and the Oppressed: the Roman Catholic Church in Contemporary Poland', paper presented to 'Church-State Relationships in Central and Eastern Europe Conference', Krakow, December.

Zatęcki, P. (1999) 'Domination, Subordination and the Roman Catholic Church in Contemporary Poland', in I. Borowik *Church-State Relations in Central and Eastern Europe* (Krakow: Nomos) pp. 346–63.

Zielinski, T. (1992) 'A Para-religious state', *Rzeczpospolita*, 24 August, p. 3.

Zubaida, S. (1992) 'Islam, the State and Democracy', Merip, November–December.

Index

Religion and Civil Society